"Which American murderer killed over 200 people?

What bandit was John Dillinger's role model?

Who gave the signal for his own execution?

BLOODLETTERS AND BADMEN will answer these questions and hundreds more."

—*Cleveland Press*

Here are the most notorious outlaws, thieves, brothel keepers, syndicate gangsters, arsonists, rapists, kidnappers, murderers, lovers, forgers, embezzlers, bombers, assassins, bank robbers and hijackers who have punctuated our history with crime. Every story is different. Some are a paragraph; others run several pages depending on the fascination of the crimes and their perpetrators.

"Gaudy and gorgeous . . . Nash has a lively eye, an inquiring and skeptical mind . . . a keen sense of the absurd . . . distinct flair for dramatic exposition."
—*Kansas City Star*

"A definitive document of America's criminal past . . . an illuminating book."

—*Buffalo Courier-Express*

"Filmmakers, writers, researchers, lawyers and sociologists should be interested in this fascinating gallery . . . a must for libraries."
—*Publishers Weekly*

"One of the year's best." —*American Libraries*

★ ★ ★

ALSO AVAILABLE FROM WARNER BOOKS

Bloodletters and Badmen, Book 1:
Captain Lightfoot to Jesse James

Bloodletters and Badmen, Book 3:
Lucky Luciano to Charles Manson

JAY ROBERT

Abridged

BLOODL
AND BA

WARNER BOOKS

A Warner Communications Company

NASH

ETTERS
ADMEN

BOOK 2

**Butch Cassidy To
Al Capone**

WARNER BOOKS EDITION

Copyright © **1973, 1975** by Jay Robert Nash
All rights reserved under international and Pan American Copyright Conventions.

This Warner Books Edition is published by arrangement with M. Evans and Company, Inc., 216 E. 49th Street, New York, N.Y. 10017

Designed by Milton Batalion
Cover design by Gene Light
Cover sculpture by Nick Aristovulos

Warner Books, Inc.
666 Fifth Avenue
New York, N.Y. 10103

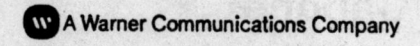

W A Warner Communications Company

Printed in the United States of America
First Warner Books Printing: March, 1975
Reissued: May, 1987

10 9

This book is for Bob Abel, who thought it necessary; for Jack Conroy, novelist and friend to young writers; and in memory of two great reporters—William L. "Tubby" Toms of the *Indianapolis News* and Ray Brennan of the *Chicago Sun-Times*.

FOREWORD

The rise of the gangster in America was a trend that developed from the old ethnic gangs in the urban and over-developed cities of the East. The once typical all-Irish Whyos gang in New York became lost in the welter of immense immigration of polyglot peoples. The American criminal brotherhoods of the past were expanded to include killers, thieves and robbers as the old ways died and the blatant desperado disappeared. Capone's army of more than a thousand gunsels during the 1920s absorbed underworld denizens with Irish, Italian, Polish, German and other heritages. It was no longer a case of being tied together through blood lines, albeit the secret criminal societies thriving at the turn of the century, the Camorra, the Mafia, and Unione Siciliane, advocated blood rituals to bind their members together. The New York gang in which Jack "Legs" Diamond (John T. Noland), an Irishman, first learned his criminal trades of bootlegging, extortion, and enforcement, possessed several ethnic types. Jewish gangsters Jacob "Gurrah" Shapiro and Louis "Lepke" Buchalter, and Sicilian gangster Charles "Lucky" Luciano also belonged to the same Little Augie (Orgen) mob.

Gangsterism itself suggested a lurking evil that hid secretly from the law while operating in shadowy alleys. Mobsters diligently worked to maintain a respectable front to cloak their lawless ways. Capone owned a furniture store. Dion O'Bannion, called the "arch killer of Chicago" with twenty-five dead men at his hand, operated a flower shop, Dutch Schultz a restaurant. These were not the stand-up bandits of old but a subtler breed of criminal in America, a melting-pot species that blended into the crowds, wore conservative suits, went home from their hidden breweries and stills like the Genna brothers to sip wine and eat with the family. Vincent "Mad Dog" Coll slipped his automatics between the seat cushions of his Marmon and posed like any tourist wide-grinned with his girl and gang members before Coney Island backdrops. "Machine-Gun Jack" McGurn donned tennis shorts and skipped rope in gyms, played the ukelele at county fairs. Theirs, from the 1910s on, was an acting game where the masks were dropped only when the business of crime for money without apology was at hand.

For a brief moment in the early 1930s a throwback type of American criminal, almost always rural-bred, operated on the old levels. John Dillinger from back-county Indiana, Charles Arthur "Pretty Boy" Floyd in the untamed Cookson Hills of Oklahoma, Clyde and Buck Barrow and Bonnie Parker across the desolate sweep of Texas performed as did the old Western outlaws. Their criminal pattern, in fact, was almost identical and began when an old-fashioned outlaw Henry Starr, supposedly Belle Starr's nephew, put his horse to pasture and began to rob banks with an automobile.

The car supplanted the horse and the machine-gun and the automatic the six-shooter. But not much else changed for this atavistic genre. Ma Barker and her brood, "Baby Face" Nelson, and Gerald Chapman did not operate in public for long. They ran from state to state, hiding in lonely places much as did Frank and Jesse James, for in their mania they allowed themselves to be identified, often announcing to startled bank customers who was robbing them, childishly boasting as Jesse himself did when robbing the Glendale train in 1881, cavalierly introducing himself and each member of his gang to the bug-eyed engineer. The outlaws of the 1930s ("gangster" is less appropriate, applying more to city mobsters) knew the striking histories of their antecedents and emulated them the way country folk had decades before. They, the Dillingers, the Floyds, were country folk themselves who had been weaned on the tarnished exploits of the hard-riding Westerners. Pretty Boy Floyd once wrote to lawmen: "Jesse James was no punk hisself (sic)."

They identified with and attempted to exemplify the dead of Boot Hill, and they followed, especially when interstate flight was blocked by federal law, the old desperadoes to the grave, shot to pieces for the most part while embracing their bloody kinship with the past. The city gangster, no less brazen in his early days, managed to survive through stealth, though the more belligerent of his type was weeded out with shotguns, "choppers" and one-way rides.

Except for Coll, Schultz, Diamond, Francis "Two Gun" Crowley, who chose to shoot it out in spectacle and open gore, the mobsters of the East quickly streamlined their criminal pursuits, avoiding the broad-day gunfight. In the West, the gangster was still in transit toward a more dignified and acceptable role model. Seven men were lined up against a wall in Chicago as late as 1929 and mowed down; machine-gunners on a bright morning in 1933 shot lawmen to bits in a busy train station in Kansas City. Knowledgeable leaders in the underworld sneered in contempt at such archaic tactics, and the public, once mildly indifferent and often amused at criminal escapades, was shocked into demanding punitive action. The daylight gunmen had to go, and they did, one by one and in groups like angry blood clots through the nation's arteries.

It was inside this epoch and hopefully shown in this second volume of *Bloodletters*, that crime shocks made way for ever-increasing crime shocks. First murder wedded glamor in such high-society killings as the slaying of noted architect Stanford White by millionaire Harry K. Thaw. But that was a bizarre lover's revenge that many excused in 1906. There was less explanation for the ego-dominated murder of Bobbie Franks by two rich youths, Leopold and

Loeb, in 1924. There was nothing but scorn for Judd Gray and Ruth Snyder when they bashed in Mr. Snyder's head with a sashweight in 1927. The shock of the American criminal continued as his pattern became more and more unpredictable and exotic. That weird Earle Leonard Nelson could strangle almost two dozen landladies from coast to coast in 1926 and 1927 and a strange old man, Albert Fish, could waylay, dissect, and cannabalize unknown scores of children up to 1928 was a hideous but distant reminder to the public of the American criminal's changing nature. For most, these oddball rarities vanished with yesterday's disgust wrinkled in yellowing newspapers. They would return.

And changing, too, were the city mobsters who no longer curled their lips into "yeahs" and "scrams," slipping manicured hands inside pin-striped suits for holstered heaters. These days faded into blurry memories of the American gangster obscurely thought of as grit-good, his image slipping nostalgically onto the movie screen, his era over, all over.

With the imprisonment of Capone, the bloody gundowning of Schultz, the electrocution of dapper Harry Pierpont, it was the end of the gangster.

A new breed of American criminal loomed larger and fiercer than even these bloodletters. And they would be awful.

Jay Robert Nash
Chicago, 1974

ACKNOWLEDGMENTS

I wish to thank the following people and organizations for their extensive assistance in helping me research this book and for the wonderful cooperation they extended in providing photos, information, and encouragement: Kevin John Mosley Collection; Roland Restle Collection; Henry Scheafer and Faytonia Fair of UPI's Chicago office; William and Edie Kelly of Wide World's Chicago office; Peter A. Evans, Librarian of the California Historical Society; James H. Davis, Picture Librarian of the Denver Public Library (Western History Department); Mrs. Leona S. Morris, Editorial Secretary of the Missouri Historical Review (State Historical Society of Missouri); G. F. O'Neill, Director of Personnel, Pinkerton's, Inc.; Jack D. Haley, Assistant Curator, Western History Collections, University of Oklahoma; New York Historical Society; Wyoming State Historical Department; Kansas State Historical Society; Arizona Historical Society; Terry Mangan, The State Historical Society of Colorado; Holly B. Ulseth, Curator of Special Exhibits & Collections, Detroit Historical Museum; Malcolm Freiberg, Editor of Publications, Massachusetts Historical Society; William M. Roberts, Reference Librarian, University of California, Berkeley; Ken Burton, *Tucson Daily Citizen*;

James, John, and Patrick Agnew; Prof. Andre Moenssens; Raymond Friday Locke, Editor, *Mankind Magazine*; Robert Connelly; Thomas Buckley; Richard Case of the Chicago Historical Society; Jack Paul Schwartz; Mrs. Jerrie L. Klein; Neil H. Nash; Jack J. Klein, Jr.; Ray Puechner; Peter Kotsos; Stan Kaiser; Dr. Richard Talsky; Barry Felcher of the *Chicago Daily News*; Curt Johnson; Leonard Des Jardins; Al Devorin; John Gehlman; Mike Berman; James Small; James Stein; Arthur Von Kluge; Brett Howard; Sidney Harris; Arnold Edwards; Jerry Goldberg of the *Los Angeles Free Press*; Warren Stamer; Arnold L. Kaye; Joseph Pinkston; James McCormick of *Chicago Today*; Jack Lane, Jeff Kamen; Herman Kogan of the *Chicago Sun-Times*; William Kirby, Associate Director of the Louisiana Division of the New Orleans Public Library; the dozens of police force officers of all ranks, criminologists, and penologists across the country who gave their time and information; and to my intrepid typist and friend, Carolyn Zozak, whose fingers ceaselessly danced across her typewriter's keyboard on my behalf.

AIELLO, JOSEPH
Bootlegger • (1891-1930)

After the Genna gang had been smashed in Chicago by Al Capone, Milwaukee-bred Joey Aiello and his brothers, Dominick, Antonio and Andrew, attempted to seize control of the *Unione Siciliane*, fraternal organization which controlled Sicilian rackets in Chicago. Aiello reorganized the old Genna mob in October, 1927, and joined forces with North and West Side gangs under the leadership of hoodlums George "Bugs" Moran, William Skidmore, Barney Bertsche and Jack Zuta.

Capone, who coveted the presidency of the *Unione*, went to war with Aiello. It was a short one. The Aiellos tried to bribe the chef at the Little Italy Cafe where Capone regularly dined. They wanted him to put prussic acid in Capone's soup and offered the chef $10,000. The nervous cook weepily told Capone of the treachery and the plot failed.

Next, Aiello offered $50,000 to any Chicago hoodlum who would "show us a Capone notch."

"Nobody puts a price on my head and lives!" Capone reportedly screamed when he heard of the Aiello-offered

Joey Aiello offered $50,000 to any gunman who could kill Al Capone during Chicago's 1920s bootleg wars; Scarface got him first on 10/23/30 with machine guns. (UPI)

bounty. Weeks later, when Scarface learned that Joe Aiello had been picked up for questioning in a murder, he sent a troop of gunmen to the Chicago Detective Bureau headquarters.

As detectives on duty watched, eight taxis drew up in front of the Bureau. More than twenty men, all Capone gangsters, climbed out.

"What the hell do they think they're gonna do?" one officer stated, "lay siege to this building?"

Three men headed straight for the door of the headquarters. One was recognized as Louis "Little New York" Campagna, Big Al's personal bodyguard.

"It's the Capone crowd!" a detective yelled; he and some others ran to the street and arrested Campagna, Frank Perry and Sam Marcus for carrying guns. The three thugs were all placed in a cell next to Aiello's which turned out to be their real intent.

A policeman, who understood Italian, was hidden next to the cells and heard the following conversation:

Aiello: "Can't we settle this? Give me just fifteen days—just fifteen days—and I will sell my stores and house and leave everything in your hands. Think of my wife and baby and let me go."

Louis Campagna laughed and then spat: "You dirty rat! You started this. We'll end it. You're as good as dead!"

Aiello was terrified and, upon his release from jail, did exactly as he had promised the Capone henchmen. He disappeared from Chicago for eighteen months. In his absence, his brother Dominick was shot to death by Capone men. When Aiello did return, he caused no damage to either Capone's empire or prestige.

For three years, Aiello dodged Scarface's triggermen. They finally caught up with him October 23, 1930, when he emerged from the home of one of his aides, Pasquale Prestigiocomo (alias Presto). Several bursts from machine guns tore Aiello to pieces.

Aiello's futile thrust to take over the Chicago rackets ended all serious underworld opposition to Capone.

ALTERIE, LOUIS ("TWO-GUN")
Bootlegger • (1892-1935)

Of all Dion O'Bannion's daffy gunners in his Prohibition-fed North Side Chicago Gang, Louis Alterie (nee Leland Verain) was the wackiest. He was born in Colorado and owned a small ranch there before moving Eastward to join O'Bannion in the early 1920s.

Alterie was a minor partner in O'Bannion's wide-open

gambling casinos and bootlegging operations and was addicted to wearing two pistols Western-style on his hips.

One of Alterie's close pals in the churgh-going, sentimental O'Bannion organization was Samuel J. "Nails" Morton who fronted for the mob, a well-dressed, cultured gentleman who had won the *Croix de Guerre* during the First World War after leading several heroic charges against German machine-gun emplacements. Morton was a horseman of some note, riding each day along the Lincoln Park bridle path. On one of these rides, a spirited horse threw him and kicked him to death.

Hearing his pal was dead, Alterie went berserk; he went to the stables, rented the same horse and, taking it to the exact spot where Nails had been killed, shot the animal through the head (a scene repeated in the classic gangster film, *Public Enemy*).

Alterie then called the stable owner and said: "We taught that goddamn horse of yours a lesson. If you want the saddle, go and get it."

Even more infuriating for Two-Gun was the assassination of his chief, Dion O'Bannion, in 1924. He wept openly at O'Bannion's funeral and then, in a rage, turned to reporters and said: "I have no idea who killed Deanie, but I would die smiling if only I had a chance to meet the guys who did, any time, any place they mention and I would get at least two or three of them before they got me. If I knew who killed Deanie, I'd shoot it out with the gang of killers before the sun rose in the morning and some of us, maybe all of us, would be lying on slabs in the undertaker's place."

The logical dueling ground, he pointed out, would be the world's busiest corner—Madison and State Streets—at high noon.

Reform Mayor Dever was flabbergasted when he heard of the Alterie challenge. "Are we still abiding by the code of the dark ages?" he stormed.

The brag had created heat for the North Side Mob and its new nominal leader, George "Bugs" Moran, went to Alterie and told him: "You're getting us in bad. You talk too much. Beat it."

Alterie took the hint and caught the next train west to

his Colorado ranch, where he lived out his days in obscurity.

Louis "Two Gun" Alterie hijacked beer trucks for Chicago gangster Dion O'Bannion during Prohibition; he offered to shoot it out with his boss's killers in the heart of the Loop at high noon but left for his Colorado ranch when things got too hot in 1924. (UPI)

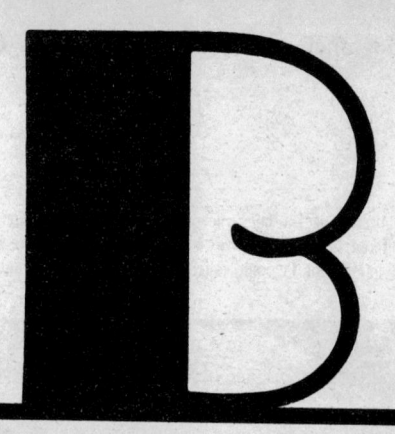

BARKER, ARIZONA DONNIE CLARK ("KATE," "MA")
Gangleader • (1872-1935)

BACKGROUND: BORN NEAR SPRINGFIELD, MO., 1872. MARRIED GEORGE BARKER, A SHARECROPPING FARMER, IN 1892. GAVE BIRTH TO FOUR SONS, THE NOTORIOUS BARKER BROTHERS: HERMAN, LLOYD, ARTHUR, AND FRED. DESCRIPTION: 5'2", BROWN EYES, BROWN HAIR, STOUT. ALIASES: UNKNOWN. RECORD: PLANNED SEVERAL BANK ROBBERIES IN THE MIDDLE 1920S AND RAN A HIDEOUT IN TULSA, OKLA. DURING THIS PERIOD FOR ESCAPED CONVICTS AND BANKROBBERS BEING SOUGHT; UPON THE RELEASE OF HER SONS FREDDIE AND DOC FROM PRISON, MA BARKER PLANNED SEVERAL PAYROLL, POST OFFICE AND BANK ROBBERIES IN THE EARLY 1930S; FINALIZED PLANS FOR THE HAMM AND BREMER KIDNAPPINGS OF 1933 AND 1934. MA BARKER AND HER SON FREDDIE WERE KILLED IN A WILD GUN BATTLE WITH FBI MEN IN A REMOTE RESORT ON LAKE WEIR OUTSIDE OF OKLAWAHA, FLORIDA, 1/16/35. MA BARKER HAD NEVER BEEN ARRESTED FOR ANY CRIME DURING HER LIFETIME, REMAINING BEHIND THE SCENE AND SENDING OUT HER SONS AND OTHER CRIMINALS TO PERFORM ROBBERIES.

The grandmotherly woman shown in these snapshots (the only photos ever taken of her during her lifetime) is "Ma" Barker with paramour Arthur V. Dunlop; she organized bankrobberies and kidnappings for her killer sons. (UPI)

BARKER, ARTHUR
("DOCK" OR "DOC")
Murderer, Bankrobber • (1899-1939)

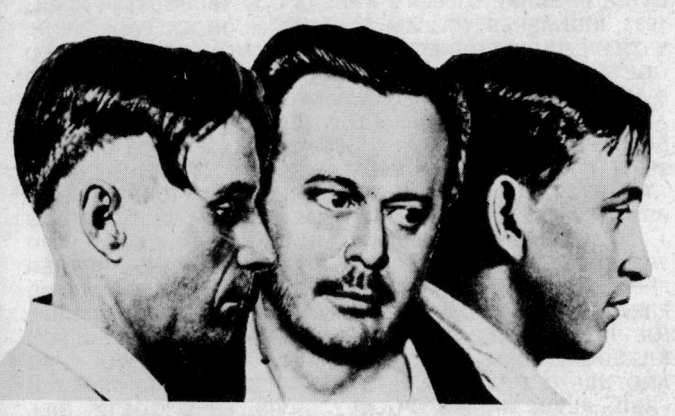

The "Bloody Barkers" (left to right)—Herman, Arthur ("Doc"), and Freddie, 1930s kidnappers and bankrobbers. (UPI)

BACKGROUND: BORN IN AURORA, MO., 1899. MINOR PUBLIC EDUCATION. DESCRIPTION: 5'3", BROWN EYES, BLACK HAIR, STOCKY BUILD. ALIASES: UNKNOWN. RECORD: ARRESTED SEVERAL TIMES ON ADOLESCENT CHARGES, 1910–15, IN WEBB CITY, MO.; RELEASED TO THE CUSTODY OF HIS MOTHER; STOLE A GOVERNMENT-OWNED CAR, 1918, ESCAPED, WAS RECAPTURED; ESCAPED; KILLED A NIGHT WATCHMAN AT THE ST. JOHN'S HOSPITAL IN TULSA WHILE ATTEMPTING TO STEAL A DRUG SHIPMENT; SENT TO THE OKLAHOMA STATE PENITENTIARY FOR LIFE WHERE HE SERVED THIRTEEN YEARS BEFORE BEING PAROLED 9/27/32 BY WILLIAM H. "ALFALFA BILL" MURRAY, GOVERNOR OF OKLAHOMA; ROBBED WITH HIS BROTHER FRED, ALVIN KARPIS, JESS DOYLE, BILL WEAVER, VERNE MILLER, AND LARRY DEVOL THE THIRD NORTHWESTERN BANK IN MINNEAPOLIS, MINN. ($20,000) 12/16/32, KILLING TWO POLICEMEN WITH MACHINEGUNS AND WOUNDED A CIVILIAN; ROBBED WITH HIS BROTHER FRED, ALVIN KARPIS, JESS DOYLE, FRANK NASH, VOLNEY DAVIS, AND EARL CHRISTMAN THE FAIRBURY, NEBRASKA BANK ($151,350), WOUNDING A BANK PRESIDENT AND GUARD (CHRISTMAN WOUNDED BY THE GUARD, DYING A DAY

21

LATER IN VERNE MILLER'S KANSAS CITY HIDEOUT) IN APRIL, 1933; KIDNAPPED WILLIAM A. HAMM, JR. IN ST. PAUL, MINN. WITH HIS BROTHER FRED, ALVIN KARPIS, MONTY BOLTON, FRED GOETZ ("SHOTGUN ZIEGLER") AND CHARLES J. FITZGERALD 6/15/33, DEMANDING $100,000 RANSOM; RANSOM PAID 6/17/33 AND HAMM RELEASED 6/18/33 (ROGER TOUHY, CHICAGO BOOTLEGGER, MISTAKENLY TRIED BY THE JUSTICE DEPARTMENT FOR THE CRIME); ROBBED THE SWIFT COMPANY PAYROLL AT THE SOUTH ST. PAUL, MINN. POST OFFICE WITH HIS BROTHER FRED, ALVIN KARPIS, LARRY DEVOL AND CHARLES J. FITZGERALD, ($30,000), KILLING ONE POLICEMAN AND WOUNDING ANOTHER, 8/15/33; ROBBED WITH HIS BROTHER FRED, MONTY BOLTON, BILL "LAPLAND WILLIE" WEAVER, AND FRED GOETZ A FEDERAL RESERVE MAIL TRUCK IN CHICAGO (GETTING SEVERAL SACKS OF USELESS CHECKS), BOLTON KILLED PATROLMAN MILES A. CUNNINGHAM AND WOUNDED ANOTHER OFFICER, 8/22/33; KIDNAPPED WITH HIS BROTHER FRED, ALVIN KARPIS, VOLNEY DAVIS, FRED GOETZ, BILL WEAVER, AND HARRY CAMPBELL MILLIONAIRE BANKER EDWARD G. BREMER IN MINNEAPOLIS, MINN. 1/17/34, HOLDING HIM FOR $200,000 RANSOM; RANSOM PAID 2/7/34 AT WHICH TIME BREMER WAS RELEASED; KILLED DR. JOSEPH P. "DOC" MORAN WITH HIS BROTHER FRED, AUGUST, 1934, CAPTURED BY FBI MEN, LED BY SPECIAL AGENT MELVIN PURVIS, IN CHICAGO 1/8/35; CONVICTED OF THE BREMER KIDNAPPING AND SENTENCED TO LIFE IMPRISONMENT AT ALCATRAZ; KILLED IN AN ATTEMPTED ESCAPE FROM "THE ROCK" 6/13/39.

BARKER, FRED
Murderer, Bankrobber • (1902-1935)

BACKGROUND: BORN IN AURORA, MO., 1902. MINOR PUBLIC EDUCATION. DESCRIPTION: 5'4", BROWN EYES, BROWN HAIR, SLIGHT BUILD. SEVERAL GOLD-FILLED TEETH. PLASTIC SURGERY SCAR ON FACE. ALIASES: UNKNOWN. RECORD: ARRESTED IN HIS YOUTH FOR VAGRANCY AND ROBBERY, RELEASED TO HIS MOTHER'S CUSTODY; ARRESTED FOR ROBBING THE BANK IN WINDFIELD, KANSAS, 1926; RECEIVED FIVE-TO-TEN YEAR SENTENCE IN THE KANSAS STATE PENITENTIARY AT LANSING WHERE HE MET AND FORMED HIS ASSOCIATION WITH BURGLAR

AND SNEAK-THIEF ALVIN KARPIS; PAROLED 3/20/31; ROBBED WITH KARPIS SEVERAL JEWELRY AND CLOTHING SHOPS IN MISSOURI AND KANSAS, SUMMER, 1931; ARRESTED FOR BURGLARY IN CLAREMORE, OKLA., SUMMER, 1931, ESCAPED; ROBBED STORE IN WEST PLAINS, MO., WITH ALVIN KARPIS, JULY, 1931, KILLING THE LOCAL SHERIFF, C. R. KELLY; ROBBED THE MOUNTAIN VIEW, MO. BANK WITH ALVIN KARPIS, BILL WEAVER AND JAMES WILSON ($7,000) EARLY FALL, 1931; STOLE CLOTHING, CARS, CIGARETTES (BY THE TRUCK LOAD), HIJACKED WHISKEY (FENCED BY ST. PAUL, MINN. CRIME KINGPIN, JACK PEIFER), AND CRACKED SAFES THROUGHOUT THE FALL OF 1931 WITH ALVIN KARPIS IN MINNESOTA; KILLED CHIEF OF POLICE MANLEY JACKSON OF POCAHOLTAS, ARK., NOV. 1931, SHOOTING HIM FIVE TIMES IN THE BACK; ROBBED A BRANCH OF THE NORTHWESTERN NATIONAL BANK OF MINNEAPOLIS WITH ALVIN KARPIS, ($81,000 CASH, $185,000 BONDS); ROBBED OTHER BANKS IN THE WINTER OF 1932 IN BELOIT, WISC., FLANDREAU, S.D., REDWOOD FALLS, MINN. WITH ALVIN KARPIS, LARRY DEVOL AND ONE OR TWO OTHER MINOR HOODLUMS; ROBBED THE FORT SCOTT, KAN. BANK IN MAY, 1932 WITH ALVIN KARPIS, LARRY DEVOL, PHIL COURTNEY, AND HARVEY BAILEY, ($47,000); THREE ESCAPEES FROM THE OKLAHOMA STATE PENITENTIARY AT THIS TIME—JAMES CLARK, EDWARD DAVIS, AND FRANK SAWYER—MISTAKENLY ARRESTED FOR THE FORT SCOTT RAID AND RECEIVED TWENTY TO ONE HUNDRED YEARS AT LANSING STATE PRISON IN KANSAS; ROBBED THE WAHPETON, N.D. BANK IN LATE JUNE, 1932 WITH ALVIN KARPIS, JESS DOYLE, HIS BROTHER DOC, AND LARRY DEVOL ($7,000); ROBBED THE CLOUD COUNTY BANK AT CONCORDIA, KAN., ($250,000) 7/25/32 WITH ALVIN KARPIS, JESS DOYLE, FRANK NASH, EARL CHRISTMAN, AND LARRY DEVOL; ROBBED THE CITIZEN'S SECURITY BANK, BIXBY, OKLA., ($1,000) 8/8/32 WITH VOLNEY DAVIS AND LARRY DEVOL; ROBBED SEVERAL BANKS AND PARTICIPATED IN TWO KIDNAPPINGS 1932-34 (SEE ARTHUR "DOC" BARKER FOR DETAILS); KILLED WITH HIS MOTHER, "MA" BARKER, AT LAKE WEIR IN FLORIDA 1/16/35 IN A 45-MINUTE GUN BATTLE WITH FBI AGENTS.

BARKER, HERMAN
Murderer, Bankrobber • (1894-1927)

BACKGROUND: BORN IN AURORA, MO., 1894. MINOR PUBLIC EDUCATION. DESCRIPTION: 5'5", BROWN EYES, BLACK HAIR, STOCKY BUILD. ALIASES: UNKNOWN. RECORD: ARRESTED FOR PETTY THEFT WHILE A YOUTH; RELEASED TO THE CUSTODY OF HIS MOTHER; ORGANIZED THE CENTRAL PARK GANG IN TULSA, OKLA., 1910, AN ADOLESCENT GROUP DEDICATED TO MINOR BURGLARIES; ARRESTED IN 1915 FOR ROBBERY IN JOPLIN, MO., RELEASED TO THE CUSTODY OF HIS MOTHER; BECAME A MEMBER OF THE KIMES-TERRILL GANG IN EARLY 1920S, ROBBING BANKS IN TEXAS, OKLAHOMA AND MISSOURI. SEVERELY WOUNDED AFTER ROBBING A STORE IN NEWTON, KAN. AND KILLING POLICEMAN J. E. MARSHALL, HERMAN BARKER TURNED HIS LUGER ON HIMSELF, COMMITTING SUICIDE 9/19/27.

BARKER, LLOYD
Robber • (1896–1949)

BACKGROUND: BORN IN AURORA, MO., 1896; MINOR PUBLIC EDUCATION. DESCRIPTION: 5'4", BROWN EYES, BROWN HAIR, SLENDER. ALIASES: UNKNOWN. RECORD: ARRESTED FOR PETTY THEFT WHILE A YOUTH, RELEASED TO THE CUSTODY OF HIS MOTHER; ORGANIZED THE CENTRAL PARK GANG IN TULSA, OKLA., 1910; CAUGHT WHILE ROBBING A POST OFFICE IN RURAL OKLAHOMA, 1922 AND SENT TO LEAVENWORTH FOR TWENTY-FIVE YEARS; SERVED ALL HIS TIME AND WAS RELEASED IN 1947. LLOYD WAS THE ONLY MEMBER OF THE BARKER BROTHERS WHO DID NOT JOIN A GANG. FOLLOWING THE RELEASE FROM LEAVENWORTH, HE WAS EMPLOYED AS AN ASSISTANT MANAGER OF A SNACK SHOP IN RURAL COLORADO; KILLED BY HIS WIFE IN 1949.

No other outlaw gang of the 1930s so baffled law enforcement officials as the Barkers. Unlike other bank-robbers such as "Pretty Boy" Floyd, Dillinger, and the Barrow gang, the Barkers operated with great stealth allowing others to grab the headlines and the credit. They robbed without pattern. Geographically, the gang—its members rarely the same in number or personnel—roamed from the far northwoods of Minnesota to Texas and Oklahoma, from Illinois to Nebraska (they steered clear of Indiana as that was almost the exclusive province of John Dillinger). The types of robberies committed by the Barkers were far from consistent. One day they might knock over a bank for $250,000, a job expertly cased, well-equipped and selectively-manned. The next day they would appear rashly unprepared in another state, heisting a jewelry store for only several hundred dollars. Then they would switch to a totally new field of crime such as kidnapping.

It was this kind of unpredictability that made it so difficult to identify them and link them to specific crimes. Their crazy-quilt crime wave was more the result of neuroticism rather than planned modus operandi. The Barkers, especially Doc and Fred, were dedicated criminals who would strike happily on all levels.

Fred Barker's willingness to kill, whether or not circumstances demanded it, typified the murderous insanity that ran through the blood of the Barker breed. His brother Doc was just as wildly lethal. "Ma" Barker was slightly more level-headed, but she, too, never flinched when murder seemed the most expeditious method of handling a problem.

Also, unlike the lone bandits of their era, the Barkers found protection in cities like St. Paul, Minn., Kansas City, Kan., Hot Springs, Ark., Joplin, Mo. (towns that were almost wholly owned by local bootleggers and corrupt politicians). Here, for a cut of their enormous profits, politicians, lawyers, and police officials gave them sanctuary, informing them of any impending raid against them far enough in advance to allow them to escape. The Barkers contributed mightily to the campaign chests of politicians running for office.

Contacts were everything with the Barkers. Though they were never part of the embryonic criminal syndicate blossoming during the 1930s, the national crime cartel encouraged and shielded them. The reason, of course, was the money. The Barkers, under Ma's intuitive criminal genius, accumulated at least $3 million in their collective criminal careers and fenced huge amounts of ransom monies through political contacts, who took large percentages (without having to take any serious risk). The gang even gave certain officials their money for safekeeping, drawing funds from them when needed as one would from a bank. In turn, the political hacks would recruit dependable men for the gang, experts in safe-blowing, bankrobbing, burglary—mostly ex-convicts whose records proved them committed to crime. Political hacks would also "finger" jobs.

Even with such influential men to help them, the Barkers would, no doubt, have floundered early and been picked off one by one had it not been for the shrewd thinking and meticulous planning of Ma Barker. Though bankrobber and kidnapper Alvin Karpis, after his release from prison, denied Ma Barker's role as leader of the gang, (perhaps unwilling to think of himself being ordered about by an elderly woman) the fact is evident from all records and accounts.

Ma Barker has been portrayed from every slant imaginable: as a kind and protective mother whose boys grew up poor and got into bad company, as a bloody mama type who planned robberies and kidnappings for her boys at the cold and methodical pace of an IBM machine working overtime; as a thick-witted, slow-moving, silly old woman who knew nothing about the activities of her murderous sons and was used by them as a front.

Which story is true? Probably, a little of each.

Born 18 miles northwest of Springfield, Missouri in 1872, Arizona Donnie Clark grew up in the heartland that nursed Jesse and Frank James. Her childhood hero, Jesse, was killed by Bob Ford when she was ten, but she never forgot the handsome bandit. She had seen him ride through nearby Carthage once with the Younger brothers at his side. The image would never leave her.

Arizona Kate (or "Arrie" as friends called her) was Ozark Mountains tough and grew into a pretty, hard young woman who read her Bible and played the fiddle. She could always be found at the church "sing" on Sunday.

Kate was twenty in 1892 when the Dalton brothers were shot full of holes in Coffeyville, Kansas, after trying to take two banks at one time. That year, Kate married a farm laborer, George Barker, and moved to Aurora, Missouri.

There the four Barker boys were born: Herman, Lloyd, Arthur (nicknamed Doc) and her favorite, Freddie. Shortly after Herman and Lloyd were school age, the Barkers moved to Webb City, Mo., a mining boomtown.

The family lived in a broken-down tar-paper house and in a few years the boys, growing up wild, got into trouble. Small stuff was first: window-breaking and fights. Next came pilfering and then outright thievery. Ma always defended them against complaints.

Their father, George Barker, brushed aside his paternal responsibilities with, "You'll have to talk with Mother. She handles the boys." Years later, George Barker would recall: "She'd pack up those boys and take them to Sunday school every week. I don't know just why. Because when I tried to straighten them up, she'd fly into me. She never would let me do with them what I wanted to."

But Mother had become Ma and didn't handle the boys at all; she let them run wild and refused to see them as they were, apprentice hoodlums. Even slight criticism of her brood would inflame Ma Barker to rage. She stopped attending church with the words: "If the good people of this town don't like my boys, then the good people know what they can do."

Herman was the first to get into serious trouble. Webb City police arrested him for petty thievery in 1910. Ma raised hell in the police station and the unnerved cops released him.

In 1915, Herman was again arrested for highway robbery. Again, Ma appeared before authorities and got him released. By now, Kate Barker knew she had best get the boys out of Webb City. "They're marked," she told neighbors. "The cops here won't ever stop persecuting my boys."

The Barkers moved to Tulsa, Oklahoma, but the boys grew worse, not better. Her boys were being picked up regularly for all sorts of adolescent crimes, yet Ma always managed to get them off with tantrums, rage, tears, and promises.

After Freddie Barker visited ex-con Herb Farmer, who ran a hideout in Joplin, Mo., he invited several fugitives to stay at Ma's in Tulsa. They started to show up in 1915, people like bank robber Al Spencer. Other big-time heist men like Frank Nash, Ray Terrill, and Earl Thayer appeared. Chicago-bred holdup men Francis Keating and Thomas Holden also used Ma's Tulsa home to lay low.

It became not only a cooling-off place for fugitives but also a hotbed of plans for bank jobs and robberies. Naturally the boys were affected. The first to leave the clan was Herman who drove off with Ray Terrill to knock over banks.

Lloyd tried to hold up a post office in 1922 and was captured. He got 25 years in Leavenworth. Doc's career was not going too good, either; he was nabbed for stealing a government car in 1918, and was in and out of jail through the 1920s. The same year that Lloyd went to Leavenworth, Doc was sent to the Oklahoma State Prison for life. He was charged with killing a night watchman at a hospital in Tulsa.

Ma and Doc always insisted he didn't do it. For once, they were right. Many years later a California thief admitted the killing.

Freddie went to prison next, after dozens of arrests ranging from bank robbery to assault with intent to kill. He got 5-to-10 in the Kansas State Penitentiary in Lansing.

Herman Barker was the only son still free, but his end came abruptly and violently. After being captured with Ray Terrill while trying to rob a Missouri bank, both men escaped custody and with a stolen car raced for the Kansas border. After a holdup in Newton, Kansas, cops flagged down a suspicious-looking car traveling at high speeds. Herman Barker was driving and guns blazed from all the windows.

As police returned fire, officer J. E. Marshall fell dead. But Herman didn't escape; police caught him in another trap. After emptying his gun at them in a blistering shootout, he pulled out his "lucky piece"—a spare bullet—inserted it into his gun and sent it into his brain.

Ma denied it was suicide: "A Barker don't do things like that." She screamed that it was a police execution. But officials still listed Herman as dead by his own hand.

It was Herman's suicide and the imprisonment of her other three sons that, in the words of FBI chief, J. Edgar

Hoover, changed Ma Barker "from an animal mother of the she-wolf type to a veritable beast of prey." Perhaps the transformation was not that acute, but Ma's desire to see her boys free never waned.

At 55, gone fat and gray, her face sagging, Ma was alone. But she hadn't lost her perseverance. Kate left George Barker and raised tens of thousands of dollars by running a regular hideout for escaped cons and wanted robbers. She needed the money to pay lawyers who were seeking her sons' release.

For years Ma Barker hounded and haunted the parole boards, wardens, and governors. Finally, on March 20, 1931, her efforts paid off. Freddie was released from Lansing. He brought along his friend and cell-mate, Alvin Karpis, who had also been set free.

They both moved in with Ma and her lover, Arthur V. Dunlop. Alvin Karpis, whom Freddie called "Old Creepy" because of his strange and sinister smile, was well-liked by Ma. He reminded her of her own boys and he was after the same things she taught them to desire.

"What I wanted," Karpis later admitted, "was big automobiles like rich people had and everything like that. I didn't see how I was going to get them by making a fool of myself and working all my life. So I decided to take what I wanted."

And with Ma's help at planning and picking jobs, that's exactly what Old Creepy and Freddie did. Ma would then relax, listening to hillbilly music on the radio and working crossword puzzles.

Alvin and Freddie started small. They robbed a store in West Plains, Missouri. When C. R. Kelly the local sheriff spotted the robbery car with two men sitting in it two days later, he investigated. Freddie and Alvin let him have it.

Kelly was killed instantly.

Now the boys were hot and Ma decided to go to one of the country's cooling-off spots for criminals, St. Paul, Minnesota. They took old man Dunlop along, too, but he didn't like it and complained incessantly.

Ma was tired of Dunlop and his complaining. So were the boys. His bullet-ridden body was discovered floating along the shores of isolated Lake Freasted in upstate Wisconsin in 1932, shot up by gangsters working for the St.

Paul political fixer and bootlegger Jack Peifer. Dunlop had talked too much about the gang's operations after getting drunk one night. The gang had done many jobs for Peifer and he "knocked off Dunlop as a kind of return favor to us," Karpis later remembered.

Peifer used his club, the Hollyhocks, as a sort of clearing house for criminal operations in St. Paul. Harry Sawyer (nee Sandlovich), another crime cartel operator in St. Paul, ran the Green Lantern. It was here that every hoodlum on the lam had to check in. After letting Sawyer know he was in town, the criminal was free to operate alone, available, perhaps, for some job Sawyer might dream up.

The Green Lantern became the hangout for almost all Barker mobsters. Young, nervy toughs such as Volney Davis, part Cherokee, born in Tulsa and friend of Doc Barker's who had been sentenced with Doc for killing the night watchman, came into Sawyer's Green Lantern. Davis began his criminal career by stealing a pair of shoes and getting a three-year sentence for it. Ma Barker had arranged for his parole. Davis' eccentric girl friend, Edna "The Kissing Bandit" Murray (who had escaped from the Missouri Penitentiary) enjoyed Ma Barker's wrath. Mother Barker hated all female competition. Davis would get life in prison for his part in the Bremer kidnapping.

William Weaver, a vicious gunsel from Arkansas and one-time cell-mate of Freddie Barker's at Lansing, would also get life at Alcatraz for the Bremer kidnapping (dropping dead of a heart attack in the prison laundry in 1954). Weaver was also known as "Lapland Willie" and "Phoenix Donald."

The other major and younger members of the Barker gang included Lawrence "Larry" DeVol, a hell-bent killer who was finally killed by lawmen during a holdup; Phil Courtney, an ex-motorcycle cop turned bandit; Earl Christman, who, after being wounded in the Fairbury Bank holdup in 1933, would be buried secretly by the Barkers in Kansas City; Jess Doyle, and James Wilson.

Also in Sawyer's wide-open saloon strutted the older pros of bankrobbing who periodically teamed up with the Barkers—Harvey Bailey, the dean of American bank robbers; Thomas Holden; Francis Keating; Gus Winkler (later killed by syndicate hitmen); Fred Goetz, alias "Shotgun Ziegler," reputed to have been one of the machinegunners at the St. Valentine's Day Massacre (killed by syndicate hoods with a full shotgun blast a foot away from his face while starting his car on a Chicago street); Homer "Big Potatoes" Wilson, who had robbed banks for two decades without ever being apprehended; Tommy Gannon; Tom Philbin; Tommy Banks; Kid Can; and Frank "Jelly" Nash, one of the most notorious and durable bankrobbers in the nation, who was to meet his grimly ironic end at the Kansas City Massacre.

It was from this amazing assortment of stickup men, bankrobbers, and killers that Ma Barker and her sons selected their helpmates.

After working several successful bank jobs in the northwest, the Barkers filtered down to Kansas City. From there Ma planned the raid against the Fort Scott, Kansas, bank. The boys got $47,000 there in May, 1932 with the help of gunmen Larry DeVol, Phil Courtney, Alvin Karpis, and Harvey Bailey.

Soon, however, police were on the trail and Ma and the boys headed back to St. Paul; once in St. Paul they planned another big job in Kansas. Mobility was everything then, and Ma knew it.

Freddie and Doc Barker (who had been paroled through Ma's persuasiveness in time to help pull the Fort Scott job), Karpis, and expert gunmen Frank Nash, DeVol, and Earl Christman, then knocked over the Cloud County Bank in Concordia, Kansas.

The take was $250,000.

In December, 1932, the boys robbed the Third Northwestern Bank of $20,000. Machine-gunner Volney Davis was in on that one.

In April of 1933, after wintering in luxury in Reno, Nevada, the Barkers robbed the bank at Fairbury, Nebraska. Again the take was impressive: $151,350.

Shortly after that, Ma became inspiration-struck. They would kidnap wealthy St. Paul brewer William A. Hamm, Jr. and ransom him for $100,000. There were less risks in kidnapping, she reasoned.

They took Hamm quickly on June 14 and within three days released him forty miles north of St. Paul after getting the ransom. As in almost all of their robberies up to this point, someone else was blamed; Roger Touhy got the nod from the authorities.

Kidnapping worked so well, Ma got greedy. They would now, she said, snatch Edward G. Bremer, a wealthy Minneapolis banker, and get twice as much for him—$200,000. The following year they pulled it off, but Doc Barker left a fingerprint and the gang was now identified.

In the spring of 1934, the Barkers, feeling local and federal heat for the first time, became desperate. They were out in the open, known. Pictures of Doc and Freddie Barker, Alvin Karpis, and other gang members were prominently displayed in such magazines as *Liberty* and *True Detective*, as well as upon the thousands of FBI wanted posters.

Freddie Barker and Karpis decided to change their appearances. The two gangsters went to Joseph P. "Doc" Moran, a practicing physician who operated on the other side of the law at high fees. Moran, who maintained offices on Irving Park Blvd. in Chicago, specialized in plastic surgery and fingertip alterations. He had also spent some time in Illinois' Joliet prison for illegal abortions performed on syndicate whores.

After injecting Barker and Karpis with heavy doses of morphine, Moran worked on their noses, chins and jowls. He froze their fingertips with cocaine and scraped them with a scalpel, "sharpening the ends of my fingers just like you'd sharpen a pencil," Karpis added later.

The operations were not successful: both Karpis and Barker were in a good deal of pain and did not notice any appreciable change in their make-up. Both developed ghastly scars that would not heal on their faces. Barker's thumbs became infected and swelled. Ma and Dolores Delaney, Karpis's girl, nursed them as best they could.

One night, Fred yelled out in pain: "I'm going to kill that guy [Moran] as soon as I can hold a gun!"

But Moran, a man in his late thirties whose addiction to liquor made him look twenty years older, had not lost his usefulness. He had been paid $1,250 for the two operations but was told he could make a lot more by helping to unload the hot ransom money from the Bremer kidnapping.

Dope addict Russell "Slim Gray" Gibson acted as the

go-between for underworld figures such as "Boss" John J. McLaughlin, a Chicago politician, and Moran, doling out thousands of dollars in exchange for small percentages of "safe" money. The strain on Moran became intense, especially when McLaughlin was picked up by the FBI who had traced a hot Barker hundred-dollar bill to him. The gang, taking Moran along, moved to Toledo, Ohio, where their strong contacts with the Licavoli syndicate gang would afford them cover.

Once more, Moran drank himself into a permanent stupor while living in a Toledo whorehouse. Once, he bragged to the madam: "I've got this gang in the hollow of my hand—right there!" He offered a cupped palm. "In the hollow of my hand!" The madam called Barker and Karpis.

In late August, Doc and Freddie Barker took Moran for a ride; he never came back. Freddie told Karpis: "Doc and I shot the son of a bitch. Anybody who talks to whores is too dangerous to live. We dug a hole in Michigan and dropped him in and covered the hole with lime. I don't think anybody's going to come across Doc Moran again."

Things got hot after Moran's death and everybody scattered. Doc Barker was trailed to Chicago and taken without a fight on the night of January 8, 1935. Doc was surrounded on Surf Street by Melvin Purvis and a dozen other FBI agents after gang member "Slim Gray" Gibson, had informed on him.

Barker was taking his usual evening stroll. As agents searched him, Doc merely smirked. He had no weapon.

Purvis studied him. "Where's your gun?"

Doc half smiled. "Home . . . and ain't that a hell of a place for it?"

Purvis hustled his prize catch to FBI headquarters at the Bankers' Building in downtown Chicago. Agents grilled him hour after hour as to the whereabouts of the rest of the gang. Barker gave them nothing. Purvis wrote later: "He sat in his chair, his jaw clenched, and looked straight ahead. He was not impressive-looking; only his eyes told the story of an innate savagery." Being hand-cuffed for eight days and nights to that chair still couldn't budge Doc's memory.

He spent the rest of his life at Alcatraz until he was

killed trying to make a break on June 13, 1939. He had made it over the high walls of Alcatraz and to the rocky beach of San Francisco Bay. Frantically, he assembled what strewn waterlogged timber there was, tying it together with strips of his shirt, attempting to build a raft.

"Barker!" a voice from the guard's tower above him yelled down through a bullhorn, "throw your hands in the air."

Doc Barker glanced up at the tower only once and then went back to his frenzied work, pushing out a little until the water was at his knees. Police guns from the tower barked and Doc spun in the air, riddled, falling with a splash and dying instantly.

The FBI, through a marked map of Florida found in Doc's apartment, tracked down Ma and Freddie to a southern resort in Oklawaha on Lake Weir in Florida. Guns drawn, they asked the Barkers to come out of their cottage. Suddenly, they heard Kate Ma Barker give her youngest son his last command: "All right! Go ahead!"

After a moment, the Barkers opened up on the G-Men. FBI agents returned their fire and inside of 45 minutes the cottage was a sieve. The Barkers had stopped firing. So had the agents, who were out of ammunition, having to send for more from a Jacksonville armory.

Agents then sent a Negro handyman, Willie Woodbury, who worked for the Barkers, into the cabin. The elderly man hesitantly walked inside. Moments later he called out from an upstairs window: "Dey's heah, boss. Dey's dead." (Quote as written by FBI agent Melvin Purvis.) Entering, the agents found Ma and Freddie shot to pieces in an upstairs bedroom. They had died fighting, Fred still holding his Thompson sub-machinegun. A .300 gas-operated rifle with 40 of its 94 rounds gone was next to Ma.

Freddie had been hit eleven times, Ma three, one directly through the heart. This shot, some reported, had been self-inflicted. It's not hard to believe that Ma would end her life the same way her son Herman had chosen.

There was $10,200 in clean currency found in Ma Barker's handbag. Born of a poor family, she died comparatively rich.

George Barker, the man Ma and her four sons had deserted, remained to receive the bodies of his family in

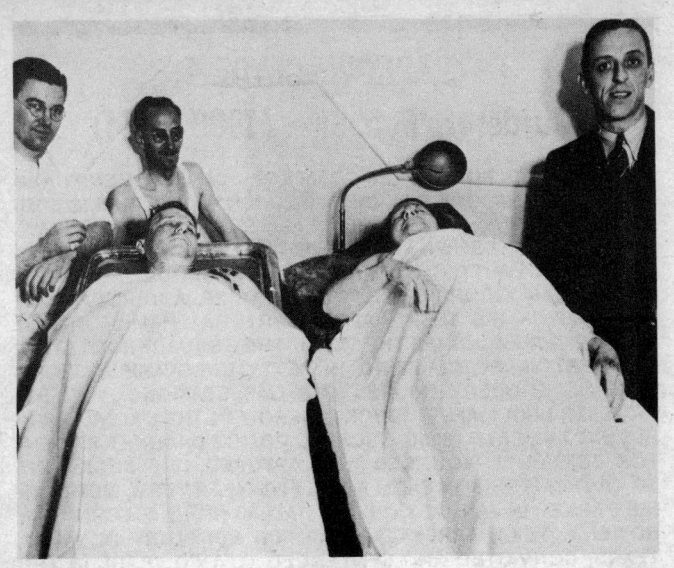

Freddie (left) and Ma Barker in the morgue after shooting it out with federal agents in a remote Florida resort, 1935. (UPI)

the small town of Welch, Oklahoma where they all now rest. Herman was dead, Freddie was dead. Ma was dead. Doc was dead. Lloyd, finally paroled from Leavenworth in 1947, died two years later, killed by his wife.

George Barker buried them all in an open field not far from where he ran a clapboard filling station. New superhighways skirted the dirt road by which it squatted, but sometimes a rare tourist would come by, kicking up dust. George Barker would amble up from his chair in the sun, fill the tank, and study the lonely road.

Once a tourist noticed the clump of graves, their markers poking oddly above the tall reeds about them.

"What's that? A graveyard?"

"That's Ma and the boys," George Barker said.

[ALSO SEE Alvin Karpis, *Bloodletters and Badmen, Book 3.*]

BARROW, CLYDE
Murderer, Robber • (1909-1934)

BACKGROUND: BORN IN TELICE, TEXAS 3/24/09 TO HENRY AND CUMIE BARROW, ONE OF EIGHT CHILDREN. MINOR PUBLIC EDUCATION. ORIGINAL OCCUPATION, FARMER. DESCRIPTION: 5'6¾", BROWN EYES, BROWN HAIR, SLIGHT BUILD. ALIASES: NONE. RECORD: COMMITTED TO HARRIS COUNTY SCHOOL FOR BOYS, 1918 AS "AN INCORRIGIBLE TRUANT, THIEF, AND RUNAWAY"; RELEASED IN HIS TEENS; ALONG WITH RAY HAMILTON AND FRANKE CLAUSE JOINED THE SNEAK-THIEF SQUARE ROOT GANG IN HOUSTON, SPECIALIZING IN PETTY BURGLARIES; BEGAN ROBBING GROCERY STORES AND GAS STATIONS WITH HIS BROTHER IVAN MARVIN (BUCK) BARROW IN THE DALLAS AREA DURING THE LATE 1920S; ESCAPED POLICE DRAGNET AT DENTON, TEX., BUCK WOUNDED AND CAPTURED, 1928; BUCK SENT TO EASTHAM PRISON FARM FOR A FIVE-YEAR TERM; MET BONNIE PARKER IN JANUARY, 1930 IN DALLAS (BONNIE BORN 1911, ROWENA, TEX.); ARRESTED, 1930 FOR BURGLARY IN WACO, TEXAS, CONVICTED AND SENTENCED TO TWO YEARS IN THE WACO JAIL; DAYS AFTER BUCK BARROW ESCAPED EASTHAM 3/2/30, CLYDE, USING A GUN SMUGGLED TO HIM BY BONNIE PARKER, ESCAPED; RECAPTURED IN MIDDLETON, O., SENT TO EASTHAM PRISON FARM; KILLED FELLOW INMATE, ED CROWDER, 1931; PAROLED 2/2/32; STOLE A CAR IN MARCH, 1932 WITH BONNIE PARKER, PURSUED BY POLICE AND OVERTAKEN IN MABANK, TEX.; BONNIE CAPTURED AND SENTENCED TO THREE MONTHS IN JAIL AT KAUFMAN, TEX.; CLYDE, WITH RAY HAMILTON, ROBBED THE SIMS OIL COMPANY IN DALLAS, 3/25/32 ($300); ROBBED A JEWELRY STORE IN HILLSBORO, TEX., ($40), KILLING JEWELER JOHN N. BUCHER; ROBBED WITH HAMILTON AND FRANK CLAUSE SEVERAL GAS STATIONS IN THE LUFKIN, TEX. AREA IN MAY, 1932; ROBBED A DALLAS LIQUOR STORE 5/12/32 ($76); KILLED SHERIFF, C. G. MAXWELL AND DEPUTY EUGENE MOORE AT A BARN DANCE, ATOKA, OKLA. 8/5/32; ROBBED THE NEUHOFF PACKING COMPANY 8/12/32 ($1,100); BONNIE PARKER REJOINED CLYDE 8/12/32; TOOK SHERIFF JOE JOHNS OF CARLSBAD, NEW MEXICO HOSTAGE 8/13/32, DROPPING HIM OFF THE NEXT DAY IN SAN ANTONIO, TEX.; ESCAPED POLICE DRAGNET ON THE COLORADO RIVER BRIDGE AT WHARTON, 8/14/32; RAIDED WITH HAMILTON THE NATIONAL GUARD ARMORY AT FORT WORTH, STEALING BOXES OF MACHINEGUNS, AUTOMATIC RIFLES, AND SHOTGUNS, SEPTEMBER, 1932; ROBBED THE ABILENE STATE BANK ($1,400) 10/8/32; ROBBED GROCERY STORE IN SHERMAN, TEX.

10/10/32 ($50), KILLING BUTCHER HOWARD HALL; ROBBED WITH BONNIE THE ORONOGO, MISSOURI BANK ($200), 11/9/32; STOLE FORD V-8 IN TEMPLE, TEX., 12/23/32, KILLING ITS OWNER DOYLE JOHNSON; ESCAPED POLICE TRAP IN DALLAS 1/6/33, KILLING DEPUTY MALCOLM DAVIS; HELD STATE MOTORCYCLE POLICEMAN THOMAS PERSELL HOSTAGE 1/9/33; BUCK BARROW, WHO HAD BEEN RECAPTURED IN 1931 PAROLED 3/20/33, JOINED CLYDE, BONNIE AND W. D. JONES; BARROW GANG ROBBED A JEWELRY STORE IN NEOSHO, MO., RAIDED A FEDERAL ARMORY IN SPRINGFIELD, MO. AND STUCK UP A LOAN OFFICE IN KANSAS CITY, KAN. IN MARCH–APRIL, 1933; ESCAPED POLICE TRAP IN JOPLIN, MO. 4/13/33, KILLING TWO POLICEMEN, WES HARRYMAN AND HARRY L. MCGINNIS; HELD H. D. DARBY AND SOPHIE STONE HOSTAGE 4/27/33, LATER RELEASED THEM UNHARMED: ROBBED THE LUCERNE STATE BANK IN INDIANA 5/8/33 ($300); ROBBED THE FIRST STATE BANK OF OKABENA, MINN. 5/16/33 ($1,500); ROBBED THE ALMA STATE BANK, TEX. 6/22/33; ROBBED A PIGGLY WIGGLY STORE, FAYETTEVILLE, TEX. 6/23/33; KILLED MARSHAL H. D. HUMPHREY NEAR ALMA 6/23/33; KILLED TRAFFIC OFFICER, OKLAHOMA CITY, OKLA., JULY, 1933; STOLE A CAR, RAIDED THE NATIONAL GUARD ARMORY AT ENID, OKLA., JULY, 1933; ROBBED THREE GAS STATIONS 7/18/33, FORT DODGE, IOWA; ESCAPED POSSE, LED BY ARMORED CAR, NEAR PLATTE CITY, IOWA, BUCK AND BLANCHE BARROW WOUNDED; POSSE SURROUNDED BARROW GANG AT PICNIC GROUNDS OUTSIDE OF DEXTER, LA., 7/24/33, BLANCHE AND BUCK BARROW CAPTURED, BUCK DIED OF SIX BULLET WOUNDS IN THIS FIGHT FIVE DAYS LATER; W. D. JONES, CLYDE BARROW, BONNIE PARKER ALL WOUNDED BUT ESCAPED; ELUDED POSSE NEAR GRAND PRAIRIE, TEX. 11/22/33, BOTH BONNIE AND CLYDE WOUNDED IN LEGS; BROKE RAY HAMILTON, JOE PALMER AND HENRY METHVIN OUT OF EASTHAM PRISON 1/16/34; ROBBED A BANK IN LANCASTER, TEX. 1/20/34; ESCAPED POLICE DRAGNET OF 1,000 POLICE AND NATIONAL GUARDSMEN IN THE COOKSON HILLS, 2/17/34; KILLED TWO STATE MOTORCYCLE POLICEMEN, E. G. WHEELER AND H. D. MURPHY, WHO INTERRUPTED A PICNIC NEAR GRAPEVINE, TEX. 4/1/34; KILLED BY POSSE ON THE ROAD BETWEEN SAILES AND GIBSLAND, LA., 5/23/34.

The year was 1933 and the place, Oklahoma City, Oklahoma. It was hot and the young, somewhat well-dressed couple in the black Ford had the windows rolled down.

As they came to a corner, the young woman driving braked the car to a stop and glanced at the corner traffic cop with his white helmet worn against the blazing hot sun. An unnatural smile twisted upward on the right side of her face. She poked her companion, a sleepy-eyed youth.

"Watch this," she said to him as she worked the sawed-off shotgun upward from the driver's well until it rested between her legs. She moved the car forward slowly, pausing in the intersection.

"How do I get to Sixth and Main?" she said innocently in a sweet voice.

The traffic cop gave her the directions, smiled and touched the tip of his helmet. Then the girl brought out the shotgun and, firing both barrels, blew his head off. The headless, bloody corpse swooned slowly in the hot Oklahoma sun and then toppled backward toward the cement.

The girl let out a squeal, the youth chuckled, and they drove off. This was the real Bonnie and Clyde.

There never was, in the annals of American crime, a more pathetic, illogical, and murderous pair of social truants.

These two penny-ante outlaws—they never robbed anything but gas stations, luncheonettes and a few small-town banks—epitomized the hardscrabble 1930's and the grubbing poor dust bowl Oakies from which they came.

Unlike the legend, Bonnie and Clyde were far from Robin Hood types. They preyed on their fellow poor and killed them ruthlessly, thoughtlessly. They were hated by their own kind.

The biggest haul the Barrow gang ever gleaned was $1,500. John Dillinger, who read about their southwestern exploits in 1933 while he was still waiting to be released from the Michigan City, Indiana Penitentiary, called them "a couple of punks. They're giving bank robbing a bad name!"

They never entered John Dillinger's class or matched his heists—his biggest being $74,000 at Greencastle, Indiana in 1933. But they possessed, for those who did not know them, the devastating and down-home image of the displaced person whose cool resignation to oblivion was embodied in their slogan: "They wouldn't give up till they died."

Born into a brutally poor farm family in Telice, Texas

in 1909, Clyde was the third youngest of eight children. His boyhood was pockmarked with pranks and just plain trouble. His older brother Buck was his bad example and Buck was hellbent for young death, progressing early from selling stolen turkeys to stealing cars. Clyde was right behind him.

At an early age, Clyde developed a taste for music, so he stole a saxophone. As a teenager, Clyde went to Houston, Texas, where he rolled drunks, stole cars, and enjoyed some "high livin."

But the high living cost money, so Clyde, armed with an old horse pistol that wouldn't fire, held up a gambling den. The take was small but he managed to get his hands on two very real .38s. From then on it was running all the way.

Clyde, joined by his brother Buck, pulled a string of robberies in the Dallas area. Then the boys held up a gas station in Denton, Texas. The law jumped them and a highspeed pursuit at 90 mph developed with Clyde, who was normally an excellent driver, at the wheel. Taking a sharp turn, the car rammed into a ditch, breaking both axles. Buck had been wounded during the chase and Clyde left him for the law. Buck received a five year term at Eastham prison farm.

Clyde went on with his smalltime holdups and in January, 1930, he met five-foot, golden-haired, 90-pound Bonnie Parker. He walked into a little Dallas cafe where she was a waitress. Bonnie was nineteen years old and married to Roy Thornton, a convict at Eastham prison farm doing a 99-year term for murder.

Bonnie had not been faithful to Thornton, even though she had his name and two hearts tattooed on her right thigh. She dated everybody and that included Clyde.

Life in Dallas in 1930 was tedious and, in her own words, Bonnie was "bored crapless." Clyde Barrow was a mover and shaker to her. He was doing something, even if it was outside the law. They began living together. Bonnie liked it that way; Clyde was going somewhere.

He certainly was ... straight to jail. Dallas lawmen came for him while he and Bonnie were necking on the sofa in a small, threadbare apartment. Clyde was arrested for a burglary committed in Waco, Texas, where he had ne-

Clowning it up, Bonnie Parker "gets the drop" on Clyde, 1933. (UPI)

glected to wear gloves; the fingerprints he left behind convicted him. He received two years in the Waco jail.

Then Buck escaped from Eastham prison on March 2, 1930. Good old Buck, he knew how to work things out, Clyde thought as he planned his own escape. A few days later, Bonnie Parker walked into the Waco jail with a .38 Colt equipped with a Bisley handle thin enough to squeeze through bars. She had it taped to her thigh and slipped it to Barrow. He forced his way out that night and headed for Abilene, leaving Bonnie behind. Clyde ran as far as Middleton, Ohio, where train police grabbed him as soon as he jumped from a fast freight. This time he was sent to Eastham, known as "The Burning Hell."

If his poverty-striken home life didn't make Clyde Barrow into a criminal, then Eastham surely did.

At Eastham, Clyde was beaten with whips and tortured on the "barrel cavalry"—made to mount a pickle barrel on top of a sawhorse and sit until he collapsed in the burning sun. There he also killed his first man.

An informer, Ed Crowder, told prison authorities Clyde had been gambling. Later, after being punished, Barrow armed himself with a lead pipe and smashed Crowder's head to pulp.

After Clyde had served twenty months in this sore-festering prison, his mother, Mrs. Cumie Barrow, went to Texas Governor Ross Sterling. She pleaded for his release. A month later, the governor granted it.

It was February 2, 1932 and Clyde Barrow would never see the inside of another prison. "I'll die first," he said. He did.

Bonnie teamed up with Clyde in March, 1932, but after they stole a car lawmen sighted them and another spectacular chase developed. Clyde crashed the car into a tree and the two ran across the fields attempting to escape. Deputies caught Bonnie, locked her in jail for three months, and then released her. Meanwhile, Clyde went on robbing tank town cafes and filling stations throughout Texas. His take for the month: $76. In Hillsboro, Texas, Clyde shot 65-year-old John M. Bucher to death while robbing him of ten dollars in his jewelry store.

Governor Sterling put a $250 reward on Clyde's head, but this didn't stop Clyde from shooting Sheriff C. G. Maxwell and Deputy Eugene Moore in Atoka, Oklahoma at a barn dance. The officers had the nerve to ask him what he was doing there lurking in the shadows. Clyde killed them both.

Bonnie and Clyde, with a gunsel named Ray Hamilton, headed for New Mexico where Bonnie had relatives. It was the fall of 1932 and Bonnie and Clyde had twenty-one months to live.

Their life together on the open road was a strange one. Though Clyde was portrayed as being impotent, his real bent was homosexuality; that was another "lesson" he learned at Eastham. It was Ray Hamilton who slept with Bonnie . . . and Clyde. Later W. D. Jones, the gas-station attendant who joined the Barrow gang for kicks, would serve as lovers to both. Bonnie bordered on nymphomania and she slipped across that border many times.

All through 1932, Bonnie and Clyde went their wild, reckless way. On October 8, 1932, they knocked over the Abilene State Bank for $1,400. It was small pickings but times were tough.

Stopping for groceries a few days later in Red River Valley, Clyde tussled with a butcher whom he tried to rob. The man attacked him with a cleaver but missed. Clyde fired six rounds into him from his .45, scooped up some tin goods and took $50 from the till. The butcher died hours later.

The two young outlaws slept in the open, made coffee over campfires and ate peanut-butter-and-jelly sandwiches. The only real beds they knew were in remote tourist cabins and fishing grounds.

On November 14, 1932, while Bonnie manned the wheel of the car, Clyde robbed the Oronogo, Missouri state bank. The take was awful, a few hundred dollars. Then the two, homesick, sped to Dallas to see Bonnie's relatives.

It was on this trip that Bonnie and Clyde picked up the gas station attendant turned apprentice robber, W. D. Jones. The awe-struck Jones joined them immediately and began to live through "18 months of hell," as he later described it.

He was forced to rob banks, fire a machinegun and was constantly ravaged by both Bonnie and Clyde. They even tied him up at night with chains so he couldn't escape. That was his tale, at least.

The trio drifted aimlessly in and about the Southwest through the early part of 1933, continuing to hold up small-town banks and stores. Then, Blanche Barrow, Buck's wife, went to the Texas Governor, wept and carried on. She had three children and no support and another baby

A typical picnic for Bonnie Parker and her mass slayer boyfriend, Clyde Barrow (shown cleaning part of his arsenal). This photo was taken by Buck Barrow in a wooded area near Dexter, Iowa, 7/24/33; minutes later a hundred-man posse burst through the trees behind them. Buck, mortally wounded, and his wife Blanche were captured; Bonnie and Clyde got away.

on the way. Please, please, please release Buck, she begged.

Governor Sterling had been replaced by kind-hearted Mrs. Miriam A. "Ma" Ferguson who was absolutely wild about pardons—she had given out two thousand of them in her first term during the Twenties. Buck Barrow got one, too.

Buck and Blanche immediately joined brother Clyde, Bonnie and W.D. They headed straight for the federal armory in Springfield, Missouri. Days later, brandishing their new machineguns, the Barrow gang held up a loan office in Kansas City.

They were roaring now and the nation's press lavished front-page stories on their most meager exploits. Clyde, who was named the "Texas Rattlesnake," received most of the attention. But Bonnie wasn't far behind. An enterprising newsman dubbed her "Suicide Sal."

The Barrows were snapshot fanatics and would often pose menacingly with automatic rifles, pistols, and other assorted weapons of their vast arsenal. Bonnie posed once with Clyde, both holding pistols on each other, grinning. On one occasion Bonnie dangled a pistol from her hip and clenched a cigar in her mouth, portraying the deadly gun moll.

Later, Bonnie told one of the gang's many hostages, Police Chief Percy Boyd: "Tell the public I don't smoke cigars. It's the bunk."

But Bonnie enjoyed her publicity, and she wrote a long poem about their exploits which was published in many newspapers. By then, she had begun to realize that instead of "going some place" with Clyde Barrow, she was "just going." And she also knew death wasn't far behind.

Bonnie told her mother in the early months of 1934, "When they kill us, Mama, bring me home. Please don't let them lay me out in a funeral parlor."

The Barrow gang roared on through all the small towns, hiding, hitting, running. Bonnie knew death was closing in when they barely escaped a trap in Joplin, Missouri. In a wild shoot-out the Barrows escaped, killing two lawmen, constable Wes Harryman and detective Harry McGinnis.

After the escape, lawmen found Bonnie's poem on the kitchen table, unfinished. She later completed it. Her doggerel was a curious blend of self-exoneration and fatal prophecy:

THE STORY OF SUICIDE SAL
by "Bonnie" Parker

We, each of us, have a good alibi
For being down here in the joint;
But few of them are really justified,
If you get right down to the point.

You have heard of a woman's glory
Being spent on a downright cur.
Still you can't always judge the story
As true being told by her.

As long as I stayed on the island
And heard confidence tales from the gals,
There was only one interesting and truthful,
It was the story of Suicide Sal.

Now Sal was a girl of rare beauty,
Though her features were somewhat tough,
She never once faltered from duty,
To play on the up and up.

Sal told me this tale on the evening
Before she was turned out free,
And I'll do my best to relate it,
Just as she told it to me.

I was born on a ranch in Wyoming,
Not treated like Helen of Troy,
Was taught that rods were rulers,
And ranked with greasy cowboys . . .

The Joplin raid interrupted the poem at this point. Bonnie finished her tale weeks later and mailed it to a newspaper. The last stanzas read:

You have heard the story of Jesse James,
Of how he lived and died.
If you still are in need of something to read,
Here is the story of Bonnie and Clyde.

Now Bonnie and Clyde are the Barrow gang.
I'm sure you all have read
How they rob and steal,
And how those who squeal,
Are usually found dying or dead.

There are lots of untruths to their write-ups,
They are not so merciless as that;
They hate all the laws,
The stool-pigeons, spotters and rats.

If a policeman is killed in Dallas
And they have no clues to guide—
If they can't find a fiend,
They just wipe the slate clean,
And hang it on Bonnie and Clyde.

If they try to act like citizens,
And rent them a nice little flat,
About the third night they are invited to fight,
By a submachinegun rat-tat-tat.

A newsboy once said to his buddy:
"I wish old Clyde would get jumped;
"In these awful hard times,
"We'd make a few dimes
"If five or six cops would get bumped."

They class them as cold-blooded killers,
They say they are heartless and mean,
But I say this with pride,
That once I knew Clyde
When he was honest and upright and clean.

But the law fooled around,
Kept tracking him down,
And locking him up in a cell,
Till he said to me,
"I will never be free,
"So I will meet a few of them in hell."

This road was so dimly lighted
There were no highway signs to guide,
But they made up their minds
If the roads were all blind
They wouldn't give up till they died.

The road gets dimmer and dimmer,
Sometimes you can hardly see,
Still it's fight man to man,
And do all you can,
For they know they can never be free.

They don't think they are too tough or desperate,
They know the law always wins,
They have been shot at before
But they do not ignore
That death is the wages of sin.

From heartbreaks some people have suffered,
From weariness some people have died,
But take it all in all,
Our troubles are small,
Till we get like Bonnie and Clyde.

Some day they will go down together,
And they will bury them side by side.
To a few it means grief,
To the law it's relief,
But it's death to Bonnie and Clyde.

The police closed in fast after Joplin. They captured Blanche Barrow and shot holes into Buck in Dexter, Iowa, July 24, 1933 on a deserted fair grounds where the gang had been hiding. Bonnie and Clyde got away, Bonnie wounded.

Throughout 1934, the two were on the run, but on May 23, set up for a trap by a friend, Henry Methvin, the two were killed at a roadblock ambush near Gibland, Louisiana. A well-armed posse led by Texas Ranger Frank Hamer pumped 187 shells, such was their fierce legend, into Bon-

"It's the bunk about me smoking cigars," Bonnie Parker told a police hostage after this photo (found in a Joplin, Mo. apartment along with Bonnie's poem, "Suicide Sal") was widely published by newspapers in 1933. (UPI)

nie and Clyde, killing them instantly. Clyde had been driving in his socks and Bonnie had a sandwich in her mouth.

Hamer had tracked the two outlaws for 102 days. His telephone report of the shooting to the Texas Highway Patrol was laconic: "There wasn't much to it. They just drove into the wrong place. Both of them died with their guns in their hands, but they didn't have a chance to use them."

Unlike Bonnie's prediction, the killer-lovers were not buried side by side. Clyde was buried next to his brother Buck in West Dallas cemetery. Bonnie was first buried miles away in Fish Trap Cemetery and later removed to Crown Hill Memorial Park.

At Bonnie's burial, a local quartet sang "Beautiful Isle of Somewhere." On her tombstone ran the mawkish verse (not her own):

As the flowers are all made sweeter
By the sunshine and the dew,
So this old world is made brighter
By the lives of folks like you.

BECKER, CHARLES
Murderer, Extortionist • (1869-1915)

BACKGROUND: BORN AND RAISED IN NEW YORK CITY, MARRIED. ROSE THROUGH THE RANKS OF THE NEW YORK CITY POLICE DEPARTMENT, REACHING THE RANK OF LIEUTENANT. MINOR PUBLIC EDUCATION. DESCRIPTION: 6'2", BROWN EYES, BROWN HAIR, HEAVYSET, SWARTHY. ALIASES: NONE. RECORD: EXTORTED MONEY FROM ILLEGAL GAMBLING CASINOS IN THE BROADWAY, TENDERLOIN, AND HELL'S KITCHEN AREAS OF NEW YORK FOR YEARS. ORDERED THE KILLING OF GAMBLER HERMAN

"BEANSIE" ROSENTHAL ON 7/21/12. AFTER TWO LENGTHY TRIALS, BECKER WAS CONVICTED OF MURDER AND SENTENCED TO DEATH. EXECUTED IN THE ELECTRIC CHAIR AT SING SING PRISON, 7/7/15.

One of America's greatest novelists, Stephen Crane, watched horrified one evening in the 1890s as a patrolman—tall, massive-shouldered, and with the largest pair of hands he had ever seen—sauntered up to a small, white-faced prostitute. He demanded his share of money from her latest job. She shook her head at the burly extortionist. The patrolman's gigantic hands doubled into fists and began to beat her with hammer-like blows until she crumpled to the ground, her face ripped to a bloody pulp.

Before Crane could move, the huge cop had scooped up the prostitute's miserable change and walked away. This man was not an ordinary cop as Stephen Crane and the rest of the country would later discover. He was Charles Becker "the crookedest cop who ever stood behind a shield."

Although Crane would write Becker into his novel about the little New York prostitute: *Maggie: A Girl of the Streets*, the world was yet to really know this most brutal of men.

When dapper Rhinelander Waldo became New York's police commissioner in 1911, he made Becker a lieutenant and his aide. The big cop had charmed his way into the post. He then charmed the gullible Waldo into naming him as the head of Special Squad Number One.

This squad had but one assignment: crack down on the wide-open graft, gambling and prostitution then rampant in New York. Under Becker's greedy direction this police squad became a strong-arm gang of terrorists promoting its own graft and corruption.

Becker's take came mostly from kickbacks on prostitution and gambling; under his "protection," gambling dens flourished in the Tenderloin and Broadway strips. Becker's "protection" assured him of twenty-five cents on the dollar.

When gamblers refused to kick back, Becker's squad raided their casinos, destroying everything in sight. With particularly stubborn customers, the squad faked evidence and brought in convictions, making Becker appear reliable and upright. It was cheaper, the gamblers learned, to pay off the big cop.

To collect his graft, Becker employed some of the strangest bagmen ever seen in the underworld. One was "Billiard Ball" Jack Rose, who didn't have a single hair on his head. Another was a professional killer from the Lower East Side, "Big Jack" Zelig.

Also making the rounds for Becker were Bridgie Weber, Sam Schepps and a man who had a face like a character out of Bram Stoker's *Dracula,* Harry Vallon. These unsavory criminals were immune to prosecution. "Nothing you do for me will get you in trouble with the law," Becker had promised. The big cop enjoyed his role of enforcer as he swaggered throughout Manhattan, well-tailored, glib, demanding tribute from the corner of his mouth.

Becker had been closely associated with gambler Herman "Beansie" Rosenthal for years. Rosenthal owned a gambling spa called The Hesper and, once each week, kicked back half of his take to Becker. Suddenly, as was Becker's habit over real or imagined slights, the ham-fisted cop took a dislike to "pasty-face" Rosenthal. "He's a goddamn coward and he talks too much," Becker said one day to Vallon.

Even though he owned a large piece of The Hesper, Becker demanded more of the take and Rosenthal balked. Becker went into an hysterical rage and ordered his flying squad to smash Beansie's gambling casino. Every stick of furniture was broken. No one said *no* to Charles Becker.

He placed a policeman on duty outside the closed gambling den and, incredibly, one in Rosenthal's apartment— twenty-four hours a day. Rosenthal's wife underwent a nervous breakdown and Beansie almost went berserk staring at the cop sitting placidly in his living room.

With his business closed and his house invaded, Rosenthal finally launched a plan to retaliate against his oppressor Becker. The gambler knew that Charles S. Whitman, New York City's young and aggressive District Attorney, wanted to break Becker's criminal stranglehold on Manhattan. Rosenthal also knew that Whitman had no evidence against Becker. His hatred for Becker bubbling over, Rosenthal went to the District Attorney and gave him everything he needed to indict the crooked cop—

New York Police lieutenant Charles Becker (shown in 1911) was the king of graft in Manhattan, ruthlessly ordering death for anyone, such as gambler Herman Rosenthal, who displeased him. (UPI)

names, places, dates, the amounts of graft the Becker ring had collected for years.

Whitman moved immediately to have a grand jury convene to indict Becker. Through the well-greased grapevine that fed the crooked cop his information, however, Becker learned of the impending indictment and Rosenthal's betrayal. He gathered his murderous clan, including Billiard Ball Jack Rose and Jack Zelig. Zelig brought in four East Side killers: Gyp the Blood (Harry Horowitz), Dago Frank (Frank Cirofici), Lefty Louis (Louis Rosenberg), and Whitey Lewis (Jacob Siedenshner).

"I want Rosenthal croaked!" Becker screamed at the group. "Kill him anywhere. Do it in front of a policeman and it will be all right. I'll take care of everything."

Herman Rosenthal had the habit of stopping by the Cafe Metropole for a late night coffee and brandy. The Metropole on West 43rd Street was a gambler's hangout and Beansie would trade talk there with his fellow high rollers. But when Rosenthal entered the cafe late on the night of

July 21, 1911, no one would talk to him; the gamblers, gangsters, and racetrack touts thought him a turncoat.

None of the angry looks or snarling remarks his friends gave him upset the small gambler. He moved about freely, ignorantly showing everyone a newspaper which told his tale in bold headlines. "That's what the newspapers think of me," he commented.

At 2 a.m., a voice from the doorway called out, "Herman, somebody wants to see you."

Without a sign of apprehension, Rosenthal casually walked out the door and stood blinking under the bright marquee lights of the cafe.

Another voice called out from the darkness: "Over here, Beansie."

As Rosenthal moved in the direction of the voice, four shots quickly rang out and the gambler collapsed to the cement. Then one of Charles Becker's murder group ran forward and leveled his pistol at Rosenthal's head while he lay bleeding on the sidewalk. The killer blew away part of Beansie's skull with the final shot.

The killing occurred in full view of dozens of Metropole customers. It was one of the most blatant and ill-conceived murders in American crime, yet the killers were confident that Becker would protect them.

Becker had boldly instructed police to "lose" the license number of the murder car should some zealous citizen turn it in. Smugly, he thought his order would be sufficient to quash any investigation. But District Attorney Whitman spoiled the killer cop's arrangements. Through a tipster, Whitman learned that police were hiding an eyewitness to the Rosenthal slaying in a back cell of a remote station. He appeared, demanding to talk to the witness.

Ludicrously, there was even a scuffle with the sergeant in command before Whitman spirited his witness away. Through this man, the District Attorney was able to trace the license number of the murder car to its owner, Billiard Ball Jack Rose.

Brought in for questioning, Rose admitted nothing. Ten days passed and when Becker did not intervene on his behalf as promised, Rose panicked. "I'm being thrown to the wolves," he wailed and then asked to see Whitman.

Billiard Ball's mouth didn't close until he had named Rosenthal's killers. Gyp the Blood and the others were quickly arrested. They, too, named Becker as their boss. Rose was given immunity for his testimony but the gunmen were promptly convicted and electrocuted.

The two trials of Lieutenant Becker dragged on for almost three years. Finally, he was sentenced to death after being found guilty of planning Rosenthal's murder.

The powerfully-built Becker was led into the electrocution room at Ossining on July 7, 1915 and several jolts of electricity were sent through his massive body. He was so strong, however, that it required repeated jolts to finally kill him. The execution was one of the clumsiest in Sing Sing's history.

By the time Becker came to be executed, Whitman had become Governor of New York, largely on the strength of convicting the crooked cop. He refused to stay Becker's death sentence.

After the execution, Becker's faithful wife had a plaque (later removed) placed on the crooked cop's tombstone which read:

> CHARLES BECKER
> Murdered July 7, 1915
> By Governor Whitman

BLACK HAND, THE

Contrary to popular belief, The Black Hand was anything but a single organization officially associated with such secret brotherhood groups as the Mafia and the Camorra. It was essentially an extortion racket practiced by Sicilian and Italian gangsters (many of whom were members of the evil brotherhoods) for approximately thirty years—1890 to 1920—against the unschooled, superstitious immigrants of the "Little Italy" settlements sequestered in major Eastern, Southern, and Midwestern cities.

The racket consisted of sending an unsigned note to a prominent and well-to-do member of the Italian or Sicilian community, demanding money under the penalty of death. The sender usually threatened to kill the victim's family and, to create an air of outright terror, would mark the extortion letter with ominous symbols such as daggers, skull and crossbones, hatchets, and sabers dripping blood. In most cases, the outline of a hand dipped in heavy black ink was impressed at the bottom of the note. This was usually sufficient to frighten the recipient into delivering large amounts of extortion monies to the Blackhander at a specified secret place.

New York, Chicago, New Orleans, St. Louis, and Kansas City were centers of this activity, all of these metropolitan areas containing the largest segments of Italian and Sicilian immigrants in the country.

In New York, the top Blackhander for three decades was Ignazio Saietta, known to inhabitants of Little Italy as Lupo the Wolf. Others who operated in Brooklyn and Manhattan during Saietta's Black Hand supremacy were Frankie Yale (Uale), Johnny Torrio, and Ciro Terranova, who later became the rackets czar known as "The Artichoke King."

Saietta concentrated his Black Hand terror against Sicilians living in the Harlem district; he was more than once arrested for Blackhanding by Lieutenant Joseph Petrosino, the intrepid head of the NYPD's special Italian squad, whose almost impossible job it was to track down the extortionists. Saietta's Black Hand fortune, however, permitted him the best lawyers in the community and he squeaked past one indictment after another. He was finally put out of action by his own greed when he thought counterfeiting would be more lucrative than extortion; he was caught by Secret Service agents and sent to prison for thirty years.

Lieutenant Petrosino got it into his head that most of the Blackhanders probably had criminal records in Sicily. If the New York authorities could prove nothing against

New York's Ignazio Saietta, a vicious Blackhander known to the Italian community he terrorized as Lupo the Wolf. (UPI)

these extortionists, he reasoned, they could at least be permanently deported to Sicily if they were wanted there. He began lengthy correspondence with Sicilian authorities, sending them the NYPD records of Sicilians arrested for Blackhanding. His work paid off. Police in Palermo, Sicily sent back wanted sheets on many of these, and more than 500 Sicilian gangsters were subsequently deported to their native country to face prosecution and imprisonment.

In some instances, Petrosino, a hulking six feet, 200 pounds, did not wait for the mail from Sicily. When his good friend, the internationally famous tenor, Enrico Caruso, received a Black Hand note, Joe tracked down the sender by himself. He broke the man's arms and personally threw him onto a boat headed for Sicily with the warning that he would "blow out" the man's brains if he ever came back to the U.S.

The guile which personified the Blackhanders was not for Joe Petrosino. He faced the extortionists squarely in alleys and dark hallways, most often alone, and handled them with his fists and police revolver. On one occasion he tracked down Enrico Alfano, a ranking member of the murderous Camorra brotherhood of criminals, who had killed several helpless persons in New York after they refused to pay Black Hand notes. Alfano was wanted, Italian police notified Petrosino, for killing and mutilating an entire family in Naples.

It was the kind of job Petrosino liked. He located Alfano's room. Drawing his .38 caliber service revolver, Petrosino raised his heavy foot and slammed it against the door. It banged down on two men who were waiting on the other side with drawn guns. Petrosino jumped onto their stomachs with each foot and leveled his gun at Alfano who was making for a window.

"Go ahead, rat!" the policeman yelled. "My bullet will take away your head." Alfano meekly dropped his gun and surrendered. Petrosino roped all three Blackhanders together with their own ties and a bedsheet and dragged them down four flights of stairs and through the gutters of Little Italy on Mulberry Street for two blocks to the station, telling the startled Italian spectators along the way: "Is this what you're afraid of, these gutter rats? How fierce is the Black Hand now? Spit on them!" But none dared to spit.

Petrosino's life was lived against razor-thin odds. He himself received over a thousand Black Hand notes telling him to leave New York or die. He was repeatedly shot at on the street. Knives flashed in bustling crowds, slashing out at him. Poison was put into his food in restaurants. But still he lived, honored by the city of New York and by the Italian and Sicilian governments for his service. Italian authorities presented him with an enscribed gold watch.

Petrosino decided that instead of sending makesheets on those suspected of Blackhanding in New York to Sicily and Italy, he himself would journey to Palermo. There, he concluded, it would be easier if he merely went through the police files checking mugshots to locate wanted criminals he knew were living in the U.S.

Joe convinced Police Commissioner Bingham to send him to Palermo, Sicily in 1909. Arriving in Palermo, Petrosino energetically tackled the police archives there, unearthing hundreds of wanted cards on fugitives known to the NYPD. These he mailed in large batches to Bingham, who promptly had the criminals arrested and arraigned for deportation.

But Petrosino was living inside a hornet's nest. His investigation ran headlong into the core of the Mafia and the Mafia dons wanted him exterminated; he was getting too close to knowledge concerning their own activities and power. *Capo di tutti capi* (boss of bosses) "Don" Paulo Marchese, head of the Mafia's Grand Council in Sicily, actually entertained Petrosino in an exclusive restaurant to learn if the policeman knew of the Mafia hierarchy. When he discovered that Petrosino was hot on the trail, he ordered him murdered.

The next evening, March 12, 1909, Petrosino waited at the base of the Garibaldi statue in the large Piazza Marina in the very center of Palermo. He had been tipped that an informant would meet him there with a complete list of all the important Mafia chiefs in Sicily and the U.S. He was met, however, by more than a hundred shots fired from the darkness and killed.

His death caused an international uproar and produced profuse apologies from the Italian Government. His killers were never apprehended.

Petrosino's effects were shipped to his wife Adelina (who was given a permanent $1,000-a-year pension by the NYPD and $10,000 from friends for the care of her young son). The courageous policeman's belongings were returned to her; they consisted of one "gold watch and chain, pair gold cuff links, cane, two dress suitcases containing personal effects, package of letters and a check for $12.40." After 26 years in desperate pursuit of the Black Hand, this was Joseph Petrosino's legacy.

Marchese, who found Sicily too hot for him after the killing, immigrated to the U.S., living briefly in New York under the name Paul Di Cristina. He then journeyed to New Orleans where he plied the Black Hand trade.

As head of the Mafia in New Orleans, Di Cristina felt powerful enough to operate openly. He delivered his Black Hand notes in person. Fearing instant death, none dared resist—none except stubborn Pietro Pepitone, a grocer. After Pepitone told Di Cristina's strong-arm men that he would not pay any Black Hand money, the boss himself showed up to collect. As Di Cristina casually alighted from his wagon, drawn up in front of the grocer's store, Pepitone stepped out to the sidewalk with a shot gun and emptied

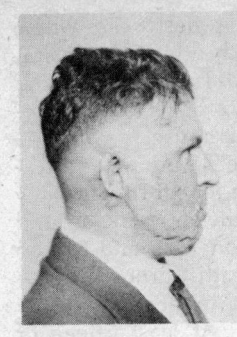

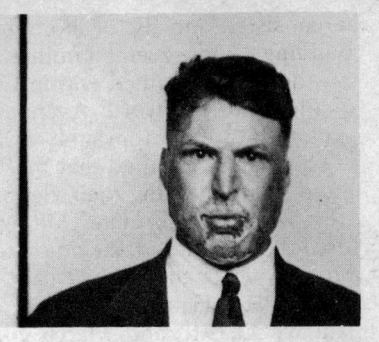

Joseph "Scarface" DiGiovanni, notorious Kansas City Blackhander, who was horribly disfigured when a still blew up in his face.

it into the boss Blackhander, killing him. This killing touched off one of the fiercest vendettas ever experienced in America by Mafia factions (see MAFIA). Pepitone got twenty years in the Louisiana State Penitentiary but was paroled in six years.

The Italians of Kansas City were plagued by Blackhanders from 1912 to the early 1920s, the most notable offender being Joseph "Scarface" DiGiovanni. Sicilian-born in 1888, DiGiovanni immigrated to K.C. in 1912 and only days after receiving his naturalization papers there went into the Black Hand business, with his brother Peter "Sugarhouse Pete" DiGiovanni. The brothers were arrested by Kansas City detective Louis Olivero in 1915 after the police received complaints from about twenty Black Hand victims. Detective Olivero was shot in the back and killed days laters. The victims wilted in court and remembered nothing.

Black Hand thugs made it a practice to attend any and all court cases involving Blackhanders. Witnesses against them were silenced in seconds after getting the high sign from one of the thugs. The sign was delivered in many ways—drawing a finger across the throat, displaying a red handkerchief, pointing an index finger to the temple—all of them meant death to any witness who dared to testify.

Chicago's history of the Black Hand, like New York's, dated back to about 1890. The violence displayed by Chicago Blackhanders against their victims was devastating;

it consisted mostly of bombings that destroyed whole buildings and several families in each attack. Little Italy—the area contained within Oak and Taylor Streets and Grand and Wentworth Avenues—was a Black Hand playground, more appropriately a slaughterhouse.

For years, it seemed that Blackhanders were more interested in annihilating their victims than in extorting money from them. Black Hand killings reached a peak around 1910-11 in Chicago. At one intersection, Oak and Milton Streets, which the Italians named "Death Corner," thirty-eight Black Hand victims were shot to death between January 1, 1910 and March 26, 1911. At least fifteen of those killed were dispatched by a professional Black Hand assassin referred to by the residents as "Shotgun Man." This killer, never apprehended, walked about openly in Little Italy and was well known. He had no loyalty to either victim or Blackhander. He hired out his gun and would murder without flinching, carrying out death sentences decreed by Blackhanders who could not collect. Blackhanders paid him handsomely for his services.

One criminal historian estimated that close to eighty Black Hand gangs terrorized Chicago's Little Italy during the first two decades of the present century. Some of these gangs, wholly unrelated to each other signed their notes as "The Mysterious Hand," or "The Secret Hand," but it meant the same thing: Pay or Die.

The notes Chicago Blackhanders sent their victims were couched in unbearably polite words, making them all the more sinister. The letter received by a wealthy Italian businessman typified the courteous but deadly Blackhander of this era:

> "Most gentle Mr. Silvani: Hoping that the present will not impress you much, you will be so good as to send me $2,000 if your life is dear to you. So I beg you warmly to put them on your door within four days. But if not, I swear this week's time not even the dust of your family will exist. With regards, believe me to be your friends."

This letter was not signed but police still managed to

trace it to one Joseph Genite (who was discharged for lack of evidence), in whose house they found a stockpile of dynamite, two dozen revolvers, several sawed-off shotguns, and other assorted weapons.

Other Black Hand notes were less formal:

> "You got some cash. I need $1,000. You place the $100 bills in an envelope and place it underneath a board in the northeast corner of Sixtyninth Street and Euclid Avenue at eleven o'clock tonight. If you place the money there, you will live. If you don't, you die. If you report this to the police, I'll kill you when I get out. They may save you the money, but they won't save you your life."

The police in most instances were helpless; the notes were all but impossible to trace. When witnesses did come forward they quickly retracted their statements after being contacted by Black Hand enforcers. In desperation, police raided Chicago's Little Italy in January, 1910, and rounded up close to two hundred known Sicilian gangsters suspected of running Black Hand extortion rackets. All were released within twelve hours for lack of evidence.

For a five-year period—1907 to 1912—upstanding business leaders of the Italian community banded together to form the White Hand Society which actually supplied its own police force and money to prosecute Black Handers. Many extortionists were put in prison, but were shortly paroled through contacts with corrupt local and state officials. Dr. Joseph Dimiani, one of the White Hand leaders, explained why the Society threw in the sponge. "They [the White Handers] were so discouraged by the lax administrations of justice that they were refusing to advance further money to prosecute men arrested on their complaints."

A rash of bombings came next. Experts used by the Black Hand were brutal enforcers such as Sam Cardinelli, his chief lieutenant, eighteen-year-old Nicholas Viana, known as "The Choir Boy," and dim-witted Frank Campione. The three, all later hanged for murder, were responsible for at least twenty bombings in which dozens of Italians were killed. One police estimation reported that more than 800 bombs were directed against Black Hand victims in Chicago between 1900 and 1930, most of them during the period from 1915 to 1918.

A whole generation of professional bombers who had once worked for Black Hand gangs found heavy-duty work in the dawn-of-the-1920s bootleg wars between gangs in Chicago. Many of these were used in Chicago union wars, as well. The Italian and Sicilian Black Handers in earlier days preferred to use non-Italian bombers to prevent identification. When the Black Hand operations fell off in the early 1920s, these non-Italian bombers went to work for union gangsters. One of these, Andrew Kerr, was arrested in 1921 and boasted that he employed the best bombers in the business to enforce his edicts over the Steam and Operating Engineers union.

Kerr named Jim Sweeney as a boss bomber. Sweeney's group of killers included "Soup" Bartlett and "Con" Shea, who had murdered whole families with bombs for decades. Shea, Kerr swore, had been a professional bomber since he was sixteen years old.

Boss of the barber's union in Chicago, Joseph Sangerman took Sweeney's position as king of the bombers after Sweeney was arrested and sent to prison. Sangerman's top bomber was George Matrisciano (alias Martini) who manufactured his own "internal machines" of black powder. This berserk bomber, who had terrorized Black Hand victims for twenty-five years, always walked about with two sticks of dynamite in his pockets. Before Sangerman had him killed, Matrisciano could be seen approaching total strangers in Little Italy and proudly showing them a newspaper clipping which described him as "a terrorist."

A sharp decline of Black Hand operations followed Matrisciano's death, and finally the racket ceased to flourish. Police had failed to snuff out the Black Hand terror; it was the coming of Prohibition and its big-moneyed rackets which ended the terrible extortions. Like stock market investors, almost everybody happily plunged into bootlegging—even the courteous murderers of Little Italy, much to the gratitude of its hounded residents.

C

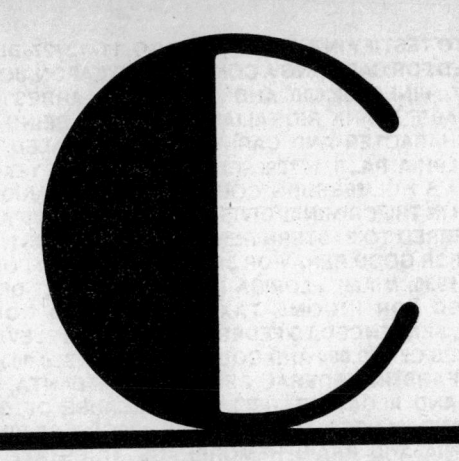

CAPONE, ALPHONSE ("SCARFACE")
Murderer, Crime Czar • (1899-1947)

BACKGROUND: BORN IN NYC, 1/17/1899 OF GABRIEL AND TERESA CAPONE (PRONOUNCED CAP-OWN, NEE CAPONI) WHO IMMIGRATED TO THE U.S. IN 1893 FROM NAPLES, ITALY. CAPONE WAS THE FOURTH OLDEST OF NINE CHILDREN INCLUDING JAMES, RALPH ("BOTTLES"), FRANK, JOHN ("MIMI"), ALBERT JOHN, MATTHEW NICHOLAS, ROSE, AND MAFALDA. MARRIED MAE COUGHLIN 12/18/18. SON ALBERT FRANCIS ("SONNY") BORN IN 1919. MINOR PUBLIC EDUCATION. DESCRIPTION: 5'10½", GRAY EYES, DARK BROWN HAIR, STOUT BUILD, OBLIQUE SCAR OF 4" ACROSS LEFT CHEEK 2" IN FRONT OF LEFT EAR; VERTICAL SCAR OF 2½" ON LEFT JAW; OBLIQUE SCAR OF 2½", 2" UNDER LEFT EAR. ALIASES: AL BROWN, ALFRED CAPONI, A. COSTA. RECORD: ARRESTED FOR DISORDERLY CONDUCT IN OLEAN, N.Y., 1919, DISCHARGED; ARRESTED FOR SUSPICION OF MURDER IN NYC, 1919, DISMISSED; ARRESTED FOR ASSAULT WITH AN AUTOMOBILE, DRIVING WHILE INTOXICATED, CARRYING A CONCEALED WEAPON, CHICAGO, 1922, CHARGES DROPPED AND EXPUNGED FROM POLICE RECORDS; ARRESTED FOR BLOCKING TRAFFIC, CHICAGO, CHARGE DISMISSED, 1923; ARRESTED FOR SUSPICION OF MURDER, CHICAGO, 5/8/24, RELEASED; ARRESTED FOR SUSPICION OF MURDER, NYC, DECEMBER, 1925, DISMISSED; ARRESTED FOR VIOLATION OF THE NATIONAL PROHIBITION ACT, CHICAGO 6/7/26, DISMISSED; ARRESTED FOR MURDER, CHICAGO 7/28/26, CHARGE WITHDRAWN; ARRESTED FOR VIOLATION OF THE NATIONAL PROHIBITION ACT, CHICAGO 10/1/26, DISMISSED; ARRESTED FOR RE-

FUSING TO TESTIFY IN KILLING, CHICAGO, 11/12/27, DISMISSED; ARRESTED FOR CARRYING A CONCEALED WEAPON, JOLIET, ILL., 12/22/27, FINED $2,600 AND DISMISSED; ARRESTED WITH BODYGUARD, FRANK RIO (ALIAS KLINE) FOR BEING A SUSPICIOUS CHARACTER AND CARRYING A CONCEALED WEAPON, PHILADELPHIA, PA., 5/17/29, SENTENCED TO ONE YEAR IN PHILADELPHIA'S HOLMESBURG COUNTY PRISON BY JUDGE JOHN E. WALSH IN THE CRIMINAL DIVISION OF THE MUNICIPAL COURT, TRANSFERRED TO EASTERN PENITENTIARY, AUGUST, 1929, RELEASED FOR GOOD BEHAVIOR 3/17/30; ARRESTED FOUR TIMES IN MAY, 1930, MIAMI, FLORIDA FOR "VAGRANCY," DISMISSED; ARRESTED FOR INCOME TAX EVASION AND CONVICTED 10/24/31, SENTENCED TO FEDERAL PRISON FOR ELEVEN YEARS WITH FINES OF $50,000 AND COURT COSTS OF $30,000; SERVED EIGHT YEARS IN FEDERAL PRISONS IN ATLANTA, LEAVENWORTH, AND ALCATRAZ; RELEASED BECAUSE OF GOOD BEHAVIOR AND ILLNESS, 11/16/39; DIED 1/25/47 OF BRONCHIAL PNEUMONIA AND BRAIN HEMORRHAGE AT ESTATE IN PALM ISLAND, FLA.; BURIED AT MOUNT OLIVET CEMETERY IN CHICAGO, BODY LATER SECRETLY REMOVED TO MOUNT CARMEL CEMETERY.

All of the doors of the Hawthorn Hotel in Cicero, Ill., were barred. The windows were sealed and draped expensively. Inside, at a long table in the private dining room, dozens of swarthy men in tight tuxedos gulped blood-red wine and devoured *linguine* coated with shrimp sauce. Al "Scarface" Capone sat smiling at the head of the table.

At the other end of the table sat three equally happy men—John Scalise, Albert Anselmi, and Joseph "Hop Toad" Giunta. These men were Big Al's ace gunners, a trio of cold-eyed killers who had, for the past ten years, mercilessly chopped down rival gangsters and balking politicians by the scores. Scarface was grateful.

"Saluto, Joe," Capone said to Giunta and raised his brimming glass of chianti.

"Saluto, Scalise, saluto, Anselmi!"

The three men raised their glasses in glee at the boss' toast. Al was such a wonderful guy.

"These are my boys," Capone bawled and with a sweep of the arm took in his three guests who beamed. "Such good boys, too. Always loyal to Al. Never a question. Tell 'em to do this, do that, and they do it." Capone pushed back from the table and got up leisurely, still smiling.

"If it wasn't for these three fine boys, where would I be, I ask you?" Capone held onto his smile but his stare was like ice as he took in the now frozen band of gangsters. "Yes, where would I be?"

Capone walked heavily around the table as his three honored guests clung to half smiles, amused. "I'll tell you where I would be," Capone said softly. And then he screamed, "I would be safe from a bullet in the head!"

He was quick for his five feet ten inches and 225 pounds. He reached beneath the banquet table and withdrew a baseball bat and then raced around the table behind his now petrified three guests.

"Bastards! You were gonna get me killed and take over, huh? Bastards!"

Crash, the bat came down on Joe Giunta's head, crushing his skull and killing him instantly. He moved over to Scalise next and slammed the ballbat down to cave in his head also. Eyes begging and lips bitten so hard the blood ran down his chin, Albert Anselmi took the same death blow looking straight ahead.

Capone's eyes bulged and his porcine, florid face glistened with sweat. He breathed heavily, hushed swearwords gushing from his mouth like spittle. He glared down at the three corpses and noted the splashes of blood from their heads staining the starched tablecloth. "Get 'em outa here!" he roared and several men scrambled to remove the bodies.

This was a typical Capone dinner in Chicago, May 7, 1929, a few short months after the very men Scarface murdered had killed seven of Bugs Moran's gang for him in the St. Valentine's Day Massacre.

The three murdered men had been disloyal and Al Capone liked to think of himself as a loyal man. In the space of a dozen bullet-torn years he rose from an obscure bouncer in Big Jim Colosimo's posh restaurant on Wabash Avenue, to the total blood-drenched ruler of Chicago. By then he was only thirty years old and he made $5,000,000 a year.

"Scarface" was born in Brooklyn in 1899. He was raised in the violent hell of Brooklyn's Williamsburg section.

Always a large, chunky kid with murderously big hands, Al climbed rapidly through the hierarchy of the street gangs and became a member of the notorious Five Points Gang. He was a labor union "slammer" who muscled union leaders unwilling to kick back dues to the gang.

Early in his Brooklyn days, Capone took a job as a bouncer and bartender in a notorious brothel-saloon, the Harvard Inn. One evening he passed an uncomplimentary remark about one of the girls at the bar. Unfortunately for Capone, the girl's brother, Frank Galluccio, a known felon, suddenly leaped over the bar, stiletto in hand, slashing out revenge. The result of Galluccio's fast carving became Capone's involuntary trade-mark for life—three ugly, jagged scars on the left side of his face that stood out white and hairless (Capone used mountains of talcum powder to soften the appearance).

Capone never sought revenge for the act against Galluccio. Ironically, Capone later hired his attacker as a bodyguard at $100-a-week, proving again, when it was important to his press, that he could be magnanimous. Al claimed (and several criminal historians bought the story) that he had been wounded by shrapnel while fighting with the famous "Lost Battalion" in France, but this, like so many of his self-constructed legends, was created to gain him sympathy.

Capone's career as an apprentice hoodlum in Brooklyn was mainly directed and inspired by an older boy, Johnny Torrio. Before he went West to help his wife's cousin—Big Jim Colosimo of Chicago—run his immense brothel empire, Torrio was the leader of the Five Points Gang in Brooklyn. Al worshipped the bantam killer, called him "Johnny Papa," and once told newsmen: "I'd go the limit for Johnny." He did, including murder.

Torrio never tired of playing *patron* to his hulking protege. After both men married Irish girls ("They make the best wives, Al; they don't run around."), Torrio became the godfather to Capone's only son, Albert Francis, nicknamed Sonny. Every year on his birthday, Torrio bought his godson a $5,000 bond.

Once situated with Colosimo in Chicago—in charge of Big Jim's hundreds of brothels in the Red Light districts— Torrio sent for his boy Capone. Al was happy to leave

Brooklyn. A police officer had been pistol-whipped to death there and Capone was wanted for questioning.

So in through the gilt-edged doors of Colosimo's nightspot came Scarface in the year 1919 wearing a thirty-dollar suit, scuffed shoes, and no tie. His only baggage was a .38 pistol tucked inside his waistband.

Capone was only 19 then, crude, loud, and Torrio's gunman . . . as Colosimo was to find out too late. Big Jim taught Al an appreciation for life's finer things: a taste for opera (his favorite was Verdi), tailored clothes, expensive cars, society contacts.

The Scarface went to work, first as a bouncer at Colosimo's plush cafe, then as a gun toting aide-de-camp for Torrio, policing brothels, keeping all the madams in line, bagging the daily take and, incidentally, sleeping with Chicago's best whores. He began as a $75-a-week tough and by 1922 he was raking in two thousand a week.

Capone's "front" was printed on his business card which read: "Alphonse Capone, Second Hand Furniture Dealer, 2222 S. Wabash." To make the front seem more real, Capone even put up a few cheap displays of broken-down furniture in the bay windows of some of the whorehouses he managed for Big Jim and Torrio.

When Prohibition became law in 1920, Torrio realized the golden opportunity. Everyone wanted to drink and bootlegging would be big business. There would be millions! But Big Jim Colosimo with his fine clothes and swanky restaurants and well-paying whorehouses couldn't see it. He was making money, life was sweet and he had his reserved seat at the opera. Why go looking for trouble?

"It's business, it's business, Jim," Torrio argued.

"I don't understand it. We stay out. That's final."

It was final. A few days later, Alphonse Capone waited behind the glass doors of a telephone booth in Colosimo's nightclub . . . doing a favor for "Johnny Papa." Big Jim never knew what hit him as he crashed to the tile floor of his club's vestibule. Capone fired through the glass of the door, catching his boss with a shot under the left ear, killing him instantly. Al stepped from the phone booth, tore Big Jim's clothes apart as if a robber had been searching for a money belt, and then quietly left the restaurant.

Torrio and Capone were hauled into police headquarters for questioning. They were angry and tears streamed down their faces. "Big Jim was like a father to me. Colosimo was the kindest man I ever met . . . who would want to hurt Big Jim? God, captain, it's terrible, killing that wonderful old man, a cultured gentleman like that." They were released. "No evidence"—a phrase which was to become standard for Chicago's gang murders during the next ten years.

The day following Colosimo's execution—March 21, 1920—Torrio, with Capone as his right-hand man sharing in 25% of all profits, took over Big Jim's empire.

Capone's first arrest was in 1922. Drunk, his car loaded with several ladies of the night, Scarface smashed into a taxicab. He was doing sixty miles an hour down Wabash Avenue. Three bodyguards sat in the back of his car.

The cabdriver staggered from his taxi holding his head and cursing, "You crazy son-of-a-bitch! You almost killed me!"

Capone jumped from his expensive car and rushed the driver. His pistol was out and pointed at the amazed cabbie. "Goddamn you little bastard, don't talk that way to me!"

"Hey, now wait a minute, fella. How come you got a gun on me?"

Capone stopped and thought a moment. Then he produced a special deputy sheriff's badge. "I'm a law officer."

This was too much for Capone's nervous companions, who could hear the approaching clang of police gongs. They left the hot-head on the street and took off.

Police collared Capone and took him in while cabdriver Fred Drause had his head bandaged. The arrest—Scarface was booked as "Alfred Caponi"—came to nothing. The clout was in by then—Torrio and Capone owned too many judges and police chiefs for notice to be made of such "mischief."

The kind of protection from the law enjoyed by Torrio, Capone, and other Chicago gangsters of the era was never more in evidence than on the night of May 8, 1924. That night in Heinie Jacobs' bistro on South Wabash, "Ragtime" Joe Howard was boasting of how easy it was to hijack beer trucks, particularly those owned by Johnny Torrio.

Howard was a criminal product of another age. He did not carry a gun: such a weapon was not necessary in his day at the turn of the century, and it wasn't necessary in 1924, he told his pal Heinie. "Brass knuckles to the jaw is good enough. Them wop beerboys fold up like old newspapers after one chop."

At that moment, Howard spotted Jake "Greasy Thumb" Guzik, Capone's financial wizard, ambling out of the bar. Howard barred his way. "This is one of them wop workers," Ragtime Joe said. He slapped the small, portly Guzik across his wattles and then added a couple of kicks to the shins. Terrified, Guzik merely took the abuse and then sheepishly walked away—straight to Al Capone.

Minutes later, Capone walked through the doors of Heinie Jacobs' place and Howard, apparently expressing a change of heart toward Italian bootleggers, smiled and put out his hand. "Hello, Al," he said affably.

Grabbing Howard by his coat, Capone shook the independent hijacker. "Why did you kick Jake around, Joe?" he yelled.

Howard, still smiling, became indignant at being manhandled in front of his friends. "Aww, go back to your girls, you dago pimp!"

Capone produced a pistol, placed it to Joe Howard's temple, and emptied all six bullets into his head. Scarface then sauntered out of the saloon.

Three amazed witnesses at that late hour—Heinie Jacobs and two customers, George Bilton and David Runelsbeck, stared at the floor where Ragtime Joe lay, still grinning. When police arrived they immediately inventoried Joe's estate: "1 pair cuff buttons; cash $17." The witnesses swore in anger that Al Capone had been the killer.

The Chicago Tribune published Capone's picture the next morning for the first time, a face that would become synonymous with Chicago and such inglorious terms as "the rubout," "the one-way ride," and "the cement overcoat." A month went by before Capone walked into a police station, stating, "I hear the police have been looking for me. What for?"

Captain James McMahon of the Cottage Grove station instantly hustled Capone to the Criminal Courts Building, where he was interrogated by a young assistant state attorney, William H. McSwiggin.

"You killed Joseph Howard, Capone," McSwiggin charged. "We've got witnesses."

"Who, me?" Capone responded with raised eyebrows. "Why, I'm a respectable businessman. I'm a second-hand furniture dealer. I'm no gangster. I don't know this fellow Torrio. I haven't anything to do with the Four Deuces. Anyway, I was out of town the day Howard was bumped off. You had better do your talking to my lawyer."

McSwiggin's witnesses suddenly lost their memories. Bilton disappeared. Runelsbeck couldn't identify the killer; Heinie Jacobs was at the end of the bar when the shooting occurred.

The coroner's jury at Howard's inquest handed down a familiar verdict: "Joe Howard came to his death at the hand or hands of one or more *unknown*, white male persons . . ."

A year and ten months after Howard's death, State Attorney McSwiggin, along with two West Side gangsters, James J. Doherty and Tom Duffy, was slain by a machine-gunner outside of a Cicero saloon. The heavyset man wielding the "chopper" was identified as Al Capone. This charge, too, was dismissed.

After Big Jim Colosimo's $20,000 funeral—the first of the splashy gangster send-offs—Torrio and Capone celebrated. Big Jim was dead and they had his rackets, his nightclub and his women. They could also run their booze into the Windy City. Chicago was all theirs. Well, almost.

A tough, church-going, street-fighting Irishman on Chicago's North Side had different ideas. His name was Dion O'Bannion and he knew what Prohibition meant, too. And Deanie, as his fellow Irish mobsters affectionately called him, wasn't alone.

Facing Torrio and Capone were whole armies of ambitious gangsters cutting themselves in on the boozy empire of Prohibition. Allied with the Torrio-Capone mob were the six terrible Genna brothers, killers all. The Italians could also count on Ralph Sheldon, Frankie Lake, Frank McErlane, and Terry Druggan.

But the rest . . . "those Irish bastards," Capone would complain, were Deanie's boys. There were the South Side

Five of Capone's top gunmen who made Scarface's power in Chicago for a decade (left to right): William "Klondike" O'Donnell, William "Three-Fingered Jack" White, Murray "The Camel" Humphreys, Marcus Looney, and Charles Fischetti. (UPI)

O'Donnell brothers, six of them to match the Gennas. Then there were the West Side O'Donnells, Klondike and Miles.

The North Side, naturally, was all O'Bannion's. His hired hijackers and killers and rumrunners were the most colorful. Earl "Hymie" Weiss was his right-hand man—a shrewd murderer with an obsession for showgirls. Vincent "The Schemer" Drucci would yank out his cannon in broad daylight, threaten a cop writing him a traffic ticket, and get away with it. Two-gun Louis Alterie actually wore two six-guns which he would whip out instantly, twirl, and replace and was called the Cowboy because he owned a ranch in Colorado. George "Bugs" Moran, Deanie's enforcer, was known as "The Shootin' Fool."

It was a frightening array of killers that stood in Torrio's path. He could count, however, on Capone's 300 top gunsels.

For four years these underworld armies worked their own territories by mutual agreement (O'Bannion had Chicago's North Side, Torrio-Capone, the South Side—Madison Street was the dividing line—with smaller gangs to the west and southwest, snatching what they could from the other side of the fence. But it was not open warfare. Torrio and Capone had seen to that by holding a gangster summit meeting where the city was cut up like a pie and everybody agreed not to get out of line or kill each other.

Capone always had eyes for the North Side. "O'Bannion's nuts," he said once to "Machine-Gun" Jack McGurn. "Not one cat house up there. The phony church-going turkeyneck. Says its immoral. Whores immoral? What the hell kind a guy is that, I ask you, Jack? Cat houses mean money! The buck! Business."

So Capone tried to cut into Deanie's territory in the 42nd and 43rd wards, installing his high-priced prostitutes. O'Bannion, who had been a choir boy at Holy Name Cathedral (and across from which he had his "front"—a flower shop) learned about it and exploded.

He was also upset that Capone had done in his friends the O'Donnells and taken over their South Side territory. The O'Donnells had referred to Capone as a "dago punk" and a "stinking greaseball." Scarface didn't care for that so he sent Danny McFall and Frank McErlane out and they sprayed the whole O'Donnell gang with machinegun fire. Within weeks, only Spike O'Donnell was alive.

"Those killings weren't Torrio's orders," O'Bannion said later in his flower shop. Hymie Weiss nodded. "They were all done by that dirty atheistic dago! Did you see poor Jerry O'Connor's face at the funeral home. It was blown off. Nothing left to it. And Walter O'Donnell, too. And all those other lads. That Capone kills like a beast in the jungle!" The ever-faithful Weiss nodded to that, too.

O'Bannion was addressing a Capone associate who was friendly with the Irishman. Then Weiss turned to the Capone man and said, "You can tell Capone this for me. If he ever pulls anything like that on us, I'm going to get him if I have to kill everybody in front of him to do it. You can tell him that, and if I see him I'll tell him." The message was delivered and Al Capone started to sweat.

O'Bannion and his boys weren't like the O'Donnells. Deanie had congressmen and judges and half the police force on his payroll. His army of torpedoes was almost as large as the Italian contingent. Capone also remembered the words of Chicago Police Chief Morgan Collins: "Dion O'Bannion is Chicago's arch criminal who has killed or seen to the killing of at least twenty-five men."

Before Capone moved North, O'Bannion came up with a scheme to "take them spaghetti-benders," as he called Torrio and company. He called "Johnny Papa" and told him that he wanted to sell one of his breweries—Siebens by name—and would Torrio be interested. Hell, yes.

Torrio gave O'Bannion $500,000 cash for the brewery. Only days later, police, led by a chief reportedly on O'Bannion's payroll, raided the place and locked up Torrio who was taking inventory of his new property. Coincidence? Capone didn't think so.

Deanie had also been hijacking Genna beer. Weiss told him that the terrible Gennas might begin a full-scale war. "Aw," O'Bannion said, "to hell with them Sicilians."

Scarface heard about the remark and didn't think that was a nice way to talk. O'Bannion had to go.

On November 8, 1924, three men—New York gangster Frankie Yale, imported especially for this occasion, John Scalise, and Albert Anselmi—walked into O'Bannion's flower shop on North State Street. Deanie, who had three guns on him at all times (in specially-sewn pockets of his pants) was holding a pair of shears. He had been trimming chrysanthemums.

O'Bannion had no apprehensions. Mike Merlo, president of the *Unione Siciliane* had just died (a natural demise) and all of gangdom was ordering flowers from his shop for the funeral. "Hello, boys," the Irish killer said and held out his hand to Yale. "You come for Mike Merlo's wreath?"

Yale smiled and took O'Bannion's hand and held onto it. Scalise and Anselmi came up fast on either side firing rapidly into Deanie. The gangster hit the floor, his head in a bucket of flowers. Yale leaned forward and made sure. He fired a bullet into O'Bannion's head. The three calmly walked out of the shop and drove away.

"Hymie Weiss became a raving lunatic," one report says,

"when he heard the news of Dion's murder. He took a solemn oath to kill Capone, and Torrio and everyone else in the Syndicate he could find."

And little Hymie tried his best. Weiss, Moran, and Drucci caught up with Johnny Torrio as he was coming home one night, January 24, 1925, after shopping with his wife.

"Shotguns, Johnny!" Torrio's wife screamed, but Torrio was leaning into his car for packages and didn't move fast enough. Moran and Drucci let him have four barrels from ten feet away.

Moran ran up and put a pistol to "Johnny Papa's" head. He squeezed the trigger. "Goddammit!" Bugs yelled. The gun was jammed. A truck was grinding down the South Side Street and the O'Bannion mobsters thought it was the police. They took off on a run.

When the police did arrive, Torrio looked up weakly. He had been hit in the abdomen, chest, jaw and arm. "Bullets . . . tipped with . . . garlic," he managed to say before passing out.

Though given up for dead by doctors, Torrio managed to survive, but he knew what was coming. He had had Chicago. "It's all yours, Al," he told Capone, and packed. After serving a short term in jail for his Sieben brewery operations, he and his wife left for Italy.

Now Capone, at twenty-five years of age, was the Number One Man in Chicago. He was chairman of the board with an income of $5,000,000 a year, but he had a full-scale war on his hands.

Weiss was a fanatic. He almost got Torrio. At least he drove him out of town. He got on the phone to Capone and demanded that he turn over Scalise and Anselmi to him.

"What? I wouldn't do that to a yellow dog!" Capone yelled back. He slammed the phone down and turned to a bodyguard. "You hear that?"

"Yeah," the bodyguard said.

"Hymie's gotta go," Al said.

Scarface was too slow. Weiss, Moran, and the boys planned their next move.

Capone was sitting with his tough bodyguard Frank Rio in the restaurant of the Hawthorn Hotel. It was September

20, 1926. His hot coffee steamed before him and just as he hooked his thumb around the cup and leaned forward, he heard it. "Typewriters," he gasped and his hand slid into his coat to the left armpit where his gun rested.

This was Cicero, Scarface's fortress to the west of Chicago. He ruled supreme here yet the sound of machineguns came drilling down the street. Rio stood up and looked out the window. People were yelling and running down the sidewalk. The restaurant waiters scampered for the kitchen. A lone car cruised past the hotel, stitching it with machinegun bullets.

Capone started to rise but Rio was quick. He pushed Al down to the floor and shielded him with his body. "It's a stall, boss," he said, "to get you out. The real stuff hasn't started. You stay here."

The real stuff was another eight touring cars brimming with machinegunners. It was crazy; the bootleg war had reached its peak of fury. Here in broad daylight was an open attack on Big Al's stronghold. At high noon! The eight cars came abreast of the hotel spraying everything in sight. Not only that; they stopped and little Hymie Weiss got out and stood boldly in front of the hotel holding his Thompson; Moran was right behind him.

Capone controlled the hotel and all the shops around it. He had 100 men there, all armed. But they dove for cover rather than face the withering fire. Weiss took careful aim and fired from the hip into the hotel's entranceway.

"He used a ukelele with one hundred shells, and his typewriter was set for rapid fire," newsmen wrote later. "That means six hundred shots a minute, including reloading, as an expert can slide in a new drum in four seconds . . ."

Weiss' aim was perfect. "As he pressed the trigger he moved the gun slowly back and forth the width of the passageway. The results are still visible—neat horizontal lines of .45-caliber bullet holes against the wall, some the height of a man's waist, some breast-high."

After Hymie finished his serenade to Scarface, he calmly walked back to his car. Three honks on the horn and the cavalcade drove off leisurely. Every glass pane in the hotel was shattered. But surprisingly, no one was killed.

Capone got up slowly from the restaurant floor, bug-

Capone's top killers, the sinister John Scalise and Albert Anselmi.

eyed, trembling. "Those goddamn bastards! Comin' in here, in here!" He grabbed Rio. "Frank, did you see 'em. Huh?"

"Yeah," Rio said. "It was Weiss. It was Drucci. It was Moran."

"Those bastards are dead," Scarface screamed as he ran through the hotel lobby to inspect the awful damage. His torpedoes gathered about him. They were all shaken. "They're all dead, do you hear me? Dead! Dead! Dead!"

Weiss had his moment of glory and revenge for Deanie's murder. He went down before two Capone gunmen—Scalise and Anselmi—in front of O'Bannion's flower shop. "Hymie," Capone explained to newsmen openly, "is dead because he was a bullhead.

"Forty times I've tried to arrange things so we'd have peace and life would be worth living but he couldn't be told anything!" Drucci went next, killed by a young cop.

Two-gun Louis Alterie was through. His partners on the North Side had no staying power. He retired to his Colorado ranch.

That left only George "Bugs" Moran. Outnumbered and outgunned, Moran knew he was the only real threat left to Scarface but he wouldn't give an inch. He earned the name Bugs the hard way.

Capone took care of Moran by long distance. While living it up in his half million dollar Palm Island retreat outside Miami, he called Chicago. He had some fresh work for Scalise and Anselmi . . . sort of a Valentine.

Early in the morning of February 14, 1929, five men parked a squad car outside a garage at 2122 N. Clark Street. Two were in plainclothes and three were dressed as police officers.

The five marched into the garage—Moran's bootleg headquarters—and lined up seven of the Irish mobsters, who were waiting for a shipment of booze, against the wall. Moran's boys didn't think it unusual, a routine pinch. Bugs would bail them out by noon.

Arriving late, Bugs himself had seen the cops go into the garage and ducked into a nearby coffee shop to wait out the pinch. Inside, however, the "cops" leveled their machineguns at the Moran gang and systematically raked them. They fell away from the wall like lifeless dolls, six of them killed instantly.

Frank Gusenberg lived for a few hours. When questioned, all he had to say was, "Coppers done it."

Moran had more to say, for the first time breaking the underworld code of silence. When he learned of the massacre, he spat out: "Only Capone kills like that!"

Capone's empire was crumbling. Even the hangers-on were getting big ideas. A kinky newspaperman, Jake Lingle of the *Chicago Tribune*, bragged, "I fixed the price of beer in this town!" And he was on Capone's payroll.

Lingle was found in a subway underpass on Michigan Avenue, his brains blown out. Capone, who had given Jake a diamond-studded belt-buckle, lamented in public (as he always did). "Jake was a dear friend of mine," he said. Jake had also taken $50,000 from Capone, promising to use his influence to clear a dog track operation with the city. He never delivered.

Still it seemed nothing could touch Big Al, the Butcher. He had a fortune of $50,000,000, an island estate off Miami, two armored-plated McFarland cars especially made at $12,500 apiece. He was supreme.

But for all his wealth and street savvy, Al had forgotten one thing. He had neglected to pay his income taxes for ten years. Urged by the press and an enraged public at the mass killing on North Clark Street, federal agents moved in.

After offering the government $4,000,000 to forget his income tax oversight (which was promptly turned down), Al Capone went to trial.

Scarface sweated while the government built a strong case against him. He talked freely to the press, trying to explain his position. "All I ever did was to sell beer and whiskey to our best people . . . Why some of the leading judges use the stuff . . . If people did not want beer and wouldn't drink it, a fellow would be crazy for going around trying to sell it.

"I've seen gambling houses, too, in my travels, you understand, and I never saw anyone point a gun at a man and make him go in . . ."

But the government ignored Al's little-boy-innocent act and found him guilty of tax evasion. He was sentenced to eleven years and $80,000 in fines and court costs. They

Chicago's king of crime, Al Capone plays cards with a federal guard on a train taking him to Leavenworth in 1932. (UPI)

sent Scarface to Leavenworth and then the Rock, Alcatraz, where he served out eight years.

Paroled in 1939, Capone was a physical wreck. His high living in the 1920s had made a shambles of his body. He had contracted syphilis years ago from one of "Johnny Papa's" whores. It developed into paresis of the brain and the bug ate him alive. He lived, a powerless recluse, at Palm Island until 1947. He was 48 when he died.

Al Capone had ordered the deaths of over 500 men in Chicago, and more than 1,000 were killed in his bootleg wars. The wholesale slaughterhouse Scarface had made of Chicago was a strange and ironic monument to his own words: "I want peace and I will live and let live!"

[ALSO SEE James "Big Jim" Colosimo, Vincent "The Schemer" Drucci, Dion O'Bannion, O'Donnell Brothers (Chicago, South Side), O'Donnell Brothers (Chicago, West Side); "Machine Gun" Jack McGurn, George "Bugs" Moran, Johnny Torrio, *Bloodletters and Badmen, Book 3.*]

CASSIDY, "BUTCH" (ROBERT PARKER)
Bankrobber, Trainrobber • (1866- ?)

BACKGROUND: BORN ROBERT LEROY PARKER IN CIRCLEVILLE, UTAH, 4/6/1866, ONE OF TEN CHILDREN. NO PUBLIC EDUCATION. ORIGINAL OCCUPATION, COWBOY. DESCRIPTION: 5'9", BLUE EYES, LIGHT BROWN HAIR, MEDIUM BUILD, MUSTACHE (ON OCCASIONS), TWO SCARS ON BACK OF HEAD, SMALL SCAR UNDER LEFT EYE. ALIASES: "BUTCH" CASSIDY, GEORGE CASSIDY, INGERFIELD, MAXWELL, LOWE. RECORD: BEGAN RUSTLING CATTLE WITH OUTLAW MIKE CASSIDY IN THE UTAH-COLORADO RANGES WHILE STILL A TEENAGER; ROBBED WITH TOM AND BILL MCCARTY THE DENVER AND RIO GRANDE TRAIN NEAR GRAND JUNCTION, COLO, 11/3/1887; ROBBED WITH THE MCCARTY BROTHERS AND MATT WARNER (WILLIARD CHRISTIANSEN), THE FIRST NATIONAL BANK IN DENVER, COLO., 3/30/89, ($20,000); ROBBED WITH THE MCCARTY BROTHERS THE SAN MIGUEL BANK IN TELLURIDE, COLO., 6/24/89, ($10,500); ARRESTED BY SHERIFF JOHN WARD IN AFTON, WYO. IN 1894 AND SENTENCED TO TWO YEARS IN THE STATE PENITENTIARY FOR RUNNING A PROTECTION RACKET IN WYO.; RELEASED 1/19/96; RODE TO DIAMOND MOUNTAIN, COLO. WHERE NOTORIOUS OUTLAWS HID OUT AT THE HOLE-IN-THE-WALL, A VAST MOUNTAIN FORTRESS PROTECTED ON THREE SIDES BY SHEER CLIFFS, WITH OUTLAWS ELZA LAY AND BOB MEEKS; ROBBED WITH ELZA LAY A PAYMASTER IN CASTLE GATE, UTAH IN APRIL, 1897, ($8,000); ROBBED THE UNION PACIFIC'S OVERLAND FLYER WITH GEORGE CURRY, HARVEY LOGAN ("KID CURRY") AND ELZA LAY, BLOWING UP THE EXPRESS CAR WITH DYNAMITE, 4/25/98, ($30,000); ROBBED WITH HARVEY LOGAN, CHARLES HANKS ("DEAF CHARLEY"), AND BILL CARVER UNION PACIFIC'S TRAIN NO. 3 AT TABLE ROCK, NEAR TIPTON, WYO., 9/29/1900, ($5,014); ALLEGED TO HAVE ROBBED THE FIRST NATIONAL BANK OF WINNEMUCCA, NEV., WITH HARRY LONGBAUGH (OR LONGABAUGH, ALIAS "THE SUNDANCE KID") 9/19/1900; ROBBED WITH HARVEY LOGAN, HARRY LONGBAUGH, CHARLES HANKS THE GREAT NORTHERN TRAIN NEAR WAGNER, MONT., 7/3/01, ($40,000); FLED TO SOUTH AMERICA WHERE HE AND LONGBAUGH PURPORTEDLY ROBBED SEVERAL BANKS AND THE PAYROLLS OF AMERICAN BUSINESSES IN ARGENTINA AMOUNTING TO $20,000–$30,000; ALLEGEDLY KILLED BY BOLIVIAN SOLDIERS IN SAN VICENTE, BOLIVIA AFTER ATTEMPTING A MINE HOLDUP IN 1908. SOME OF CASSIDY'S RELATIVES INSIST TO

Butch Cassidy of the Wild Bunch, a most happy-go-lucky outlaw. (Wyoming State Archives and Historical Department)

THIS DAY THAT BUTCH RETURNED TO THE U.S. ABOUT 1910 AND LIVED OUT A QUIET LIFE ON A WESTERN RANCH.

Butch Cassidy is unique in the annals of Western outlawry. Not only did he begin late as a train and bank thief, robbing successfully from one century and into another, but he imported his considerable criminal skills to another country where he was just as successful. And there is still the strong possibility that Butch survived the many attempts made on his life by determined posses, and died of old age in a West grown modern.

Cassidy was born Robert LeRoy Parker on a small farm in Circleville, Utah, one of ten children. All but two of the Parker brood, Robert and his younger brother Daniel, became law-abiding citizens. Robert turned to criminal activities in his early teens.

Mike Cassidy, a Western outlaw who had survived many a shoot-out since the 1850s, was a neighbor; young Parker grew so fond of him that he subsequently took the name

81

Cassidy himself. Mike taught his young protege how to shoot better than any apprentice outlaw in the territory. Some stories had it that the teenager became so accurate with a six-gun that he could shoot a playing card dead center from fifty paces away. He was fast on the draw, too.

The elder Cassidy soon introduced his charge to cattle rustling, taking him on long drives in and about the Henry and Colorado Mountain ranges. Soon Butch assumed second-in-command of the Cassidy gang. He took over completely when Mike Cassidy disappeared into Texas after shooting down an angry Wyoming rancher.

Butch was a natural leader—calm, easy-going, softspoken, always reluctant to draw his gun in an argument. Violent, much-sought-after outlaws rode into Robber's Roost, his mountain retreat. There Cassidy met the train-robbing McCarty brothers, Tom and Bill, and Matt Warner, whose real name was Williard Christiansen. Warner was the son of a Mormon bishop.

Cassidy didn't hesitate when the McCarty brothers asked him to come along to Grand Junction, Colo., on a train raid they had planned. Butch's first robbery was a bust. The McCartys and Butch stopped the Denver and Rio Grande express on November 3, 1887. However the express guard gave them trouble from the start by not opening the safe as ordered. The McCartys pointed their six-guns at his head and he still refused.

"Should we kill him?" one of the brothers said.

"Let's vote," Butch said.

The vote went in favor of the guard and he was allowed to live. The train roared off leaving the bandits with nothing and cursing the obstinate guard. The trio switched to bank-robbing the following spring, hitting the large First National Bank of Denver, March 30, 1889.

Tom McCarty, who apparently possessed a macabre sense of humor, coolly approached the bank president and said: "Excuse me sir, but I just overheard a plot to rob this bank."

The bank president became apoplectic. "Lord," he finally managed. "How did you learn of this plot?"

"I planned it," the bandit said. "Put up your hands!"

The take was better this time. Butch, Matt Warner, and

the McCarty brothers walked out of the bank without a shot being fired—and with $20,000 in notes. Matt Warner used his share of the robbery to open a saloon. Behind the bar he nailed a $10,000 bank note to the wall. Its denomination prevented any gang member from cashing it.

Next came the bank in Telluride, Colo. Butch and the McCartys brought $10,500 in currency out in a sack, again without gunplay, on June 24, 1889. The lawmen in the area, however, were leading massive posses against the raiders and the bandits decided to lay low.

Cassidy spent two years, from 1890 to 1892, working small ranches in Colorado and Utah as a cowboy. In Rock Springs, Wyoming he even put in some time as a butcher in a local store—from which sprang his nickname. But going legitimate was not for Butch. A drunk picked a fight with him one night and Cassidy knocked him out; a local lawman locked him up for disturbing the peace.

After his release, Butch vowed never to work for a living again. Teaming up with a small-time cattle thief, Al Rainer, Cassidy rode about the ranches in Colorado selling, of all things, "protection." If ranchers wanted to avoid having their cattle stolen, they could pay Butch and Rainer a fee. They would drive off any rustlers, Cassidy promised. If the ranchers refused, Butch and Rainer drove off the cattle. It was the kind of extortion that became a specialty with Al Capone, the Black Hand, and modern-day gangsters half a century later.

Sheriff John Ward of Wyoming tracked down the two protection specialists in early 1894, arresting them with stolen cattle near Afton. Ward crept up on Rainer and quickly had him tied to a tree. Butch was in a cabin. Ward went in after him with gun in hand. Cassidy dove for a chair where his pistol was holstered, but two fast shots from the Sheriff's gun creased his scalp and sent him flying unconscious to the floor.

Butch got two years in the Wyoming State Prison. There he heard about a fabulous hideout and gathering place for the toughest gunmen and bandits in the West called the Hole-in-the-Wall, a mountain fortress in Colorado. When released from prison on January 19, 1896, this is exactly where Butch headed, along with two other ex-convicts: crafty, self-taught Elza Lay and gunman Bob Meeks.

There Butch met every notorious gunman and thief still operating in the West. The Logan brothers, Harvey and his younger brother Lonnie, were already experienced bandits by their early twenties. Harvey Logan, the deadliest killer in the Wild Bunch, was also known as Kid Curry, taking his name from an older outlaw, Big Nose George Curry, who also hid out in Hole-in-the-Wall.

Butch got word, while in the mountains, that his old friends the McCartys had met disaster while attempting to rob the bank in Delta, Colo. Bill and Fred McCarty were shot to pieces by the townspeople, who had been informed of their raid by a gang member. The McCartys were displayed dead for one and all on wooden planks. Matt Warner was lucky. He was captured and sent off to do a long prison term for robbery (he would reform, however, and live to a ripe age, dying in 1937).

With Elza Lay as his lone companion, Butch struck the mining camp at Castle Gate, Utah in April, 1897, robbing the paymaster there of $8,000. The take was not as much as Butch expected, so he decided to go back to train-robbing.

Butch, George Curry, Harvey Logan, and Elza Lay stopped the Union Pacific's Overland Flyer on a small trestle near Wilcox, Wyo., June 2, 1889. There were problems right from the beginning when engineer W. R. Jones refused to uncouple the express car after the train ground to a halt. Though Logan viciously pistol-whipped Jones, Elza Lay finally had to move the train himself, jamming down the throttle.

The gang forgot a charge of dynamite they had placed beneath the trestle, but fortunately Lay got the train moving in time. The trestle exploded into fragments just as the Flyer got across.

Surrounding the express car, Cassidy and his men called to the guard inside, a man named Woodcock, to open up and come out.

"Come in and get me!" came Woodcock's brave reply.

A charge of dynamite was placed next to the car and the gang scattered. When it went off, the whole side of the express car was blown away and Woodcock was thrown out unconscious. Logan wanted to kill him, but Cassidy

Cool gunman and close Cassidy chum Elza Lay. (Pinkerton, Inc.)

Shot to pieces, Bill McCarty's corpse was propped up by boards and photographed an hour after his abortive raid against a Delta, Colo. bank. (Pinkerton, Inc.)

stepped in front of his guns. "Leave him be, Kid," Butch is quoted as saying. "A man with his nerve deserves not to be shot."

After blowing up the safe, the bandits had to scurry along the tracks, picking up bills that had been scattered by the blast. Their haul was substantial—$30,000 in currency and bonds.

This last raid brought in the Pinkertons; such relentless pursuers as Charlie Siringo and N. K. Boswell were soon on their trail. A posse cornered Logan, Curry, and Lay at Teapot Creek in Wyoming but the trio shot their way through; Harvey Logan shot and killed the posse's leader, Sheriff Joe Hazen, when the lawman was foolish enough to lead a frontal attack against the outlaws as they hid behind the rocks.

Butch and his gang struck next outside of Tipton, Wyo., by stopping Train No. 3 of the Union Pacific Railroad. By mere chance, the same guard, Woodcock, was in the express car. Cassidy was nonplussed for a minute; then he told the engineer to inform the guard "to open up the door or this time we'll blow him and the car sky-high."

The engineer pleaded and the plucky Woodcock submitted. The outlaws blew the safe with dynamite and made off with more than $50,000. A superposse headed by the feared Joe Lefors was hot on Cassidy's trail, but the gang escaped once again into its impenetrable hideout, the Hole-in-the-Wall.

From there, the gang rode out once more—Cassidy, Logan, Deaf Charley Hanks, and a new man, an outlaw whose draw was the fastest ever seen in the West—Harry Longbaugh, better known as the Sundance Kid.

Longbaugh had served eighteen months in the Sundance jail in Wyoming when a boy, for horse stealing; he took the name The Sundance Kid from this experience. He wore only one gun but his aim was deadly. No member of the Wild Bunch ever tangled with Sundance. While Butch was raiding with the McCarty boys, Sundance had been robbing trains and banks. He held up the Great Northern train at Malta, Mont., in December, 1892 with Bill Madden and Harry Bass. Madden and Bass were captured and got ten years in jail; Sundance escaped, teaming up with Harvey Logan, Tom O'Day and Walt Putney to rob the bank in

Harry Longbaugh, known as The Sundance Kid, the fastest gun in the West.

Belle Bourche, S.D. on June 27, 1897. The entire gang was captured. Longbaugh was booked under the alias of Frank Jones. He and Logan escaped from the Deadwood, S.D. jail October 31, 1897, just before their trial.

Some time in 1900, Sundance and Cassidy met at the Hole-in-the-Wall and became great friends. Both men were somewhat introverted, casual and hard to anger.

The gang hit the Great Northern Flyer almost in the same spot where Sundance had once waylaid the train near Malta, Mont. on July 3, 1901. Logan sneaked into the baggage car. Sundance sat in one of the coaches until it reached the outskirts of Wagner. There Logan jumped from the tender into the locomotive cab and, bristling two six-guns, ordered the engineer to stop the train. The Sundance Kid ran up and down the passenger cars, firing his pistol occasionally into the ceiling and yelling to riders: "Keep your heads inside!"

Butch and Charley Hanks got on the train when it came to a stop over a small bridge. The two had been staying at a nearby ranch. With them was one of the girls, Laura

Bullion, who periodically stayed with the gang at Hole-in-the-Wall. Laura tended the horses while Butch and Hanks joined Logan and Sundance. Butch, employing his favorite tool, set a massive charge of dynamite under the Adams express car and blew off its side. The take was more than $40,000 in incomplete bank notes. The fact that the notes lacked the bank president's signature meant little to the gang. They merely forged a signature and cashed the notes.

A hundred-man posse chased after Butch and the gang following the Wagner robbery. Cassidy and company rode fast mounts and knew the territory well. They again escaped, this time heading for Fort Worth, Texas, where they stayed in Fannie Porter's luxurious brothel.

It was while languishing at Fannie's that Butch took up bicycle riding and Sundance took up with Etta Place, an uncommonly beautiful teacher and housewife who craved excitement.

Fort Worth was the end of this last great cowboy-outlaw band. Harvey Logan and others rode North in search of more plump banks to rob; Cassidy and Sundance decided against it. Butch tried to explain to Kid Curry that their free-booting days in the West were numbered. There were too many lawmen and law-abiding communities, and too few places left where outlaws could hide.

When some of the gang spent notes taken from the Wagner job, Fort Worth detectives began asking around town about the strangers from up North. Butch and Sundance decided to leave for South America. Etta Place went with them.

The Pinkerton Detective Agency, which had so relentlessly pursued Cassidy and Sundance over the years, completely lost their trail. Then they picked it up in Argentina when banks there were suddenly robbed by two American cowboys.

Etta Place acted as a scout on these raids, entering the South American banks ostensibly to open an account, casing each bank and its guards, and then making her report to her two outlaw friends. For a while Butch and Sundance worked at the American-owned Concordia tin mine in Bolivia as day laborers. It was as good a dodge as any.

But their employer, Percy Seibert, discovered their iden-

Etta Place, schoolteacher turned robber's accomplice; she traveled to South America with Butch and The Sundance Kid when they made their escape. (Pinkerton, Inc.)

tities and they departed after two years of legitimate work. In 1907, tired of the reckless life with her two bandits, Etta asked to go home. Sundance accompanied her to New York, where she had an appendicitis operation, and then on to Denver to recuperate. There Harry Longbaugh got drunk, shot up a saloon, and left his girl forever, making his way back to New York and then to the Grand Hotel in La Paz, Bolivia to once more join up with Butch.

It has been reported that the two friends continued their robbing and were finally trapped by a mounted company of soldiers near San Vincente, Bolivia in 1908, where the two men were passing themselves off as the Lowe brothers. Surrounded, the two bandits made a dash for their rifles and ammunition, which were on the other side of a large, open patio. As they ran, they story goes, the soldiers fired repeatedly, shooting Sundance several times. He fell in the dust and died. Butch, upon seeing his friend dead, simply turned his six-gun to his temple and fired.

Another story has it that Cassidy alone survived the

Bolivian ambush and made his way back to the U.S., visiting his family in Utah as late as 1929 and dying about 1937 in Johnny, Nevada, where some claim his grave is located.

[ALSO SEE The Wild Bunch, *Bloodletters and Badmen, Book 1.*]

CHAPMAN, GERALD
Murderer, Robber, Jewel Thief • (1890-1926)

BACKGROUND: BORN AND RAISED IN BROOKLYN, N.Y. OF IRISH-AMERICAN PARENTS (NEE CHARTRES). MINOR PUBLIC EDUCATION. DESCRIPTION: 5'9". BLUE EYES, LIGHT BROWN HAIR, THIN, WIRY. ALIASES: NONE. RECORD: ARRESTED IN 1907, NYC, FOR PETTY THEFT; IN AND OUT OF PRISON FOR UNSUCCESSFUL ROBBERIES IN THE NYC AREA UP TO 1920; MOST SENTENCES SERVED AT NEW YORK'S AUBURN PRISON; ROBBED, WITH DUTCH ANDERSON (IVAN DAHL VON TELLER), A MAIL TRUCK OF THE PARK ROW POST OFFICE 10/24/21 ($1,454,129) CONTAINING REGISTERED MAIL—THE LARGEST THEFT IN AMERICAN HISTORY TO THAT DATE; APPREHENDED AND ESCAPED DAYS LATER FROM THE NYC JAIL, RECAPTURED; AFTER BEING CONVICTED AND SENTENCED TO ATLANTA PENITENTIARY, CHAPMAN ESCAPED TWICE; ROBBED DEPARTMENT STORE IN NEW BRITAIN, CONN., KILLING A POLICEMAN; APPREHENDED AND SENTENCED TO DEATH; HANGED IN CONN. 4/5/26.

There was nothing unusual about the birth of Gerald Chapman in 1890. His family name had originally been Chartres and he was raised in one of New York's more motley Irish districts where apple-stealing and street gang warfare was as ordinary as taking a breath.

Perhaps Chapman, who from 1907 to 1920 amassed a long series of arrests, would have wound up as a common and forgotten thief if he hadn't been locked in the same cell with a European dandy.

While waiting out a stretch in Auburn Prison in upstate New York, a criminally warped man from Denmark named Ivan Dahl von Teller was shown into Chapman's cell as his new mate. Von Teller's name in America was George "Dutch" Anderson.

Anderson was one of the most twisted men ever held in an American prison. He was cunning and intellectual. The son of a wealthy Dutch family, Anderson had attended such European citadels of learning as the Universities of Heidelberg and Upsala.

Dignified, aristocratic, Anderson glibly spoke five languages. His polish and worldly airs deeply impressed Chapman, who idolized the crafty crook. Anderson, in turn, took Chapman under his wing.

A swindler, con man, and embezzler, Anderson taught his young protege Chapman the refinements and high art of crime. When Chapman was finally released, he did not resume his normal routine. He bought some fancy clothes, several homburg hats, and bided his time until Anderson was released. When Dutch was finally paroled, he and Chapman moved to the Midwest, where they fleeced suckers by the dozen. In the space of several months they were $100,000 richer.

They then moved back to New York and took a swanky apartment in Gramercy Park to live the high life of leisured gentlemen. Chapman took to dressing like his mentor Anderson, wearing spats, waist-tight tailored suits, and a monocle. He even carried a stylish and expensive cane.

Gerald Chapman had become every inch the gentleman . . . yet underneath his glossy exterior there lurked the pathological robber and killer.

The good food, fancy nightclubs, and Broadway chorus girls were expensive and soon the pair were short of funds. While casting about for some activity, Anderson and Chapman ran into an old crony of Auburn days, a cheap purse-snatcher, Charles Loeber.

Loeber had a plan. He explained that he had watched several unguarded mail trucks moving from Wall Street to the main New York post office.

"Inside those trucks there's millions, registered mail with money orders, bonds, securities . . . a fortune. But the job's too big for me alone . . . now with the three of us . . ."

Loeber had to say no more. The trio immediately made plans to rob the U.S. mails. They watched several mail trucks taking the Wall Street route to the main post office and then, in a stolen Cleveland car, on the night of October 24, 1921, they made their move.

Mail truck driver Frank Havernack slowly geared his truck up deserted Broadway. He paid no attention to the approaching Cleveland which suddenly swerved from behind and raced alongside his truck. A drunk, Havernack thought, and let the big car zoom in front.

Then the car dropped back again so that it was pacing the truck. Havernack was annoyed but decided to ignore the pesty motorist. Suddenly, the car door on the right swung open and Gerald Chapman, always agile, jumped onto the running board of the mail truck.

"Pull over and don't make any noise," Chapman ordered. There was a big, ugly pistol in his hand pointed at Havernack's stomach. The mail truck driver pulled over, got out, and opened the back of the truck, on Chapman's orders.

The trio pushed Havernack aside, tying him up with a laundry sack about his head. Then, digging under 33 sacks of regular mail, the robbers found five sacks of registered mail. Quickly, they scooped them up and fled.

They didn't know it until the sacks were opened, but the robbers had made the greatest haul in mail theft history to date, $1,424,129!

In their hideout on Long Island, the thieves unhappily discovered that only $27,000 of their loot was in cash, the rest being in securities. These could be converted to cash, but the process was long and complicated.

And it would cost them. Fences would demand as much as 40¢ on the dollar. But the thieves had no other choice, so Anderson and Chapman left for Muncie, Indiana where they had a contact.

Holed up on a farm owned by Ben Hance, Chapman and Anderson converted $100,000 of the stolen bonds. Then they returned to Broadway and lived it up, spending upward of $1,000 a day on expensive cars and women.

Dapper Gerald Chapman, who pulled off a $1 million mail robbery in 1921, is shown in his jail cell five years later, pensive and waiting to be hanged for murder. (UPI)

Their butler and chauffeur was none other than their partner in crime, Charlie Loeber. His lack of brains, Chapman and Anderson figured, rated him a reduction in status. His lack of brains also got them caught.

Loeber did not have the contacts out of town that his partners had, so he foolishly tried to convert his share of the mail robbery loot in New York. This quickly led to his arrest by detectives. He immediately blabbed about Anderson and Chapman and each were speedily picked up.

While waiting to stand trial in New York, Chapman attempted to escape by climbing along a ledge 75 feet above the ground. Though he was apprehended, newsmen inflated his image to that of another Jesse James. Chapman, never tired of having his picture taken, appeared in the New York papers behind bars. He posed with dignity, a gentleman crook, the image he liked best.

Both Chapman and Anderson were convicted and sent to prison for 25 years. The penitentiary to which they were sent was a tough one—Atlanta, but this didn't worry Chapman. He vowed to escape. The massive publicity he had received while under detention in New York had gone to his head.

Shortly after Chapman went into his cell in Atlanta he planned his escape. He drank an entire bottle of disinfectant and was sent to the prison hospital with a very sore throat. Once there, he slugged an unsuspecting guard, sawed through the bars, and slid to the yard on a rope made of tied-together bedsheets.

Chapman's sensational escape made headlines throughout the country, but he was captured two days later. Police had to shoot him three times before he would surrender.

Following his recovery, Chapman again escaped from Atlanta, again using his bedsheet trick. This time he was successful and went immediately to the Hance farm in Indiana to hide out.

Dutch Anderson soon joined him after he, too, escaped from Atlanta by tunneling his way under the prison wall. This time the confederates thought to reverse their roles. They would commit crimes in the East and live in Chicago.

The two teamed up with an apprentice hoodlum, Walter Shean, and soon they attempted another big caper. They attempted to rob the largest department store in New Britain, Conn., but police intervened and the escaping robbers shot it out, killing one officer.

Shean was soon captured and bragged to police: "My pal was Gerald Chapman."

Chapman was captured in Muncie and taken to Hartford. Avid news readers waited daily for the latter-day Jimmy Valentine to escape just once more—but he didn't.

At his trial, Shean and others identified Chapman as

the man who had killed the New Britain cop and he was convicted, sentenced to hang.

Chapman's reaction was laconic. "Death itself isn't dreadful," he said, "but hanging seems an awkward way of entering the adventure." Chapman went awkwardly into death on April 5, 1926.

Dutch Anderson, still at large, lost his mind at the death of his younger associate and convinced himself that the farmer Ben Hance had betrayed Chapman. He was wrong, but he killed Hance and his wife anyway and set their house on fire.

Dutch tried to kill Shean as well, but the informer was too well guarded. This one-man vendetta was finally halted when a policeman in Muskegon, Michigan recognized Anderson, even though he was wearing one of his many disguises. Both men fired at the same time and killed each other.

COLL, VINCENT ("MAD DOG")
Gangster, Murderer • (1909–1932)

BACKGROUND: BORN AND RAISED IN NEW YORK CITY, THE SECOND SON OF IMMIGRANT PARENTS FROM COUNTY KILDARE, IRELAND. MINOR PUBLIC EDUCATION. DESCRIPTION: 6'1", BLUE EYES, BROWN HAIR, SLENDER. ALIASES: UNKNOWN. RECORD: ARRESTED WHILE A TEENAGER AS A DISORDERLY CHILD AND PLACED IN IMMACULATE VIRGIN MISSION; ARRESTED BEFORE HIS 21ST BIRTHDAY FOR BREAKING AND ENTERING, THEFT, GRAND LARCENY, AND VIOLATION OF PAROLE; SENT TO ELMIRA, N.Y. REFORMATORY FOR A SHORT PERIOD; FROM 1930–32, BECAME A BOOTLEGGER AND POLICY RACKETS GANGSTER; MURDERED VINCENT BARELLI AND HIS GIRL FRIEND MARY SMITH, 1931; KILLED FIVE-YEAR-OLD MICHAEL VENGALLI, 1932 IN AN ATTEMPT TO SLAY ANOTHER GANGSTER; KILLED IN A TELEPHONE BOOTH IN A MANHATTAN DRUGSTORE IN 1932 BY GUN-

MEN ON ORDERS FROM THE MOBSTER LEADER DUTCH SCHULTZ.

The short bitter life of Vincent Coll was marked by incredible violence that caused revulsion even in his fellow gangsters. Coll more than earned the sobriquet "Mad Dog" in his brief and awesome twenty-three years.

In the Irish ghetto poverty of Hell's Kitchen, stealing soon became second nature to Coll and his brother Peter. Their childhood twisted from one petty theft to another, from overturned pushcarts to looting department stores. Coll's rise was similar to that of Jack "Legs" Diamond in that it was meteoric and ruled by the gun. His span of criminal success and notoriety, however, was considerably less than Diamond's.

After a number of petty arrests and a hitch in the reformatory at Elmira, Coll became determined to make the big money; he hired out to Dutch Schultz as a gunman and rumrunner at $150-a-week. He enforced the Dutchman's mandate in every saloon that squatted in Schultz's Bronx and Harlem territories. Friends described Coll as mentally unbalanced, a sadistic brutal young man who enjoyed beating up bartenders.

Although Coll enjoyed his job, he disliked working for Schultz, or anybody else for that matter. He had ideas of his own. He, Vinnie Coll, would form his own gang and steal the Dutchman's empire. Enlisting his brother Peter and two young hoodlums, Arthur Palumbo and Frank Giordano, Coll went foraging for an army. His first selection was a trusted Schultz lieutenant, Vincent Barelli, who had solid connections on the bootleg front.

Barelli turned out to be a loyal sort and twice refused to join Coll's embryonic gang. The second time Barelli and his girl Mary Smith met Coll in 1931 guns exploded. When Barelli again turned Coll down, the youthful mobster yanked out a pistol and shot both Barelli and Miss Smith dead.

To make matters worse for the Dutchman, Coll had the impudence to set up headquarters in a speakeasy only a half block from Schultz's office. From this vantage point,

Coll began pirating several top gunmen from the Dutchman's employ.

Schultz thought to teach his ex-aide a lesson. He kidnapped Peter Coll and had him shot to death on a quiet street in Harlem.

"That yellow rat!" Coll screamed when he heard how his brother had died. "I'm gonna burn the Dutchman to hell!" Vinnie went to work with unbridled passion. He stole the Dutchman's beer trucks by the dozens and killed the drivers. He took over a huge section of Schultz's Manhattan policy racket. He didn't stop at Schultz but attacked and made inroads against the rackets controlled by crime czars such as Owney Madden and Legs Diamond, who were the Dutchman's friends and associates. He kidnapped Madden's second-in-command, George "Big Frenchy" DeMange and held him captive until receiving $35,000 in ransom money. But his vengeance was mostly vented on Schultz. He harassed the gangster so much that the Dutchman placed a $50,000 reward for Coll's dead body and moaned to his men: "Get Coll off my back! Get the Mick off my back!"

One of Dutch's men attempted to do exactly that. Joey Rao, Schultz's enforcer in the policy racket, took two of his best gunmen and stalked Vincent Coll through the streets of New York. Coll, on the other hand, had learned of the price on his head and Rao's intent. He and his men went looking for Rao.

In July of 1932, Coll spotted Rao and his two henchmen walking down East 107th Street. It was a hot day and every child in the neighborhood was on the sidewalk playing. Rao wended his way through the playing groups of children. Just as he approached one group, a car suddenly swept past and Coll, holding a machinegun out the car's window, sprayed the street.

Rao and his bodyguards ducked but the children didn't. Residents were horrified to see five small children, ages two to four, writhing on the sidewalk, some of them shot four and five times. All survived except five-year-old Michael Vengalli, whose stomach had been blown away by Coll's .45-caliber slugs.

Coll was identified and the newspapers screamed he was a "Mad Dog Killer" who had to be eradicated. The young

Vincent "Mad Dog" Coll (center) shakes hands with his lawyer, Samuel Leibowitz, following a 1931 acquittal for murder. (UPI)

murderer knew it would be only a matter of time before he was caught and tried. He wanted the best lawyer in town for that: Samuel Liebowitz, but lawyers like Liebowitz were expensive. To raise a defense fund, Coll kidnapped another top aide of Owney Madden's and held him for ransom. Bootlegger Madden paid $30,000 and got his man back. Coll paid Leibowitz and got an acquittal.

To celebrate his freedom, Coll married heavyset Lottie Kreisberger, his chorus girl sweetheart. The honeymoon was brief.

Four of Dutch Schultz's gunmen, one of them Rao (who reportedly swore vengeance on Coll for killing the Vengalli child), caught up with the Mad Dog as he was talking on the phone to none other than Owney Madden, then one of Coll's shakedown victims.

Coll was jabbering threats to Owney's life from a phone booth in a drugstore located on West Twenty-Third Street. Schultz's torpedo merely stepped up to the booth and yanked a submachinegun from beneath his coat. Coll's eyes grew big behind the small glass doors of the booth as he watched the man raise the weapon and aim. There was no room for Vincent Coll to draw his own gun and when the burst of .45-caliber shells tore into him he could do nothing but die helplessly.

Oddly enough, Vincent Coll had been hired by Salvatore Maranzano to kill Lucky Luciano and Vito Genovese during the Mafia's 1930 Castellammarese War in New York. Maranzano, however, was murdered by Luciano and Genovese first. One wonders how the national crime cartel would have developed if the Mad Dog had fulfilled his "contracts."

The mobster who wanted to be a big shot had been hit by fifteen bullets in the head and chest. Police found a miserable $101 in his pockets. Vincent Mad Dog Coll was down on his luck to the last.

COLOSIMO, JAMES ("BIG JIM")
Gangster, Brothel Keeper • (1877-1920)

Immigrating with his father Luigi from Consenza, Italy in 1895, Colosimo began humbly as a newspaper boy in Chicago who shined shoes on the side. He also labored long as a section-gang water boy and then graduated to the sanitation department, pushing a broom through the streets of the notorious First Ward, known in the Nineties as the Levee, a vice-ridden red light district crawling with crime and overlorded by two of the most colorfully corrupt politicians of the era—Alderman Michael "Hinky Dink" Kenna and his erstwhile side-kick Bathhouse (he once worked as a rubber) John Coughlin.

Colosimo, who had tried his hand at petty thievery and pickpocketing, attempted to make a living as a pimp but was arrested at eighteen and went to work for Kenna and Coughlin instead, serving as their bagman. It was Colosimo's chore to collect the kickbacks of those brothels operating in the First Ward.

In this capacity, Colosimo met Victoria Moresco, an obese and aging madam who ran an Amour Avenue whorehouse and was attracted to his swarthy animal magnetism. She offered him the managership of her brothel and he immediately accepted, marrying Victoria two weeks later in the bargain.

From 1902 Colosimo's fortunes grew. He added one new brothel after another to his chain with the blessings of his political sponsors Kenna and Coughlin. Big Jim became the king of pimps, owning thirty to forty $1 and $2 cribs and two swanky brothels, the Saratoga and the Victoria (named for his wife), which were frequented by every high roller of the day. Kenna and Coughlin received handsome kickbacks.

The take for Colosimo was colossal. He raked in $1.20 for every $2 trick. Dozens of Colosimo saloons, connected to his brothels via side-doors and tunnels, added to his daily coffers. As a labor racketeer he had also moved strong-armed thugs into a dozen unions, skimming mightily from union membership dues. He became a young millionaire. Jim took to wearing well-tailored suits and ostentatious arrays of diamonds—diamond belt buckles, diamond shirt studs, diamond rings, diamond cufflinks.

To add to his personal glitter, the gangster opened the gaudiest, poshest, most elegant nightclub west of the Alleghenies—Colosimo's Cafe at 2126 South Wabash Avenue. It boasted a mahogany and glass bar unequalled in craftsmanship, and a dining room of green velvet walls trimmed with gilded filigree. The sky-blue ceiling was adorned with baroque paintings of nymphs, pucks, and pans frolicking among Nirvana-like surroundings; solid gold chandeliers hung overhead. Crystal chandeliers graced the dancehall, which featured a dance floor that was lowered or raised by a hydraulic lift.

Colosimo made it a point to hire the best entertainment available; the cream of Chicago's society rushed in to sit at his elbow-jamming tables where out-of-town personalities and close friends of Big Jim's like opera stars Amelita Galli-Curci, Luisa Tetrazzini, Cleofonte Campanini, and Enrico Caruso would regularly be seen.

Here the elite of society mixed with the elite of the underworld. Social butterflies played name-games as they pointed out tuxedoed gangsters such as "Issy the Rat" Buchalsky; Vincenzo "Sunny Jim" Cosmano, a notorious Blackhander who had often extorted money from Big Jim; gamblers Mont Tennes and Julius "Lovin' Putty" Annixter; union overlords like Joey D'Andrea and *Unione Siciliane* chief Mike Merlo; and whoremasters such as Charlie Genker, Dennis "Duke" Cooney, and "Mike de Pike" Heitler; political bosses Kenna and Coughlin; newspaper reporters Jack Lait, Ben Hecht, Ring Lardner; gunmen Tommy O'Connor, Samuel J. "Nails" Morton, Dion O'Bannion—a polyglot *Who's Who* that would stagger the mind of any dedicated reformer.

As Colosimo's empire spread out through the Levee and other areas of the city, his enforcement arm blossomed. To keep tight control of his vast interests, Big Jim enlisted the aid of some of the toughest gunmen in the Midwest. His bully boys included Jim "Duffy the Goat" Franche, Mac Fitzpatrick (alias W. E. Frazier), Joseph "Jew Kid" Grabiner, Billy Leathers, Harry Gullet, and his pistol-packing brother-in-law Joseph Moresco. These men swore to die to defend Big Jim in an elaborate ceremony which included taking the oath on Colosimo's family Bible.

Irrespective of this formidable assemblage of muscle and gunpower, Big Jim was easy prey for Blackhanders who threatened to blow up his cafe or whorehouses unless he forked over sizable amounts of money. At first, Colosimo and his troops fought back by dumping the payoffs at specified secret spots and then ambushing the extortionists when they came to collect, but it proved too hazardous.

To correct the problem, Colosimo, in 1910, sent for his gangster nephew, Johnny Torrio, who led the ruthless Five

Points gang in New York. Torrio, fleeing a murder charge in Brownsville, eagerly accepted the new post and the Blackhanding stopped months after his arrival.

For a decade, Big Jim enjoyed his wealth and power. He divorced his fat whorehouse wife, Victoria, and married showgirl Dale Winter, a sweet-faced, nineteen-year-old ingenue from Ohio who had starred in the roadshow of *Madame Sherry*, a comic operetta.

Colosimo doted on Miss Winter and became not only her husband but sponsor, arranging music lessons for her, introducing her to Caruso, escorting her to Chicago's most dazzling social functions. Instead of attending to his brothels, Big Jim spent most of his time either with Dale or inside his plush cafe hob-nobbing with celebrities. His taciturn, organization-minded nephew, Torrio, was left to run everything.

Torrio, who was once called "the father of modern American gangsterdom," did run everything, pocketing $1 million a year from Colosimo's booze and brothel kingdom. But he was not the boss and Johnny Torrio was an ambitious man.

In 1919, Torrio all but got on his knees before his opera-loving uncle, begging Big Jim to branch out into hijacking and bootlegging. The National Prohibition Act, Torrio argued, was heaven-sent for the likes of them; there would be millions, super millions, to be made by selling illegal hooch. But Colosimo had grown fat and content with what he had. "We stay with the whores, Johnny," he said and scoffed at Torrio's wild schemes.

Sorrowfully, Torrio sent for a bloodthirsty plug-ugly who had served as his enforcer in the old Five Points gang—a heavyset, cheek-scarred, egotistical gangster named Al Capone. Ostensibly, Capone's new job with Torrio was that of a bouncer and bag man for Big Jim's brothels. His real mission in Chicago was to kill Colosimo, a job for which Torrio had neither the stomach nor the heart.

On May 11, 1920, Torrio called his uncle and told him that a shipment of whiskey would be delivered to his cafe that afternoon, promptly at 4 p.m. Big Jim would have to sign for it personally. Colosimo was there, waiting in the vestibule of his club at precisely that time.

Capone was hiding at that moment in a glass-paneled telephone booth. He fired two shots through the glass when Colosimo passed him, the first bullet entering Big Jim's head behind the right ear, the second slamming into a wall.

Big Jim toppled heavily to the tiled floor of the vestibule, face down, dead. Capone rushed from his hiding spot, turned the crime czar over, ripped open his shirt front, withdrew his money-crammed wallet, and fled. (A porter at the cafe had seen Capone enter but testified to police that the man was a "stranger.")

Old World crime ceased in Chicago after that. Big Jim's idea of enforcement was brass knuckles; Torrio and Capone would employ the machinegun. Big Jim's flashy showmanship gave away to Torrio's secrecy and Capone's stealth.

It was still quite fashionable to be a gangster after Colosimo's murder, but it was no longer "a safe bet."

[ALSO SEE Al Capone, *Unione Siciliane*; Johnny Torrio, *Bloodletters and Badmen*, Book 3.]

CROWLEY, FRANCIS ("TWO-GUN")
Murderer, Bankrobber • (1911-1931)

BACKGROUND: BORN 10/31/11 IN NEW YORK, N.Y., PLACED IN A FOSTER HOME AS AN INFANT. FINISHED THIRD GRADE IN ELEMENTARY SCHOOL; FORCED TO WORK AS A DAY LABORER AT AGE 12. DESCRIPTION: 5'6", BROWN EYES, BROWN HAIR, SLIGHT BUILD. ALIASES: NONE. RECORD: PURCHASED A .38-CALIBER PISTOL ON HIS NINETEENTH BIRTHDAY AND WENT ON A ROBBERY SPREE IN THE SPRING OF 1931, ROBBING A BANK AND COMMITTING SEVERAL HOLDUPS, ONE OF WHICH RESULTED IN HIS MURDERING A STOREKEEPER; WITH HIS PARTNER RUDOLPH "FATS" DURINGER, MURDERED DANCE HALL HOSTESS VIRGINIA BANNER IN APRIL, 1931; SHOT AND KILLED PATROLMAN FREDERICK HIRSCH NEAR NORTH MER-

RICK, L.I. THE SAME MONTH WHILE ESCAPING; TRAPPED BY NYPD OFFICERS AT 303 W. 90TH ST. IN AN APARTMENT, SHOOTING IT OUT WITH THE COPS IN WHAT WAS TERMED "THE SIEGE OF W. 90TH STREET"; APPREHENDED AFTER BEING WOUNDED, TRIED FOR MURDER, CONVICTED, AND SENTENCED TO DEATH IN THE ELECTRIC CHAIR AT SING SING PRISON; EXECUTED A FEW DAYS BEFORE HIS TWENTIETH BIRTHDAY, 1931.

Francis "Two-Gun" Crowley would probably have remained a smalltime hood had it not been for his abiding faith in his own press clippings. From a penny-ante sneak-thief, Crowley, in his scant lifetime of nineteen years, managed to rise to the image of the stand-up and shoot-it-out desperado of old, fascinating a Depression-torn Manhattan.

Just as he was the product of a broken home, like many another gangster, Crowley was also the invention of the press. He stopped calling himself Francis after the newspaper dubbed him "Two Gun." And he believed himself to be the toughest man in New York.

Crowley was born just outside of Manhattan, illegitimate. His mother, a German household worker, placed him in a foster home at an early age. His education was halted at the third grade and except for what he learned on New York's streets and from the pages of cheap detective magazines and gangster movies, Crowley remained an illiterate.

He hated policemen. His foster mother told him that his grandfather had been a police captain, and in his loneliness Crowley looked upon all policemen as cruel and heartless animals who would abandon their own flesh at any moment.

In his late teens, Crowley fell in with a dim-witted clod of a man, Rudolph "Fats" Duringer, whom he referred to as "Big Rudolph." Together, after work, the two planned and executed several minor holdups in and around Manhattan. Their take was miserable but Crowley was delighted. He had found his *milieu* in the excitement of robbery and the risk of death. Like novelist Willard Motley's Nick Romano in *Knock On Any Door*, he wanted to "live hard, die young, and have a good-looking corpse."

Munching on candy, the boy bandit and Duringer robbed

a small bank in early 1931. Then they knocked over several gas stations and stores, killing one grocery store owner when he resisted. Crowley and Duringer took to hanging around dance halls after Francis learned that gangster Jack "Legs" Diamond frequented these nickel-and-dime dives.

Crowley never met Diamond, but he and his friend Duringer did get friendly with pretty Virginia Banner, a hostess at one of the halls. When she refused to go out with Duringer, he and Crowley waited for her one night and after she left the hall, the two shoved her into their green coupe and drove to an isolated spot. There Duringer raped her repeatedly. Then Crowley, using the pistol he had given himself as a present on his nineteenth birthday, shot her to death. Duringer shot her also for good measure. "I heard she was going to marry someone else," he later confessed. "I was jealous of him."

The two raced on with their crime spree. The police were stymied. Ballistic experts matched the bullets from Miss Banner's body with those from the grocery store murder, but clues ended there.

Then on a warm April night just outside North Merrick, N. Y., two officers, Patrolmen Frederick Hirsch and Peter Yodice, drove up to a deserted spot called Black Shirt Lane to shoo away lovers parked in their cars. There was only one car in sight, a dirty green coupe.

"Probably some kids," Hirsch told his partner. "We'd better get them out of here before someone holds them up."

Hirsch got out of the patrol car and advanced on the green coupe with his flashlight bouncing about in the darkness. His thin yellow light settled on a pasty-faced youth sitting next to a pretty teenage girl. Yodice walked to the front of the car and wrote down the license number just in case.

"It's pretty late to be out here," Hirsch said to the youthful driver. "Let me see your license."

"Sure, sure," mumbled the young man and he slowly moved his arm from around the girl. In a moment he opened the car door, slamming Hirsch off balance. As the officer fell backward, Francis Crowley fired three rapid shots into him. Before Hirsch died, he managed to draw his gun and get off one shot which went wild. Crowley jumped from his car and snatched the policeman's pistol, then leaped back into his car and, dodging patrolman Yodice's shots, escaped.

Now police knew who they were looking for and they placed a "shoot-to-kill" order out on Crowley. But he had buried himself in the city. For weeks, it appeared as if the boy murderer had vanished. Then a newspaper reporter for the *New York Journal* tracked down a friend of Crowley's, dance hall girl Billie Dunne. She exploded at the mere mention of the outlaw's name. Crowley, Duringer, and Crowley's girl, sixteen-year-old Helen Walsh, had evicted her from her cheap apartment. They were living there now, she screamed, and she gave the address as 303 W. 90th.

The reporter, along with a photographer, hurried to the apartment after notifying the police. Billie had warned him not to see Crowley. "That guy will shoot his own mother," she said.

News photographer Jerry Frankel didn't wait for the police to arrive. He wanted his pictures for the next edition. After lugging his equipment up the stairs, he stood in front of Billie's apartment and knocked.

A thin voice on the other side yelled out: "Get out of here! We don't want any!"

Before Frankel could reply, police detectives who were hiding in the hall yanked him backward toward the stairs. Suddenly, the door flew open and there stood Francis Crowley, ready for battle. Two guns were strapped to his hips, another was tucked into a shoulder holster. His pants were rolled up to the knees and strapped around each calf were two more guns.

Two-Gun whipped out the pistols on his hips and began shooting down the hallway, his roaring six-guns chunking away plaster that showered down on the policemen as they dove for cover. He emptied his pistols and then jumped back into the apartment, slamming the door and barricading it.

In that moment of eerie silence, policemen raised their heads to peer down the hallway still filled with Crowley's gunsmoke, and heard that oft-delivered classic line snarled from behind the door: "Come and get me, coppers!"

The siege was on. Down in the street, police roped off two blocks and brought an army of officers to train machineguns, shotguns, and high-powered rifles on the apartment. They began to pepper the building as carloads of reinforcements arrived by the minute. (Police were to fire 700 shots throughout the battle.)

Crowley acted out his role in the true Hollywood tradition. Jumping from window to window, he fired a vicious fusillade down to the street, reloading his guns as he ran. Machineguns answered him, shattering the windows overhead; he laughed and brushed away the glass, firing back coolly, plunking his shells dangerously close to where policemen took cover behind parked cars in the street. Then he would dart to the hallway door, spray both ends of the halls with bullets and then return to the windows.

The scene was incredible. Over 300 officers were in the street below, firing back, a tremendously withering fire that chipped away brick, mortar and wood from the building's facade. Two-Gun would wait for a lull and then, from his five-story perch, rapidly squeeze off his rounds, loudly cursing the police below.

Rudolph Duringer and Helen Walsh hid beneath the bed, screaming. Crowley ignored them. He sat on the bed and reloaded. "You're yellow, all yellow," he castigated them.

Fifteen thousand people were in the streets watching the battle. More spectators foolishly watched from neighboring buildings, leaning out of the windows and using pillows for armrests.

While the police regrouped for a final charge preceded by tear-gas, Crowley and Helen prepared to die. Duringer still sobbed beneath the bed as the star-crossed lovers wrote out their farewells to the world.

Two-Gun wrote:

"To Whom It May Concern:
I was born on the thirty-first [of October]. She was born on the thirteenth [Helen was born on the 13th of October]. I guess it was fate that made us mate. When I die put a lily in my hand, let the boys know how they'll look. Under my coat will lay a weary, kind heart that wouldn't hurt anything. I hadn't anything else to do, that's why I went around bumping off cops. *It's the new sensation of the films* [italics added]. Take a tip from

me to never let a copper go an inch above your knee. They will tell you they love you and as soon as you turn your back they will club you and say the hell with you. Now that my death is so near there is a couple of bulls at the door saying "come here." I'm behind the door with three thirty-eights—one belongs to my friend in North Merrick [officer Hirsch]—he would have gotten me if his bullets were any good."

Helen wrote:

"To Whom It May Concern:
I was born on the 13 of Oct. and he was born on the 31. If I die and my face you are able to see, wave my hair and make me look pretty and make my face up. Dress me in Black and White in a new dress. Do my nails all over. I don't use this kind of polish. It's too dark. I use a very pale pink. I always wanted everybody to be happy & have a good time—I had some pretty good times myself. Love to all but all my love to Sweets. [Helen called Crowley Sweets]. Everybody happy & how."

Moments later, the police resumed firing after asking Crowley to come out. Again, he retorted à la James Cagney: "You ain't gonna take me alive, coppers!" and blasted away with his pistols. The police returned his fire with a hail of tear-gas shells which thudded into the apartment. Two-Gun picked up several smoking tear-gas shells and tossed them out the window; some officers below were overcome by their own cannisters. As he threw the tear-gas shells out, Crowley was a perfect target and police bullets hit him again and again, knocking him to the floor.

He staggered up, his eyes swollen from the gas, shooting blindly out the windows. A brave squad of police volunteers finally rushed the apartment door and crashed in. Crowley was staggering blindly about. He leveled his two guns in their direction and squeezed the triggers. Nothing happened. He was out of ammunition. As officers approached him, he swore and collapsed, leaking blood from four bullet wounds. Duringer and Helen Walsh were yanked from beneath the bed.

When Two-Gun Crowley was taken to the hospital the

Francis "Two-Gun" Crowley (right) on his way to Sing Sing and the electric chair (UPI)

police took no chances. They strapped him to the stretcher and a guard held a gun to his head until he arrived in the emergency room. His trial was anti-climactic.

His faithful sweetheart Helen turned on him, testifying against his defense (she was released). When she stepped from the witness stand she winked at her lover but Two-Gun did not wink back. Duringer, indicted for the killing of Virginia Banner, tried to pin the blame solely on Two-Gun, but he, too, was sentenced to death.

Crowley sat through the entire trial amused and delighted at the attention he received. He smart-cracked for the newsmen. He laughed when the death sentence was pronounced. The only visible sign of annoyance to cross his face occurred when his own lawyer called him "a moral imbecile" before the open court.

The press played up Crowley's bravado. Two-Gun was tough, they said. Two-Gun would go to the chair laughing.

From the moment Crowley entered Death Row at Sing Sing to await his execution, he attempted to prove just how tough he was. Two-Gun was brought through the gates of Sing Sing by a dozen deputies and immediately searched. Inside one of his socks, they found a spoon handle which could have been eventually shaped into a knife.

During his first day on Death Row, Crowley cursed his guards and kicked over his tray of food. The other condemned prisoners applauded him. Thus encouraged, the nineteen-year-old killer proceeded to create pandemonium.

A letter arrived from Helen Walsh. In it she called him yellow. Crowley went berserk. In a matter of days he had destroyed his cell. He stuffed his clothes down the toilet and flooded his cell. Though denied matches, Crowley managed to set fire to everything in sight and a squad of guards had to put out the blaze. He then twisted the wire away from his bunk and wrapped it around a heavy magazine, clubbing one guard unconscious in a futile break.

Warden Lewis Lawes took drastic measures.

He had Crowley's cell stripped of everything. Two-Gun was also stripped naked. A mattress was thrown into his cell at night and removed each morning. At first, Crowley only laughed at such punishment. He spent his time trapping flies with sugar from his meals, and then slowly killing them. He was placed in an isolated cell away from the other prisoners and without an audience to goad him on, he became docile. One day a starling flew into his cell, but Two-Gun didn't kill it. Like Robert Stroud, the "Birdman of Alcatraz," he fed it from his food allotment and the bird returned each day.

The bird's appearance seemed to calm the killer. He asked for his clothes and a bunk and Lawes granted these to him. He asked for a sketch pad and began to draw pictures. One of his drawings was of the electric chair. This Crowley pasted to the wall of his cell. He then drew a figure of a man lying inside of a coffin. He labeled this sketch: "Francis (Two-Gun) Crowley." This drawing too, he stuck up on his wall.

Later, Crowley was taken to New York to testify in a review trial of Rudolph Duringer's case. Before he left, Crowley took one of the death house porters aside and said: "Take all my things. I won't need them again. Once I leave here, I won't come back. You can be sure of that." Two-Gun was planning to make a break but he never got the chance.

Four guards sat around him during the trial. At lunch time, Crowley waited impatiently in the ante-room for his food. "No eats, no testimony," he snarled at a guard. His lunch appeared minutes later. In the afternoon, Crowley played to the gallery, making what he termed "wise cracks." When some of his remarks brought on laughs he began clowning.

"Did you notice how busy those newspapermen got every time I made a hit?" he asked his guards later.

On his return to Sing Sing, Crowley got a good view of the George Washington Bridge. Once back in his cell he asked for some light wood and Lawes gave it to him. Meticulously, with a magazine photo to guide him, he reconstructed the entire bridge. He built a miniature Empire State Building and a rambling structure he labeled "Crowley's Hotel," complete with elevators and miniature workmen. Two-Gun trapped a beetle and, tying it down with a thread, compelled the insect to act as a watchman at Crowley's Hotel.

Two-Gun began to confide in Warden Lawes, one of the best penologists of modern times. He told Lawes that he used to attend church regularly, but that he always wore his two guns, even during the services.

"Why didn't you shoot the minister?" a tough guard sarcastically inquired.

"I never shoot my friends," Crowley said smiling. "Only my enemies—policemen."

Crowley's fame had not subsided. The press kept running a series of articles about his spectacular exploits and just before his execution several requests from newspapers for a final interview with the killer crossed Lawes' desk. One syndicate had written Two-Gun's life story without ever consulting the facts or its subject. It offered $10,000 if Crowley would only sign the phony autobiography. He didn't, but later Two-Gun told Lawes that "if mother [his foster mother] had that money when I was a kid, maybe things would have been different." He also told Lawes: "I knew when I bought that gun it would land me in the electric chair."

The night he was due to march to the death chair, Lawes came into Crowley's cell to find Two-Gun staring at a water bug shooting about the floor. "See that?" he said, "I was about to kill it. Several times I wanted to crush it. It's a dirty-looking thing. But then I decided to give it a chance and let it live."

Twenty-five newspapermen were on hand in the gallery seated before the electric chair as witnesses when Crowley was led into the chamber. Rudolph Duringer had just been electrocuted minutes before. Noting the journalists, Crowley returned to his swagger and banter.

Two-Gun stopped in his tracks and turned to the warden. "I got a favor to ask you," he said.

"Name it," Lawes said.

"I want a rag," Two-Gun said.

"A rag? What for?"

"I want to wipe off the chair after that rat sat in it."

Lawes had seen this kind of braggadocio displayed many times before by killers on their way to the chair. (He had witnessed all kinds of bizarre behavior, such as the time a Negro murderer was led to the death room humming and whistling, dancing up to the electric chair which he stroked and kissed several times, calling it his "sweet chariot that takes me over Jordan.") Lawes ignored Crowley's remark but the newsmen began to write furiously about the killer they called "the game kid."

Two-Gun was smoking a cigar when he calmly sat down in the chair. He looked at the newsmen who had created the warped legends about him, and, before the straps were applied to his arms, he withdrew the cigar and flipped it at them, hitting one in the middle of the forehead. "You sons-of-bitches," he hissed.

His arms were then strapped down. Just before the black hood was placed over his head, Crowley turned to Warden Lawes and said softly: "Give my love to mother."

Then the executioner jerked a switch downward and the lethal current raced through Francis Two-Gun Crowley, celebrity.

D'AUTREMONT BROTHERS
Trainrobbers, Murderers

BACKGROUND: ROY, RAY (TWINS) AND HUGH D'AUTREMONT WERE BORN AND RAISED IN RURAL OREGON NEAR THE CITY OF EUGENE. THE THREE BROTHERS RECEIVED MINOR EDUCATION. OCCUPATIONS, LUMBERJACKS. DESCRIPTION: ALL WERE OF MEDIUM HEIGHT, FAIR COMPLEXIONS. ALIASES: GOODWIN, BRICE, ELLIOTT. RECORD: STOPPED TRAIN NUMBER 13 OF THE SOUTHERN PACIFIC RAILROAD ON 10/11/1923 BETWEEN PORTLAND AND SAN FRANCISCO NEAR THE TOWN OF SISKIYOU, ORE., IN AN ATTEMPT TO ROB THE MAIL CAR; KILLED FOUR MEMBERS OF THE CREW AND ESCAPED; CAPTURED IN MARCH, 1927; CONFESSED TO THE ROBBERY AND MURDERS AND ALL THREE WERE SENT TO THE OREGON STATE PENITENTIARY FOR LIFE.

Probably no other train robbery in American history was so stupidly mismanaged as that attempted by the D'Autremont brothers in 1923. By then the act was archaic; the dubious art of robbing trains belonged to another age and to a different breed of men long dead. But time had passed by the D'Autremont brothers without impressing upon them the futility and risks of train robbing.

Living out their young lives in the remote wilds of Oregon, however, the D'Autremonts—twins, Roy and Ray, and their older brother Hugh—believed that this was still a good way to get rich quick. Nothing in their combined backgrounds suggested a bent toward crime. They were all hard-working boys who labored in the deep forests of Oregon as lumberjacks. Their decision to rob the Southern Pacific's mail train was, perhaps, a whim.

Since boyhood, the D'Autremonts had watched the mail trains snake in and out of Eugene, Ore., their home. They had even joked about robbing one. After all, Jesse James had been in his grave less than forty years. The memory of his daring train raids were still vivid in the minds of the American young. This idle summer dream became a crazy reality for the D'Autremonts on the morning of October 12, 1923.

An hour before noon on that day the three brothers—Hugh was the nominal leader—got up from their passenger seats on train Number 13 just after it had pulled out of the little station of Siskiyou, Ore. and began to walk to their positions. They wore heavy overcoats and beneath these they carried sawed-off shotguns.

A long tunnel cut through half a mountain outside of Siskiyou. Just as the train, slowing and working its way up a steep grade, entered this tunnel, Roy and Ray D'Autremont wriggled over the engine tender and quietly let themselves down into the locomotive cab where engineer Sidney Bates and fireman Marvin Seng were laboring.

The twins probed the crewmen's backs with their shotguns. Startled, the men turned about. "Stop the train," Roy D'Autremont ordered and waved the engineer toward the brake with his shotgun. Bates obediently grabbed for the brake lever. Half the train was out of the tunnel when it stopped.

Ray D'Autremont then motioned the crewman from the cab. "Get out now. Quick. Come with us." At shotgun point, the two trainmen were forced to walk up a small hill where the twins made them sit down, looking away from them. Bates and Seng then saw another bandit, Hugh D'Autremont, race toward the mail car. He nervously placed a cumbersome package on the window sill of the mail car and ran back into the tunnel. Moments later, the car was rocked by an explosion. The bomb, however, did not perform as expected. Instead of merely blowing away the locked door on the mail car, it caused the entire car to erupt into roaring flames.

The burning mail car was half in and half out of the tunnel. Hugh signaled his brothers to bring their prisoners down the hill. They came on the run.

"We've got to get it out of this tunnel!" Hugh screamed. He held a pistol on Bates and ordered him to climb into the engine's cab. "Get it started. Pull her out a bit." Bates climbed inside the cab and tried to start the engine. It wouldn't move. He explained to the bandits below that he had stopped the train too soon. Certain mechanisms in the old iron horse were jammed.

"Get back down here," Hugh ordered. He was sweating. His brothers were glancing anxiously about. The money and jewels they expected to find in the mail car were being destroyed by the fire. Just then brakeman Charles Johnson, holding a lantern, came running from the tunnel, investigating the sudden stop and subsequent explosion.

"You!" Hugh yelled. "Get over there and uncouple the mail car from the rest of the train." Johnson took one look at Hugh's pistol and complied. He could not uncouple the car. As he was returning to explain his failure, Hugh D'Autremont, now in a rage at the ridiculous situation, raised his pistol and fired. His shot hit Johnson in the head, killing him. His brothers then turned and, without a murmur, discharged their shotguns into Bates and Seng, killing them, too.

A fourth crewman was already dead. Edwin Daughtery, the mail clerk, had been roasted alive by the fire consuming the mail car.

The brothers stared down at the dead men. Then they panicked. Hugh, who had planned so carefully and long, lost all presence of mind and threw down his pistol, running wildly up the hill next to the tunnel. The twins ran after him.

At the top of the hill, the three men slipped out of the overalls they had donned for the raid. Bundling these, they raced on. Roy D'Autremont's overalls fell from his grasp. He kept running.

The three young men, once back in Eugene, decided to keep on running. The raid had been a fiasco, a bloody crazy mess. Train robbing had brought them nothing but impetuous murder. Hugh decided to join the army; Roy and Ray, always inseparable, would go East and try to find jobs.

When authorities got to train Number 13 they were met with the horrible sight of three men brutally slain, lying next to the still-steaming locomotive. The mail car was a cinder. Clerk Daughtery's remains were charred bones.

Chief of the Southern Pacific's train police, Daniel O'Connell, had never seen anything like it. What was worse, he had no clues to guide him to the identity of the bandits. None of the passengers had gotten so much as a glimpse.

It was days later when a brakeman spotted Hugh's pistol near the roadbed. A farmer brought in Roy's overalls. That was it. O'Connell was stumped. This pistol, the detective was convinced, could not be traced. The first three serial numbers on its face had been filed away. That left him with a pair of overalls, which meant he was left with nothing.

He was about to close out the case as "unsolved" when he remembered an odd little criminologist named Edward Oscar Heinrich, who ran an experimental crime lab in Berkeley, California. O'Connell took the pistol and overalls to Heinrich.

This man, who was to become known as the "Wizard of Berkeley," had a reputation for solving the most baffling criminal cases in modern times. He was an expert in ballistics, chemistry, botany, geology—a master criminologist in the Holmesian tradition. Though his peers jeered at him, O'Connell had confidence in Heinrich's capabilities.

The criminologist asked for two days to work on the clues. At the end of this time, he showed up in O'Connell's office with some astonishing information. "These overalls," he said, holding them out, "were worn by a left-handed lumberjack who has worked around fir trees somewhere in the Pacific Northwest." Heinrich went on to state that the suspect was a white man between the ages of 21 and 25, had medium light brown hair, was not taller than 5'10" weighed about 125 pounds and was "very definitely fastidious in his habits."

When O'Connell recovered his speech, he asked how Heinrich had come to such amazing conclusions. Simple, the criminologist explained. The fir pitch staining the overalls and tiny Douglas fir needles found in the pockets (indigenous to the Northwest territory), which Heinrich examined under a powerful microscope, along with small tree chips found in the righthand pocket of the overalls pointed to the fact that the suspect was a left-handed lumberjack. "A left-handed lumberjack, you know, stands with his right side to the tree he's cutting, and chips fly to the right, not to the left." Henrich determined the man's size by simply measuring the overalls. The fact that he was "fastidious" was established by Heinrich when he found some neatly cut fingernail slivers in the seam of a pocket. The suspect's age, hair color, and race were determined by examining a hair caught on the button of the overalls.

The Colt pistol was no challenge at all to Heinrich. True, the first three serial numbers had been filed away, but, little known to law officials then, there was another set of serial numbers hidden inside the gun. Heinrich merely dismantled the weapon and found the number. (Manufacturers of firearms had been doing this for a number of years for the explicit purpose of establishing ownership, albeit this process was publicized little.) Heinrich also found a mail receipt tucked into the bib pocket of the overalls.

Armed with this storehouse of information, O'Connell, the local police, postal inspectors, and the FBI fanned out.

The receipt was for a registered letter, Post Office investigators revealed, sent by a Roy D'Autremont to his brother Hugh. O'Connell's men journeyed to Eugene, Ore. and interviewed Roy's father. His sons were away, he said. He didn't know where. Roy was a lumberjack, yes. He was also left-handed. The detectives scooped up several effects the brothers had left behind, and departed.

The serial number on the Colt pistol led police to a

Seattle store. Records showed that a Mr. William Elliott had signed for it. Heinrich, using samples taken from the D'Autremont home, compared this signature with Roy D'Autremont's handwriting and concluded they were one in the same.

Now the authorities knew who they were looking for, but the D'Autremont brothers had vanished.

For four years the search went on. As manhunts go, it was unequalled in modern times. More than two million circulars prominently displaying the photos of the D'Autremont brothers were distributed to almost every city and town in the country. Foreign countries were deluged with wanted posters on the brothers and $15,000 in reward money was offered for their capture.

Sergeant Thomas Reynolds of the U. S. Army finally broke the case in March, 1927. While leafing through some wanted posters, he recognized Hugh D'Autremont as a man who had served with him in the Philippines, known to him at that time as a soldier named Brice. He informed postal authorities and official wires were sent to the army command in Manila. Hugh was arrested and shipped back to the States.

Weeks after Hugh was taken back to Oregon to stand trial, Albert Cullingworth of Steubenville, Ohio, was reading a magazine article about a thrilling train robbery that had occurred in Oregon four years before. He spotted the photos of Roy and Ray D'Autremont and gasped: "The Goodwin twins working at the mill!"

The old man contacted the FBI through a neighbor and the outlaw brothers were arrested and sent to Oregon for

Trainrobber Hugh D'Autremont upon his release from the Portland Penitentiary in 1958. (UPI)

trial. There, all three D'Autremonts confessed. Their confession saved them from the rope. The brothers were sent to prison for life.

Hugh was paroled in 1958, dying in March, 1959. Ray was paroled in 1961. Roy D'Autremont, whose discarded overalls betrayed him, still resides in an Oregon mental institution. He is considered just as insane as the criminal adventure which led him there.

DIAMOND, JOHN THOMAS (JACK "LEGS")
Racketeer • (1896-1931)

BACKGROUND: BORN AND RAISED IN PHILADELPHIA. (CHRISTENED JOHN T. NOLAND) MINOR PUBLIC EDUCATION. SERVED BRIEFLY IN THE U.S. ARMY (DESERTED) DURING THE FIRST WORLD WAR. ONE BROTHER, EDWARD. MARRIED ALICE KENNY, 1920. ORIGINAL OCCUPATION, LABORER. DESCRIPTION: 5'11", BROWN EYES, BROWN HAIR, THIN. ALIASES: "LEGS," JOHN HIGGINS, JOHN HART, JACK DIAMOND. RECORD: BEFORE 1910, AS A CHILD IN PHILADELPHIA, DIAMOND, WITH HIS BROTHER EDWARD, BELONGED TO THE BOILER GANG WHICH PRACTICED PETTY THIEVERY; UPON MOVING TO NEW YORK CITY WITH HIS BROTHER, JOINED THE HUDSON DUSTERS, A SNEAK-THIEF GROUP SPECIALIZING IN ROBBING PACKAGES FROM DELIVERY TRUCKS; ARRESTED 2/4/14 FOR BURGLARY IN NEW YORK CITY; SENT TO NYC REFORMATORY FOR A BRIEF TERM; ARRESTED FOR ASSAULT AND ROBBERY 5/12/16, DISCHARGED; ARRESTED FOR GRAND LARCENY 5/27/16, DISCHARGED; ARRESTED FOR ASSAULT 7/15/16, DISCHARGED; ARRESTED FOR DESERTION FROM THE U.S. ARMY, 3/24/19; SENTENCED TO ONE YEAR AT GOVERNORS ISLAND DISCIPLINARY BARRACKS, LATER TRANSFERRED TO LEAVENWORTH PENITENTIARY; RELEASED IN EARLY 1920; ARRESTED FOR GRAND LARCENY, 6/1/21, DISCHARGED; ARRESTED FOR ASSAULT AND ROBBERY, 10/27/21, DISCHARGED; ARRESTED FOR BURGLARY, 11/18/21, DISCHARGED; ARRESTED FOR ROBBERY, 11/28/23, DISCHARGED; ARRESTED NEW YORK FOR ROBBERY, 6/14/24, DISCHARGED; WORKED AS A LIEUTENANT TO NEW YORK CITY GANGSTER JACOB "LITTLE

AUGIE" ORGEN AS A BOOTLEGGER, NARCOTICS SMUGGLER, AND HIJACKER; ARRESTED FOR SMUGGLING NARCOTICS, 9/9/26 IN MOUNT VERNON, N.Y., DISCHARGED; ARRESTED ON SUSPICION OF MURDER IN OCT., 1928, DISMISSED; SHOT AND KILLED WILLIAM "RED" CASSIDY AND SIMON WALKER, 6/13/29, IN HIS HOTSY TOTSY CLUB WITH CHARLES ENTRATTA, ARRESTED FOR MURDER, DISMISSED; ARRESTED FOR VIOLATING THE NATIONAL PROHIBITION ACT, 5/13/31; RECEIVED AN $11,000 FINE AND SENTENCED TO FOUR YEARS IN PRISON 8/13/31; RELEASED ON $15,000 BAIL BOND PENDING APPEAL; ARRESTED FOR ASSAULTING AND TORTURING BOOTLEGGER GROVER PARKS AND KIDNAPPING JAMES DUNCAN, BARTENDER, BOTH OF ALBANY, N.Y., 12/11/31, ACQUITTED; SHOT AND KILLED BY UNKNOWN GANGSTERS (ALLEGED TO BE WORKING FOR DUTCH SCHULTZ) IN AN ALBANY ROOMING HOUSE, 12/18/31.

In the underworld of his day, he was known as the "Clay Pigeon." Jack "Legs" Diamond had been shot at and wounded so many times in his criminal career that even his fellow bootleggers were aghast at his amazing ability to survive. "The bullet hasn't been made that can kill me," Legs once boasted.

Of all the New York gangsters of the 1920s, Legs Diamond was the flashiest, a disarming charmer. He was also the deadliest gunman in the rackets.

Legs got his beginning as a sneak thief and earned his nickname while hanging around the West Side Winona Club owned by racketeer Owney Madden. Diamond, a member of the Hudson Dusters then (about sixteen years old) robbed packages from the backs of delivery trucks parked in front of Madden's swank nightclub. His ability to elude pursuing policemen quickly earned him the name "Legs."

He and his brother Eddie, after moving from Philadelphia, were arrested for a series of petty thefts and burglaries up to the time of the First World War when America called Legs to arms. He was not enthusiastic about serving his country and soon went AWOL. Diamond was apprehended and served a year and a day in Leavenworth as a deserter.

Prison was Diamond's training ground and there he met

Nathan "Kid Dropper" Kaplan; he ruled New York rackets until Legs Diamond figured a way to have him shot to death.

Legs Diamond's first underworld boss: Little Augie Orgen.

tough New York mobsters who put him in touch with a showy racketeer, Jacob "Little Augie" Orgen, upon his release. Orgen was a zany killer who had worked his way into the garment industry racket using strong arm goon squads under the command of another rising gangster, Louis Lepke Buchalter. Little Augie was also in need of tough gunmen to help him in his bootlegging enterprises.

Legs Diamond, recently released from prison, with his brother Eddie went to work for Little Augie at the dawn of Prohibition. First, they hijacked beer and liquor trucks carrying Canadian shipments in upstate New York. They worked their way into Little Augie's smuggling rackets, dealing largely in narcotics and stolen gems.

In the early gang wars Legs more than once proved his nerveless skill with a gun. Little Augie was also surprised at Diamond's ability to organize and plan; he soon made him his chief lieutenant and right-hand man. His first important assignment was getting rid of Nathan "Kid Dropper" Kaplan, Little Augie's chief rival in the labor rackets and bootlegging territories in midtown Manhattan.

Kaplan was no easy prey. He surrounded himself with an army of hoodlums and never hesitated to order a killing either for business or personal reasons. He had even attempted to kill Little Augie once with a knife, when both men were younger and vying for control of a street gang; Kaplan left Orgen with a vicious looking scar that ran from his left ear across his cheek to his nose.

An egotistical gangster, Kaplan insisted that his men and even his wife call him "Kid Dropper," or "Jack the Dropper," after an oldtime boxer he had admired. New York's young, tough mobster-gangs were beginning to flourish about the time Diamond and his brother were developing their package thievery. Three men—Owney Madden, Nathan "Kid Dropper" Kaplan, and Johnny Spanish (Joseph Weyler)—were the rising kingpins of New York's underworld.

Madden went to prison for murder in 1915. Spanish and Kaplan followed him there shortly after but were both released in 1917. Then began Manhattan's first bloody gang war. Kid Dropper and Spanish ran the rackets in New York but the competition was tough. The two gangsters sent out platoons of killers and soon open warfare bloodied the streets. For two years, the Dropper-Spanish legions battled. Then, as he emerged from a restaurant on Second Avenue on the night of July 29, 1919, Johnny Spanish was killed. The Dropper and two of his bodyguards merely slipped up behind Spanish and emptied their pistols into his back. Kid Dropper reigned supreme.

The first man to challenge his authority within a year of the Spanish killing was Little Augie Orgen, a product of the Dopey Benny gang on the Lower East Side. Financed by gambler and underworld money man Arnold Rothstein, Orgen moved into the garment racket, amassing a formidable gang of ambitious terrorists culled from the toughest street gangs in the city—Charles "Lucky" Luciano, Lepke and his faithful killer ape, Gurrah, Waxey Gorden, and the Diamond brothers.

This gang clashed openly with Kid Dropper's troops in an industry and bootleg war between 1919 and 1920. In one gun battle between the factions on Essex Street, two bystanders were shot to death. Little Augie still had no luck in getting rid of Kaplan. Legs Diamond came up with a solution.

He proposed that Jacob Gurrah Shapiro file a complaint

with the police department, charging Kid Dropper with assault (Dropper had fired at Gurrah in a recent gun battle). When Kid Dropper was brought in to face that charge, the Little Augie gang would simply shoot him. "Get him into court," Diamond insisted. "Once we pinpoint him, we can get to him."

Gurrah filed the complaint and Kid Dropper was brought in for questioning. When police found a gun on the Dropper, Kaplan yelled: "I had to carry it! Self-defense . . . Little Augie and the Diamonds are after me! They want to kill me!"

When the Dropper emerged from the Essex Market Court on August 18, 1923 after listening to Shapiro's charges, Louis Kushner, an Orgen gangster, was waiting for him with a gun in his pocket. Kushner was a hanger-on whom the Little Augies used as a messenger boy. Diamond convinced Kushner that his status in the gang would rise considerably if he killed the Dropper as he came out of court. Kushner didn't need too much urging. Kid Dropper had been blackmailing him for the beating of a garment worker.

As the Dropper walked down the courthouse stairs, squads of police swept in about him to escort him to the West Side Court for another hearing. Legs Diamond watched elatedly across the street as Kushner made his way to the back of the police car carrying Kid Dropper. The undersized Kushner awkwardly jumped on the bumper and, in front of hundreds of witnesses, fired rapid shots through the car's back window. The first shot wounded the driver of the car in the ear, the second tore off a straw hat from the head of Police Captain Cornelius Willemse. Seeing Kid Dropper fall to the floor of the car to avoid being hit, Kushner battered out the police car's window to get a better shot.

The Dropper's wife, Veronica, who was standing on the sidewalk, rushed up to the little gangster and tried to hold him, screaming: "Don't shoot him, don't shoot him!" Kushner pushed her down and squeezed off another round into the car, hitting Kid Dropper in the head. "They got me," Jack the Dropper moaned and died.

Dozens of policemen surrounded Kushner, pistols aimed

at his head. The killer was ecstatic and proud over his feat. He smiled and handed his gun to an officer. "I got him," he beamed. "May I have a cigarette?"

The bizarre scene, witnessed by a satisfied Legs Diamond from across the street, was not complete until Veronica Kaplan, hysterical, threw herself across the Dropper's body, hanging from a car door, pleading into the dead man's ears: "Nate! Nate! Tell me that you were not what they say you were!" Kushner turned, with a bevy of policemen holding him, and happily posed for the cameras of newsmen who had come to cover Kaplan's hearing. "I got him, I got him," he continued to say as he was led away.

Little Augie was now master of the New York rackets and he had Legs Diamond to thank. He showed his gratitude by giving Diamond lucrative chunks of his bootleg-and-narcotics empire which stretched from Manhattan to Albany, New York.

Suddenly in the big money, Diamond haunted nightclubs, Broadway shows, and dance halls. He had once been a semi-professional dancer, hiring out to wealthy women who wanted to fast-step. Chorus girl Marion "Kiki" Roberts (Marion Strasmick) caught his eye and he quickly made the bosomy, florid-faced jazz baby his mistress.

Diamond's love life never distressed his wife, Alice, who married him in 1920. Alice was the patient sort and proudly sported her wedding ring. Kiki may have had her husband's attentions, she told newsmen, but she possessed the man. Mrs. Diamond hero-worshipped her husband. Pictures of the lean, hollow-eyed gangster adorned every wall of their luxurious apartment. On one above the fireplace, Alice had scrawled in large letters the words: "My Hero."

Kiki Roberts didn't need any photos of her lover, she reasoned. The jewels and money Legs showered on her were enough. Kiki didn't know it, but she was not the only girl-on-the-side Diamond supported. The Hotsy Totsy Club, a second-floor speakeasy on Broadway between 54th and 55th Streets, was owned by Diamond and Hymie Cohen. The place was a veritable Diamond harem. It was also a deathtrap.

Here Legs held court and directed Little Augie's rackets. The speakeasy also served as a killing spot. Several would-be crime czars were lured to the Hotsy Totsy Club only to be carried out hours later, feet first.

By 1927, Legs was a powerful figure in New York's underworld. He ranked with Dutch Schultz, Lepke, Big Bill Dwyer, and Charles "Lucky" Luciano. Top mobsters such as Vannie Higgins, Owney Madden, Waxey Gorden, and Larry Fay, head of the city's mild rackets, paid him homage. Even "Mr. Big"—Arnold Rothstein—took him into his confidence (Diamond had performed bodyguard services for Rothstein while moving up in Little Augie's troop).

But 1927 was also the year in which Legs Diamond's luck turned sour. On October 15, 1927, Diamond was escorting his boss Little Augie from his Lower East Side headquarters near Delancy and Norfolk Streets. The bodyguard chore usually fell to Eddie Diamond but he was in jail, right where Legs wanted him. Diamond, serving as a stand-in bodyguard for Little Augie, explained to his boss that his brother was tubercular and that jail was the best place for his lungs until he could make arrangements for him in a Colorado sanitarium.

Little Augie told Diamond about his present worries, particularly about Lepke Buchalter and Gurrah Shapiro. They were ungrateful punks, kids he himself had trained for the rackets. Now they were muscling in on his garment industry rackets. They would have to be taught a lesson. Diamond nodded.

Moments later, as the gangster pair turned onto Norfolk Street, a fast-moving cab, a Chevrolet, swept past them and stopped. Little Augie was about to get in, when the cab door flew open and a machinegunner, crouched low in the back, opened up on him with a quick short burst. Twelve bullets went into Orgen and the little hoodlum fell to the sidewalk, dead. Diamond, wounded in the arm and leg, staggered down the street and collapsed inside a doorway. He was ambulanced to Bellevue Hospital where he barely managed to stay alive. He had lost so much blood, doctors at first thought he would certainly die.

The minute Legs was able to talk, police rushed into his hospital room. The gangster weakly propped himself up on an elbow and shouted: "Don't ask me nothin'! You hear me! Don't ask! And don't bring anybody here for me to identify. I won't identify them even if I know they did it!" He fell back on the bed unconscious.

Legs didn't have to point anyone out. He knew the machinegunner in the back of the cab on sight—Lepke Buchalter. And the obese, scowling cabdriver had been none other than Jacob Gurrah Shapiro. Little Augie's troubles with these two gangsters were over.

Upon recovery, Diamond settled for his booze and narcotics rackets, leaving Lepke to take over Little Augie's garment industry interests. But Dutch Schultz, by then the most vicious beer baron of New York, wanted some (perhaps all) of Diamond's territory. War broke out again with a rash of hijackings and killings.

Rothstein backed Diamond in his war against the Dutchman and Legs spent a fortune recruiting gun talent. His goon squads were headed up by a trigger-happy killer named Charles Entratta (alias Charlie Green). Others of Diamond's hit-men troop included A. J. Harry Klein, A. Treager, Salvatore Arcidicio, and a sadistic gangster who enjoyed torturing bartenders reluctant to push Diamond's needle beer, W. Talamo (alias John Scaccio).

For a period of about two years, Legs made great inroads against the Dutchman's empire. He cut a great bootleg swath out of upstate New York, actually controlling several major highways down which Canadian liquor was being bootlegged.

Diamond's fortunes dipped drastically in 1928 following the mysterious murder of his benefactor, Arnold Rothstein. He was then involved in a senseless killing inside his Hotsy Totsy Club.

William "Red" Cassidy, a minor hoodlum, was standing at the bar on the night of June 13, 1929 with a group of friends. Cassidy's demeanor was anything but cordial. He asked for service by banging on the bar with his hamhock fists and shouting: "C'mon you punks, give me some goddamn service!"

Legs and his favorite henchman, Entratta, were in the bar and jumped up excitedly. "Behave yourself," Diamond warned Cassidy.

"Go to hell, you pimp!" Cassidy roared, throwing a punch in Diamond's direction. Without further word, Diamond and Entratta pulled out their pistols and fired a barrage into Cassidy's group which was advancing upon them, fists raised. When the smoke cleared, gangster Simon Walker, recently paroled from Sing Sing, was dead, his head resting on the bar rail, two loaded .38-caliber revolvers still stuck in his belt. Red Cassidy was badly wounded in several places. His friends frantically dragged him down the Club's stairs to the street where an ambulance was called. He was dead within an hour.

Diamond and Entratta disappeared while police hunted them throughout the state. Dutch Schultz, never a man to miss an opportunity, moved in on Legs' bootleg interests while Diamond was in hiding until the Cassidy murder cooled off. When he did surface and surrender to police he was quickly dismissed of the murder charge for "lack of evidence," (although twenty-five people saw the shootings) but Schultz had grabbed off large portions of his beer territory.

Before the guns roared again, Joey Noe, a Schultz gunman, arranged a truce talk with Diamond in 1929. Both gang leaders were apprehensive of each other.

"I don't trust the Dutchman," Diamond said. "He's a crocodile. He's sneaky. I don't trust him."

"I don't trust Legs," the Dutchman said. "He's nuts. He gets excited and starts pulling a trigger like another guy wipes his nose."

The two arch criminals met in spite of their distrust and agreed to a truce. The meeting took place in the old Harding Hotel. Diamond told Schultz he could keep the midtown beer territory he had stolen if he paid an equitable price for it. Legs wanted out of that area anyway, he said. His other rackets were taking up too much of his time to worry about it. Schultz paid the price, an alleged half million dollars, on the spot and in cash.

Minutes later, as the Dutchman and Noe were walking down the street, two men jumped from an alley and shot Noe down. Schultz whipped out his revolver and drove the two off. The Dutchman then raced off toward the Harding Hotel, leaving Noe to bleed on the sidewalk. Schultz arrived to find the room where he had met Diamond empty. One of his own men was still there.

"The goddamn double-crosser just shot Joey!" Dutch screamed. "I'm gonna kill him for this!" He meant it.

Eddie Diamond, who had traveled to Denver to seek the pure air for his bad lungs, was trapped weeks later in a cabaret his brother Legs had financed. Five gunmen shot him several times and left him for dead. Though Eddie lived, Legs vowed revenge.

Within a year, the five gunmen were dead. Frank "Blubber" Devlin, was shot through the back of the head only once on March 3, 1929, in Somerville, New Jersey. Next Eugene Moran was riddled and his body cremated on a bonfire in August, 1929. James Batto, Monkey Schubert, and Harry Veasey wound up in similar conditions by 1930.

While Diamond was systematically attempting to rub out Schultz's army, the Dutchman made his own plans. Three of his men barged into Kiki Roberts' suite in New York's Hotel Monticello in October, 1929. Kiki and Legs were dining in their pajamas and the gunmen unleashed a wall of shells in their direction. Legs was wounded five times but lived. Kiki was unharmed.

It was getting hot for Legs. Dutch was not going after his men but after him. To avoid such personal attention, Diamond decided to tour Europe. He sailed on the *Baltic* in 1930. Authorities in England, however, aware of the gangster's notorious reputation, refused to let him off the boat. It was the same story in Belgium. Dejected, Legs returned to New York. No sooner was he home with his wife in Acra, N. Y., than Schultz struck again. Legs was shot several times as he emerged from the Aratoga Inn in April, 1931. Again he lived.

The newspapers thought it phenomenal. Diamond had been put on the spot three times and lived. He was a clay pigeon that couldn't be shattered. Schultz started to get nervous. "Can't anybody shoot that guy so he won't bounce back up?"

In early December, 1931, Legs, trying to expand his upstate operations, threatened a bootlegger, Grover Parks, with death unless he turned over his shipments to his men. Parks told Legs to "go to hell." John Scaccio abducted Parks and a partner, James Duncan, one night and took them to an Albany hotel room. There, while Legs and his girlfriend Kiki got drunk, Scaccio and others repeatedly burned

Jack "Legs" Diamond (right) following a court acquittal in 1931; he was shot to death only hours after this photo was taken. (UPI)

the two men with lighted cigarettes, flaming matches jammed beneath their fingernails, and a white hot poker run up their backsides. The two stalwart bootleggers finally gave in and consented to work with Diamond.

Upon their release, however, Parks and Duncan went to the police and reported the whole story. Diamond and Scaccio were arrested and tried in Troy, N. Y. Legs squeaked out of a conviction by sacrificing his henchman Scaccio (who got ten years in Sing Sing and Diamond's promise that he would get him out shortly).

Back in Albany, Legs decided to celebrate. He gave a roaring party at a local speakeasy on the night of December 17, 1931. Dozens of his hoodlum friends, as well as his wife Alice, were in attendance. About 1 a.m., Legs slipped away from the party to secretly rendezvous with his sweetheart, Kiki Roberts. After spending three and a half hours with her, Diamond, still somewhat drunk, shakily hailed a cab in his employ at Clinton and Tenbroeck and told his man, Jack Storey, to take him home. Home was a small room in a boarding house at 67 Dove Street.

Diamond got out of the cab and staggered upstairs to bed. His driver took off. At 4:45 a.m., the landlady, Mrs. Wood, was suddenly awakened from her bed by five clear shots coming from Diamond's upstairs room. She heard feet running down the stairs and, from her window, saw three men sprint down the street.

Within minutes, Alice Diamond was called; the police came right behind her. They found Legs Diamond still in bed, five bullets in his head and torso, quite dead.

Alice Diamond threw her large body over the corpse, screaming, "Help me, somebody! They've shot Jack! They've killed him!" Great tears swelled up in her green eyes and ran down her face. A police doctor pronounced Diamond dead. Alice shook her head wildly, her long red hair swirling. She dove for the bed, grasping the bedposts. "No! No! You can't have him! He's mine! He belongs to me! Let me stay with Jack . . ."

It took close to ten minutes before two officers could pry Alice's hands loose. They led her sobbing from the room. Before leaving, she turned and said quietly, "I didn't do it."

Detectives found no money on Diamond. His signet ring, brandishing a large D, was in a drawer. Also in the drawer were dozens of letters from women written to Legs at the time of his trial. Most of these ladies wanted to marry and reform him.

When she heard the news of Diamond's death, Kiki Roberts contacted the *New York American,* telling reporters in an exclusive interview: "I was in love with Jack Diamond. I was with him in Albany, New York before he was killed. But I don't know who killed him or anything about the murder."

Apparently, neither did anyone else. Jack Legs Diamond's killers were never apprehended, though most concluded that Dutch Schultz's boys had done the job on orders.

Alice Diamond was the only person to attend her husband's funeral. Marion Kiki Roberts had disappeared. Two years later, Alice Diamond was murdered in Brooklyn. Her killer was never found. Kiki Roberts was found at the time of Alice's death. She had resumed her real name, Marion Strasmick, and was living alone in a tenement.

"I don't know anything about those people," Marion insisted. "They were gangsters, weren't they?"

DILLINGER, JOHN HERBERT
Bankrobber • (1903- ?)

BACKGROUND: BORN IN INDIANAPOLIS, INDIANA 6/22/03 TO JOHN AND MOLLIE DILLINGER. ONE SISTER, AUDREY. COMPLETED ELEMENTARY SCHOOL IN INDIANAPOLIS. ORIGINAL OCCUPATION, MACHINIST. SERVED BRIEFLY ON BOARD THE BATTLESHIP "UTAH" IN 1923 AFTER JOINING THE U.S. NAVY. MARRIED BERYL ETHEL HOVIUS IN 1924, DIVORCED IN 1929. DESCRIPTION: 5'7¼", BLUE EYES, LIGHT BROWN HAIR, MEDIUM BUILD, ½" SCAR ON BACK OF LEFT HAND, SCAR ON MIDDLE OF UPPER LIP. ALIASES: FRANK SULLIVAN, JOSEPH HARRIS, JOHN HALL, "DESPERATE DAN" DILLINGER, JOHN DONOVAN, CARL HELLMAN. RECORD: ARRESTED FOR STEALING A CAR BELONGING TO OLIVER P. MACY OF MOORESVILLE, IND. ON 7/21/23, NO CHARGES MADE; DESERTED U.S. NAVY 12/4/23 IN BOSTON, MASS., $50 REWARD OFFERED FOR HIS CAPTURE; ATTEMPTED TO ROB FRANK MORGAN, A GROCER IN MARTINSVILLE, IND., 9/6/24; SENTENCED 9/15/24 BY JUDGE JOSEPH WILLIAMS OF MARTINSVILLE, AFTER DILLINGER THREW HIMSELF ON THE MERCY OF THE COURT, TO CONCURRENT SENTENCES OF TWO TO FOURTEEN YEARS AND TEN TO TWENTY YEARS FOR CONSPIRACY TO COMMIT A FELONY AND ASSAULT WITH INTENT TO ROB; SENT TO THE INDIANA STATE REFORMATORY AT PENDLETON; ATTEMPTED TO ESCAPE 10/15/24; RECEIVED SIX MORE MONTHS ON TOP OF HIS SENTENCE; ATTEMPTED TO ESCAPE 9/28/24 FROM GUARD AFTER TESTIFYING AGAINST EDGAR SINGLETON, AN ACCOMPLICE IN THE MORGAN ROBBERY AND WHILE BEING RETURNED TO PENDLETON; NAVY OFFICIALS DROPPED CHARGES AGAINST DILLINGER AT THIS TIME FOR

DESERTION, ISSUING HIM A DISHONORABLE DISCHARGE; ATTEMPTED TO ESCAPE PENDLETON IN DECEMBER, 1924; SIX MORE MONTHS ADDED TO HIS SENTENCE; CAUGHT GAMBLING BY REFORMATORY GUARDS 2/25/25, THIRTY DAYS ADDED TO HIS SENTENCE; ACCUSED OF BEING "DISORDERLY" IN AUGUST, 1926, THIRTY MORE DAYS ADDED TO HIS SENTENCE; ACCUSED OF DESTROYING PRISON PROPERTY, 10/17/28, THIRTY DAYS ADDED TO HIS SENTENCE; TRANSFERRED BY INDIANA GOVERNOR HARRY G. LESLIE, AT DILLINGER'S OWN REQUEST, TO MICHIGAN CITY, INDIANA STATE PRISON IN JULY, 1929; PAROLED 5/22/33; ROBBED WITH WILLIAM SHAW SEVERAL SMALL STORES AND FACTORIES IN RURAL INDIANA AND INDIANAPOLIS DURING JUNE, 1933; ROBBED WITH SHAW AND PAUL "LEFTY" PARKER THE NATIONAL BANK OF NEW CARLISLE, IND., 6/10/33 ($10,600); ROBBED WITH HARRY COPELAND THE COMMERCIAL BANK IN DALEVILLE, IND., 7/17/33 ($3,500); ROBBED WITH HARRY COPELAND THE FIRST NATIONAL BANK OF MONTPELIER, IND., 8/4/33 ($10,110); ROBBED WITH HARRY COPELAND AND SAM GOLDSTINE THE CITIZENS NATIONAL BANK IN BLUFFTON, OHIO, 8/14/33 ($2,100); ROBBED WITH HARRY COPELAND AND HILTON CROUCH THE MASSACHUSETTS AVENUE STATE BANK OF INDIANAPOLIS, IND., 9/6/33 ($24,800); ARRESTED BY POLICE OFFICERS IN DAYTON, O., 9/22/33; SENT TO LIMA, O. JAIL TO AWAIT TRIAL FOR THE BLUFFTON ROBBERY; TEN CONVICTS ESCAPED THE MICHIGAN CITY, INDIANA STATE PRISON 9/26/33—A BREAK FINANCED AND ENGINEERED BY DILLINGER—ESCAPEES INCLUDED WALTER DIETRICH, JIM "OKLAHOMA JACK" CLARK, JAMES JENKINS, JOSEPH BURNS, JOSEPH FOX, EDWARD SHOUSE AND DILLINGER'S FORMER CLOSE PRISON ASSOCIATES, BANKROBBERS HARRY PIERPONT, JOHN HAMILTON, RUSSELL CLARK, AND CHARLES "FAT CHARLEY" MAKLEY; TO OBTAIN FUNDS TO FINANCE DILLINGER'S ESCAPE FROM THE LIMA, O. JAIL, PIERPONT, HAMILTON, CLARK, MAKLEY, AND SHOUSE ROBBED THE FIRST NATIONAL BANK IN ST. MARY'S, O. 10/3/33 ($14,000); DILLINGER ESCAPED FROM THE LIMA, O. JAIL 10/12/33, HIS RELEASE EFFECTED BY PIERPONT, MAKLEY, CLARK, HAMILTON AND SHOUSE; PIERPONT AND MAKLEY KILLED SHERIFF JESS SARBER DURING THIS BREAK; ROBBED WITH PIERPONT, MAKLEY, HAMILTON, AND CLARK THE POLICE ARSENAL OF PERU, IND., 10/20/33 (TAKING TWO MACHINEGUNS, TWO SAWED-OFF SHOTGUNS, FOUR .38-CALIBER POLICE SPECIALS, TWO 30.30 WINCHESTER RIFLES, BULLETPROOF VESTS, THREE POLICE BADGES AND AMMUNITION); ROBBED WITH PIERPONT, MAKLEY, CLARK, AND HAMILTON THE CENTRAL NATIONAL BANK OF GREENCASTLE, IND., 10/23/33 ($75,346 IN CASH AND BONDS); ESCAPED POLICE TRAP IN CHICAGO 11/15/33; ROBBED WITH PIERPONT, MAKLEY, CLARK, AND HAMILTON THE AMERICAN BANK AND TRUST COMPANY OF RACINE, WISCONSIN, 11/20/33 ($27,789); ALLEGEDLY ROBBED

WITH HAMILTON THE FIRST NATIONAL BANK IN EAST CHICAGO, IND., 1/15/34 ($20,736) AT WHICH TIME POLICEMAN PATRICK O'MALLEY WAS KILLED BY ONE OF THE BANDITS; ARRESTED WITH MAKLEY, CLARK, PIERPONT IN TUCSON, ARIZ. BY LOCAL POLICE 1/25/34; EXTRADITED TO INDIANA TO STAND TRIAL FOR ROBBERIES THERE AND FOR THE MURDER OF POLICEMAN O'MALLEY; PLACED IN CROWN POINT, IND. JAIL; ESCAPED CROWN POINT JAIL USING A WOODEN GUN 3/3/34; ROBBED WITH BABY FACE NELSON (LESTER GILLIS), HOMER VAN METER, JOHN HAMILTON, EDDIE GREEN, AND TOMMY CARROLL THE SECURITY NATIONAL BANK IN SIOUX FALLS, S.D., 3/6/34 ($49,000); ROBBED WITH NELSON, VAN METER, HAMILTON, GREEN, AND CARROLL THE FIRST NATIONAL BANK OF MASON CITY, IOWA—DILLINGER AND HAMILTON WOUNDED—ON 3/13/34 ($52,000); ESCAPED FBI TRAP IN ST. PAUL, MINN., 3/31/34; ESCAPED FBI ATTACK AT LITTLE BOHEMIA LODGE NEAR MANITOWISH WATERS, WISCONSIN, 4/22/33; ALLEGEDLY ROBBED THE MERCHANTS NATIONAL BANK OF SOUTH BEND, IND., 6/30/34 ($18,000); FBI CLAIMED TO HAVE KILLED DILLINGER 7/22/34 OUTSIDE THE BIOGRAPH THEATER IN CHICAGO BUT ALL PERTINENT FACTS OF THE SHOOTING CONTRADICT THIS AND POINT TO THE FACT THAT ANOTHER MAN WAS KILLED IN HIS PLACE AND THAT THE INDIANA BANDIT DISAPPEARED COMPLETELY.

John Herbert Dillinger is America's classic bankrobber. No other criminal ever approached his exploits and reputation. Within the space of twelve months Dillinger robbed more banks and stole more money than Jesse James did in the sixteen years he was at large. It took the combined forces of five states and the FBI to pressure his operations to a halt and there exists today no real evidence that he was ever finally apprehended and killed.

Unlike the city gangsters of the Thirties, Dillinger sprang from humble rural beginnings. School and work dominated his early life. He was not a "born" criminal in any sense; only a precocious child who could reasonably be considered as average as any man's offspring.

Born in his father's Indianapolis home June 22, 1903, John Dillinger was delivered by a midwife. His mother Mollie was not a well woman and she died prematurely in 1907 following an apoplectic attack and a subsequent operation. Little Johnnie was left to the care of his fifteen-year-old sister Audrey and his father John Wilson Dillinger, who operated a grocery store on Bloyd Street and maintained several houses which he owned and rented.

In 1912, Dillinger's father remarried. His second wife was Elizabeth Fields of Mooresville, Ind. Evidence indicates that Audrey Dillinger spent more time with Johnnie than anyone else during this period. Elizabeth Dillinger gave birth to Hubert Dillinger in 1914, John and Audrey's half-brother. A half-sister, Doris, was born in 1916.

John Dillinger, age three, with his sister Audrey.

As a sixth-grader, Dillinger was hauled into juvenile court one day, charged with stealing coal from the Pennsylvania Railroad yards and selling it to neighbors. He was defiant in court. When the magistrate demanded he stop chewing a wad of gum, Dillinger complied, removing it from his mouth and sticking it to the bill of his cap. "Your mind is crippled!" the judge shouted. Johnnie only grinned.

He was turned back to the custody of his parents. After his graduation from Washington, Dillinger was suddenly uprooted from his Indianapolis home. His father—some later said for reasons of getting John away from corruptive city influences—sold his house and store and bought a modest farm outside of Mooresville, Indiana, a farming community seventeen miles south of Indianapolis.

Here, everything changed for John Dillinger. He refused to help his father farm and vowed never to return to school. Instead, he took a job in Indianapolis as an apprentice machinist at the Reliance Specialty Company, commuting each day from Mooresville on his prize possession, a motor bike. He did attempt to return to school, to please his stepmother, but quickly dropped out of his first semester at Mooresville High.

Dillinger as a teenager with his father on the porch of the family farm in Mooresville, Ind.

When not working in Indianapolis, Dillinger drove south to Martinsville, the county seat, where he had friends. There he played pool in Big John Gebhardt's pool room. He was not good with a cue but took his losses quietly. One man remembered him coming into the pool room, playing for a half hour and regularly losing two dollars to the local sharks. Without a word he would then put on his cap and stroll out.

Dillinger joined the Martinsville baseball team, proving to be a remarkably good second baseman. He dated Frances Thornton, his uncle Everett's stepdaughter. The affair bloomed into love and Dillinger asked his uncle for Frances' hand.

Everett Dillinger refused, the two were too young. The uncle wanted Frances to marry a prosperous boy from Greencastle, Indiana.

Embittered by this rejection, Dillinger returned to Indianapolis where he was seen by neighbors patronizing prostitutes. He contracted gonorrhea. On the night of July 21, 1923, he impulsively stole a car belonging to Oliver P. Macy from the parking lot of the Friends Church in Mooresville. Hours later, Dillinger abandoned the auto in Indianapolis. Fearing arrest, Dillinger enlisted in the U.S. Navy (unknown to John, Macy refused to press charges). He gave his real name and a false St. Louis, Mo., address when enlisting.

After basic training at Great Lakes, fireman third class Dillinger was assigned to the battleship, U.S.S. *Utah* (which would be destroyed at Pearl Harbor in 1941). He went AWOL several times and was thrown in the brig. While the ship was anchored off Boston, Dillinger, on December 4, 1923, permanently jumped ship. The Navy listed him as a deserter and posted a $50 reward for his capture.

Back in Indiana, Dillinger met and courted sixteen-year-old Beryl Ethel Hovius of Martinsville. The young couple married in the spring of 1924 and moved in with Beryl's parents. There wasn't much to it. Dillinger spent more time playing baseball and shooting pool in Gebhart's than he spent with his wife.

After drinking several beers with Edgar Singleton, 31, a former convict and umpire for the Martinsville baseball team, a robbery plan ensued. Singleton excitedly told John that 65-year-old Frank Morgan, a grocer in Mooresville, carried his week's receipts home late on Saturday nights. It would be terribly easy to waylay him and steal the money.

Dillinger agreed. On the night of September 6, 1924, the two men jumped Morgan in front of the Mooresville Christian Church at 10:30 p.m. as the grocer was making his way home. One of them (it was never determined which) hit Morgan with a large bolt wrapped in a rag, opening his skull. He got up and was hit again. One of the robbers brandished a pistol but the intrepid Morgan

Dillinger (left) with Navy buddies in 1923 (taken while he was serving on board the battleship Utah).

knocked it away with his hand and a shot was accidentally fired. The two men, thoroughly frightened, ran.

Morgan's head wound required eleven stitches. He told Deputy Sheriff John Hayworth he couldn't identify his attacker, but the lawman, through information supplied by Mooresville youths, believed John Dillinger was behind the crime and drove out to the family farm. Morgan went with him.

When the grocer confronted John, he recalled how the young man had purchased candy in his store as a child.

"Why, John," Morgan said, "You wouldn't hurt me, would you?"

"No, Mr. Morgan," Dillinger replied.

Hayworth took the would-be bandit in for questioning, placing him in the county jail. When Dillinger's father arrived at the jail, John tearfully admitted the hold-up attempt. The prosecutor promised the elder Dillinger that his son would receive a lenient sentence if he threw himself on the mercy of the court. The old man convinced his son to do so and, without counsel, twenty-year-old John Dillinger pleaded guilty.

It was his bad luck to have been brought before Judge Joseph W. Williams, the most severe jurist in the county. Williams gave Dillinger concurrent sentences of two to fourteen years and ten to twenty years on the two charges of conspiracy to commit a felony and assault with intent to rob. He also fined the youth $100 on each charge and disenfranchised him for a period of twelve years. Edgar Singleton, through his lawyer, received a change of venue and a much lighter sentence (he was paroled inside of two years).

Deputy Sheriff Russell Peterson, who delivered Dillinger to the Indiana State Reformatory at Pendleton where he was to serve out his sentence, felt that John "was just a kid. He got a raw deal. You just can't take ten years away from a kid's life."

Dillinger felt the same way. When he faced Warden A. F. Miles at Pendleton for the first time, he calmly stated: "I won't cause you any trouble except to escape."

"I've heard that kind of talk before," Miles responded.

"Yeah, well, I'll go right over the administration building."

Within weeks, Dillinger tried exactly that but was caught. Next, when Deputy Peterson was returning Dillinger to Pendleton, after he had been escorted to Singleton's trial as a witness, the youth attempted another escape. He kicked over a table in the train station and sent Peterson sprawling. The Deputy chased his charge down a deadend alley and Dillinger surrendered after Peterson fired a warning shot into the air.

Dillinger obstinately continued break attempts at Pendleton. On the night of October 10, 1924 he was discovered missing from his cell. Guards located him under a pile of excelsior in the foundry. In November of the same year, working with a makeshift saw, Dillinger broke out of his cell and into a corridor where he was caught. He tried again in 1925 and was captured.

About this time, Dillinger met the man who was to shape his criminal career, handsome Harry Pierpont, a young bankrobber first arrested for trying to kill a man in Terre Haute, Indiana in March, 1922. Pierpont, soft-spoken and considered quite a ladies' man, had knocked over a Kokomo, Ind. bank singlehandedly and, upon his capture, was sent to Pendleton.

There, Dillinger and Pierpont became close friends and were soon joined by another youthful bankrobber, Homer Van Meter, a crafty habitual criminal who played jester to Pendleton's high court of criminals. Pierpont and Van Meter, who disliked each other, earned Dillinger's admiration by being the toughest, most incorrigible convicts at Pendleton. They spent more time in solitary confinement than in their cells. When officials could no longer control them they were both shipped off to the state prison at Michigan City, Indiana to serve out their long sentences.

After Dillinger's wife divorced him in 1929, he came up before the parole board. His record had been spotty and the board chairman told him that "maybe you'd better go back for a few years."

Dillinger eyed the members of the board. Indiana Governor Harry Leslie was sitting in on the meeting. The Governor had seen Dillinger play baseball in the reformatory's yard once and remarked: "That kid ought to be playing major league baseball." Dillinger had heard of this and now used Leslie's observation as a ploy to obtain a transfer. He asked that he be sent to Michigan City.

"Why do you want to go to Michigan City?" he was asked.

"Because they have a real team up there," John replied.

Leslie quickly convinced the board that such a transfer might lead to "an occupation for him later." Dillinger was sent to the Big House on July 15, 1929 and happily fell in with Pierpont and Van Meter upon arrival.

His old Pendleton classmates introduced him to John Hamilton, another bankrobber, who was apprehended after stealing a car in 1927. Doing a twenty-five year sentence, Hamilton, 34, began to teach Dillinger, as he had Pierpont, the ins and outs of robbing banks. He was an intelligent tough con who talked quietly and was known to the prison population as "Three-Fingered Jack." Hamilton had lost the index and middle fingers of his right hand years earlier in an accident. (It is interesting to note that though Hamilton was considered a "tough customer" by jailers, he was punished only once at Michigan City and that was for skipping rope in the machine shop in 1932.)

In Pierpont's elite bankrobbing alumni was Charles "Fat Charley" Makley who had been in and out of prison in the last ten years, and who was doing twenty years for robbing a Hammond, Ind. bank. Ohio-born Makley was 44 and the clown of the group when Van Meter wasn't about. There was also Russell Lee Clark, a large, big-boned bankrobber with steely nerves and an introverted disposition. Clark had been sent up in 1927 and had caused prison authorities no end of headaches. He had led attempted prison breaks, riots, and had tried to kill his guards on several occasions.

These men, who would figure in Indiana's largest prison break four years later (an escape engineered by Dillinger), would form a super gang of bankrobbers whose incredible thefts would astound the country.

The group cultivated Dillinger as their future contact man on the outside; he would be up for parole before any of the others. It would be his job to rob a string of small town banks from a list prepared by Pierpont and Hamilton and use funds from these robberies to finance a massive break from Michigan City.

Dillinger's parole came about in the spring of 1933. For four years he had led the life of a model prisoner. In addition, Governor Paul McNutt received a petition from John's Mooresville neighbors, asking that he be released to help out his father on the farm. Even Judge Williams, who had sentenced Dillinger, signed the petition, perhaps regretting the brutal judgment he had handed down in the case.

McNutt relented and signed Dillinger's parole. He was released May 22, 1933 and immediately rushed to his father's Mooresville farm where his stepmother was

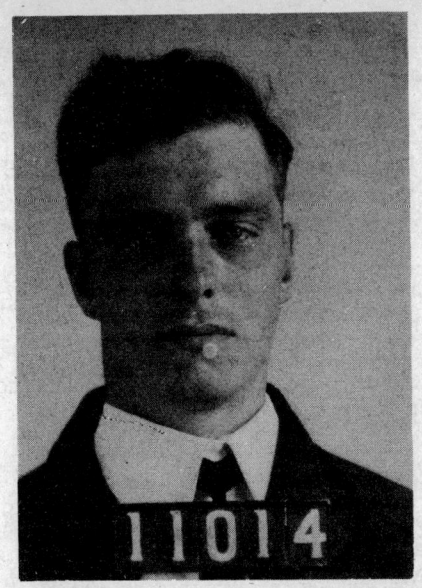

Inmate 11014 Harry Pierpont, professional bankrobber who taught Dillinger the ropes at Michigan City.

seriously ill. He arrived an hour after Elizabeth Fields Dillinger died.

Two weeks later, after recruiting an Indianapolis thug named William Shaw, Dillinger began robbing small stores and companies. Using Pierpont's list, Dillinger, Shaw, and Paul "Lefty" Parker robbed the bank at New Carlisle, Indiana, getting $10,600. (Pierpont's list was somewhat obsolete; many "ripe" banks had already failed during the Depression and Dillinger was met by empty buildings and locked doors.)

Shaw, an egotistical small-time hoodlum, wanted everyone in the gang to don white caps as an identifying symbol sure to strike terror into their victims. Dillinger declined and wore a straw boater. He also insisted that Shaw and Parker call him Dan Dillinger, the only name by which they knew him.

Days later Dillinger and Harry Copeland approached Shaw's home in Indianapolis through an alley. Copeland, a bankrobber from Muncie, Ind., was another ex-convict from Michigan City and had been newly recruited for the gang. Dillinger, driving a stolen Chevrolet, spotted Shaw and Lefty Parker with their hands in the air and a swarm of police about them.

Quickly, Dillinger put the car in reverse and gunned it backward out the alley. Shaw watched him escape. "He drove faster than some people drive forwards," he remembered.

With Copeland as his only aide, Dillinger next struck the small Commercial Bank at Daleville, Ind. on July 17, 1933. It was a one-room red brick affair with a five-foot railing separating the vault and customer areas.

Cashier Margaret Good was the only person in the bank when Dillinger sauntered in wearing his straw boater and a neat blue suit. He pulled out a gun and said to Miss Good: "This is a stick-up, honey." With an agile movement, Dillinger leaped over the railing and entered the vault. Harry Copeland left the getaway car parked in front of the bank and walked inside. He, too, flourished a pistol, lining up customers against a wall as they came into the bank.

Dillinger quickly scooped up $3,500 and then ordered everyone inside the vault. The two bandits casually walked to their car and drove slowly out of town. Miss Good opened the vault door from inside and moments later, trembling, told local police that Dillinger was the most courteous of bankrobbers. "I think he knew I was a kid and was sorry to scare me. He didn't want to scare me any worse than he had to."

Dillinger's identity as the daring, leaping bankrobber was cemented by witnesses, and police throughout Indiana were suddenly searching for him.

He was by then in another state, Ohio, seeing a new girlfriend, Mary Longnaker, who lived in Dayton. Dillinger

John Dillinger with his girl friend Mary Longnaker at Chicago's World Fair, summer, 1933; he had already robbed several banks by then (this photo was taken by an unsuspecting policeman at the Fair, an incident which amused Dillinger no end).

took Mary to the World's Fair in Chicago where he humorously photographed a policeman and then impudently asked if he would snap a picture of him and Mary.

On August 4, 1933, Copeland, Dillinger, and another unknown man robbed the National Bank of Montpelier, Indiana. Dillinger was elated to find $10,110 in the bank's small safe and remarked: "This is a good haul." He then spotted the bank president's .45-caliber automatic in a drawer. "And this is a good gun," he added and took that, too.

To supplement the escape fund Dillinger had been assembling for his friends still in Michigan City, he, Copeland, Sam Goldstine, and two other unknown men hit the Citizens National Bank in Bluffton, O. Dillinger and Copeland, wearing straw hats and expensive grey suits, walked into the bank while two other men stood guard outside. "Stand back," Dillinger said to cashier Roscoe Lingler as he drew his gun, "this is a stickup!" He began to go through the tellers' cages gathering up the cash. The take was thin and Dillinger turned to bookkeeper Oliver Locher saying, "You've got more money in here. Where is it?"

Locher pointed a quaking finger at the vault. Just then the bank's alarm went off. One of the lookouts poked his head in the door. "They're after us! Let's go!"

Dillinger ignored the remark and continued filling a sack with small bills. The lookouts started firing aimless shots into the air to frighten away the curious.

After collecting only $2,100, Dillinger and Copeland joined the two men on the street. They hurriedly piled into a large sedan and sped away.

Dillinger was angered over the small take. He required much more to finance the Michigan City break. Again, he and Copeland went searching for a "soft" bank. They settled on the large Massachusetts Avenue State Bank in downtown Indianapolis.

Using Hilton Crouch, a professional racetrack driver, as a get-away wheelman, Dillinger and Copeland entered the bank and John immediately vaulted over a high railing and ransacked the tellers' cages. Copeland held a machine-gun on at least ten customers.

Dillinger took everything in sight including $500 in half dollars, dumping the coins into a white sack. "Hurry up, will you," Copeland said as he nervously glanced out the bank window. Minutes later the two robbers ran from the bank and Crouch raced the green DeSoto down the street.

With his major share of the $24,800 taken on the Indianapolis raid, Dillinger moved to Chicago where he heavily bribed a foreman of a thread-making company to doctor one of the thread barrels being sent to the shirt shop at Michigan City, Indiana prison. Several guns were placed inside the barrel. It was resealed, and according to a pre-arranged Pierpont plan, a red "X" was marked on its top in crayon.

This was Dillinger's second attempt to free Pierpont and the others. In early September, 1933, Dillinger had crept up to the Michigan City prison wall under the cover of darkness and tossed three loaded guns wrapped in newspapers over the 30 foot barrier into the athletic field where Pierpont was expected to find them. Other inmates, how-

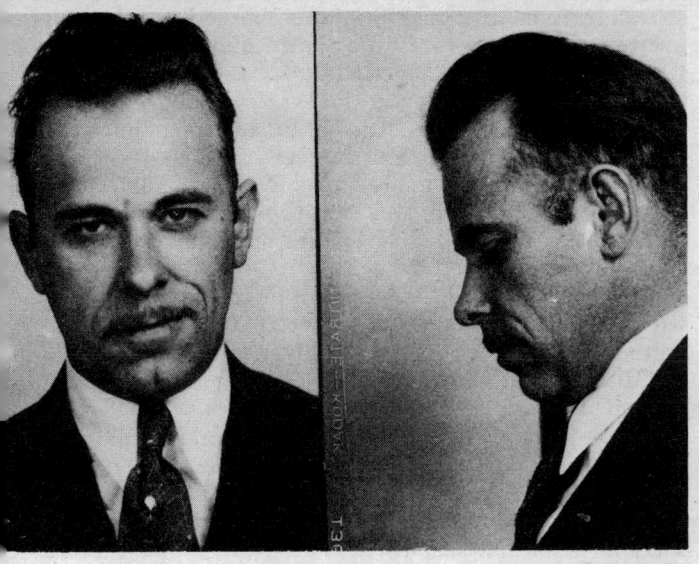

Police photos of John Dillinger taken in Tucson, Ariz., 1/25/34, following the gang's capture. The diamond stickpin was worth about $4,000.

ever, discovered the guns and turned them over to Warden H. D. Claudy.

While the thread barrel was being shipped to Michigan City, Dillinger drove to Dayton once more to see Mary Longnaker. Someone else was looking for the same girl. Dayton police detective Russell K. Pfauhl had been tipped that Dillinger had been seeing a Dayton woman. The tip came from the Pinkerton Detective Agency which had been at work investigating several bank robberies committed by the Indiana bandit. The warden of Michigan City Prison told Pfauhl that Mary Longnaker was James Jenkins' sister. Jenkins was part of the Dillinger-Pierpont clique in Michigan City.

Pfauhl and his partner, Charles E. Gross, staked out Mary's plush rooming house on West First Street in Dayton. At 1:30 a.m. Pfauhl and Gross went in to arrest Dillinger after receiving a call from Lucille Stricker, Mary's landlady, who told them Dillinger was in the house. The two detectives, carrying shotguns, barged into Mary's apartment. A man was standing in the middle of the room holding snapshots. Dillinger had just been showing Mary the photos of them taken at the World's Fair.

"Stick 'em up, Johnnie," Pfauhl ordered and aimed the shotgun square at Dillinger's head.

The photos fluttered to the carpet. Dillinger's hands went upward, then hesitated, and began to inch downward.

"If you do, John," Pfauhl warned, "I'll kill you on the spot."

John Herbert Dillinger was back in custody. Four days later, as Dillinger waited to be indicted for the Bluffton Bank robbery in the Lima, O. jail, his friends came crashing out of Michigan City Prison, wielding the pistols he had smuggled in to them.

Before Dillinger's capture he had left funds with Mary Kinder, a gang contact. Using this money, Pierpont outfitted his men with new clothes, a new car and an arsenal of weapons. To make sure they had enough traveling money, Pierpont led a raid against the First National Bank of St. Mary's, O., on October 3, 1933. St. Mary's was Makley's home town and once inside the bank Makley ran into an old friend, W. O. Smith. Makley passed small talk with bank president Smith like a man causally discussing crops around a cracker barrel. The gang, with $14,000 in a sack, left the bank without firing a shot.

For days, Dillinger had been telling his cell mate, Art Miller, in the Lima jail that his men would deliver him. On October 12, 1933, Pierpont, Makley, Clark, Hamilton, and Shouse did come.

At 6:20 p.m. that night, armed with pistols, Pierpont, Makley, and Clark entered the jail office. Sheriff Jess Sarber, his wife Lucy, and Deputy Wilbur Sharp were reading newspapers after their dinner of pork chops and mashed potatoes. Sarber looked up and spoke pleasantly to the visitors. "What can I do for you?"

"We're officers from Michigan City," Pierpont said. "We want to talk to the prisoner John Dillinger."

Sarber didn't move from his desk. His wife continued working a crossword puzzle. Sharp never put down his paper. "I guess that will be all right," Sarber said. "But first let me see your credentials."

Pierpont's eyes narrowed. Then he drew out a pistol from beneath his expensive suit and aimed it at Sarber. "Here's our credentials."

Sarber's mouth sagged a bit and he put his hand toward the gun as if to ward it away. "Oh, you can't do that," he said.

Pierpont fired two shots. Both hit the Sheriff, one in the stomach, the other in the hip. He sank to the floor. Stunned, Lucy Sarber and Wilbur Sharp stared in wonder.

"Give us the keys to the cells," Pierpont demanded.

Sarber tried to rise on his elbow. Makley dashed forward and brought his gun butt down on the Sheriff's head, opening it to the bone. He hit him a second time.

"I'll get the keys," Lucy Sarber screamed. "Don't hurt him any more."

At the first shots, Dillinger put down the cards in his hand. Art Miller, the other player, had also heard the firing. "John," he said, "your gang has come for you." Dillinger snatched his coat and went to the cell door. Pierpont, grinning, was there in a minute, opening it and handing him a gun.

"Wanna come?" Dillinger asked Miller.

"No, thanks."

The two men rushed out into the jail office. Other prisoners clamored to be let free. Pierpont stuck his head in the corridor leading to the cells and shouted: "Get back there, you bastards! We came for John. The rest of you can leave when we've gone."

Dillinger knelt down to inspect the damage done to the Sheriff. Sarber, who had been kind to the Indiana bandit, blinked in agony.

"You have to do this?" Dillinger asked without looking at Pierpont.

Handsome Harry made no reply.

Suddenly, Sarber moaned his last: "Oh, men, why did you do this to me?" He then inched his face about slightly to look at his weeping wife and said, "Mother, I believe I'm going to have to leave you."

By then the gang had fled down the jail steps and into a waiting car. Sarber died moments later.

The Terror Gang, as the press first dubbed Dillinger and the others, headed for Indianapolis where Mary Kinder, who had taken up with Harry Pierpont, and Evelyn "Billie" Frechette, a part Menominee Indian girl Dillinger had met in Chicago, were waiting. There the gang made plans to equip themselves for a string of bank raids.

There was no real leader of the second and most important Dillinger gang. Pierpont was the most daring and nerveless of the group but his impulsiveness oft-times outweighed his considerable intelligence. Hamilton was the old pro. Whenever any bank job was discussed, he could offer the soundest advice based on experience. Makley and Clark, for the most part, listened.

Pierpont appreciated and more or less encouraged Dillinger's role as leader. He once kidded the Indiana bandit about his name, telling him that it was euphonic and memorable, and it could be employed as a tool to properly unnerve robbery victims. (The name Dillinger, with French-German origins, was actually pronounced with a hard "g," but the press and the public uttered the name with a soft ending which somehow reminded everyone of the pistol, derringer.)

Indiana State Police Captain, Matt Leach, was a dogged pursuer of the Dillinger gang. He thought that by giving statements to the press in which he named Pierpont the leader of the gang, Dillinger and others would be angered and dissension among the members would develop. Nothing of the sort happened.

Many stories surrounding Dillinger and Leach were purely fictitious. Leach stated that Dillinger was a megalomaniac who once called him, stating: "We'll get you. Watch your ass."

Leach went further, saying that Dillinger had mailed him an 1898 publication entitled "How to Be A Detective," but this stunt was performed by two Indiana newsmen who could not abide Leach's pompous statements about how he would snare the Dillinger gang. One of the newspapermen was William L. "Tubby" Toms of the *Indianapolis News*.

Chicago became the base of operations for the gang. They lived in twos and threes in several North Side apartments, changing addresses every two or three weeks. None of the members drank hard liquor, only an occasional beer.

Their women did drink liquor but the gangsters frowned on it.

Dillinger never bought liquor for his girl Billie Frechette. "She's an Indian," he told Pierpont. "It's not good for her . . . or for us . . . if she drinks."

While preparing their first major bank robbery together, Dillinger, Pierpont, and Hamilton sat around a dining room table with detailed maps and timetables. While in prison, they had learned from Walter Dietrich (he, Jim Clark, and Joseph Fox were apprehended shortly after the Michigan City break) an amazing formula for robbing banks.

Dietrich had once been a member of a gang headed up by a Prussian ex-officer, who had deserted the Kaiser's service before the First World War, a strange bankrobber named "Baron" Herman K. Lamm (whether or not the term "taking it on the lam" stems from his name is unknown). Lamm immigrated to the U.S. and operated in Utah as a stickup man until his arrest in 1917, spending a year in the state prison. There he perfected what he thought to be a foolproof system of robbing banks.

Upon his release he gathered a gang of experts and initiated his system. First he would case a bank, visiting it several times while posing as a newsman or investor, pinpointing its alarm system, position of guards and the location of safes, vaults and tellers' cages. Then he would draw an actual floor plan of the bank and sometimes the interior of the bank would be created in a vacant warehouse or country barn where his gang members would rehearse their roles. The vital part of the plan was Lamm's stopwatch. He figured the exact time the bandits would have to work safely inside the bank before customers or lawmen could interfere. He insisted that his men leave the bank when the allotted time was up, whether or not they had all the money in the bank.

This kind of precision bank-robbing worked well for thirteen years as Lamm and his gang ran pell mell through the Western states. In 1930, Lamm's incredible exploits came, quite by accident, to a halt.

On December 16, 1930 he entered the Citizens State Bank in Clinton, Ind. with three other men—26-year-old Walter Dietrich, James "Oklahoma Jack" Clark, and

G. W. "Dad" Landy, a bankrobber in his late sixties whose criminal career trailed back to stagecoach days. The robbery went off smoothly as the bandits jammed several paper bags with $15,567 and walked to their getaway car, a large Buick, parked across the street from the bank.

Here, Lamm's third stage of robbing a bank, the carefully planned getaway with all back roads carefully marked and all street lights (if any) timed to the second, fell apart. The driver, upon seeing a vigilante walking toward the bank cradling a shotgun, panicked and made a reckless U-turn, puncturing a tire.

The bandits were forced to commandeer a number of cars and trucks that either broke down or had very little gas. Their trail was quickly picked up and two hundred vigilantes and policemen converged on the group as they stood helplessly around a stalled car next to a cornfield in rural Southern Illinois.

Lamm and his boys decided to fight it out. A wild gun battle raged for several hours. Lamm and his driver were shot dead. Dietrich and Clark surrendered. Old "Dad" Landy hid behind the car while the lawmen called for him to come out. "No prison for me," they heard the old man cry out, "not again." A single shot echoed across the open fields. Landy had sent a bullet into his brain.

Walter Dietrich, who was then sent to Michigan City with Clark for life, was the man who outlined the Lamm strategy for the Dillinger gang. They would use it well.

The super gang drove up to the Central National Bank in Greencastle, Indiana at 2:45 p.m. on October 23, 1933. Clark sat behind the wheel of a Studebaker touring car while Pierpont, Dillinger and Makley went inside. Hamilton stood by the bank's entrance as the "tiger," whose job it was to spot anyone acting suspiciously in the street. Makley stood near the door with a stopwatch. Dillinger and Pierpont knew the bank's interior intimately. They had both acted as "jugmarkers"—casing the bank days before as newsmen—and could have found the vault and important tellers' cages blindfolded.

Dillinger, still the showoff, leaped over a small railing and went rapidly through the cages, scooping money into a sack while Pierpont and Makley held guns on employees.

"Keep your hands at your sides and don't move," Pierpont said. "We're not advertising."

Makley kept glancing down at the stopwatch in his hand.

An elderly woman, foreign-born, hurriedly walked out of the bank.

Hamilton, surprised, gently held onto her arm. "Better go back inside, lady," he said.

She pulled away from him and brushed his drawn gun aside. "I go to Penny's and you go to hell," she said and walked off down the street.

Makley called out: "It's five minutes." Dillinger stopped filling his sack—he had just about everything anyway—and abruptly turned about, hopped back over the railing. The bandit spotted a farmer standing at one of the teller's cages. His hands were stiff at his side. In front of him on the counter was a small stack of bills.

Dillinger glanced at the money. "That your money or the bank's?" he asked.

"Mine," the farmer said.

"Keep it. We only want the bank's." (This act was later wrongly attributed to Bonnie and Clyde; even a cursory study of the Barrow gang would reveal that the niggardly Texas thieves would not only have taken the farmer's money but also shot him on the spot for thrills.)

The men quietly left the bank without ever firing a weapon. Taking dirt roads and following pre-coded maps, the gang drove leisurely out of the country, avoiding every major roadblock set up by state and local police.

When they opened the sack in the car, the bandits found they had taken $75,346 in cash and negotiable securities. It was Dillinger's biggest strike.

Newsmen pressing Matt Leach for a lead on the gang were told by the police captain that Dillinger had again called him on the phone, arrogantly shouting: "This is John Dillinger. How are you, you stuttering bastard?" When there were no facts to relay Leach was inclined toward fiction, but it made good copy anyway. The police captain reasoned that if he inflated Dillinger's reputation as a cavalier, wise-gun bandit, his own ego would eventually cause his downfall.

Almost a month later in Chicago, Dillinger came close

to doing exactly that. He was suffering from barber's itch, a skin disorder, and went to Dr. Charles Eye for treatment. Ed Shouse, who had been kicked out of the gang because he drank and made advances toward some of the members' women, had been caught and informed Chicago police that Dillinger was being treated by Dr. Eye.

The Dillinger Squad planned to snare the bandit on the night of November 15, 1933. But the wily outlaw, with Billie Frechette at his side, suspected a trap when he saw several unmarked cars next to Dr. Eye's office on Irving Park Boulevard. They were facing the wrong way.

Dillinger was driving his favorite car, a Hudson Terraplane. He quickly changed gears, roaring down the street. In a moment several police cars were on his tail. Flooring the accelerator, Dillinger soon lost all but one police car driven by Sergeant John Artery. With his partner, Art Keller, leaning out the window with a shotgun, Artery brought his car alongside of the Terraplane. Both cars were doing eighty miles an hour down Irving Park, a spin-crazy chase in which they both narrowly avoided several autos, streetcars, and pedestrians.

When the two cars were hood-and-hood, Keller began pumping shells at Dillinger.

"Hey," Billie Frechette said almost lamely, "somebody's shooting at you." Dillinger smiled at her and jammed his foot almost through the floorboard. The Terraplane shot ahead briefly. Spotting a narrow side street, Dillinger whipped the wheel around and took the corner at terrific speed. Artery shot past him down Irving Park. By the time the two officers had turned about, Dillinger's car had disappeared.

"That bird can sure drive," Keller said and disgustedly threw his shotgun in the back seat.

The gang immediately guessed the informant had been Shouse. He had been a troublemaker from the beginning, even attempting to convince John Hamilton to join him in independent bank robberies.

Mary Kinder had overheard Shouse talking and broke in with: "You ain't gonna do a damn thing. There ain't nobody going no place until we all talk it over. This has always been a friendly bunch and you ain't gonna take no two or three and go rob a bank."

Following the incident, Dillinger threw a thousand dollars in a fat wad at Shouse and said, "There's your money. Now get your ass out." Shouse got out. His recklessness led to his capture.

The gang moved to Milwaukee and made plans to rob the bank in Racine, Wisconsin. It was there they learned that Harry Copeland, who had been with Dillinger on earlier bank robberies, had gotten drunk and arrested.

"We ain't gonna miss neither of them two," Makley commented.

Days later, November 20, 1933, a well-dressed, nonchalant Harry Pierpont walked into the American Bank and Trust Company in Racine just before closing time. Bookkeeper Mrs. Henry Patzke watched, puzzled, as Pierpont unraveled a huge Red Cross poster in the lobby and pasted it in the middle of the bank's large picture window. Mrs. Patzke shrugged and went back to work.

Then Makley, followed by Dillinger and Hamilton, entered.

"Stick 'em up," Makley said to head teller Harold Graham.

"Go to the next window, please," Graham said, thinking the stout man was joking.

"I said stick 'em up," Makley repeated. Graham made a sudden movement and Makley fired, sending a bullet into the teller's elbow and hip. Graham fell and hit the alarm button. The alarm, which did not sound in the bank, went off at Racine Police Headquarters.

Dillinger, Hamilton and Pierpont fairly ran down the aisle behind the cages, gathering up money. "Everybody flat on their stomachs," Pierpont shouted. Everybody in the bank went flat on their stomachs.

Two local policemen, Wilbur Hansen and Cyril Boyard, drove slowly toward the bank after being notified that an alarm had gone off. They were in no hurry. The alarm had gone off accidentally several times before when careless tellers had triggered the button.

When Boyard and Hansen did amble into the bank, Pierpont disarmed them. Hansen took his time surrendering his machinegun and Makley shot him. The women in the bank began screaming. Dillinger came out of the vault. "I've got all of it," he said. An off-duty policeman then walked into the bank. Dillinger poked him with his pistol. "Come on in and join us," he said.

A large crowd had assembled outside when the first shot was fired. Dillinger and the others pushed several women out the front door in front of them as hostages. Policemen were firing at them from across the street, the shots sent high to avoid hitting bystanders.

Dillinger and the others turned around and scurried out a back entrance where Clark was waiting in a large Buick. The gang piled into the car, taking the bank's president and Mrs. Patzke with them as hostages. After several minutes of racing along pre-marked back roads, the two terrified hostages were let out.

Before pulling away, Dillinger looked at Mrs. Patzke and grinned. "Maybe we ought to take you along. Can you cook?"

"After a fashion," Mrs. Patzke said.

"Some other time."

The take from the American Bank and Trust Company was less than what the gang expected—$27,789—but it would have to do. The outlaws decided to winter in Florida and headed for Daytona Beach, where they rented several cottages at the water's edge. They played cards, listened to the radio, fished, and ate steak and potatoes cooked by Mary Kinder and Billie Frechette.

From Daytona Beach, they motored in separate cars to Tucson, Ariz. Between the time the gang left Daytona Beach and the time they arrived in Tucson, the First National Bank of East Chicago, Ind., was robbed of $20,736 on January 15, 1934. A policeman, Patrick O'Malley, attempted to stop two unidentified bandits and was machinegunned to death. The crime was attributed to Dillinger and Hamilton.

Dillinger was named as the killer of O'Malley, but he always denied being there. Mary Kinder to this day denies he ever left the gang to pull this robbery. So did Billie Frechette when interviewed in 1968 before her death by cancer.

Tucson turned out to be a mistake. Clark and Makley were apprehended there first after a fire broke out in their hotel. They paid firemen hundreds of dollars to rescue two of their suitcases. One of the firemen became suspi-

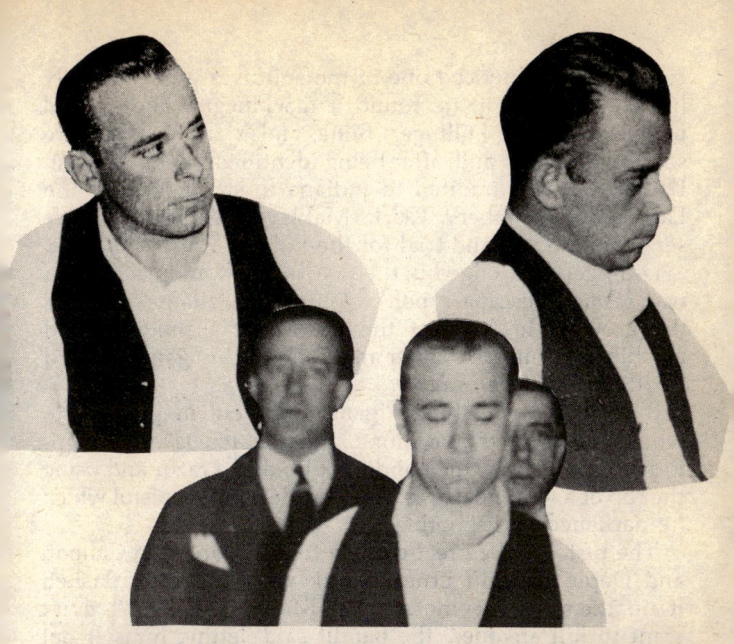

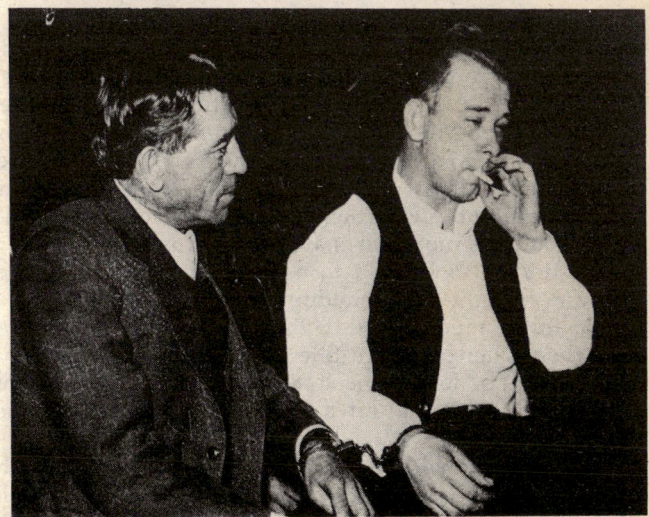

Photos of John Dillinger at hearing in Crown Point Jail, Crown Point, Ind., March, 1934; Dillinger escaped from this "escape-proof" jail days later using a wooden gun to bluff his way past guards.

cious when he noticed one of the suitcases was extremely heavy. Opening it, he found a machinegun and several pistols. Pierpont, Dillinger, Billie, and Mary Kinder were soon rounded up and, after being identified, sent back East. Dillinger was extradited to Indiana to stand trial for the East Chicago robbery. Clark, Makley, and Pierpont were sent to Ohio to stand trial for the killing of Sheriff Sarber.

Dillinger was lodged in the Crown Point, Ind. jail, which was termed "escape-proof." Dozens of vigilantes roamed the grounds in front of the jail carrying shotguns and machineguns in case other members of his gang decided to attempt to free him.

But all of the Dillinger gangsters were in prison. He would have to escape alone, he told his lawyer, Louis Piquett. Somehow, the bandit got hold of a razor and using the top of a washboard, carved a crude-looking pistol which he darkened with bootblack.

The pistol looked real enough to attendant Sam Cahoon and Deputy Sheriff Ernest Blunk when Dillinger flashed it on them on the morning of March 3, 1934. "I don't want to kill anyone," the bandit said, letting himself out into a corridor. "Now you do as I tell you."

In minutes, Dillinger had rounded up a dozen guards, made his way down a flight of stairs and, with Herbert Youngblood, a Negro prisoner awaiting trial for murder, escaped in Sheriff Lillian Holley's car, taking Blunk and a mechanic, Ed Saager, along as hostages. He drove on back roads until he crossed into rural Illinois. There he let Blunk and Saager out, giving them $4 for food and carfare. "I'd give you guys more but that's all I can spare."

He drove away. The two men heard him singing, "I'm heading for the last roundup." Before the car turned a bend in the muddy road, Dillinger waved at them.

When Dillinger drove Sheriff Holley's car across state lines, the FBI joined the hunt for him (although agents had been on his trail for months at the request of police in several states).

Chicago seemed to be the most likely place to hunt the bandit, but Dillinger had moved to St. Paul, Minn. Billie Frechette, who had been freed with Mary Kinder after the Tucson arrests, joined him there. Dillinger quickly went to work building a new gang.

Michigan City Prison parolee Homer Van Meter, who

had been robbing banks in Michigan and Kentucky, became his right-hand man. Van Meter brought in Eddie Green and Tommy Carroll. John Hamilton, who had gone to Chicago from Daytona Beach, showed up. One more man was needed. A Chicago gangster who had worked with the Capone and Bugs Moran mobs was recruited. He was Lester Gillis, better known as Baby Face Nelson, an insane killer who had been a bootlegger in California and had robbed banks all over the Midwest.

Van Meter and Nelson argued constantly and Dillinger had to step between them more than once before their guns went off. Dillinger didn't like the situation but knew he had to move fast to obtain a large amount of cash and Nelson was important to reach that end. Dillinger had been planning a permanent escape for some time now and he also wanted to help Pierpont, Clark, and Makley, who were standing trial for Sarber's killing.

The new Dillinger gang struck the Security National Bank and Trust Company in Sioux Falls, S. D. on March 6, 1934, only three days after the spectacular escape from Crown Point which had made Dillinger's name a byword in almost every American home.

The robbery went along without incident until Nelson spotted an off-duty policeman getting out of a car. He jumped on a desk and fired several shots through the bank window, wounding Hale Keith. "I got one of them! I got one of them!" he squealed.

Tommy Carroll stood in the middle of the street gripping a machinegun. By the time Dillinger and the others came out of the bank, Carroll had lined up Sioux Falls' entire police force, including the chief. Thousands of spectators milled around the bank, bemused. The good citizens thought the robbery was part of a film being made. A Hollywood producer had been in town a day previous telling everyone that he intended to make a gangster film there. The film producer had been Homer Van Meter!

The gang poured into a large Packard with $49,000 in a white sack and raced out of town. After going several miles, Dillinger ordered the car halted. He got out and, with Hamilton, sprinkled roofing nails all over the road for several yards. "That ought to slow them up," he said. Once again the gang escaped.

Eddie Green was sent out as a jugmarker and soon

discovered a plum in Mason City, Iowa, the First National Bank. Green discovered that the bank's vault contained more than $240,000.

On March 13, 1934, the gang entered the bank. Nelson stayed with the getaway car. One complication after another set in from the start. When the bank president, Willis Bagley, saw Van Meter approaching him with a gun he thought "a crazy man was loose." He ran into his office and locked the door. Van Meter, knowing Bagley had the key to the vault, fired several shots through the door but then gave up and began helping Hamilton and Dillinger clear out the cages.

A guard in a specially-equipped seven-foot steel cage above the main lobby then fired a tear-gas shell at Eddie Green. It hit Green in the back, almost knocking him down. He swung his machine gun around and sprayed the cage. Some of the bullets went through a tiny slot and hit guard Tom Walters.

A female customer, minus one shoe, ran from the bank and down an alleyway where she bumped into a short man wearing a cap. "Get to work and notify somebody," she screamed. "The bank is being held up!"

"Lady, you're telling me?" Baby Face Nelson said, and waved her back with his machinegun.

Meanwhile John Hamilton faced a dilemma. Inside the bank, cashier Harry Fisher stood on the other side of a locked, barred door from Hamilton. The vault was to Fisher's back. Since Hamilton could not open the door, he ordered Fisher to pass the money through the bars of the door to him. Fisher wisely began handing him stacks of one dollar bills.

Dillinger was in the street outside, guarding prisoners. An elderly policeman, John Shipley, could see him from his third-floor office. Firing an old pistol, Shipley winged Dillinger in the arm. The outlaw whirled about and let loose a burst from his machinegun. His bullets spattered off the face of the bank building. Shipley was unhurt, having ducked back into his office after firing his one shot.

"Tell them it's time to leave," Dillinger yelled to Van Meter who rushed into the bank.

Hamilton was frantically waving his pistol at cashier

Fisher. The bandit could see stacks and stacks of currency just inside the vault where Fisher stood.

"Open up this door," Hamilton yelled.

"I can't," Fisher lied. "I already told you I don't have the key. All I can do is continue to shove the money out through the bars." He passed several more stacks of one dollar bills to Hamilton.

Van Meter was at the bank door. "Let's go!"

"If you don't hurry up, I'm going to shoot you," Hamilton told Fisher.

"C'mon!" Van Meter yelled.

"Just give me another minute!" Hamilton yelled back. Then to Fisher: "Gimme the big bills!" Fisher kept handing him one dollar bills.

"We're going now!" Van Meter almost screamed.

"It's hell to leave all that money in there!" Hamilton's sack contained only $20,000 in small bills. There was still about $200,000 in full view behind the bars in the vault.

Gritting his teeth John Hamilton turned around and ran from the bank. The crafty Fisher sighed, and closed the vault door, fondly patting it in relief.

The moment Hamilton ran from the bank, Shipley, back at his window, fired another round and wounded the outlaw in the shoulder. He and Dillinger rounded a corner and ran to a large Buick in which the rest of the gang waited. Twenty hostages were on the running boards, fenders, and back bumper, holding on to the back window frame where the glass had been removed.

One hostage was on the ground, bleeding from a leg wound. Dillinger looked at Nelson, who was nearby holding a gun. "Did you have to do that?"

Nelson shrugged.

The car took off at a slow speed, sagging under the weight of the six gang members and twenty hostages. The police did not pursue closely; it was hopeless. Only the hostages would get killed in a running gunfight, thought Police Chief E. J. Patton. Patton's car followed at a safe distance but several times Nelson got out and fired bursts from his machinegun. The police finally gave up, turning into a farmer's driveway.

Taking back roads and moving at twenty-five miles an

hour, the Buick let off its last reluctant passenger two hours later. The gang then headed for St. Paul. The raid netted the outlaws a little over $52,000. John Hamilton brooded all the way to the Twin Cities. "I should have killed that man," he finally said.

The city health officer for St. Paul, Dr. N. G. Mortenson, treated the mild shoulder wounds Dillinger and Hamilton had received in the robbery. Mortensen thought of calling the police but was sure Homer Van Meter, who was fondling a machinegun, would return and kill him.

FBI agents, however, had gotten a tip that a Carl Hellman was living in a rooming house somewhere in St. Paul with a woman they thought to be Billie Frechette. Hellman answered Dillinger's description.

While they worked to pinpoint Dillinger's hideout, the outlaw rested, recuperating from his wound and writing letters to his family in Indiana. In one letter to his sister Audrey, Dillinger revealed his sense of self-confidence, boasting easily about his escape from Crown Point. The letter read:

"Dear Sis:

I thought I would write a few lines and let you know I am still perculating. Don't worry about me honey, for that won't help any, and besides I am having a lot of fun. I am sending Emmett [Audrey's husband, Emmett Hancock] my wooden gun and I want him to always keep it. I see that Deputy Blunk says I had a real forty five thats just a lot of hooey to cover up because they don't like to admit that I locked eight deputys and a dozen trustys up with my wooden gun before I got my hands on the two machineguns and you should have seen their faces. Ha! Ha! Ha! Don't part with my wooden gun for any price. For when you feel blue all you have to do is look at the gun and laugh your blues away. Ha! Ha! I will be around to see all of you when the roads are better, it is so hot around Indiana now that I would have trouble getting through so I am sending my wife Billie [Dillinger had not married Billie Frechette]. She will have a hundred dollars for you and a hundred dollars for Norman [another Dillinger relative]. I'll give you enough money for a new car the next time I come around. I told Bud [his half-brother Hubert] I would get him one and I want to get Dad one. Now honey if any of you need any thing I wont forgive you if you dont let me know. I got shot a week ago but I am all right now just a little sore. I bane one tough sweed. Ha! Ha! Well honey I guess I'll close for the time give my love to all and I hope I can see you soon. Lots of love from Johnnie."

Not only was it impossible for Dillinger to go to his family in Indiana but he realized that his friends—Pierpont, Clark, and Makley—were doomed. There was no way to reach them either.

Dillinger, on the other hand, had his own troubles. Agents R. L. Nalls and R. C. Coulter finally discovered that Dillinger and Billie were living in the Lincoln Court Apartments in St. Paul. They went in after their man on the night of March 31, 1934.

Billie answered their knock and explained that her husband, Carl Hellman was asleep and she was not dressed. They insisted they talk with Carl. Billie told them to wait, relocked the door and ran into the bedroom, telling Dillinger that policemen were outside. He got dressed hurriedly and grabbed a machinegun.

Waiting on the other side of the door, the FBI agents were startled to see a man coming up the stairs.

"Who are you?" Coulter asked the young man.

Homer Van Meter smiled disarmingly. "I'm a soap salesman."

"Yeah?" Coulter said, eyeing him. "Where are your samples?"

"In my car. Come down stairs and I'll prove my identity to you."

Coulter followed Van Meter down the stairs. At the first floor Van Meter whirled about, displaying an ugly-looking pistol. "You asked for it, so I'll give it to you!"

Coulter ran for the front door and raced down the stairs. The outlaw was so nonplussed that he did not fire. Remembering the other lawman upstairs, Van Meter himself ran out to the street, jumped on a horse-drawn delivery wagon, donned the driver's cap and whipped the horses down the street, a unique getaway for a modern bandit.

Agent Cummings, who had gone downstairs to investigate, left the way clear for Dillinger and Billie to escape via a flight of back stairs. The outlaw sprayed the hallway with his machinegun just to be sure. Cummings followed him out and shot him in the leg from the back door but Dillinger managed to get into his Hudson Terraplane and backed it out of the alleyway at high speed.

Eddie Green found another doctor to treat John's leg wound. The gang then decided to leave St. Paul. It was getting too hot. Pat Reilly, a fringe member of the gang, told Dillinger about a quiet resort he knew of in Wisconsin called Little Bohemia. It wouldn't officially open until May. They could all go there and rest up without being disturbed. Who would look for them at a remote fishing resort?

First Dillinger took a quick trip to Chicago with Billie. He told his lawyer Piquett to keep certain monies available; he would be going on a long trip. From there, Dillinger and Van Meter raided the police station in Warsaw, Indiana, taking several guns and bullet-proof vests.

The gang then drove into the woods of Wisconsin to Little Bohemia Lodge to relax and plan another robbery.

Melvin Purvis, head of the FBI office in Chicago, got a tip from a resort owner in Rhinelander, Wis. that Dillinger was staying at Little Bohemia. Within hours he moved dozens of his agents from Chicago and St. Paul to the Wisconsin woodlands. The group converged upon the lodge on the night of April 22, 1934.

When Purvis led his men against the front of the lodge, three customers emerged and climbed into a parked car. As the car's engine started, Purvis called out for the men to stop, but they failed to hear the warning. A shower of bullets followed and Eugene Boiseneau, a CCC worker, was killed on the spot, his two companions wounded.

Hearing the gunfire, Dillinger, Van Meter, Carroll, and Hamilton raced out the back, running along the shore in the moonlight. Baby Face Nelson, in a cabin nearby with his wife Helen, emerged and fired some random shots at Purvis and then disappeared into the woods.

The FBI pounded the lodge all night thinking the gangsters were still inside. By morning, their only captives were the gang's girls who had been hiding in the basement.

Dillinger, Hamilton, and Van Meter stole a car and drove

out of the trap to St. Paul. Nelson, after killing an FBI agent at another resort, stole a car and headed for Chicago. Tommy Carroll stole yet another car and drove to Michigan.

The FBI fiasco put Purvis and J. Edgar Hoover on the spot. The raid did nothing but cause the death of an innocent man, an FBI agent, and the destruction of a fishing lodge.

Hoover placed a shoot-to-kill order out on Dillinger and a $10,000 reward. Another $10,000 was offered by five states where Dillinger had robbed banks.

In the next two months half a dozen men who looked like Dillinger were arrested or almost shot. The bandit, however, was nowhere to be found. He appeared briefly at his father's farm for a Sunday chicken dinner in May. At that time, the outlaw told the elderly Dillnger that he was going on a long trip and that he wouldn't have "to worry" about him anymore.

When the Merchants National Bank of South Bend, Ind. was robbed on June 30, 1934, the FBI and local police insisted that Dillinger had done the job. Not only that, but his companions in the robbery were identified by police as Baby Face Nelson and Pretty Boy Floyd.

All evidence points to the fact that Dillinger, Nelson, and Floyd did not commit this robbery. Nelson was already on his way to California, thoroughly unnerved by the Little Bohemia raid and seeking isolation. Floyd was in Ohio at the time. And Dillinger was on the road north, heading toward Minnesota to make certain contacts in preparation for a trip West.

In early July, 1934, Chicago Police Captain John Stege was approached by Detective Sergeant Martin Zarkovich of the East Chicago, Ind. Police Dept. Zarkovich told Stege he could, through his long-time friend and whorehouse madam, Anna Sage, deliver Dillinger. There was, however, one condition. Dillinger had to be killed, not taken alive.

Stege refused, kicking Zarkovich out of his office and telling him: "I'd even give John Dillinger a chance to surrender."

Next Zarkovich went to the FBI. Purvis jumped at the plan. Anna Sage would set up Dillinger, Zarkovich stated, but the FBI had to promise to stop deportation proceedings then being enacted against her. Purvis promised.

On the night of July 27, 1934, Anna Sage, the much publicized "Lady in Red," led a young man named "James Lawrence" into the FBI trap outside of the Biograph Theater. He was shot to death (by Zarkovich) as he left the theater.

The FBI called in the press and announced to the world that John Dillinger was dead.

The author has extensively written about this aspect of the Dillinger case in another book and cannot, for reasons of space, detail the miasmic proportions of this underworld plot. James Lawrence, killed by Martin Zarkovich outside the Biograph Theater could not have been, according to this evidence, John Dillinger.

An autopsy of the dead man (which was missing for three decades) performed by Dr. J. J. Kearns, the Cook County Coroner's chief pathologist, utterly disproved James Lawrence's corpse as being Dillinger's. Lawrence's eyes were brown. Dillinger's eyes were blue. The dead man possessed a rheumatic heart condition chronic since childhood. Dillinger did not. (It would have been impossible for Dillinger to play baseball, join the Navy or perform his athletic bank-robbing feats with such a condition.) Lawrence was shorter and heavier than Dillinger would

"James Lawrence" in the morgue, his head held up for photos by Dr. Charles D. Parker; dead man had brown eyes, Dillinger's were blue.

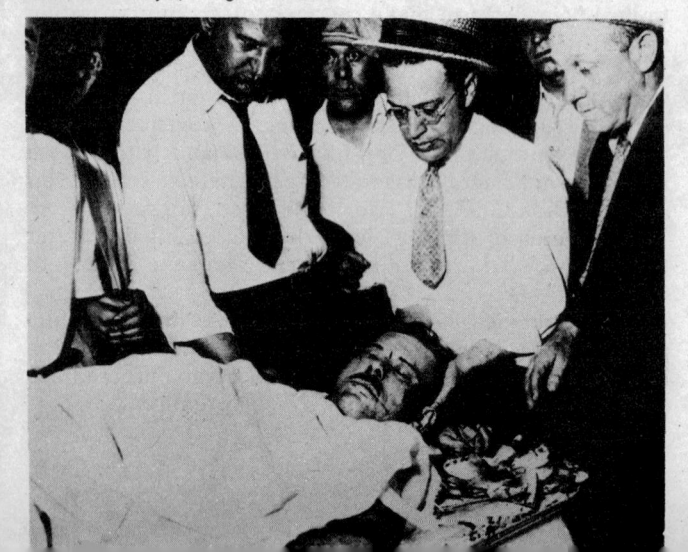

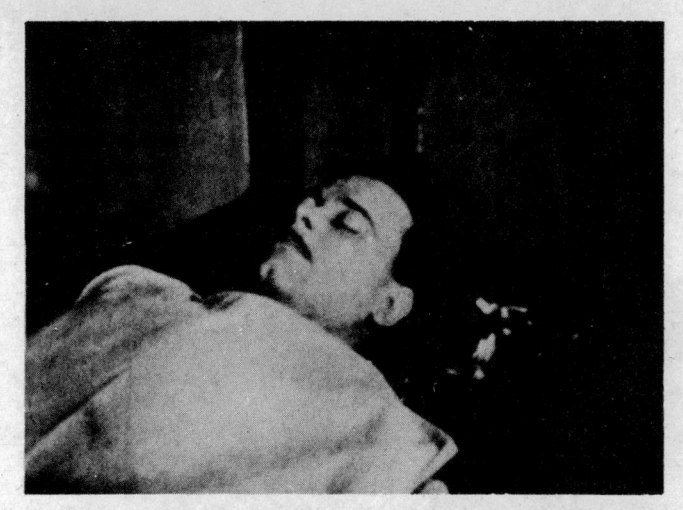

Another morgue photo of "James Lawrence"; to explain the differences in facial appearance between Lawrence and Dillinger, FBI offered preposterous theories about plastic surgery.

have been. He also lacked all of Dillinger's scars, wounds and birthmarks. His face was not altered through plastic surgery as explained by the FBI (to compensate for his obvious facial differences with that of Dillinger's).

The fingerprint card offered up by the FBI alleging that Dillinger's and the dead man's fingerprints were one in the same was obviously "planted" in the Cook County Morgue days before the killing.

The FBI was simply duped into believing the dead man was Dillinger and then had to cover up their error after the shooting.

Who then was Jimmy Lawrence? From what this writer has been able to determine he was a small time hoodlum who came from Wisconsin to Chicago about 1930. He was seen in the neighborhood of the Biograph for at least two years, long before John Dillinger, inmate 13225 of the Michigan City Prison, was ever paroled.

That he was involved in an underworld scheme to provide Dillinger with a permanent escape there is no

Dillinger's favorite girl friend, Evelyn "Billie" Frechette, with a man who bears an amazing resemblance to "James Lawrence"; this photo was taken from Billie's purse when she was arrested in Chicago short months before the Biograph shooting.

doubt. Whether or not he was a willing dupe to the Sage-Zarkovich plot (both had a fifteen-year record of strong ties to the underworld) is unknown. Perhaps, because of his heart condition, Lawrence may have volunteered for the role. That, too, is unknown.

But it is known that John Herbert Dillinger, a pragmatic but spectacular escape artist, eluded the law in the end.

The last Dillinger gang went to pieces in late 1934. Tommy Carroll was killed by policemen in Waterloo, Iowa, June 5, 1934. Eddie Green was shot in the back by FBI officials April 3, 1934. Homer Van Meter was gunned down in an alleyway, betrayed by friends, in St. Paul, August 23, 1934. Baby Face Nelson, in a wild shoot-out with two FBI men (both killed by him) was shot to death near Barrington, Ill., November 27, 1934. John Hamilton's body was never found; reports have it that after receiving a fatal wound in a fight with police, his body was buried in an isolated quarry outside of Aurora, Ill. in April 1934. Russell Clark was paroled in 1970 and died of cancer months later.

In September, 1934, Pierpont and Makley tried to duplicate Dillinger's Crown Point ruse. They carved pistols from cakes of soap and attempted to escape death row in the Ohio State Penitentiary in Columbus. Makley was shot to death and Pierpont wounded.

The following month Handsome Harry Pierpont sat down almost jubilantly in the electric chair. Through a wide smile he said: "Today I am the only man who knows the 'who's and how's' and as my end comes very shortly, I'll take this little story with me."

[ALSO SEE Baby Face Nelson]

DRUCCI, VINCENT ("THE SCHEMER")
Bootlegger, Jewel Thief • (1885-1927)

Close friend of Chicago gangster Dion O'Bannion, Drucci began his criminal career as a teenager by robbing coins from telephone boxes. He graduated to safecracking with O'Bannion, George "Bugs" Moran, and Earl "Hymie" Weiss, who formed the leadership of the North Side Irish gang dominating Chicago's Forty-second and Forty-third Wards.

This cold-blooded killer got his sobriquet from his fanciful, wild schemes to rob banks and kidnap wealthy citizens. When O'Bannion went to war with Capone and the Genna brothers brothers over certain Chicago bootleg territories, Drucci, along with Weiss, became a chief enforcer. Drucci was known as the "Shootin' Fool" of the outfit.

He is credited by Chicago Police as being the killer of at least two Capone-Genna gangsters, Giuseppe Nerone, better known as "The Cavalier," a Capone man, on July 8, 1925 and Samuzzo "Samoots" Amatuna, a Genna satellite who had set himself up as president of *Unione Siciliane* and was murdered November 11, 1925.

Drucci and a henchman of the West Side O'Donnell clan, Jim Doherty (the O'Donnells and the O'Bannionites had by then joined forces against the Capone-Genna forces) found Samoots in a Cicero barber shop getting a shave and a haircut. Drucci waded in immediately firing four shots from his pistol. Jim Doherty added another four shots for good measure. Samoots tried to avoid execution by hiding behind the barber chair but was fatally wounded. Hospitalized he begged that he be allowed to marry his childhood sweetheart, Rose Pecorara. Samoots died in his hospital bed, half-way through the wedding ceremony.

Drucci sent a large floral piece to his funeral.

In 1926, Capone made a concerted effort to rid himself of the plaguing North Siders. On August 10, 1926, he sent gunman Louis Barko and three others to kill Drucci and Hymie Weiss. At 9 a.m. that morning, Weiss breakfasted with Drucci in the latter's eighth-floor suite at the Congress Hotel. The two gangsters then took a leisurely stroll down Michigan Avenue, heading for the Standard Oil Building on Ninth Street.

At the entrance of the building, four men jumped from a car and ran toward the O'Bannionites with drawn automatics, Barko in the lead. Weiss and Drucci pulled their guns, hiding behind a parked car. The street erupted with gunfire. Windows were smashed. Concrete flew in great chunks from buildings as bullets chipped and whanged into them. Thousands of horrified shoppers saw the shooting. Some ran. Some threw themselves to the pavement. Others merely stood frozen in terror.

Weiss backed away down the line of cars. Drucci did not, advancing toward his sworn enemies, pistol cracking. The four would-be assassins were driven back to their double-parked car by Drucci's fire. They climbed on the running board to get better aim. Drucci, on the sidewalk by then, danced wildly about like a fighter shadow-boxing to avoid their shots. Bullets snapped and clunked at his feet. He laughed hysterically and banged away at the Capone men.

Thirty shots had been fired and none of the participants were hit; James Cardan, a spectator, was slightly wounded in the leg.

A police car roared up with a squad of men and the four Capone gunmen fled in their sedan. Drucci was not content to allow their retreat. He jumped on the running board of a passing auto.

"Follow that goddamn car," he yelled at the driver, wagging his fierce-looking weapon. Police ran after him and dragged him to the pavement.

"What the hell is this, Drucci?" a policeman who recognized the gangster asked.

"It wasn't no gang fight," Schemer blurted. "A stickup, that's all. They wanted my roll." When police searched him they discovered amid "whews" and whistles that Drucci's roll consisted of $13,500. The lawmen surmised that Drucci and Weiss were headed for the offices of Morris Eller, political boss of the Twentieth Ward, to make a protection payoff for their illegal speakeasies.

Eller emphatically denied any such hanky-panky.

Louis Barko (alias Valerie) was picked up by police and brought in front of Drucci. "I never seen him before," The Schemer snarled. All were released.

Five days later, Capone's men tried again, almost at the same time and spot, shooting volley after volley at Drucci and Weiss as they once again tried to enter the Standard Oil Building. This time the pair were attacked as they drove down Michigan Avenue in a large sedan. They elected to run for it, deserting the bullet-smashed car and finding sanctuary in an office building.

Drucci, Weiss, and Moran then gave their violent retort to Scarface Al. On September 20, 1926, the trio led eight cars full of men past Capone's headquarters, the Hawthorn Hotel, and at high noon, stood on the sidewalk with blazing machineguns and riddled the place with more than a thousand bullets.

Louis Barko was the only gang casualty, wounded in the arm as he stood in the hotel lobby—by none other than Vincent "The Schemer" Drucci. When Drucci was brought before him by police, he returned The Schemer's compliment. "Never saw him before," Barko snapped.

During the following election year, Drucci labored hard to get William Hale "Big Bill" Thompson elected. His tactics were a bit unorthodox. The Schemer didn't bother with canvassing voters. He terrorized the political bigwigs backing incumbent Mayor Dever. One such person was Dorsey R. Crowe, Alderman of the Forty-second Ward. Drucci broke into Crowe's offices on April 4, 1927 and wrecked the place, beating up Crowe's secretary. The Schemer had planned to kidnap Alderman Crowe and keep him incommunicado until after the election on April 5.

Police Lieutenant William Liebeck and a squad of men picked Drucci up on the corner of Diversey Parkway and Clark Street that afternoon. With him were two aides, Henry Finkelstein and Albert Single. A .45 automatic was taken from The Schemer's inside pocket; all three men were arrested for creating mayhem and taken to a local station. After twenty minutes of grilling ("I don't know nothin' coppers," was Drucci's favorite response), The Schemer was ordered to go to the Criminal Courts Building where his ever-available lawyer, Maurice Green, was waiting with a writ of *habeas corpus.*

Four officers—Danny Healy, Matthew Cunningham, Dennis Kehoe, and a driver packed up Drucci and his friends for the trip downtown. Healy was a tough cop who abided no back-talk from gangsters. Months before he had shot it out toe-to-toe with three bandits on Armitage Avenue, killing one and driving the others off. A chunky man, Healy had also taken on giant gangster Polack Joe Saltis with his fists and reduced Joe to bleeding pulp. He would tolerate no guff from Drucci and told him so.

The Schemer's violent temper exploded in the police car during the trip. "Nobody talks that way to me, cop," Drucci said, working up his anger. "You son-of-a-bitch. I'll get you. I'll wait on your doorstep for you!"

"Shut your mouth and sit back," Healy ordered.

"Go on, you kid copper. I'll fix you for this!"

Healy held his gun steady on Drucci. "I said shut up."

"You take your gun off me or I'll kick hell out of you!"

Healy only stared. Then Drucci stood up on one leg and swiped his fist down against Healy's right temple, screaming: "I'll take you and your tool [pistol]! I'll fix you!" The Schemer reached down for the revolver in Healy's right hand. The policeman shifted the weapon to his left hand and fired four shots into Drucci at point blank range.

The 31-year-old hoodlum fell to the floor of the police car cursing Healy. He died within minutes, an oddball gangster demise that elated Capone and saved his torpedoes from further gunplay with the Shootin' Fool.

When Maurice Green's client arrived at the Criminal Courts Building, he was a stiffening corpse. Green wanted Healy arrested for murder.

Chief of Detectives William Shoemaker ("Old Shoes") snorted: "I don't know anything about anyone being murdered. I know Drucci was killed trying to take a gun away from an officer. We're having a medal made for Healy."

Drucci's funeral was as lavish as any gangster sendoff of the 1920s. He was placed in a $10,000 silver and aluminum casket and lay in state at Sbarbaro's Funeral Home for a day and a night. (Sbarbaro was also Assistant State Attorney; his funeral home received all the business from the North Side mob. He had buried gangleader Dion O'Bannion and his aid, Hymie Weiss.)

Flowers worth $30,000 surrounded the casket. Drucci's weeping widow, Cecilia, placed a heart of blood-red roses at his feet. Her card read, "To My Darling Husband." A broken wheel of white and purple flowers was placed at his head by gang buddy (and last of the O'Bannion leaders), George "Bugs" Moran, with an inscription reading: "Our Pal."

The Schemer was put to rest at Mount Carmel Cemetery.

As Cecilia Drucci, a pretty blonde flapper with beestung lips, walked from the graveyard, she smiled at reporters and quipped: "A policeman murdered him, but we sure gave him a grand funeral."

[ALSO SEE Al Capone, Dion O'Bannion, *Unione Siciliane*; George "Bugs" Moran, *Bloodletters and Badmen, Book 3*.]

DRUGGAN-LAKE GANG (THE VALLEY GANG)

Terry Druggan and his oafish partner Frankie Lake looked at all times like two businessmen down on their luck. These two terrorist-killers controlled a vast West Side area between Chicago's Little Italy and Cicero during Prohibition and were staunch allies of Al Capone during the bootleg wars, the only Irish gang to side with Scarface.

Their mob was built upon the remnants of the Old Valley Gang, begun in the early 1890s, a group of labor sluggers which included "Big Heinie" Miller, Walter "Runty" Quinlan, and Paddy "The Bear" Ryan—guns for hire to the highest bidder. Druggan, dwarfish in size, and Lake apprenticed with the Valley Gang and by 1919 had taken over, controlling all the rackets in the area, specializing in burglary and booze.

Druggan was the leader, a lisping gangster devoted to wide-brimmed fedoras and horn-rimmed glasses. Lake mimicked his boss' style of dress and obeyed Druggan's every order, whether it was a beating or for murder. Frankie, who had been a fireman and later a railroad switchman, was a bumbling giant who through his awkward antics produced galloping guffaws in the underworld.

Both men were ardent Catholics and took their religion

seriously. Once, while hijacking a truckload of beer in front of a church, Druggan identified the drivers as Jewish hoodlums. He and Lake pulled out their guns, jamming them into the driver's faces. Druggan thundered: "Hats off, you Jews when you're passing the house of God or I'll shoot them off!"

Prohibition made Druggan and Lake rich men, especially after wealthy brewer Joseph Stenson gave the pair a fifty per cent interest in his five mammoth breweries. They rode in chauffeur-driven limousines. Druggan's $12,000-a-year apartment boasted such luxuries as solid gold doorknobs and a solid silver toilet seat engraved with the gangster's initials.

In all of the wars with the Genna brothers, with the North Side O'Bannions, and with the South and West Side O'Donnell clans, the Druggan-Lake mob fought with Capone. They supplied Capone with the best beer in town (except for the beer in the O'Bannion-controlled Forty-second and Forty-third Wards, which came from the quality-minded Sieben's Brewery). In return Capone surrounded their territory with a protective army of gunsels under the command of Danny Stanton.

Capone got a sizeable chunk of the Drugan-Lake beer concessions, an estimated 40 per cent. In turn, Terry Druggan got protection. Capone-Stanton men such as Frank "Dutch" Carpenter, Raymond Cassidy, Thomas Johnson, Hughey "Stubby" McGovern, and the kill-crazy William "Gunner" Padden successfully fought off encroachments of rival gangs seeking to penetrate the Druggan-Lake domain. All of these torpedoes died in this effort before 1925.

With such muscle backing them up, Druggan and Lake operated at whim. Terry Druggan took a liking to a nightspot called Little Bohemia, owned by one Emil Wanatka. He walked into the bar one day and announced: "I'm in, Wanatka; you're out."

The feisty Wanatka told him to go to hell and began to walk up the stairs leading to his second-floor apartment. Druggan followed, scrambling after on stubby legs.

"You don't understand," Druggan yelled. "I'm taking over!" He grabbed at Wanatka's leg. The beefy young proprietor turned angrily about and landed a haymaker which knocked Druggan down the stairs. Druggan never

Terry Drugan and Frankie Lake allied themselves with Capone in Chicago's bootleg wars; both went to jail, but a well-bribed sheriff let them out during the day to conduct business as usual. (UPI)

carried a gun, but Frankie Lake and his other boys did. The elfish gangster scurried off cursing, vowing that his partner would settle this business with Wanatka.

Emil brooded for a half hour and then realized the consequences of his impetuous act. He packed up his family, took the week's receipts out of his safe, hopped into a car, and drove at high speeds for the Wisconsin border. He never came back, establishing another Little Bohemia resort in the North woods of Wisconsin. He wanted no part of Terry Druggan or any other gangster. Ironically, Wanatka was to reluctantly host the John Dillinger gang in April, 1934, a visit that resulted in an abortive FBI raid to capture that gang and which all but destroyed his lodge. There seemed to be no way for Wanatka to avoid the limelight.

In 1924 a federal injunction against the Druggan-Lake-owned Standard Beverage Corporation was issued, ordering the firm to cease operations. After refusing to comply, both gangsters were sentenced to serve a year in Cook County Jail. They were unperturbed. They had connections. Corrupt Sheriff Peter Hoffman was glad to have the new guests stay at his jail, especially after the pair gave him $20,000 for "conveniences and considerations." To insure good treatment, political boss of the Twentieth Ward Morris Eller, told Hoffman to "treat the boys right."

Hardly a day of their sentence was spent in jail. When a reporter showed up to interview Druggan one morning, a jailer told him that "Mr. Druggan isn't in right now." The reporter asked to see Frankie Lake. "Mr. Lake is also out . . . an appointment downtown. They'll return after dinner."

The press exposed this ridiculous situation and Hoffman was fined $2,500 and sentenced to 30 days in jail. Such unorthodox political conduct in Prohibition-torn Chicago was typical and would remain long after Repeal. A latter-day Chicago alderman, Mathius "Paddy" Bauler, summed it all up with the words: "Chicago ain't ready for reform yet."

The Druggan-Lake machine ground to a halt in 1932 when both men were convicted of income-tax evasion and sent to Leavenworth. Druggan received two and a half years. Lake got eighteen months.

When they were released, the pair found their empire eaten up by other gangsters, particularly by members of the newly-formed syndicate. Big Al, their protector, was gone, doing a long stretch. He also neglected to pay his taxes. The duo became front men for the syndicate and died in obscurity during the 1950s.

EASTMAN GANG

The Eastmans were ruled by a giant of a man, Edward Monk Eastman (nee Osterman) a wild, berserk skull-cracker who delighted in street brawls and murder. The Eastman gang dominated an area in New York City between the Bowery and the East River, Monroe and 14th Streets.

Organized about the turn of the century, the Eastmans practiced wholesale robberies in their area, protected by powerful politicians such as Tammany Hall sachem Big Tim Sullivan. Monk Eastman was a scarred, broken-nosed monster who began as a bouncer in the New Irving dancehall, a dive notorious for its rapes and robberies.

Eastman employed a sawed-off baseball bat in his donnybrooks and sliced a notch into it for every head he had cracked open. One story has it that upon discovering he had forty-nine notches on his club, he jumped up from a barstool and bashed in the head of a fellow drinker, killing him. His explanation: "I wanted to make it an even fifty."

The Eastman gang dissolved after Monk was picked out of a line-up and identified as the man who had robbed a grocery store. Tammany didn't shield Eastman this time; he had disregarded Big Tim Sullivan's edict about further street brawls and had recently beaten to death some of Sullivan's cronies. Monk was sent to Sing Sing for ten years.

Monk was released before the First World War, joined the Army, and served with distinction on the Western Front. Upon his discharge, Eastman reformed but was mysteriously shot to death by unknown gangsters on the night of December 26, 1920 as he emerged from the Blue Bird Cafe in Manhattan.

EGAN'S RATS

An old line criminal gang in St. Louis that dated back to the turn of the century, the Rats were first organized by "Jellyroll" Egan, a strongarm gunsel who was known as a professional "legbreaker" for anti-union business bosses. This mob was revamped in the 1920s by a vicious hoodlum named Dinty Colbeck.

Egan's Rats, under Colbeck's direction, specialized in safecracking, jewel thefts, and bootlegging in the St. Louis-Kansas City area. Colbeck's headquarters was a notorious poolhall called Buckley's frequented by Irish gangsters. Dinty was the cock-of-the-walk in St. Louis for years. He paid off corrupt politicians and policemen with enormous sums of money so that his wide-open rackets could operate unmolested. Colbeck was killed by rival gangsters in the late 1930s.

The most infamous graduate of Egan's Rats was murderer Leo Brothers. Another noted member was safecracker Morris "Red" Rudensky.

FIVE POINTS GANG

From the turn of the century, the bloody Five Points (or Five Pointers) gang ruthlessly controlled a large area of New York's Lower East Side. Its name was derived from a five-pointed intersection between the Bowery and Broadway which later became the intersection of Baxter, Park, and Worth.

This was a terror gang of murderers and cutthroats whose musclemen and gunners were hired by businessmen as strikebreakers or by other mobs who issued them murder contracts.

Some of the most notorious modern-day gangsters served criminal apprenticeships as Five Pointers. Johnny Torrio, Five Point leader from 1903 to 1910, was introduced to the mob by the unshaven, cap-wearing Jack Sirocco, lieutenant of the first leader of the gang, Paul Kelly (nee Paolo Vaccarelli).

Kelly's headquarters was his New Brighton Club, a murky saloon off Third Avenue which attracted socialites eager to shake hands with gangster Paul, whose ferocious street battles with arch rival Monk Eastman were legendary.

Under Kelly's leadership, Torrio developed a sub-gang for the Five Pointers named the James Street gang. Torrio's youthful minions, which included Al Capone, Lucky Luciano, and Frankie Yale (Uale), served initially as runners for the Five Pointers and were gradually absorbed into the older group.

The Five Points gang broke up with the advent of Prohibition in 1920.

FLOYD, CHARLES ARTHUR ("PRETTY BOY")
Bankrobber, Murderer • (1901-1934)

BACKGROUND: BORN AND RAISED AT AKINS, OKLAHOMA (COOKSON HILLS). MARRIED 16-YEAR-OLD WILMA HARGROVE IN 1921. SON, JACK DEMPSEY FLOYD, BORN 1922. MINOR PUBLIC EDUCATION. ORIGINAL OCCUPATION, FARMER. DESCRIPTION: 6'2", BROWN EYES, BLACK HAIR, HEAVYSET, MUSCULAR. ALIASES: JACK HAMILTON. RECORD: ROBBED PAYROLL SHIPMENT IN ST. LOUIS, MO., 1925; ARRESTED, TRIED, CONVICTED, AND SENTENCED TO MISSOURI STATE PENITENTIARY FOR FIVE YEARS, 1925; PAROLED, 1929; ROBBED SYLVANIA, OHIO BANK 3/11/30; APPREHENDED BY STATE POLICE SAME DAY; SENTENCED TO OHIO STATE PENITENTIARY FOR 15 YEARS ON BANKROBBING CHARGE; ESCAPED FROM GUARDS ON TRAIN 5/25/30 ENROUTE TO PRISON; ESCAPED FROM POLICE TRAP IN KANSAS CITY, MO., 3/23/31; MURDERED WALLACE AND WILLIAM ASH 3/25/31; ROBBED FROM MAY–JUNE, 1931 MOUNT ZION TRUST COMPANY ($4,000), MOUNT ZION, KENTUCKY; ELLISTON BANK ($2,700), ELLISTON, KENTUCKY; WHITEHOUSE BANK ($3,600), WHITEHOUSE, OHIO; KILLED IN EARLY JUNE, 1931, PATROLMAN RALPH CASTNER IN BOWLING GREEN, KENTUCKY DURING GUN BATTLE TO APPREHEND HIM AND FELLOW ROBBER BILL MILLER, ESCAPED; KILLED PROHIBITION AGENT CURTIS C. BURKS 7/21/31 WHEN DISCOVERED IN A KANSAS CITY SPEAKEASY; OCTOBER–NOVEMBER, 1931, FLOYD AND GEORGE BIRDWELL ROBBED THE OKLAHOMA BANKS OF SHAMROCK, MORRIS, KONAWA, MAUD, EARLSBORO, PADEN, CASTLE, TAHLEQUAH FOR SMALL AMOUNTS; ESCAPED POLICE TRAP IN TULSA, OKLAHOMA, 2/11/32; KILLED SPECIAL INVESTIGATOR

(FOR THE STATE OF OKLAHOMA) ERV A. KELLEY 4/7/32 WHILE EVADING POLICE TRAP AT BIXBY, OKLAHOMA; ROBBED THE SALLISAW BANK ($2,530), SALLISAW, OKLAHOMA WITH AUSSIE ELLIOTT AND GEORGE BIRDWELL 11/1/32; ROBBED BANK IN HENRYETTA, OKLAHOMA ($11,352.20) 11/7/32 WITH ELLIOTT, AND BIRDWELL; ROBBED THE CITIZENS' STATE BANK ($50,000)' TUPELO, MISS., 11/30/32; ROBBED DANCE HALL, 3/33 IN WEWOKA, OKLA. WITH ADAM RICHETTI; ABDUCTED SHERIFF JACK KILLINGSWORTH OF BOLIVAR, MO., 6/16/33; CLAIMED TO BE THE MACHINEGUNNER OF THE KANSAS CITY MASSACRE, 6/17/33, KILLING FBI AGENT RAYMOND CAFFREY AND LOCAL KANSAS CITY DETECTIVES GROOMS, HERMANSON, REED, AND FRANK NASH, A PRISONER UNDER GUARD; CLAIMED TO HAVE ROBBED MERCHANTS NATIONAL BANK ($22,000), SOUTH BEND, INDIANA, 6/30/34 WITH JOHN DILLINGER, BABY FACE NELSON, AND HOMER VAN METER; ESCAPED POLICE TRAP IN RURAL IOWA, 10/11/34; KILLED BY FBI AGENTS NEAR EAST LIVERPOOL, OHIO 10/22/34.

There was very little difference between Charles Arthur "Pretty Boy" Floyd and John Dillinger. Both were poor farm boys, God-fearing and with a Jesse James complex of imagined fair-play about them. And both were professional bankrobbers. The difference was that where Dillinger was romanticized in the newspapers of the day, Pretty Boy got the worst press of any outlaw in the 1930s, and for a crime—the Kansas City Massacre— many believe he never committed.

Like all of the dust-ridden, hard-scrabble people of Oklahoma who were later to be immortalized as "Okies" in John Steinbeck's *Grapes of Wrath*, Floyd began simply enough.

Born and raised near the small town of Akins, Oklahoma, Floyd worked like a dog on his father's dirt-poor farm, clawing at the dust for crops, dust that increased each year through storms and erosion until the area became the "Great Dust Bowl." It was hard work and the unschooled Floyd didn't complain.

In the evenings and on weekends, Floyd would find release in "hellin" about Akins, nearby Sallisaw, and as far as Siloam Springs and Fort Smith, Arkansas. He loved a local brew called Choctaw Beer so much that he got the nickname Chock. His constant drinking of these down-home suds put more beef onto an already tall and muscular frame.

Wilma Hargrove was only sixteen when Floyd married her in 1921 and she was to be the one true love of his life. But the marriage was hard-pressed from the beginning. Wilma and Chock got along all right. There just wasn't any money to earn in the fast-deteriorating Oklahoma farmlands.

The local banks were small and solid. They practiced a tyranny of foreclosures on farms mortgaged to the tree-tops. Floyd tried hard at first to stay within the law. Months after his marriage he moved northward, seeking harvest work from farm to farm and usually ending in hobo camps for the night.

He grew bitter and angry at not being able to make a living—he was a strong man and willing one, but there was no work. But Floyd knew where there was money. He obtained a pistol and rode the rails to St. Louis where he committed a quick payroll robbery. Then he raced for Oklahoma and his preganat wife.

The Floyds had a few weeks of glorious living. They bought new clothes and big meals. Then police arrived, and arrested Floyd for the robbery after recovering some of the St. Louis payroll money on his farm. Floyd was sentenced to five years in the Missouri State Penitentiary in Jefferson City.

While Floyd was being introduced to the hell of the Jeff City pen—an old fashioned Big House that bellowed authority through a leather lash, sweatbox, ball and chain, and cold baths—Wilma gave birth to their son, Jackie. This little boy was to be the dearest thing in Charles Arthur Floyd's short life.

After three agonizing years, Floyd was released, vowing he would never see the inside of a prison again. He kept that promise to himself. Upon returning home, Floyd learned that his father had been shot to death by one Jim Mills, a man who had carried a mountain feud from Kentucky from which the Floyds had fled dozens of years before.

Floyd sat quietly in the Sallisaw Court House and listened as Mills was acquitted of the murder. He went home, loaded his rifle and followed Mills to the nearby Cookson Hills. Mills was never seen again.

"Chock done what he had to," an Akins resident said later. The Okies had their own way of handling things. But the law was looking for Floyd so he fled to Kansas City, "Tom's Town" it was then called, a wide-open, roaring anything-goes city under the protection of boss Tom Pendergast.

It was here in 1929 that Floyd mixed with successful gangsters, heistmen, jugmarkers, hired gunsels, learning the use of the machinegun which was to become his professional tool. A Kansas City madam, Ann Chambers, spotted Floyd immediately when he entered her brothel and said to him, "I want you for myself, pretty boy." The name stuck even though Floyd hated it.

Floyd met Red Lovett, a fellow ex-inmate from Jeff City, in Kansas City and through him two other bank robbers, Tom Bradley and Jack Atkins. The group had a neat little list of juicy banks in northern Ohio and Floyd joined them to make the Big Money.

Working out of a rented Akron bungalow, the three men knocked over several small-town banks but hit a snag after robbing the bank in Sylvania, Ohio on March 11, 1930. Speeding into Akron, the trio went through a red light and a traffic cop gave chase.

Someone in their car punched out the back window and sprayed patrolman Harlan F. Manes with bullets. The policeman splattered all over the highway but the driver swerved in his haste and the get-away-car smashed into a telephone pole.

Police pried the bankrobbers out and they were tried for murder. Bradley was sent to the electric chair for murdering Manes; Atkins received life imprisonment and Charlie Floyd was acquitted . . . until they connected him with the Sylvania bank job. He was sentenced to fifteen years in the Ohio State Penitentiary.

Floyd apparently remembered his own words after Jeff City and on the way to prison, while deputies dozed in their railcar seats next to him, Floyd kicked out a window and jumped from the speeding train. After rolling down an embankment, Floyd bounced up and ran. By the time the train was halted, he was a half mile away, still running, and heading for Toledo, Ohio.

It was May 25, 1930. While Floyd was bounding through the Ohio cornfield John Dillinger was sleeping in his cell at Michigan City, Indiana State Prison; Clyde Barrow had just chopped off two of his own toes to get out of work detail at Eastham Prison Farm in Texas; George "Machine Gun" Kelly was doing a short term in Leavenworth; and Freddie Barker and Alvin Karpis, bunkmates, had just bedded down in the Kansas State Penitentiary.

Floyd would never stop running after that until the fall of 1934.

Once in Toledo, Floyd teamed up with Bill "The Killer" Miller and the two of them knocked over a string of banks in northern Michigan. They returned to Kansas City, picked up two girls from Mother Ash's whorehouse (after killing the girls' boyfriends, William and Wallace Ash) and headed toward Kentucky.

Floyd and Miller started another bank robbing spree there: Mount Zion Trust Company, $4,000; Elliston, Kentucky bank, $2,700; Whitehouse, Kentucky bank, $3,600. Finally, they rested in Bowling Green, Ohio.

It was here that police chief Galliher grew suspicious of their license plates, checked them out and discovered that they were burning hot. With officer Ralph Castner, he approached Miller and the two girls as they were about to enter a store.

"Hold on there," Galliher shouted and Miller whirled about.

"Duck, Bill," Floyd shouted from across the street where he had planted himself for cover. Miller threw himself down and Floyd, pistols in each hand, blazed away at the two lawmen. Castner crumpled, dead. Galliher darted behind a car. When Miller tried to join Floyd, Galliher ripped half his neck away with a well-placed shot.

Miller spun in mid-air and dropped to the cement, dead. Floyd spread his legs wide apart like an outlaw of the old west and kept blazing away at Galliher. One of the girls, Beulah Baird yelled hysterically and reached for Miller's gun. She aimed it at Galliher but he was quicker and shot her in the head.

Floyd saw the situation was hopeless and dashed down

the street to the gang's car, roaring off with gears grinding.

When reporters came with the news to Madam Ash whose two sons Floyd had killed in Kansas City, she asked anxiously, "Did they get Pretty Boy?" The name was electric and it went through the wire services and into almost every headline in the country. Overnight, black fame had come to Charles Arthur Floyd.

After hiding out in Toledo and paying high protection costs to the Licavoli mob, Floyd returned to Kansas City and stayed in a partitioned room above a flower shop—headquarters for a local rum-running operation.

Prohibition agents broke into this secret room on July 21, 1931 and Floyd answered them with two roaring .45s. He blew special agent Curtis C. Burks' head off and ran out in the typical "hail of bullets."

Now Floyd ran for the only place on earth he knew he could find protection—the Cookson Hills of Oklahoma among the hill folk, who had never hurt Floyd because he was one of their own. They remembered how Chock in mad delight had ripped up first mortgages in banks he robbed, hoping they had not been recorded and thereby saving a fellow farmer's homestead.

As John Steinbeck's Pa Joad later said in *The Grapes of Wrath:* "When Floyd was loose and goin' wild, law said we got to give him up—an' nobody give him up. Sometimes a fella got to sift the law."

Floyd stayed with the back county people and became known as "The Robin Hood of the Cookson Hills." He teamed up with George Birdwell, a preacher who "had lost the callin" and the two of them went on a bankrobbing spree unequalled in the southwest.

The two men robbed the banks in Shamrock, Morris, Konawa, Maud, Earlsboro, Tahlequah, and on December 12, 1931, Floyd did what every bank bandit dreamed of doing. He robbed two banks in one day—the one horsers at Paden and Castle, Oklahoma.

In his home town of Sallisaw, Floyd got casually out of his car and strolled to the bank with a machinegun under his arm. He waved to men he knew lounging outside the local barbershop.

"How de, Chock. What you doin' in town?"

"The Robin Hood of the Cookson Hills"—bankrobber Charles Arthur "Pretty Boy" Floyd, a folklore hero to his Okie neighbors, a menace to every bank in the Southwest, and a deadly killer to police everywhere. (UPI)

"How you, Newt," Floyd waved. "Going to rob the bank."

"Give 'em hell, Chock," another man yelled admiringly.

He did.

Floyd robbed so many banks that the insurance rates in Oklahoma doubled in one year and the governor of the state went on the airwaves to denounce him and place a $6,000 reward on his head, dead or alive.

Floyd was indignant and wrote to detectives from Altus, Oklahoma: "I have robbed no one but moneyed men."

He was even beginning to believe the image of Robin Hood but that ended on the morning of June 17, 1933.

On that day, five men, one of them FBI agent Raymond Caffrey, were machinegunned to death in the Kansas City train station by three gunmen abortively attempting to deliver desperado Frank Nash. Nash was killed and four lawmen shot to death. Floyd and his new partner Adam Richetti were identified as the killers.

To his dying day, not far off, Floyd insisted he had not been in on the Kansas City Massacre. Blackie Audett, who was there watching the entire massacre wrote later in *Rap Sheet* that the real killers were Maurice Denning, Verne Miller, and William "Solly" Weissman. But the FBI, local police and the press tagged Floyd for the mass slaying.

Time ran out on Pretty Boy on October 22, 1934. Trying to escape a local dragnet, Floyd ran across an Ohio field and FBI bullets cut him down. Melvin Purvis, agent in charge, ran to him as he lay dying.

"Are you Pretty Boy Floyd?" Purvis asked.

"I am Charles Arthur Floyd."

"Were you at the Kansas City Massacre?" another agent asked.

"I didn't do it. I wasn't in on it." He rose defiantly on one elbow. "Who the hell tipped you off? I'm Floyd all right. You've got me this time." And he died there in the open field under a hazy Ohio sun.

Steinbeck's immortal character in *The Grapes of Wrath*, Ma Joad, would have the last word about this Oklahoma bandit who had ten notches on his watch fob for each man he had killed: "I knowed Purty Boy Floyd . . . I knowed his Ma. They was good folks. He was full of hell, sure, like a good boy oughta be . . . He done a little bad thing an' they hurt 'im, caught 'im and hurt 'im so he was mad, an' the next bad thing he done was mad, an' they hurt 'im again. An' purty soon he was mean-mad.

"They shot at him like a varmint, an' he shot back, an' then they run 'im like a coyote, an him a-snappin' an' a-snarlin', mean as a lobo. An' he was mad. He wasn't no boy or no man no more, he was jus' a walkin' chunk a mean-mad.

"But the folks that knowed 'im didn't hurt 'im. He wasn' mad at them. Finally, they run 'im down and killed 'im. No matter how they say it in the paper how he was bad—that's how it was."

GENNA BROTHERS
Bootleggers, Murderers

BACKGROUND: THE SIX GENNA BROTHERS—ANGELO ("BLOODY ANGELO"), ANTONIO ("TONY THE GENTLEMAN"), MIKE ("THE DEVIL"), PETE, SAM, AND VINCENZO ("JIM")—WERE BORN AND RAISED IN MARSALA, SICILY. IMMIGRATED TO THE U.S. IN 1910, FATHER A RAILROAD SECTION HAND, MOTHER ALREADY DEAD. DIAMOND JOE ESPOSITO, BOSS OF CHICAGO'S NINETEENTH WARD, SPONSORED THE GENNAS' MOVE FROM ITALY. THE ELDERLY GENNA DIED A FEW YEARS AFTER THE FAMILY SETTLED IN CHICAGO. DESCRIPTION: ALL SIX BROTHERS WERE MEDIUM-HEIGHT, SWARTHY, DARK EYED AND BLACK-HAIRED. ALIASES: NONE. RECORD: SAM, ANGELO, AND MIKE GENNA BEGAN THEIR CRIMINAL CAREERS CIRCA 1912 AS BLACKHANDERS; JIM GENNA OPERATED A BROTHEL ABOUT THIS TIME; ALL SIX BROTHERS ESTABLISHED AN ALKY COOKING EMPIRE IN CHICAGO'S LITTLE ITALY IN 1919, SUPPLYING CHEAP (AND DANGEROUS) LIQUOR TO JOHNNY TORRIO AND AL CAPONE; THE GENNAS WERE INVOLVED IN THE 1921 POLITICAL BATTLE BETWEEN NINETEENTH WARD ALDERMAN JOHN POWERS AND CHALLENGER TONY D'ANDREA, TAKING SIDES WITH THE LATTER AND KILLING SEVERAL POWERS SUPPORTERS: PAUL A. LABRIOLA, 3/8/21, DOMINICK GUTTILLO, 8/27/21, NICOLA ADAMO, 11/26/21; MIKE GENNA WITH ALBERT ANSELMI AND JOHN SCALISE KILLED POLICE OFFICERS HAROLD OLSON AND CHARES WALSH IN A GUNFIGHT ON WESTERN AVENUE 6/13/25; ANGELO GENNA KILLED BY VINCENT "THE SCHEMER" DRUCCI, GEORGE "BUGS" MORAN, AND EARL "HYMIE" WEISS 5/25/25; MIKE GENNA

KILLED IN THE ABOVE-MENTIONED POLICE FIGHT; TONY GENNA KILLED BY GIUSEPPE NERONE (TONY SPANO, ALSO CALLED "THE CAVALIER") AND ACCOMPLICES, 7/8/25; SAM AND PETE GENNA WENT INTO HIDING IN 1925, JIM FLED TO MARSALA, ITALY; THE THREE BROTHERS EVENTUALLY RETURNED TO CHICAGO, COMPLETELY DIVORCED FROM THE RACKETS, RUNNING AN IMPORT FIRM SPECIALIZING IN CHEESE AND OLIVE OIL. THEY DIED IN OBSCURITY.

Angelo Genna, "Bloody Angelo," stood on the curb with his three bodyguards, watching a man he hated—Paul Labriola—cross the street at Congress and Halsted. Genna had just eaten a mammoth spaghetti lunch and a toothpick hung limply from his scowling mouth. Labriola, a bailiff for the Municipal Court in City Hall, was a strong supporter of incumbent Alderman Johnny Powers (Johnny De Pow) in this election year of 1921. Angelo Genna wanted Tony D'Andrea, the challenger, to win. His methods of achieving such a victory were slightly unorthodox.

As Labriola nervously crossed the intersection, Angelo nodded to Samuzzo "Samoots" Amatuna, Johnny "Two Gun" Guardino, and Frank "Don Chick" Gambino. All four men, without hesitation—before dozens of pedestrians walking past them in the broad, bright afternoon—pulled out pistols and began shooting at Labriola.

The hapless victim fell in the street, his twitching body almost torn in half by the volley.

"He ain't done yet," Bloody Angelo said, and he casually sauntered over to the wounded man, straddling him with his legs. He aimed his pistol at Labriola's head and the revolver jumped three times in his hand. The back of Labriola's head disappeared.

"C'mon," Genna said to his henchmen. "He's done." Angelo threw his toothpick to the ground and the four men got into a large black Lincoln parked at the corner and drove off at a moderate speed.

This was 1921, the streets of Chicago, and whatever Angelo Genna or his five brothers chose to do in Little Italy was their business. He was a millionaire gangster whose power was so vast and reputation so fearful that he conducted open mayhem and murder with impunity. The dozen witnesses to the Labriola shooting would never testify against him, he was sure. And he was right.

The way of the Gennas, notwithstanding Angelo's public slaughter of Labriola, was normally one of guile, cunning, intrigue. They were masters of hypocrisy and deceit, more likely to ambush their victims than to shoot it out toe-to-toe.

It was an all-Sicilian clan; the Gennas trusted no one—not even their downtown sponsors, Capone and Torrio—except those who hailed from their native land and even these were suspect unless they came from the Genna village of Marsala, such as the treacherous John Scalise and Albert Anselmi.

Scalise and Anselmi were the most dreaded murderers in Chicago in the 1920s. Wanted in Sicily for murder, the unwholesome pair fled to Chicago, going to work for the Gennas as their top enforcers. They were strange-looking together; Anselmi was short, fat and balding, Scalise was tall, railroad thin and had an ugly cast to his right eye—it always appeared to be at the corner of the socket while the other stared straight ahead—creating a sinister appearance guaranteed to unnerve any rival gangster.

They were innovators of crime. Scalise and Anselmi began the practice of coating their bullets with garlic, in the mistaken belief that if their shots were not true, the additive would kill the victim by causing gangrene to set in. Gangland imitated this useless trick for several years.

The pair also inaugurated the hand-shake murder. One would walk up to an unsuspecting victim and warmly clasp him by the hand, smiling and graciously uttering the words: "Meester Joe, my fren'." The other would sneak up behind the victim and shoot him in the back of the head. This technique was applied on several occasions when the pair was busy eliminating Genna foes, notably when Scalise and Anselmi shot and killed Dion O'Bannion in 1924.

Equally fearsome killers like Orazio "The Scourge" Tropea and Giuseppe Nerone (alias Joe Pavia, Tony Spano, "The Cavalier") toted guns for the Gennas. Tropea led a sub-gang of juvenile killers who preyed on fellow Sicilians and acted as liaison agents between the Gennas and the thousands of Sicilian immigrants who ran the gang's alky-

A gathering of the "Terrible Gennas" of Chicago; the brothers (left to right) are Sam, gunmen tip garlic on their bullets. (UPI)

cooking operations in their homes. Tropea, who thought of himself as a sorcerer—the superstitious in Little Italy believed he possessed "The Evil Eye"—made his daily rounds with Tony Finalli, Felipe Gnolfo, Ecola "The Eagle" Baldelli, and Vito Bascone. These men would march peacock-proud down the streets in broad daylight with pistols drawn and shotguns cradled in their arms, unhampered by police (the Gennas reportedly paid $200,000 yearly to the police in their district for "looking the other way.").

The Gennas were the chief suppliers of liquor to dives serviced by the Torrio-Capone combine. The quality of Genna liquor was abominable. So inept were the brothers

"Bloody Angelo," Peter, Antonio, and Jim. They made bad booze and had their

as distillers that their liquor actually possessed a poisonous residue. If an unlucky speakeasy patron purchased a "bad" Genna bottle, he would wind up blind, paralyzed, or dead.

Irrespective of the dangers, Capone and Torrio couldn't buy enough of this awful rotgut, such was the demand in their bootleg domain. The Gennas, to meet the demand, first enlarged their giant Taylor Street distillery. They then turned to fellow Sicilians, installing small copper stills in homes. Day laborers quit their jobs and stayed at home in their kitchens, watching the alky-cookers gurgle at $15 a day. It cost the Gennas 40¢ a gallon to produce their booze. Torrio paid $2 for each gallon and saloons paid

$6 a gallon. The money rolled in. There was even a slush fund to handle the funeral arrangements of those hapless alky-cookers killed when defective stills exploded.

The Gennas were as status-seeking as Capone and Big Jim Colosimo. They purchased twelve front-row season tickets to the opera. After performances, they would dine *en masse* in the swanky Pompeian Room of the Congress Hotel where Tony Genna lived with his mistress, Gladys Bagwell. Gladys was the daughter of a Baptist minister in Chester, Ill. who had traveled to Chicago in 1920 seeking a stage career. She became a torch singer instead, in one of the Torrio-owned brothel bars where Gentleman Tony met her. He kept his blonde jazz cutie in a $100-a-week suite in the Congress Hotel and showered her with platinum bracelets, pearl necklaces, diamond rings, and dozens of fur coats. When asked about her relationship with the gangster, Gladys demurely answered, "Why, he's my fiancé."

All went well in the corrupt world of the Gennas until 1925. There had been the gang wars with Dion O'Bannion and other North Siders, but Big Al Capone had backed the Gennas and Big Al was always victorious. Then, a year after the death of Mike Merlo, president of the *Unione Siciliane* (a fraternal order that controlled all the Sicilian-based rackets) the Gennas rose as one man, screaming independence and defying Al Capone.

Capone lusted after the *Unione*'s presidency, but the fact that he was a Neapolitan prevented him from taking office. The Gennas moved into the *Unione*, spending heavy chunks of their $300,000-a-month bootleg income to win over high-ranking members. Angelo Genna proclaimed himself President. He also sent his deadliest of killers—Scalise and Anselmi—out to kill Capone.

The murderous pair were often rash in the ways they disposed of their victims, but in 1925 they were reasonable enough to realize that killing Capone would only insure their own deaths. (They did plot to kill Capone in 1929 when Scalise became the *Unione*'s president and were, in turn, killed by Capone.) The killers went to Capone and informed him that the Gennas had secretly declared war against him and his powerful organization. They continued to work for the Gennas, but were ever after in Capone's private employ.

Angelo Genna was the first of the scabrous clan to die. In January of 1925, Angelo married Lucille Spingola, daughter of the prestigious lawyer and politician, Henry Spingola. The wedding was another status move. Genna took out ads in newspapers which blared a "come one, come all" invitation to the lavish reception in the Ashland Auditorium. Three thousand people attended, uproariously applauding the twelve-foot, 2,000-pound cake attendants wheeled to the center of the hall. (Designer S. Ferrara gave an on-the-spot press interview stating that it took four days to bake the monstrosity; which contained 400 pounds of sugar, 400 pounds of flour, seven cases of eggs, and buckets and buckets of flavors.)

The couple honeymooned in the Belmont Hotel. Mayor William Hale "Big Bill" Thompson lived across the street. Capone, worried that Genna would form new and solid alliances with the in-power political machine, ordered Angelo killed. Bugs Moran saved his men the trouble.

On May 25, 1925 Angelo kissed his bride goodbye and hopped into his $6,000 roadster with $25,000 in cash bulging in his pocket. He was on his way to buy a house for Henry Spingola's little girl. As he approached Hudson Street on Ogden Avenue, a large sedan roared from a side street, tailing him. At the sedan's wheel was mobster Frank Gusenberg. In the back seat sat "Bugs" Moran, Hymie Weiss, and "Schemer" Drucci, all fondling their shotguns. They still seethed with hatred and vengeance over the killing of their chieftain, Don O'Bannion, by Genna killers Scalise and Anselmi.

Genna spotted them in his rear-view mirror and stepped on the gas. At Hudson, he swung the auto sharply into a vicious turn; the roadster fish-tailed and then smacked into a lamppost. Pinned behind the wheel, Angelo helplessly watched as the black sedan glided past him, shotguns from the windows emitting a fatal barrage.

At the morgue, there wasn't much left for Mike Genna to identify. He cursed for ten minutes and then called Scalise and Anselmi. They would track down Moran, Drucci, and Weiss if it took years, he told the killers.

It didn't take years for Capone to eliminate Mike. On the pretext that they were aiding Mike in his search for his brother's murderers, Scalise and Anselmi took Genna for a ride on June 13, 1925, intending to kill him. At Forty-seventh and Western, a squad car swung behind Genna's auto. Inside were police detectives Harold Olson, Charles Walsh, Michael Conway, and William Sweeney. They had recognized Genna at the wheel and decided to investigate.

Policeman Olson clanged the police gong as a signal for the gangster car to stop. It sped up. Going close to seventy miles an hour, the cars zigzagged down Western Avenue for a mile and a half. A truck suddenly veered onto the boulevard and Genna jammed down the brakes, the car spinning completely around and jumping the curb where it smashed into a pole. Genna, Scalise, and Anselmi, grabbing shotguns, flung themselves from the car.

They crouched at the ready as the squad car came up, and watched the four plainclothesmen alight. "How come you didn't stop when you heard our gong?" Conway asked.

Scalise and Anselmi opened up, their loads of buckshot hitting Olson square in the head as he stepped from the car. He was killed instantly. Walsh was half-way out of his seat when Scalise fatally shot him. Anselmi felled Conway with a blast in the chest.

That left young Sweeney.

"He's hiding behind the car," Scalise said. "We'll pick him off when he puts up his head."

Sweeney wasn't waiting to be picked off. With a pistol in each hand, the intrepid cop dove through a door and hurled himself like a javelin at the three killers. He squeezed off his rounds as he came on the run and the startled gangsters panicked and ran down an alley. Sweeney galloped after them.

For heavyset men, Scalise and Anselmi amazed the smaller Genna by sprinting ahead of him and darting down a passageway. Mike, trailing, tried to follow, but Sweeney fired a shot from the alley's mouth and sent a bullet into Genna's leg. Painfully slowed up, Mike the Devil looked about frantically for refuge. He spotted a basement window, bashed out the glass with his shotgun, and dove into the cellar head first.

Joined by two off-duty policemen, George Oakey and Albert Richert, Sweeney broke through the basement door. Genna was lying on a coal pile. Weakly, he raised his revolver and sent a wild shot at the three officers rushing toward him.

They overpowered him and dragged him into the alley. A police ambulance arrived shortly and as attendants were lifting Genna onto a stretcher, Mike raised his good leg in a mighty kick. The attendant received the blow square on the jaw and was knocked unconscious. Genna smiled crookedly. "Take that, you dirty son-of-a-bitch!" he said. These were his last words. The bullet in his leg had severed an artery and he bled to death within two hours.

Scalise and Anselmi, their shirtfronts torn open, their hair, wet with sweat, in their eyes, raced around the block like wild men. They ran north on Western and boarded a trolley car. Just as the trolley moved off, a squad car spotted them and followed. They were picked up at the next stop.

"We don't know nothin' about no shootin'," Scalise insisted.

"We are just a couple boys lookin' for work," Anselmi snorted. "You know where there's jobs?"

"I'd like to give you jobs for life," a sergeant answered and took them into custody. They were released hours later and never brought to trial. Capone got them out and kept them out. They were on his payroll. The assignment that day was to kill Mike Genna. Detective Sweeney had done it for them.

Fear came to Tony Genna. He and his remaining brothers were terrified. The two tough men of the family, Angelo and Mike, had been slaughtered in twenty days. Tony the Gentleman, the real brains behind the Genna family, knew he was next. He locked himself up in his lavish Congress Hotel suite, sending his mistress Gladys out to shop for necessities. He refused to attend meetings with his brothers. Too risky.

Several phone conversations with his chief gunner, Giuseppe Nerone, revealed that Capone was behind his brother Mike's death. Scalise and Anselmi had broken the Sicilian gangster code and had gone over to Big Al; in fact, they were now his personal bodyguards, he was told.

"I got to get out of town," Tony told Nerone.

"No, wait. First we must make plans," Giuseppe argued. "I build up the gang. We take Capone. Then you and the boys can come back. We must meet and talk first."

Tony Genna drove to a rendezvous at Curtis and Grand Avenue. Nerone waved to him from the doorway of Cutillas' grocery store, a Genna front. Genna parked his car, looked up and down the street through large smoky glasses and walked over to Nerone who put out his hand. Tony took it. In a moment, two men—Scalise and Anselmi—ran up behind him and shot him in the back.

Nerone, too, had thought it better to break the code than to buck Al Capone. The three men ran down the street and jumped into a car which roared away. This time, however, Scalise and Anselmi had been sloppy. Tony Genna still lived.

He clung to life for several hours at the County Hospital. Her mascara running with tears, Gladys Bagwell was at his bedside. "Who shot you, Tony?" she begged.

Genna's eyes fluttered open. "The Cavalier," he hissed and then died.

Police thought Tony had said "Cavallaro" and searched fruitlessly for such a man. By the time they discovered their error, the Cavalier had been machine-gunned to death in his favorite barber chair.

After Tony's slaying, everybody in the Genna cartel went down. Angelo's father-in-law, Lawyer Henry Spingola, was shot to death by Orazio Tropea and others on January 10, 1926. Tropea himself was next. "The Scourge" was hit by two shotgun blasts from a passing car on Halsted Street February 15, 1926. Vito Bascone was trapped by Capone gunners in a remote spot in suburban Stickeney. He begged for his life, hands lifted in prayer. His killers shot his hands off and sent a bullet into his brain. Vito's body was thrown into a ditch. Ecola Baldelli—"The Eagle"—was killed the same day, January 24, 1926. Scalise and Anselmi had a fight on their hands with Baldelli and took special pains, after killing him, to hack his body to pieces. The remains were strewn on a North Chicago garbage heap. Shotguns found Tony Finalli March 7, 1926, ending his career. It took three years for Capone's men to find Felipe Gnolfo; he was dispatched in 1930.

Unlike Angelo Genna, who was buried in a $10,000 bronze casket with $25,000 in flowers strewn about his grave, Tony went into the sod in a cheap wooden box and without a mourner in sight. His brothers had fled the city, their influence forever smashed. (Jim Genna ran all the way back to Marsala, Sicily, where he promptly stole the jewels from a religious statue, was caught, and went to prison for two years.)

A police sergeant at Tony's funeral, which took place at Mount Carmel Cemetery, looked about and was shocked to see Dion O'Bannion's grave only yards away. Sworn enemies in life, these two gangsters now reposed almost side by side. "When Judgement Day comes and them graves are open," the sergeant said ruefully, "there'll be hell to pay in this cemetery."

[ALSO SEE Al Capone, Dion O'Bannion, Unione Siciliane.]

GRAY, HENRY JUDD
Murderer • (1893-1928)

BACKGROUND: BORN IN NYC, 1893, HIGH SCHOOL EDUCATION, MARRIED WITH ONE DAUGHTER. OCCUPATION, CORSET SALESMAN. DESCRIPTION: 5'8½", BROWN EYES, DARK BROWN HAIR, SLENDER. ALIASES: NONE. RECORD: MURDERED, WITH THE HELP OF RUTH BROWN SNYDER, ARTHUR SNYDER, 3/20/27, TRIED, CONVICTED; EXECUTED, ALONG WITH MRS. SNYDER AT SING SING PRISON, 1/12/28.

Albert Snyder was a contented man. In 1927, he owned a sprawling three-story home in Queens, Long Island and made $115 a week as the art editor of *Motor Boating Magazine*. Married, he was relatively sure that his wife Ruth would never go beyond her casual flirtations with salesmen and delivery boys who came to their door.

Ruth was a tall, Nordic-looking woman with voluptuous curves, a hard-set jaw and an icy stare. But she was far from cold. In those flapper days, she could be aptly termed as a "red-hot mama." At thirty-two, her hair a peroxide blonde, Mrs. Ruth Brown Snyder wanted thrills and big-time adventures, not the role of the housewife and mother she compelled herself to play.

Everything in her home life annoyed her. Her husband's obsession for hunting and fishing and boating, the fuddy-duddy house she had to keep up, her nine-year-old daughter Lorraine. Her life was slipping away while the rest of the world went mad and carefree on tinny jazz, bootleg hootch and "Oh, you kid!"

But she had "Lover Boy" and that was something. "Lover Boy" or "Bud" was Henry Judd Gray, a meek-mannered, short and dapper corset salesman who wore shell-rimmed glasses and lived in Orange, New Jersey with a wife and an eleven-year-old daughter.

Ruth Snyder had been seeing Judd for almost two years. She had met salesman Gray in Manhattan in 1925, introduced by a mutual friend. When the sexy housewife learned that Judd Gray sold corsets—or corselettes as they were then called—she told that, gee, it was odd, but that's exactly what she had come down to Manhattan to buy.

Minutes later, Gray was showing Mrs. Snyder into his offices. "She removed her dress," he stated later, "and I tried on a garment to see if it was the right size and she was very badly sunburned and I offered to get some lotion to fix her shoulders . . ."

It was the beginning of their frowsy love affair. After Gray applied his lotion to Ruth Snyder's bare flesh aquiver with illegal and immoral lust, consummation followed.

They met so regularly in Manhattan hotels that sometimes Ruth would bring her daughter for lack of a baby sitter and the pathetic nine-year-old would have to sit in lobbies while her mother and Lover Boy Gray sexually attacked each other in mad bedroom antics.

Like so many sordid, little, middle-life romances, the Snyder-Gray conversations petered down to comparing notes on their separate married lives between huge gulps of booze. But as the first grey months of 1927 arrived, Ruth Snyder did more than complain to Lover Boy about her husband.

She had plans to do away with her loveless marriage and, between their love-making jousts, and through the babbling baby-talk they gurgled at each other, she told Judd all about it. It was murder, plain and simple. All they had to do was kill Albert Snyder after insuring him for a large amount of money and then they could set up their permanent love nest.

Judd Gray may have fancied himself a debonair ladies' man but the thought of murder gave him the shudders. He began to drink heavily as Ruth continued to insist they do away with her husband.

When Lover Boy repeatedly refused to kill Synder, Ruth tried several times to poison her husband. All her efforts failed. Again, Ruth went back to Gray. "Do you realize what it would mean in the eyes of God?" he naively asked her.

Eyes or no eyes, Ruth Snyder was a determined woman and she wanted her husband dead. Her insistency finally ground Judd Gray down and he agreed to the murder.

Saturday, March 19, 1927 was a cold, raw day and Judd Gray nerved himself. This was the day he had promised to kill Albert Snyder. The corset salesman mulled over the murder plan he had cooked up with Ruth.

He was to enter the Snyder home in Queens, Long Island by the back door while the Snyder family attended a late party. He was to hide in a spare room and wait.

Gray was selling corsets in Syracuse on the morning of the 19th. Solemnly, with two bottles of Mountain Dew stuffed into his handsome overcoat, he took the train to New York. There he took a bus to Queens, traveling fifteen miles and taking little nips from his pocketed spirits.

Night had fallen by the time dapper little Judd arrived in Queens. He walked around in the cold, scant blocks from the Snyder house. He acted strangely for a would-be murderer. He stopped several times beneath street lamps, yanking out his bottle and gulping the burning fluid.

Judd Gray acted as if he wanted to be caught breaking

the law of the land—Prohibition. No one paid any attention. Finally, Gray entered the Snyder home and went upstairs to the spare room.

There Ruth had already laid out the tools of murder: a heavy sashweight, rubber gloves, chloroform. Gray crouched there in the dark, drinking and waiting.

At 2 a.m., the family returned. Opening the door a crack, Ruth Snyder whispered, "Are you there, Bud, dear?"

"I'm here."

A few minutes more and she returned wearing only a slip. They fell on each other in fierce fornication that consumed an hour.

Then Gray grabbed the sashweight and Ruth led him into the master bedroom. Once there, the love duo decided not to bother with the rubber gloves and chloroform. Judd the Lover Boy raised the sashweight with all his strength and brought it down on the sleeping figure of Albert Snyder.

Gray was indeed puny for the blow merely glanced off Snyder's head, stunning him momentarily. Snyder let out a roar of pain and sat up suddenly, attempting to grab Gray.

Lover Boy became terrified; the whole thing had backfired. His voice came out of his throat like a woman's scream: "Momsie, Momsie, for God's sake, help!"

There was no panic in Ruth Snyder, who stood on the other side of the bed; only determination. With a burst of disgust and anger she wrenched the sashweight out of the quaking hands of her fellow conspirator and crashed it down on her husband's skull, killing him.

With Snyder dead, Ruth and Judd went downstairs. They had some drinks and chatted about the rest of their plan. They faked a robbery attempt by turning over a few chairs and then Gray loosely tied Ruth's hands.

Minutes after Gray left, Ruth Snyder banged on her daughter Lorraine's door. The child ran out and took the gag from her mother's mouth. "Get help" Ruth yelled to her, and the terrified girl ran to a neighbor's house where the police were called.

For all their planning, the murder-lovers had not presented a convincing robbery. All of the items Ruth said had been taken by the mysterious burglar were found in secret hiding places and detectives began to question her. The stony-hearted Ruth gave way almost at once and confessed. "Poor Judd," she said with her best Nita Naldi theatrics, "I promised not to tell . . ."

Gray was found hours later cringing in his Syracuse hotel room. He shrieked his innocence. "My word, gentlemen," he expressed to police in wounded tones, "when you know me better you'll see how utterly ridiculous it is for a man like me to be in the clutches of the law.

"Why, I've never even been given a ticket for speeding."

Judd's calm attitude broke apart on the train going to New York, and he confessed.

Almost immediately the two lovers blamed each other. Judd said that, at the moment of murder, he had weakened and required Mrs. Snyder's aid. She said she lost all her courage when the deed was done and Gray had performed the killing alone.

Damon Runyon, the celebrated newsman, said they were both inept idiots and called the whole mess The Dumb-bell Murder, "because it was so dumb."

By the time the two were tried, they were at each other's throats, each blaming the other. The trial was an extravaganza. Celebrities by the droves attended: Mary Roberts Rinehart, David Belasco, D. W. Griffith, Will Durant, Peggy Hopkins Joyce, and evangelists Billy Sunday and Aimee Semple McPherson were only a few to appear in court. Sister Aimee received a hefty sum of money from the *New York Evening Graphic* to write up the sordid mess. Sister Aimee, involved in a burning scandal of her own a year later, encouraged young men in her column to say, "I want a wife like mother—not a Red-Hot Cutie."

Both defendants had separate counsels arguing for their innocence. Mrs. Snyder's lawyer said that her husband "drove love from out that house" by carrying a torch for a departed sweetheart.

He also said that Gray had tempted her by setting up the $50,000 double indemnity insurance policy on Albert Snyder. "We will prove to you," he droned to a disbelieving court audience and jury, "that Ruth Snyder is not the demimondaine that Gray would like to paint her, but that she is a real, loving wife, a good wife; that it was not her fault that brought about the condition in that home."

Sedate and somber, sashweight murderer Henry Judd Gray awaits trial in New York in 1927; his mother gave him silent comfort. (World Wide Photos)

Her lawyer, Edgar F. Hazleton, then put the wronged woman on the stand. Over 120 reporters buzzed as she walked forward wearing a simple, black dress. Women reporters related that she looked "chic but decorous."

Ruth played the role of suffering wife and mother as never before. She told how her husband ignored her most of the time, except when taking her to an occasional movie. She was the one, she said proudly, who read the Bible to her daughter Lorraine and took the child to Sunday school, not her unfeeling husband.

Her lawyer glossed over the Gray romance as Ruth's responses were carried via a microphone at her side on the witness stand to hundreds listening in the corridors.

"He was in about the same boat I was," Ruth said of Gray. "He said he was not happy at home." Mrs. Snyder then told how Lover Boy had taken her to such speakeasy hot spots as the Frivolity Club and the Monte Carlo, where she watched him drink himself senseless. She, Ruth insisted, rarely touched even one drink and never, ever, smoked.

Then she swore that Gray insisted she take out the heavy insurance policy on her husband. "Once," she said, "he sent me poison and told me to give it to my husband."

Ruth Snyder, who murdered her husband with Judd Gray, was pensive at her 1927 trial. (UPI)

At this, the excitable little Judd began jabbering at his lawyers.

Turn about was fair play in this silly melodrama. Gray took the stand after his lawyer blasted Mrs. Snyder good and proper. Attorney Sam Miller described Judd's situation as "the most tragic story that has ever gripped the human heart."

Gray, Miller claimed, was a law-abiding citizen who was fed over twenty shots of whiskey by Mrs. Snyder to steel him for the act of killing.

"He was dominated by a cold, heartless, calculating master mind and master will," Miller chanted. "He was a helpless mendicant of a designing, deadly, conscienceless, abnormal woman, a human serpent, a human fiend in the guise of a woman.

"He became inveigled and drawn into this hopeless chasm when reason was gone, when mind was gone, when manhood was gone, and when his mind was weakened by lust and passion."

Things were looking up for Judd.

He took the witness chair dressed in a snappy double-breasted business suit, playing the victim to the hilt. As he talked, he nervously glanced at his elderly mother sitting in the court next to the famous actress, Nora Bayes, who had come to watch the fun.

Judd Gray said that Mrs. Snyder had tried to kill her husband several times. Once she put knockout drops in his prune whip, but that failed, and then she tried to gas him.

"I told her I thought she was crazy," Gray said innocently and then reported that Ruth had given her husband poison when he had the hiccups. It only made him violently sick.

"I said to her," Gray intoned mildly, "that was a hell of a way to cure hiccups. I criticized her sorely." He then added that Mrs. Snyder tried to kill her husband twice again by administering sleeping powders to him.

He also said that Ruth arranged the insurance policy on her own and had struck the death blow. It was then that Ruth Snyder sobbed loudly and Judd glanced in her direction.

The jury was spared more of this double-crossing banter;

they retired. They were out only 98 minutes and came in with a verdict of guilty. Both defendants were stunned. The sentence was death.

The warden came for Judd Gray on the bleak night of January 12, 1928. He sat smiling in his cell. He had received a letter from his wife forgiving him. "I am ready to go," he said to the warden. "I have nothing to fear."

Ruth Snyder followed her faithless lover minutes after she watched the prison lights flicker and signal his death. Reporters remembered, as she was led to the electric chair, that she had said days before that God had forgiven her and she hoped the world would.

An enterprising reporter from the *New York Daily News* smuggled a camera strapped to his ankle into the death chamber and clicked off a photo just as the current raced through Mrs. Snyder's body, hurtling her against the chair straps.

The love affair was still good for one more edition.

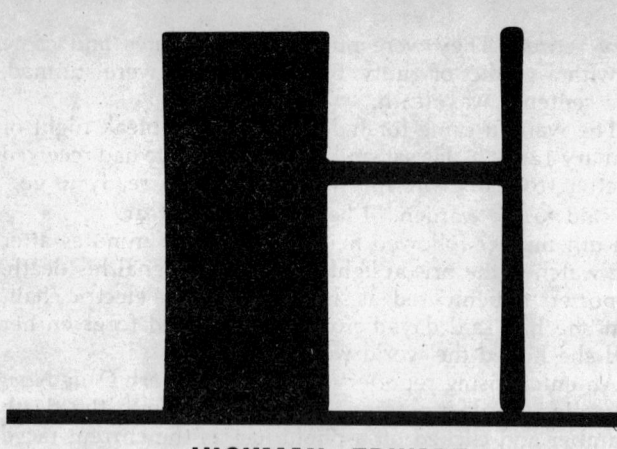

HICKMAN, EDWARD
Kidnapper, Murderer • (1907-1928)

It had been the most trying ordeal of Perry Parker's life. The Los Angeles businessman's deep love was rooted in his twin twelve-year-old daughters Marian and Marjorie. When Marian was abducted, he first went to the police and then, when the girl was not returned, agreed to pay the $7,500 ransom to the kidnapper, a young man who signed himself "The Fox."

In late December, 1927, Parker, alone in his car, met the young man in an isolated spot at the outskirts of Los Angeles. As both men glared at each other from their autos, Parker asked: "Is my daughter alive?" The curly-headed young man smiled, reached to his side and held up a blanket-wrapped child who appeared to be sleeping.

"Give me the money and I'll leave her down the road away," the kidnapper said softly. Parker threw the money from the window of his car into the young man's auto. The kidnapper's car sped away. Minutes later, following the road, Parker saw the bundle by the side of the road, stopped and ran to his daughter. Throwing back the blanket, he groaned. Marian was dead, strangled, her neck almost severed. Her monstrous killer had insanely and inexplicably cut off both her legs.

The vicious killing shocked the country and ignited one of the greatest manhunts in California history. The killer, twenty-year-old Edward Hickman, had gone to Seattle to vacation on the kidnapping money.

Hickman, a psychopath, mimicked the movie stars of the day and spent a great deal of time pitying himself and weeping over the privations he had endured as a youth. A college student, Hickman desperately fielded about for a way to amass $1,500 for tuition (at least, that was his explanation later.) In early December, 1927, he hit upon the idea of kidnapping a wealthy child and holding her for ransom.

He drove about Los Angeles' wealthy suburbs for days and finally selected prosperous Perry Parker. Hickman then went to Marian Parker's school, telling the child that "there's trouble at home," and that her father had sent him to pick her up. He drove her to a lonely shack. There he stood over Marian with a long knife pressed to her back and dictated a letter to her father. Marian, terrified, wrote down everything uttered by the maniacal kidnapper.

"Dear Daddy and Mother:
I wish I could come home. I think I'll die if I have to be like this much longer. Won't someone tell me why all this had to happen to me? Daddy please do what the man tells you or he'll kill me if you don't. Your loving daughter, Marian Parker. P.S. Please Daddy, I want to come home tonight."

After Marian finished scribbling the note, the demoniac Hickman strangled the little girl and, for reasons never explained, cut off her legs. He then mailed the note to Parker and waited. When Parker failed to correctly respond to his phone calls, Hickman began sending him his own carefully-lettered notes. They were headed by the word "DEATH," elaborately scrolled at the top of the page.

One letter read:

Kidnapper and murderer Edward Hickman in January, 1928, combing his hair and admiring himself in his jail cell; he was hanged at San Quentin Prison a month later. (UPI)

"Mr. Parker:
 Fox is my name, Very sly you know. Set no traps. I'll watch for them. All the inside guys . . . know that when you play with fire there is cause for burns. Not W. J. Burns [head of the Burns Detective Agency] and his shadowers either—remember that. Get this

straight. Your daughter's life hangs by a thread and I have a Gillette [razor] ready and able to handle the situation. This is business. Do you want the girl or the 75 $100 gold certificates U.S. currency? You can't have both and there's no other way out. Believe this and act accordingly. Before the day's over I'll find out how you stand. I am doing a solo so figure on meeting the terms of Mr. Fox, or else FATE."

Hickman's florid ego demanded he send Parker several of these notes, telling the frantic businessman that "if you want aid against me, ask God, not man."

But several very ordinary men, Seattle police, picked up Hickman at a Seattle resort and arrested him for murder after discovering he corresponded to the description offered by Mr. Parker. He was sent southward on the first fast train from Seattle. Hickman was docile in captivity but tried twice to commit suicide in the train's washroom. They were feeble efforts designed to convince his guards and later his jury that he was insane.

Thousands of curious spectators gathered at stations along the route of the train carrying Hickman. The youthful murderer idiotically waved and smiled to them. Some nervously waved back.

His trial was less farcical. The prosecution provided a witness, one of Hickman's fellow cellmates, who testified that the killer had planned to fake insanity to escape the death sentence. After a long trial, extensive psychiatric examinations and last-ditch appeals, Hickman's insanity plea collapsed. He was hanged in San Quentin Prison, February 4, 1928.

JACKSON, HUMPTY
Murderer, Gangleader • (? -1914)

A bibliophile, Jackson was partial to the works of Darwin, Voltaire, and Spencer, as well as being one of the most feared New York gang leaders in the 1890s. His extensive library and good education notwithstanding, Jackson led a gang of toughs that controlled the area bounded by First and Second avenues and Twelfth and Thirteenth streets. His headquarters was an old graveyard.

There, almost each night, Humpty Jackson, whose name was derived from his hunchback, would meet with some of the most notorious hoodlums of the era—the Lobster Kid, Spanish Louie, Nigger Ruhl, and a giant killer ominously known as The Grabber. Humpty would sit on a tombstone and outline plans for a robbery or a paid killing.

Three guns could be found on Humpty at all times. A small revolver was carried in his pocket. Another gun was tucked into a strange-looking holster slung by a strap about his hump. A third was secreted in a special compartment inside his derby. Humpty's usual price for blackjacking a person was $100. Murder cost more.

From 1890 to 1909, Jackson was arrested twenty times and sent to prison following a dozen convictions, but he always managed to obtain parole. Jackson was finally sent to prison in 1909 for twenty years after being convicted of ordering the murder of a man he never met. He died in a cell.

KANSAS CITY MASSACRE

When Frank "Jelly" Nash, one of the most successful bankrobbers of the 1920s, escaped from Leavenworth in 1930, he became the subject of a nation-wide manhunt led by the FBI and local police officers in five states. He participated in several bank robberies engineered by the Barker-Karpis gang, but when police began to close in on the Barkers, the ever-elusive Nash broke away from the gang and went into hiding in Hot Springs, Ark.

FBI agents trapped him there in early 1933. From Hot Springs the bandit would be returned to Leavenworth to finish his twenty-five year sentence. At the moment of his capture, Nash spotted gambler and pool-hall owner Dick Galatas and gave him the high sign, indicating that he was being arrested by federal agents. Galatas called Nash's wife, Frances, and then placed several long-distance calls, attempting to learn where FBI men were taking Nash.

Galatas contacted lawman-turned-bankrobber Verne Miller in Kansas City. Miller, who had robbed with the Barkers, was an old friend of Jelly's. He told Galatas: "You have Frances call me as soon as she finds out what route they'll be taking to Leavenworth."

Through connections on the Hot Springs police department, Galatas learned the agents would be driving with their prisoner along the Joplin (Missouri) Road. Galatas and Frances Nash hired a plane and flew to Joplin where they met another underworld fence, gunsmith, and hideout operator, Herbert Farmer. They learned at that moment that the FBI had gone by another route, U.S. 64, and, at Fort Smith, Ark., had boarded the Missouri Pacific Flyer en route to Kansas City.

The agents joked in their stateroom with Nash about his new disguise, a red wig to cover his bald head. "I paid a hundred bucks for it in Chicago. You do what you can," Nash explained. He went on to state that he had had his nose straightened and then asked the lawmen not to pull his mustache because that was real.

In Kansas City, Verne Miller had learned that the prisoner was heading his way on board a train. He made preparations to greet it in the morning. On June 17, 1933, there were a number of people waiting to see Frank "Jelly" Nash. FBI agents Raymond Caffrey and R. E. Vetterli and city detectives W. J. "Red" Grooms and Frank Hermanson were waiting to escort Nash to Leavenworth in their car.

Also waiting in the busy train station were five or more gangsters, the would-be deliverers of Frank Nash. One of them was definitely Verne Miller. The identities of the others are in serious doubt to this day. Just as the Flyer pulled into the station, the gangsters went out to the parking lot and took positions next to parked autos. They were not noticed by the lawmen waiting at the curb next to their own car.

Nash was led from the train by FBI agents F. J. Lackey, Frank Smith, and Otto Reed, police chief of McAlester, Okla. The bandit was still wearing his red wig; it kept slipping off. Lackey and Smith carried shotguns. The trio, joined by the four lawmen, began to get into a Chevrolet parked in the plaza. Nash got in the front seat. Lackey, Smith, and Reed got in the back. Agent Caffrey walked around the car to the driver's side and had his hand on the door handle when a booming voice yelled to the lawmen from across the plaza: "Up! Up! Get 'em up!"

Shocked and motionless, the agents and detectives

looked up to see three men standing on the running boards of cars, pointing machineguns in their direction. A heavyset man aiming his machinegun at them, the man who had yelled out the order, waved his weapon slightly. For moments, dozens of people in the parking lot stood transfixed by the incredible scene. Police detective Red Grooms then broke the spell by jerking his pistol out and squeezing off two shots at the heavyset man, hitting him in the arm.

The heavyset gangster never faltered. "Let 'em have it!" he shouted to the others and opened up on the lawmen. The deadly spray of machinegun bullets splattered the

Spectators view the carnage of the Kansas City Massacre, 6/18/33; the bodies of Kansas City detectives William Grooms and Frank Hermanson lie between the two bullet-smashed cars in the Union Station Plaza parking lot. (UPI

Chevrolet, a torrent of lead that raked the car from back to front. Agent Caffrey fell to the cement, dead. Police Chief Reed took a chest full of slugs and toppled to the floor of the car, dead. Also inside the car agents Smith and Lackey fell forward, each shot several times.

Lackey struggled up courageously with his service revolver in his hand and tried to get off a shot from the window. The weapon was shot out of his grip. Agent Vetterli and detectives Grooms and Hermanson were all wounded, pressed to the pavement for cover.

Inside the car, Nash waved frantically at the machinegunners with handcuffed wrists. "For God's sake!" he shouted. "Don't shoot *me!*" The overlapping bursts of machinegun fire quieted him forever as his head was blown away.

Mrs. Lottie West, a caseworker for the Traveler's Aid Society, witnessed the entire shooting from the station. She spotted a patrolman she knew, Mike Fanning, who had entered the lot to investigate the awful racket. "They're killing everybody!" Mrs. West screamed to him.

Slugs were now bouncing into the pavement in front of the car. They tore into the already wounded, prone lawmen, killing detectives Grooms and Hermanson.

Mrs. West screamed to Officer Fanning: "Shoot the fat man, Mike! Shoot the fat man!"

"I knew she meant the big man whose machinegun was doing such bloody work," Fanning later recalled. "I aimed at him and fired. He whirled around and dropped to the ground. I don't know whether I hit him or whether he fell to escape. In any event he got up, fired another volley into the car, and ran toward a light Oldsmobile car, which roared west toward Broadway. As the car raced out of the parking lot I saw three men in it and there may have been more."

Just as Fanning was about to walk to the lawmen's car, another auto, a 1933 Chevrolet, with more gunners swooped past the parked car and riddled it from the rear.

Fanning ran to the lawmen's auto and peered inside. "It was a shambles. In the front seat a man was dead under the steering wheel [Nash]. On the left of the rear seat was another dead man [Chief Reed]. On the right was an unconscious man but he was groaning. A third man lay face down on the floor. I could see that he was alive."

Agent Vetterli, holding a wounded arm, staggered up, staring at the blood from the bodies of Hermanson and Grooms gathering in pools at his feet. Five men were dead—FBI agent Caffrey, Chief Reed, detectives Hermanson and Grooms, and Frank "Jelly" Nash, the man the shooting supposedly had been designed to set free.

One woman, unable to take her eyes from the carnage, groaned, "It's like Chicago."

In hours, newspapers across the country were screaming headlines that read "Kansas City Massacre." The public outcry against the slaughter was deafening. Contingents of FBI men and armies of police scoured the Kansas City area searching for the killers.

Frances Nash, Dick Galatas, and Herb Farmer were traced to Joplin, Mo. through long-distance calls they had made and were soon arrested. Witnesses tentatively identified one of the machinegunners as Verne Miller. Mrs. West was sure that the "fat man" had been Charles Arthur "Pretty Boy" Floyd. FBI officials and police immediately deduced that the third gunner had been Floyd's sidekick, Adam Richetti.

When Floyd and Richetti were finally brought to ground in October, 1934, the FBI announced that they had captured the perpetrators of the Kansas City Massacre. From all subsequent reports, however, it appears that the FBI was mistaken.

According to the 1954 statements of underworld figure Blackie Audett, Floyd and Richetti had nothing to do with the K.C. killings. "I knowed better," Audett wrote, "because I seen with my own eyes who was in that car. Both of them that was in it got clean away." Audett named Verne Miller, Maurice Denning, and William "Solly" Weissman.

Events immediately following the mass killing proved Audett's claim to a great degree. Police trailed Miller to his home only hours after the shooting but found that he had fled. They also found bloody rags in his living room.

Miller's naked and mangled body was discovered in a ditch near Detroit on November 29, 1933. His death had all the earmarks of a syndicate killing. It appeared that hot flatirons had scorched his skin. He was tied up head to toe and icepicks had punctured his tongue and cheeks.

Two weeks later Weissman's body was found in the same condition on the outskirts of Chicago. Denning's corpse never surfaced. It was apparent that all three men had been killed not because they failed to effect Nash's release but because they knew who had ordered Nash killed. They also knew that Jelly was marked for death because he knew too much. It was impossible for them to mistake Nash as he sat in the front seat of the auto waving his handcuffed hands. The killing was simply a syndicate hit. The killers had been paid a considerable sum to perform the job so their attack was not made out of loyalty to Nash. Once the hit was accomplished, the killers were murdered to silence them.

The syndicate had taken root throughout the country by then; a formal board of directors would be established early the following year. Local syndicate gang bosses controlled many local politicians. In Kansas City, the local gangleaders were thickly associated with the political machine run by Tom Pendergast. From later reports it appears that everyone in power in Kansas City knew about the impending killing.

Pendergast's "front man" in K. C. was City Manager Henry McElroy. Audett stated that McElroy's daughter, Mary, had been informed of the shooting hours before it happened, and it was Mary who invited Blackie to the station to view the grisly affair. "Me and Mary McElroy watched the whole thing from less than fifty yards away," Blackie later commented.

Everything and anything went in Kansas City in those days, except a formal invitation to watch a mass murder. You had to know a special friend for something like that.

[ALSO SEE Charles Arthur "Pretty Boy" Floyd.]

KELLY, GEORGE R. ("MACHINE-GUN")
Bootlegger, Kidnapper • (1897–1954)

BACKGROUND: BORN IN TENNESSEE, 1897, RAISED IN LOWER-INCOME ENVIRONMENT, MINOR PUBLIC EDUCATION, MARRIED KATHRYN COLEMAN THORNE IN 1927. ORIGINAL OCCUPATION, SALESMAN. DESCRIPTION: 6'1", BLUE EYES, BLACK HAIR, HEAVYSET. ALIASES: J. C. TICHENOR, E. W. MOORE. RECORD: KNOWN AS A "SOCIETY BOOTLEGGER" IN MEMPHIS DURING

THE MIDDLE 1920S, KELLY WAS RUN OUT OF THAT TOWN AND TOOK UP BOOTLEGGING IN NEW MEXICO, ARRESTED IN 1925, CONVICTED AND SERVED THREE MONTHS IN THE NEW MEXICO STATE PRISON; MOVED TO THE OKLAHOMA CITY AREA AND ARRESTED THERE FOR SELLING LIQUOR TO INDIANS; CONVICTED FOR VIOLATING THE NATIONAL PROHIBITION ACT AND SENTENCED TO ONE YEAR IN LEAVENWORTH, 1930; RELEASED IN 1931; ROBBED SEVERAL SMALL TOWN BANKS 1931-1933, INCLUDING THE BANKS IN TUPELO, MISS. AND WILMER, TEX., TAKING SMALL AMOUNTS; KIDNAPPED WITH ALBERT BATES, A SMALLTIME SWINDLER AND CON MAN, MILLIONAIRE OILMAN CHARLES F. URSCHEL IN OKLAHOMA CITY, 7/22/33 AND HELD HIM FOR $200,000 RANSOM; CAPTURED 9/26/33 IN MEMPHIS BY MEMPHIS POLICE; TRIED WITH HIS WIFE KATHRYN, ALBERT BATES, MR. AND MRS. R. G. SHANNON (KATHRYN'S PARENTS WHO HAD HELPED TO GUARD URSCHEL); ALL RECEIVED LIFE SENTENCES; KELLY IMPRISONED FIRST AT LEAVENWORTH, THEN AT ALCATRAZ WHERE HE DIED IN 1954; KATHRYN KELLY RELEASED IN 1958.

There was nothing spectacular about George Kelly. He was a big, almost lovable, braggart who nearly drank up more of his own bootleg hooch than he peddled in the 1920s. He was stupid, too. But Cleo Coleman Shannon changed all that ... with a machinegun.

Cleo was born in Saltilo, Mississippi in 1904, a pretty, fetching, dark-haired girl who fantasized from childhood a life of glamor, money, and power. Her parents were dirt-poor and little Cleo would imagine her ragged homespuns to be the delicate gowns of princesses. Like many of the underfed, emotionally deprived children of the South and Southwest of those days, Cleo lived in a dream world she snatched desperately from the penny movies. There was nothing else.

When her avaricious mother deserted her father, Cleo packed her skimpy wardrobe and tagged along. Mother knew best.

By the time she was fifteen, Cleo had changed her name to the more romantic "Kathryn" and had married, giving birth to a daughter. She was divorced in 1917 and went to live with her mother.

By 1921, the seventeen-year-old girl was running booze from Forth Worth, Texas to her mother's hotel, where women as well as rooms were for rent. In 1924, Kathryn met bootlegger Charlie Thorne and it was love at first lunge.

That marriage lasted three years. One sultry night in 1927, Kathryn, her sixteen-cylinder roadster purring, stopped at a gas station in Fort Worth, Texas. She was fuming.

"Hey, Kate, what's the matter?" the attendant said.

She gave him a burning stare. "I'm bound for Coleman [Texas] to kill that goddamned Charlie Thorne." It wasn't an unusual threat since the couple carried on animal warfare with each other all the time.

But the filling station attendant was a little alarmed to hear the next day that Charlie Thorne had committed suicide. He left behind a conspicuous and not-too-believable note which read: "I can't live with her or without her, hence I am departing this life." Charlie went out with a bullet in the left temple.

That same year, 1927, George Kelly entered Kathryn's less-than-dull life.

Kelly was a big man, over six feet, with broad shoulders, a pudgy, smiling face, and a growling tough guy's voice copied from gangsters he had met. But George wasn't tough at all and Kathryn knew it.

Introduced to her in Fort Worth as a "society bootlegger," George had the criminal habits of a small-time punk and was as soft as a three-day-old cream puff in a blast furnace. "No copper will ever take me alive," Kelly was fond of sneering out of the corner of his mouth.

Kathryn became enamored of George's phony underworld image and set out to promote him as a hardnosed, high-living bank robber. There was a problem though: George had never robbed a bank.

Throughout the late 1920s and early 1930s, George Kelly had been running rotgut booze into New Mexico, Oklahoma, and Texas. He was happy with his work; as an amiable drunk who impersonated a big time mobster he was content to peddle illegal liquor to smalltown druggists. George didn't even like guns. He never hurt anyone.

"But you've got to be able to hurt people," Kathryn would plead. "You've got to be tough or nobody will

Kathryn Kelly built up her husband's desperado image and nagged him into kidnapping Oklahoma millionaire Charles Urschel. (UPI)

respect you. You gotta have that respect, George. And I know something that will get you the respect." Kathryn went out and bought George a brand new, shiny machine gun.

Next came target practice. In the baking sun that beat down on her mother's new ranch—the E. G. Shannon Ranch of Paradise, Texas—Kathryn would set up walnuts on a fence. Months went by before he knocked the walnuts off, but finally George actually became a marksman with the deadly weapon.

Kathryn was proud of him and introduced him to several of the gangsters who paid $50 a night to hide out at the

Shannon ranch while they were dodging the law. Sometimes she would drive into Fort Worth and hit the big time speakeasies there.

Kathryn would go along and carry a fistful of .45-caliber cartridges. She would hand these out to special underworld friends with a whisper: "Here's a souvenir I brought you. It's a cartridge fired by George's machine gun—Machine Gun Kelly, you know."

And the name became legend. But when asked where George was, Kathryn would imply he was away—up north pulling some high class heist jobs. Meanwhile, the legend was in a small, dirty room on the Shannon ranch, fighting off a bad case of the DT's.

In 1931, George Kelly drove a truckload of whiskey onto an Indian reservation and was promptly picked up without a fight by Prohibition agents. He got a short stretch in Leavenworth Federal Penitentiary. Again Kathryn humped the PR trail, pumping up George's reputation, telling her underworld friends that " 'Machine Gun' is in Kentucky robbing banks."

Kelly's attitude changed in Leavenworth; he began to believe the image Kathryn had been systematically building for him. When he met safecracker Morris "Red" Rudensky outside his cell one day, he couldn't resist the urge to lie about his exploits and financial assets.

"This place is getting on my nerves, Red," Kelly snarled at Rudensky. "I've got fifty grand sitting on the outside and I could throw a party that'd last for a year. But I can't get at it."

"Why don't you go over the wall," Rudensky suggested.

The thought of escape frightened Kelly. He laughed off the idea. "Hell, Red, I'm too old for that. I'll be out in a year. But if you get any ideas, I'll help you for laughs. You young guys are the ones who should be licking your chops over busting out. And if you do, you might help old George make the wheels spin a little faster."

After Kelly was released, Kathryn married her would-be desperado, took him home to the ramshackle Shannon ranch, and showed him a pile of newspaper clippings. The Barrows and the Barkers and Pretty Boy Floyd were making headlines. They robbed banks with ease. They had made the Big Time.

She got out his machine gun and after a bit more training, Kathryn landed George a job with a two-bit bankrobbing gang. Reluctantly, George hit the jug-knocker's trail.

The first Kathryn heard of him was when he and the boys hit the bank in Tupelo, Mississippi for a few thousand dollars. The take was even less when they knocked over the hayseed bank in Wilmer, Texas. And here a security guard had been machine-gunned to death.

Kathryn was proud of her roving bank robber, her own creation, and she beamed when someone whispered that the guard on the Wilmer job had been sprayed to death by none other than the hard-as-nails killer, Machine Gun Kelly.

But bankrobbing was slim pickings in the early 1930s and as the years ground on, Kathryn got tired of the small takes, George's drinking, and watching the big name outlaws grab the newspaper glory. Her clever mind whirled.

One day, George woke out of his usual drunken stupor to discover a table laden with more newspaper clippings. This time they all dealt with kidnapping. Kathryn was studying them.

Carefully, she pored over the recent Mary McElroy kidnapping, the Charles Boettcher kidnapping in Denver, the William Hamm, Jr., kidnapping in St. Paul with its $200,000 payoff.

"We've got to put the snatch on one of these birds, George," Kathryn told him. "It's the only way to make any money these days."

"Too risky," Machine Gun said.

"We're going to do it, George."

George nodded obediently.

The first person Machine Gun and Kathryn thought of kidnapping was a wealthy South Bend, Indiana businessman. But their plan failed from the start. Kathryn got drunk in Fort Worth and told of the plot to two local detectives—Ed Weatherford and J. W. Swinney—whom she thought were crooked. They weren't and a ring of security guards was thrown around the businessman's house.

The irony of the situation was that the Indiana businessman was broke and the Kellys couldn't have gotten $50 in ransom money.

The next victim of Kathryn's scheming was better off;

he was millionaire oilman Charles F. Urschel of Oklahoma City. On the night of July 22, 1933, Machine Gun Kelly and a sidekick, Albert Bates, brushed past the screen door on the porch of the Urschel home. The Urschels were playing cards on the porch with neighbors and looked up startled.

"Stick 'em up," Kelly snarled in his best gangster voice as he aimed his machine gun at the card players. "Which one's Urschel?"

Walter Jarrett, who was sitting with Urschel, remained silent. "All right," Kelly said, "We'll take both of you."

A few miles out of town Kelly had the two men empty their wallets and identified Urschel. Jarrett was thrown out on the empty road and the kidnappers drove off with their captive.

Hoover and the FBI were on the trail hours after getting a call from Mrs. Urschel and the Oklahoma City area was blanketed with agents. But they drew a blank.

The Kellys and Bates then played a cops-and-robbers game of collecting the $200,000 ransom (all in marked bills). They made a deal with Urschel's friend, E. E. Kirkpatrick, to deliver the goods. He was to deliver the money by boarding the fast train, The Sooner, speeding from Oklahoma City to Kansas City. After spotting two field fires on the way, Kirkpatrick was to toss the money from the observation car at the end of the train. But, like most everything else he tried to do in life, Machine Gun botched the deal. He flooded the gang's car and the delay caused the kidnappers to arrive late at the rendezvous without lighting their field fires. They watched helplessly as the train and $200,000 shot past them.

The kidnappers finally made contact with Kirkpatrick in Kansas City. The pickup was awkward. Kelly was so nervous he almost fumbled his relatively easy chore. As Kirkpatrick walked down Linwood Avenue, he noticed a tall, solidly-built man step from a car parked next to the curb. The large man walked abreast of him several feet, nervously glancing at the large, black bag Kirkpatrick carried which contained the $200,000 in ransom money.

"I'll take that bag, Mr. Kincaid [Kirkpatrick's cover name]," the heavyset man whispered.

"How do I know you're the right man?" Kirkpatrick said coolly.

"Hell, you know damned well I am."

The man's appearance was natty. Kirkpatrick studied the rich summer suit he wore, the rakish Panama hat creased sharply down in front, the two-tone shoes. "Two hundred thousand dollars is a lot of money," Kirkpatrick said. "I want some kind of assurance Mr. Urschel will not be harmed."

Kelly growled: "Don't argue with me! The boys are waiting!" Well, one boy was waiting anyway; meek, middle-aged Albert Bates sat blinking anxiously in a nearby car.

But Kirkpatrick held his ground. "I want a definite answer I can give to Mrs. Urschel. When will her husband be home?"

Machine Gun Kelly's huge body seemed to jangle nervously as he shifted from one foot to another. He eyed the black bag. "He'll be home in twelve hours," the kidnapper blurted.

Kirkpatrick dropped the bag to the sidewalk and strode away without turning around. Kelly scooped up the ransom and ran to the car where Bates waited.

Urschel was then released from captivity at the Shannon ranch—Machine Gun had to argue Kathryn out of killing the old man. He was driven to the outskirts of Oklahoma City, handed a hat and $10, and told to grab a cab.

Immediately, Kathryn and Kelly ran north to Chicago and St. Paul, spending their loot like drunken sailors instead of lying low. It didn't take long before the two local detectives Kathryn had blabbed to in Forth Worth led the FBI to the Shannon ranch. Picked up at the Shannon hideout was bankrobber Harvey Bailey, who was recovering from a leg wound. Bates was soon picked up in Denver.

The FBI took Mr. and Mrs. R. G. ("Boss") Shannon into custody and when Kelly learned of the apprehension of his in-laws, he exploded, foolishly writing threats to Urschel and blaming him for their arrest. One letter read:

"Ignorant Charles—
If the Shannons are convicted look out, and God help

Kidnapper George "Machine Gun" Kelly (with dyed hair), happy to be in custody and away from his shrewish wife. (UPI)

you for He is the only one that will be able to do you any good. In the event of my arrest I've already formed an outfit to take care of and destroy you and yours the same as if I was there. I am spending your money to have you and your family killed—nice, eh? You are bucking people who have cash—planes, bombs and unlimited connections both here and abroad . . . Now, sap—it is up to you, if the Shannons are convicted you can get you another rich wife in Hell because that will be the only place you can use one. Adios, smart one.

Your worst enemy,
Geo. R. Kelly

I will put my prints below so you can't say some crank wrote this."

He did. But such bravado was only superficial. Kelly did not enjoy either freedom or the ransom money. When he learned that Bates had been arrested by feds in Denver he shouted to Kathryn, "Oh, my God, it's all over!"

Before the Kellys had a chance to spend all their ransom money, it was over for them, too. The FBI tells the story that when surrounded in a Memphis flophouse, George "Machine Gun" Kelly cowered like a rat caught in floodlights, screaming "Don't shoot, G-Man!"

In reality, it was local police sergeant W. J. Raney who broke into Machine Gun's room and shoved a shotgun into the outlaw's paunch. "I've been waiting for you," Kelly said softly and smiled.

The rest was anti-climactic. The Kellys tore at each other during the resulting trial, each blaming the other. Kelly and Bates got life in prison. Kathryn got the same.

In 1954, after Kelly had been removed from Alcatraz to Leavenworth, he wrote his old victim, Charles Urschel. "These five words are written in fire on the walls of my cell." Machine Gun lamented. "Nothing can be worth this!" And nothing was. Kelly died in prison.

Kathryn Kelly survived, however, and she was released from the Cincinnati Workhouse in 1958. Like all the other gun molls of the 1930s, this once desperate woman, who saw herself as a modern Belle Star, faded unheralded into the kind of social oblivion from which she sprang.

From all reports, she is alive today with the wilting vision of the outlaw she created, a man who came to be known, sadly and tragically, as "Pop Gun Kelly."

KETCHUM, THOMAS ("BLACK JACK")
Murderer, Trainrobber • (1866-1901)

BACKGROUND: BORN AND RAISED IN NEW MEXICO. NO PUBLIC EDUCATION. ONE BROTHER, SAMUEL. ORIGINAL OCCUPATION, COWBOY. DESCRIPTION: 6', BROWN EYES, BLACK HAIR, SLENDER. ALIASES: BLACK JACK. RECORD: FORMED AN OUTLAW BAND AT WYOMING'S HOLE-IN-THE-WALL, CIRCA 1898, AND ROBBED SEVERAL STAGES AND SMALL BANKS IN NEW MEXICO THAT YEAR; REPORTEDLY KILLED TWO MINERS 7/2/99 NEAR CAMP VERDE, ARIZ.; ROBBED WITH ELZA LAY (ALIAS BILL MCGINNIS) AND G. W. FRANKS FOUR TRAINS IN ALMOST THE SAME LOCATION NEAR TWIN MOUNTAINS, N.M. 1898-99 FOR SMALL AMOUNTS; CAPTURED OUTSIDE OF CIMARRON, N.M. 7/13/99 AT WHICH TIME HE KILLED SHERIFF EDWARD FARR OF COLORADO AND ANOTHER DEPUTY, W. H. LOVE; CONVICTED OF TRAINROBBING; EXECUTED ON THE GALLOWS 4/25/01.

Black Jack Ketchum was probably the most unimaginative robber who ever held up a train.

Late in 1898, Ketchum, G. W. Franks, and Elza Lay, a member of the Butch Cassidy gang, held up an express train near Twin Mountain, N. M. The take was small, only a few hundred dollars, but Ketchum never looked down his nose or beyond his bushy, black mustache at a good thing. With the same two accomplices, Black Jack held up the same train three more times almost in the same spot, the last raid occurring July 11, 1899.

Ketchum's robbery methods never varied, which surprised no one, including Butch Cassidy and his more professional Wild Bunch riders. Black Jack and his brother Sam (who was also called "Black Jack" at times) had always been aimless cowpunchers who merely drifted into crime when times got tough.

Tom Ketchum was simply unlucky. He drank heavily and could not hold a job. Neither could he hold a woman. He was also a bit crazy. When a girl named Cora two-timed him, Ketchum went berserk. He received a letter from her in which she told him that her lover watched him kiss her goodbye before going off to a cattle drive. "No more than you were out of sight then we went to Stanton and got married." The cruelty of the letter produced an odd reaction in Tom Ketchum. He took out his pistol and, to the amazement of cowboys around him, began to beat himself on the head with the gun butt. Between blows, he yelled at himself, saying, "You will, will you? Take that! And that!"

Then Black Jack Ketchum marched down to the nearby Perico River, loudly damning all women, and gave himself another severe beating with a saddle rope while teetering at the water's edge.

Weeks later, Black Jack and his brother Sam rode to Wyoming's Hole-in-the-Wall with robbery on their minds. Butch Cassidy's men would have nothing to do with the demented bandit, but Elza Lay finally joined him. G. W. Franks, another small-time outlaw, also followed Black Jack to New Mexico where the foursome pulled several minor robberies. Then came the four train robberies of the Santa Fe Railroad near Twin Mountains.

Before the last train strike, Ketchum rode to Camp Verde, Ariz. where he killed two miners in an argument over cards. A large posse tracked down the Ketchum gang in Turkey Canyon near Cimarron, N. M. on July 13, 1899. There was a wild gun battle in which two lawmen, Edward Farr and W. H. Love, were killed. Ketchum, wounded in the shoulder, was captured with Lay; Franks escaped.

While Black Jack was in custody and awaiting trial for the trainrobbing his brother Sam displayed his own inventiveness by attempting to hold up the same Santa Fe train his brother had robbed four times. Sam was shot by an alert train conductor named Frank Harrington, but escaped to a nearby ranch. Blood poisoning set in and his arm was amputated. The surgery was badly performed by a cowboy and Sam died of shock hours later.

Though convicted of trainrobbery, Black Jack screamed his innocence while waiting to be executed on the gallows. He watched the erection of the scaffold from his prison cell with interest and when it was done called out to workmen: "You did a fine job, boys, but why not tear down the stockade so the fellows can see a man hang who never killed anyone?"

He had no words for the priest who came to visit him

Black Jack Ketchum, being executed for train robbery at Clayton, New Mexico, 4/25/1901. (Western History Collection, U. of Okla. Library)

on the day of his execution, insisting that he was "going to die as I've lived." When the warden asked Black Jack if he had any last requests, the darkly handsome outlaw smiled and said: "Have someone play a fiddle when I swing off."

Ketchum's bravado held up all through the ceremonies. He fairly ran up the steps leading to the hangman's noose and once there smiled broadly for the few witnesses standing beneath him. "I'll be in hell before you start breakfast, boys!" A black hood was put over Black Jack's head and from beneath that sinister-looking shroud came the outlaw's last words: "Let her rip!"

The rope did exactly that. When the trap was sprung, the tall bandit shot down through space and the poorly placed weights caused a terrific jolt, tearing Black Jack Ketchum's head from his torso. The outlaw's desire for self-inflicted punishment could not have been more devastating or final.

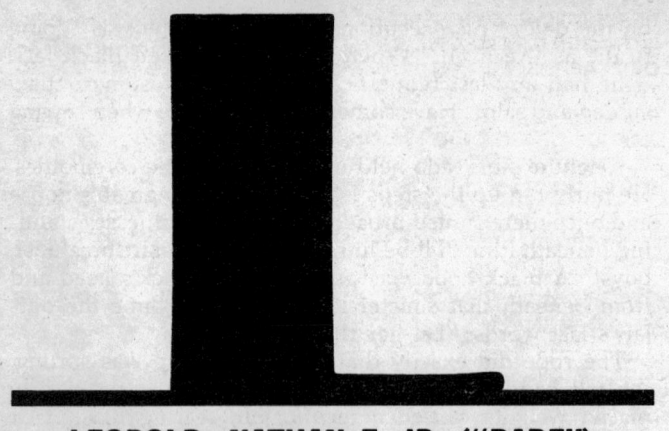

LEOPOLD, NATHAN F. JR. ("BABE")
Murderer, Kidnapper • (1906-1971)

BACKGROUND: SON OF MULTI-MILLIONAIRE NATHAN F. LEOPOLD, A SHIPPING MAGNATE. BORN AND RAISED IN THE EXCLUSIVE KENWOOD DISTRICT OF CHICAGO, ILL. GRADUATE OF UNIVERSITY OF CHICAGO, 1924, AT AGE 18. EXPERT IN ORNITHOLOGY, BOTANY, AND LANGUAGES. AUTHOR OF "LIFE PLUS 99 YEARS," 1958. DESCRIPTION: 5'8", BROWN EYES, BLACK HAIR, STOOPED, ROUND-SHOULDERED. ALIASES: MORTON D. BALLARD, GEORGE JOHNSON. RECORD: ARRESTED FOR KIDNAPPING AND MURDER OF FOURTEEN-YEAR-OLD BOBBIE FRANKS, 5/24 IN CHICAGO, ILL.; PLEADED GUILTY BEFORE JUDGE JOHN R. CAVERLY, CHIEF JUSTICE OF THE CRIMINAL COURT OF COOK COUNTY 7/21/24; DEFENDED BY COUNSEL CLARENCE DARROW IN BENCH TRIAL; SENTENCED TO LIFE IMPRISONMENT FOR MURDER PLUS 99 YEARS FOR KIDNAPPING AT NORTHERN ILLINOIS PENITENTIARY AT STATEVILLE, ILL.; PAROLED 3/13/58, DIED OF HEART FAILURE 8/30/71 IN PUERTO RICO.

LOEB, RICHARD A.
Murderer, Kidnapper • (1907-1936)

BACKGROUND: SON OF ALBERT H. LOEB, WEALTHY VICE-PRESIDENT OF SEARS, ROEBUCK AND COMPANY. BORN AND RAISED IN EXCLUSIVE KENWOOD DISTRICT OF CHICAGO, ILL. GRADUATE OF UNIVERSITY OF MICHIGAN, 1924, AT AGE 17.

DESCRIPTION: 5'11", BROWN EYES, BLACK HAIR, LEAN, ATHLETIC BUILD. ALIASES: LOUIS MASON, GEORGE JOHNSON. RECORD: ARRESTED FOR KIDNAPPING AND MURDER OF FOURTEEN-YEAR-OLD BOBBIE FRANKS, 5/24 IN CHICAGO, ILL.; PLEADED GUILTY BEFORE JUDGE JOHN R. CAVERLY, CHIEF JUSTICE OF THE CRIMINAL COURT OF COOK COUNTY 7/21/24; DEFENDED BY COUNSEL CLARENCE DARROW IN BENCH TRIAL; SENTENCED TO LIFE IMPRISONMENT FOR MURDER PLUS 99 YEARS FOR KIDNAPPING AT NORTHERN ILLINOIS PENITENTIARY AT STATEVILLE, ILL.; MURDERED BY FELLOW INMATE, JAMES DAY, 1/36.

In the spring of 1924, a Morton D. Ballard checked into the Morrison Hotel in Chicago as a salesman from Peoria. He was a short, stooped young man with bulging eyes and an even more bulging wallet. He was softspoken and a big tipper but he was no salesman and he had never been in Peoria. The wealthy youth was Nathan F. Leopold Jr. acting out the first stage of America's strangest, almost perfect murder.

Almost immediately after checking into his hotel, Leopold went to the Rent-A-Car Agency in Chicago and rented a sedan from its president, Mr. Jacobs, who asked for a reference.

Leopold was glad to supply him the name and phone number of one Louis Mason who was, in actuality, his friend, Richard Loeb. Jacobs made the call and Loeb gave "Ballard" a glowing reference.

Leopold then deposited a $50 security payment for the car and drove it around for a two hour test. He would pick it up when he needed it, he told Jacobs. Once back at the Morrison, Leopold had a lot to ponder about—he was about to become a murderer for no other reason than "intellectual" fun.

Born in 1906 to millionaire transport magnate Nathan Leopold, Babe, as the boy was called by his friends, had never been quite right. He was internally malformed with diseased adrenal, pineal, and thymus glands.

He had an overactive thyroid gland, was undersized, round-shouldered and a sexual deviate at fourteen, when he became the eager butt of thirteen-year-old Dickie Loeb's pederastic leanings.

This sexual abnormality was not developed solely by the two boys; Leopold had plenty of help from a sexually perverted governess. This sub-normal woman encouraged Leopold at an early age to practice sexual perversions on her which she, in kind, returned.

Leopold's parents showered him with gifts, money, and freedom, but they noticed his unwillingness to associate with girls. In their rank ignorance, they placed their son (along with the sex-crazed governess) into an all-girls school. To completely collapse Leopold's struggling normal sexual growth, his mother died while he was an adolescent. With his "Madonna" gone, the boy concentrated on studies, for where his physical and emotional deformities were pronounced, his mental capacities were enormous.

There is no doubt that Nathan Leopold was a brilliant student, perhaps a genius with an I.Q. of 200. By the time he was eighteen, he had graduated from the University of Chicago with a B. Ph.—the youngest ever to do so—was an expert ornithologist and botanist, and spoke nine languages fluently.

His family life was never as rewarding. Leopold lived in a loveless home and his father compensated for his lack of fatherly direction with a shower of wealth. Leopold was given $3,000 to tour Europe before entering Harvard Law School. His father also gave him a car of his own and $125-a-week allowance.

He still wasn't happy. He had devoured Friedrich Nietzsche, and the German philosopher's theory of the superman became Leopold's flaming ideal. According to historian Irving Stone, Leopold did not feel he could ever be such a superman so, instead, he longed to be "a superwoman, a female slave to some big, handsome, powerful king."

Leopold found his king in Richard Loeb, whose father was as wealthy as Babe's. As the son of the Vice President of Sears, Roebuck and Company, Dickie Loeb was given everything he wanted and even more. His weekly allowance was $250, far surpassing the monthly wage that most American men made at that time.

Where Leopold was brilliant, Loeb was clever. But where Leopold was undersized and withdrawn, seventeen-year-old Loeb was athletic, tall, handsome, a charming conversationalist. He, too, had his physical defects—stuttering, a nervous tic, fainting spells (which sometimes were interpreted as the petit mal of epilepsy) and a suicidal trend. Loeb, as his last grim days testify, was also a pronounced homosexual.

Intellectual prowess and egotism abounded in Loeb as it did in Leopold. Dickie, at seventeen, was the youngest graduate of the University of Michigan. He fancied himself a criminal detective and his dream had always been to commit the perfect crime.

Perfection for the boys was a joint obsession. To them it meant being above all others—which their station in life endorsed; they felt total immunity from laws and criticism—they were perfect.

Well, almost perfect. Both had insatiable appetites. Loeb's was crime; Leopold's, abnormal sex. These "moral imbeciles," as they were later to be called, played one desire against the next to reach their personal fulfillment.

When Leopold got down on his knees and begged his god-hero, Loeb, to satisfy his pederastic lust, he was, at first, rebuked. Then the ever-cunning Loeb had an idea.

He knew that Leopold's love for him would goad him into any kind of agreement. So Loeb said that he would be willing to submit to Leopold's sexual eccentricities if he, in turn, would agree to begin a career of crime with him. The two actually signed a formal pact to that exchange.

During the next four years, the two boys, always under Loeb's leadership, committed petty thefts, set fires, turned in false alarms, vandalized property, and even devised a system to cheat at bridge. All through this adolescent period, violent arguments took place. Both threatened to kill each other. Loeb threatened to commit suicide.

Richard Loeb's most fanatic dream was to commit an important crime perfectly. A criminal at heart, which Leopold apparently was not, Loeb insisted his sex-mate join with him in a last titanic act before Leopold went on an extended vacation to Europe.

To plan a perfect crime appealed to Leopold's Nietzschean bent. He wrote Loeb once: "The superman is not liable for anything he may do, except for the one crime that it is possible for him to commit—to make a mistake."

In this way, these two pampered, spoiled children of

vast wealth and twisted intelligence, groped toward murder.

For weeks Leopold and Loeb made intricate murder plans. They decided that whoever their victim was—his identity was of no concern to the youths—he would be kidnapped, killed, and then a ransom would be collected.

The ransom notes were to be written on a typewriter Loeb had stolen from his fraternity house at Ann Arbor, in November, 1923 when the boys attended a football game there.

Obviously they did not want to use Leopold's car for the abduction, so the Ballard-Mason identities were set up to rent a car. Further, under these aliases they opened bank accounts into which they intended to deposit the ransom money.

For several weeks Leopold and Loeb boarded the three o'clock train for Michigan City, Indiana and Loeb practiced throwing off boxes of the correct dimension and weight at places Leopold had selected (areas he had known through his bird-watching expeditions). This is how the ransom would be delivered to them.

On May 20, 1924, the boys drove the rented car to a hardware store at 43rd and Cottage Avenue where they purchased some rope, a chisel, and hydrochloric acid.

They planned to garrote their unknown victim, stab him with the chisel, if necessary, and then destroy his identity with the acid. So detailed was their plan that Loeb and Leopold argued whether or not to use sulphuric acid before deciding on hydrochloric.

The following day, the plotters met at Nathan Leopold's home where Babe took some adhesive tape and wrapped it tightly about the chisel for a better grip. They also gathered up a lap robe and rag strips with which to bundle and gag their victim.

Nothing was overlooked. Leopold also placed a pair of wading boots in the rented car. These hip boots would be worn while the victim was disposed of in a swamp the boys had already selected.

Each boy carried a loaded pistol. They read over the already-typed ransom note demanding $10,000 in cash. Although the last thing they needed on earth was cash, this would convince authorities that the kidnappers were from a lowly, money-grubbing station.

The only thing missing was the victim.

Quietly—what must have been the most macabre scene in the annals of American crime—the boys ran down a list of possible victims. First, it was suggested that they kill Loeb's younger brother Tommy, but they dismissed that idea—only on the grounds that it would be difficult for the older brother to collect the ransom from his own family without arousing suspicion.

Then they came up with little William Deutsch, grandson of millionaire-philanthropist Julius Rosenwald. But that was also still too close to home: Rosenwald was president of Sears, Roebuck and Company.

They almost agreed to kill their friend Richard Rubel who had lunch with them regularly, but they dropped him since they thought his father, a known penny-pincher, would not pay the ransom.

They shrugged. Across from Leopold's home was the Harvard Preparatory School, an exclusive institution for the sons of Chicago's wealthy. The boys decided to cruise around the school and search for a likely subject.

Loeb and Leopold agreed that their victim be small since neither felt they possessed enough strength to to subdue a strong child and one determined to fight for his life. Little John Levison was the boy they selected. They spotted him playing in the school yard.

Levison's life was spared through an oversight. The dedicated killers didn't know his address and where the ransom note could be sent. They drove away to a drugstore and looked up his address. When they returned, the Levison boy had disappeared.

Leopold spotted him across a field with his spyglasses (brought along for that purpose). As they followed him home, Levison vanished up an alley.

After more driving, Leopold pointed out some boys near Ellis Avenue. Loeb identified one of them, fourteen-year-old Bobbie Franks, as one of his distant relatives. The Franks boy was ideal for their grotesque plans. His father, Jacob Franks, was a retired millionaire who had made his mammoth fortune in the manufacturing of boxes.

Richard Loeb called to the Franks boy, who walked over to the car. He invited the youth for a ride but Bobbie said no. He must have felt some apprehension since he caught Leopold's cold stare and said he did not know the other man anyway and had to get home.

Loeb was smooth. He had played tennis with Bobbie several times and finally persuaded the boy to get into the car to discuss a new tennis racket.

Bobbie Franks got into the car.

Although at their trial both denied being the actual killer, Leopold was at the wheel of the car and Dickie Loeb was in the back, wielding the murder weapon (which he later admitted).

As Leopold drove northward in heavy traffic, Loeb dropped the idea of using the rope on the boy as being too cumbersome. Quickly, ruthlessly, Loeb lashed out at the startled boy, stabbing him four times from behind with the chisel. All of the blows were to Bobbie's head and he dropped instantly to the floor, gushing blood.

When Leopold saw the Franks boy go down, he gasped, "Oh, God, I didn't know it would be like this!"

Richard Loeb ignored him. He was all business. Even though Bobbie was unconscious, Loeb stuffed his mouth with rags. Then he wrapped the boy's body in the lap robe. As Leopold drove through twenty miles of heavy traffic, the boy slowly bled to death on the floor of the car.

While waiting for darkness to cover their body-hiding routine, the youths parked the car and had sandwiches. Leopold called his home and told his father he would return late that evening.

The boys then went to another restaurant and ate a heavy meal. After that they leisurely drove to the Panhandle tracks at 118th Street. Here a swamp drained into an open culvert, their prearranged burial site.

Leopold slipped into his hip boots and carried the Franks boy to the culvert through the mud. Both killers had stripped him. Loeb had poured the hydrochloric acid over Bobbie. Leopold struggled to shove the naked corpse into the pipe. He took off his coat to make the job easier which was to prove his "one crime . . . to make a mistake."

After stuffing Bobbie into the pipe with his foot, Leopold squished slowly back to the car. The killers felt secure that the body would not be found until long after they had received the ransom money. But in the deep darkness

Leopold failed to see one small foot edging from the culvert.

Parking the rented car next to a large apartment building, the killers went to Leopold's house. Bobbie's blood, which had seeped through the lap robe, now stained the car's upholstery. After hiding the lap robe in a yard, the youths burned Bobbie's clothes and typed out the Franks' address on the prepared ransom note.

Again in the car, the boys drove to Indiana where they buried the shoes Bobbie had worn along with everything of his made of metal, including his belt-buckle and class pin.

Then the confident pair returned to Chicago where Leopold immediately called the Franks home. "Your boy has been kidnapped," he told Bobbie's terrified mother. "He is safe and unharmed. Tell the police and he will be killed at once. You will receive a ransom note with instructions tomorrow." He hung up.

The following day, a ransom note signed "George Johnson" was delivered to Franks demanding $10,000 in old, unmarked 20 and 50 dollar bills which should be wrapped in a small cigar box, in turn wrapped in white paper and sealed with sealing wax. More instructions would follow after 1 pm.

Meanwhile, police had been notified through Franks' lawyer. They promised no publicity.

Leopold and Loeb went on with the elaborate preparations they had worked out the night previous while sipping drinks and playing cards till midnight in Babe's room.

The next day they parked the rented car in the Leopold garage and tried to clean away the bloodstains on the car seat. The Leopold chauffeur, Englund, saw them and the boys explained that they were trying to remove a stain caused by wine they had accidentally spilled.

Englund, who had no love for the boys, would later testify that Leopold's car never left the family garage on the murder night when Babe claimed he and Loeb used it to pick up two girls.

The boys took the lap robe to an empty lot outside of Chicago and there burned it. Driving to Jackson Park, Loeb yanked the keys from his typewriter. These he threw into the lagoon; the typewriter was thrown into another.

That afternoon, Richard Loeb took another train ride

to Michigan City, leaving a note addressed to Franks in the telegram slot of a stationery desk in the observation car. On the envelope he had written in long-hand: "Should anyone else find this note, please leave it alone. The letter is very important."

He then got off the train at 63rd Street and rejoined the waiting Leopold. Andy Russo, a yardman, found the letter and it was speedily sent to Franks.

Jacob Franks, however, would follow no more instructions. Bobbie's body had been found by a railroad maintenance man who spotted his foot sticking from the culvert. Police notified Franks who sent his brother-in-law to identify the pathetic little body. It was Bobbie all right and newspapers screamed extras of the murder hours later. The ransom was never delivered.

Then began one of the wildest manhunts Chicago had ever seen, witnesses and suspects picked up by the scores. Leopold said nothing, keeping to his room. Loeb, on the other hand, immediately got involved in the search, accompanying police everywhere and spouting his amateur theories about crime. Officers grew suspicious when he suddenly blurted: "If I were going to pick out a boy to kidnap or murder, that's just the kind of cocky little son-of-a-bitch I would pick," meaning Bobbie, of course.

There followed, much to the killers' apprehension, several discoveries. The typewriter was found, the keys to same, the bloody chisel wrapped with tape, and a pair of horn-rimmed glasses were picked up near the culvert where Bobbie had been hidden. Police traced the glasses to Albert Coe and Company who stated that only three pair of glasses with such unusual rims were sold.

One pair was owned by a lawyer who was in Europe. Another belonged to a woman. She was wearing them when questioned by the police. The third pair had been sold to Nathan Leopold.

Police brought both boys in for questioning. Each was gently interviewed in separate rooms.

Leopold was confronted with the glasses but he reacted shrewdly by saying that he must have lost them near the culvert days ago while on one of his bird-hunting trips.

Police Captain Wolff reported that it had rained hard

the past few days. How was it that the glasses were spotless?

Leopold shook his head. He tried to ward off the next terrible question: "He was a nice little boy. What motive did I have for killing him? I didn't need the money; my father is rich. Whenever I want money all I have to do is ask for it. And I earn money myself teaching ornithology."

The boy-killer then explained that he and Loeb had been riding around with two girls they had picked up—"May and Edna."

Pushing harder, Wolff insisted that the boys produce their girl friends. They could not. Then two novice reporters, Al Goldstein and Jim Mulroy, earned themselves a Pulitzer Prize. They obtained letters Richard Loeb had written on the stolen typewriter. The letters matched the typing of the ransom note. At that point, the youthful killers confessed.

Loeb broke down first, saying the murder was a lark, an experiment in crime to see if the "perfect murder" could be accomplished in Chicago. He then condemned, in a long tirade, Leopold's perverted sex habits. He denied being the killer; he said he had driven the car and Nathan Leopold had slashed Bobbie Franks to death.

Hearing this, Leopold said that he was the driver of the car and even posed, with police close by, in the driver's seat later as if to offer proof.

The boys were brought together. Loeb took one look at his partner-in-crime and stuttered, "We're both in for the same ride, Babe, so we might as well right together."

Leopold insisted that Loeb was the killer. Loeb sneered: "He's only a weakling after all."

Loeb's family immediately disowned him, his father dying two months after Richard was sentenced. Leopold's father went to the only man he felt could save his son. He literally got down on his knees and begged the greatest lawyer in the land—Clarence Darrow—to take the case.

Then both confessed the killing.

Darrow, accepted stating, "While the State is trying Loeb and Leopold I will try capital punishment."

For 33 days, Darrow, who knew there was no chance for mercy from a jury, pleaded before Judge John R. Caverly

Bobbie Franks being carried from his home by boyhood friends who served as pall bearers, all sons of wealthy neighbors, 5/25/24, four days after his murder. Richard Loeb, still free, was driving home and parked across the street to view this very scene. He commented later that these "small white faced boys" made him feel "a little bit uncomfortable."

in a bench trial. He pleaded his clients guilty and delivered one of the most eloquent appeals ever heard in an American courtroom.

He fought with all the vigor and brilliance in him, ending with: "I am pleading for the future . . . I am pleading for a time when hatred and cruelty will not control the hearts of men, when we can learn by reason and judgment and understanding and faith that all life is worth living and that mercy is the highest attribute of man . . . If I can succeed . . . I have done something for the tens of thousands of other boys, for the countless unfortunates who must tread the same road in blind childhood . . ."

Caverly was much moved by Darrow's pleading but he stated that his decision was based on the defendants' youth and the fact that the state of Illinois had never executed boys of their age. He sentenced them each to life imprisonment on the charge of murder and 99 years each for the crime of kindapping.

The judge stated that neither was to be paroled and that they were to be kept separate for the rest of their lives.

Though Darrow had won, he had to wait seven months for his fee (rumored to be $1,000,000). He was finally paid $30,000 by Leopold's father—the same man who had begged him to take the case—with the thankless remark: "The world is full of eminent lawyers who would have paid a fortune for a chance to distinguish themselves in this case."

Loeb and Leopold were sent to the Northern Illinois Penitentiary at Stateville just outside Joliet. Here, Judge Caverly's orders were instantly ignored.

The "fun killers" lived in luxury. Loeb's expansive cell contained rows of books on geometry and poetry, an expensive filing case and a large glass-top desk, plus toilet articles unknown to any other convict . . . except Nathan Leopold, who also enjoyed the same, if not more, special treatment.

Both men ate separately from the rest of the prisoners in the officer's lounge and their meals were cooked to their specifications. Their so-called cells were usually open and they had passes to visit each other at any time, which they did.

Leopold and Loeb washed in the officers' shower room and roamed outside the walls of the prison to visit Leopold's garden where they gathered flowers. They were brought bootleg hootch and jolts of narcotics at $1 a shot.

Special visitors could see the wealthy prisoners at almost any time. Both young prisoners were allowed to make personal phone calls from the prison storeroom at almost any time. Of course, it was the money.

Everybody, from guards up, was bribed. Loeb was the worst offender, strutting about the prison as if it were his country estate. He flaunted his homosexuality, attacking whom he liked when he liked while guards turned their backs.

Nathan Leopold, Jr. sitting on the floor of the Chicago County Jail's "bull pen," listening to a jazz concert, 6/9/24.

Leopold (second from left) stands next to Loeb before the bench of Chief Justice Caverly while being arraigned for murder. They pleaded "not guilty," 6/11/24.

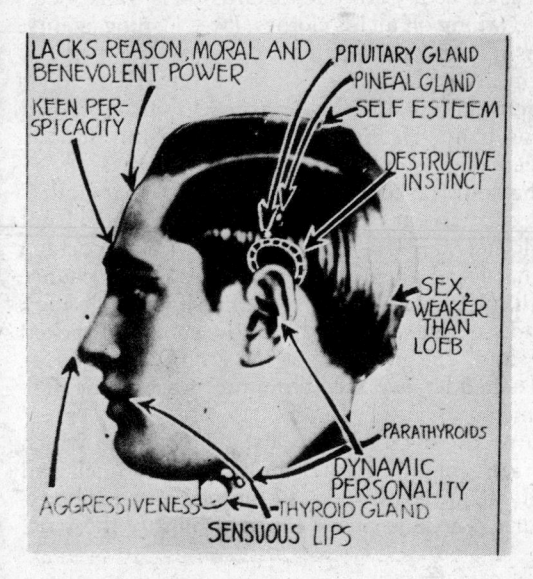

A bizarre photo diagram created by a Chicago phrenologist, which alleges Nathan Leopold, Jr. to be an intellectual "slave," 7/28/24.

Loeb spotted a young prisoner doing a seven-year term. The young man, James Day, appealed to Loeb's sexual lust and he began offering Day cigarettes and food.

Day finally got the drift when Loeb grabbed him one day in the prison library, telling him of his love and to be "broad-minded and be nice to me." Disgusted, the young prisoner pushed Loeb away and walked out.

From that moment, Loeb hounded the man. "I never had a peaceful day," the prisoner said later. "He was always after me. I became desperate. I had to get him off my back. I was looking for the right day."

It came in January of 1936. Day, after the bloodletting, described it in all its terror and gore:

"This morning after breakfast I asked Loeb if I could talk to him. Loeb was eating breakfast in his cell with Leopold. He said, 'Surely.' After dinner he came to my cell and said he was on his way to take a bath and I could see him in the bathroom.

"I went to the bathroom and waited. Loeb came in in five minutes and locked the door. He said, 'What is on your mind. Get it off quickly. I'm warning you it won't do any good as far as my attitude toward you is concerned.'

"He started taking off all his clothes. I was leaning against the wash basin. His back was to me and he bundled the clothes . . . in a towel.

"He got between me and the door and I noticed he had a razor in his hand. He had taken it out of the bundle. He said, 'Keep your mouth shut. Get your clothes off.'

"I knew the door was locked. Loeb said, 'Get your clothes off before I start in on you.' I started undressing. I got off all my clothes and left them in the shower. I decided to pretend that I had given in so I could watch my chance to do something. He followed me in the shower. He took two steps and stepped over the sill of the shower. I kicked him in the groin. He grabbed for his groin with his free hand and slashed at my face with the razor as he fell. He missed me by inches.

"I hit him on the neck with my fist. The hand in which he had the razor hit the sill and the razor hit the sill and the razor fell. He grabbed for it as I jumped over his body, and as he turned around at me I caught him by the wrist and throat and we fell to the floor together. He dropped the razor again.

"I grabbed the razor and jumped over him. He got up and swung his fist at me. It caught me on the left side of the face. I slashed at him. Blood flew in my face as he locked his arms around me. I remembered slashing at him as I fell back across the sill and felt the sharp sting across my left kidney.

"I dropped the razor. Loeb fell on top of me and he got the razor and caught me with one hand by the throat. Something told me that I would die there unless by superhuman efforts I could get out from under him.

"Somehow, I threw him off. He swung at me, laughing and saying I could fight when I had to. I got up with the razor in my hand. I slashed at him and he backed under the shower and turned on the hot water. I stepped in after him. Steam was in my eyes. I kept slashing.

"After what seemed like several minutes of fighting under the shower, he sank into a sitting position and in a funny way used two fingers of his right hand to push in some of the flesh of the abdomen, which was cut open.

"I turned to leave the shower. He started to get up. His eyes were big and staring. He lunged at me with everything he had. His hands were clenched like claws. I slashed at him some more and kept on slashing until he fell mumbling.

"I turned off the hot water. Turning on some cold, I stepped under the shower to wash off the blood. My whole body was red. I left the shower and wiped the water out of my hair and eyes. I heard laughter or a groan. Loeb stood straight up. He lunged at me and knocked me down. His body slipped over me and fell by the door.

"He got up and fumbled with the key. He ran out to the dining room tunnel. I did not see him after that."

It was one of the most shocking confessions ever heard and proved the Rasputin-like insanity that lurked in Richard Loeb.

Loeb didn't have the strength to run far. He had been slashed 56 times and guards found him sprawled in the corridor, his blood running as freely as did that of Bobbie Franks twelve years before.

Loeb's mother rushed to the prison with the family physician. Leopold stood by his lover's bedside. Loeb's eyes fluttered only once when he said, "I think I'm going to make it," and then he died.

When Clarence Darrow was told of Loeb's death, he commented, "He is better off dead . . . for him death is an easier sentence."

Leopold survived to live out the long years in prison and finally be paroled on March 13, 1958. He was allowed to travel to Puerto Rico where he became a laboratory technician at a local church. In 1961, Leopold married a widow, Trudi Feldman Garcia de Quevedo, who owned a flower shop.

Poet Carl Sandburg appearing before Illinois State Pardon and Parole Board in Stateville Penitentiary as a witness for Nathan Leopold, Jr. Sandburg supported Leopold's fourth appeal for freedom, saying that Leopold had been "struggling for the light for 33 years." The poet also stated that he would be willing to have Leopold in his home, 2/5/58.

When Leopold was released he stated: "I am a broken old man. I want a chance to find redemption for myself and to help others."

When Leopold was living in Puerto Rico and writing a sequel to his 1958 book *Life Plus 99 Years*, he gave an interview which pointed to the fact that he was still constantly hounded by the almost "perfect murder" he and Dickie Loeb committed those long decades ago.

"The crime," he said, "is definitely still the central part of my consciousness. Very often it occupies the forefront of my attention and I can think of nothing else. More often, it is not in the center of my attention, but it always is present in the background."

Nathan "Babe" Leopold died of heart failure August 30, 1971, in Puerto Rico.

Nathan Leopold, Jr., (right) waits for the plane that will take him to a $10-a-month hospital technician job in Puerto Rico after being paroled, 3/15/58.

MAFIA, THE

Of all the sinister and evil secret societies and brotherhoods—from the Thugee cult of India to Aleister Crowley's clique of devil worshippers—the Mafia has emerged as the most feared, the most powerful, and the most malignant. It was not always so.

The present-day Mafia is a vile perversion of a once patriotic and partisan secret brotherhood dedicated to freeing its native Sicily from the oppressive rule of the French Angevins in 1282. The Society's battle slogan, was, according to legend, *"Morte alla Francia Italia anela!"* ("Death to the French is Italy's cry!") The initial letters of this slogan formed the word Mafia and came to symbolize the violently anti-French movement.

For centuries the Mafia became a champion of its people, waging guerrilla warfare against the French and other invaders of Sicily. The island country's chief city, Palermo, became the hub of Mafia activities and from here the "dons" of the secret organization sent out recruiters to the country, culling from the land the young and ardent patriots who were taught the deadly uses of the dagger, the rope, and the sword.

Early members of the Mafia were experts at mutilating their enemies with the knife in order to extract information from them, a practice learned from Moslem invaders years before. Stealth, guile, and murder became the Mafia's stock in trade.

The early organization, strictly confined to those born in Sicily, absorbed all sub-secret societies in the country, including the centuries-old Camorra (although this criminal fraternity continued to operate independently in mainland Italy, its leaders vowing eternal blood feuds with the Mafia).

By the turn of the Nineteenth Century, the Mafia had evolved from a benevolent society which fed the starving and sheltered the homeless to a monolithic beast of prey that extorted money and power on a grand scale from both wealthy landowners and peasants. Its leaders, known as *capos*, directed its political destiny with businesslike methods, infiltrating politics, the police system, and even the small Sicilian army.

The brotherhood was and is organized along militaristic lines. Centuries ago, Sicily was divided into areas of responsibility by the Mafia, each faction accountable for a certain province and all factions answerable to the chief Mafia overlord in Palermo. The *Stoppaglieri* faction controlled Palermo and the province of Morreale, its rules enforced by a gang of young thugs known as the *Fratuzzi* (Little Brothers). The large agrarian province of Messina was controlled by the *Beati Paoli;* the province of Caltanisetta was dominated by the *Fratellanza* (Brotherhood).

Usually ten Mafia members constituted a unit. From these a *capo*, or leader, was elected through democratic voting. The *capos*, in turn, elected a chief of the province or "family" known as *capo famiglia*. The family or province chiefs then elected their Mafia king, or, as he would be known in the U.S., boss of bosses—*capo dei capi* or *capo de tutti capi*.

Naturally, the position of Mafia king became the most enviable and powerful position in all of Sicily. The holding of such power in Sicily mostly required the ability to make nerveless decisions and a steady diet; it was life-long. In the U.S., such a position was risky. Once elevated to this underworld throne, a *capo de tutti capi* had to guard against ruthless, ambitious Mafiosi who disregarded Old World tradition and pursued the position through the undemocratic process of murder.

For the first four decades of the Mafia's encroachment into the United States' underworld, Sicilian Mafia leaders considered the American chapter of the brotherhood irresponsible and perverted, since it paid little or no allegiance to its parent group. Ties today are much stronger, particularly through the use of the Mafia-controlled European drug traffic channeled into the U.S.

However, the *Mafiosi* who immigrated to the U.S. in the last quarter of the Nineteenth Century upheld the basic rules that governed the paternal Sicilian organization.

1. Reciprocal assistance to any Mafia faction in need without question.
2. Total obedience to the boss.
3. An attack on any Mafia member to be considered an attack on all members, to be avenged irrespective of circumstance.
4. No dealings with authorities in any circumstances.
5. The code of *omerta* (silence) to be maintained under penalty of death; the identity of Mafia members and the brotherhood's rites to be kept secret at all costs.

This fanatical credo was kept amazingly intact for five decades in America until Nicola Gentile, a Mafia member, disclosed the brotherhood's working apparatus in the late 1930s. Joseph Valachi was to do the same twenty years later when he outlined the Society's rites and pecking order. Up to the time of these revelations, the only hard core information provided to U.S. authorities about the Mafia came from the tidbits and scraps pieced together by outsiders, albeit the knowledge of an existing Mafia in America had been established as early as 1889.

Early in that year, on January 24, 1889, authorities of New Orleans came into contact with the evil operations of the Mafia quite inadvertently when investigating the murder of Vincenzo Ottumvo, a Mafia member. Vincenzo's throat was cut from ear to ear while he was playing cards.

Police Chief David Peter Hennessey suspected the existence of a powerful brotherhood in New Orleans after questioning several Sicilian immigrants who hinted darkly that a "secret society" had ordered Ottumvo's death. The puzzled Hennessey (who had an avowed dislike for all Italians and Sicilians) was further troubled a month later when investigating the brutal slaying of another immigrant, Giuseppe Mataino, whose throat had also been cut and his head shoved into the fireplace of his home and set afire.

New Orleans Police Chief David Peter Hennessey accidentally stumbled upon the existence of America's first powerful Mafia faction but was murdered by Mafia killers on October 15, 1890 before he could fully expose their operations.

Four months later Camillo Victoria was shot through the head by a bullet from a rifle poked through a window of his home one warm June night. Hennessey was plagued by citizens' groups demanding he solve the murders. The only leads his department developed ran to the existence of a secret society. Witnesses whispered in his ear and then vanished. For a year, Hennessey's detectives attempted to penetrate this organization but met small success.

Then, on May 1, 1890, Tony Matranga was shot and

wounded as he coaxed his horse-drawn wagon down Esplanade Avenue. Through this shooting, Hennessey learned that Charles and Anthony Matranga were the *capos* of the New Orleans Mafia faction. Tony had been shot by opposing Camorra leaders, members of the Provenzo family, who were hotly contesting the lucrative New Orleans dock rackets.

To learn more of the Mafia, Hennessey openly sided with the Provenzos and, when the case was scheduled for court in October, 1890, the chief of police announced that he would take the stand and relate what he had learned about the Matranga-controlled Mafia organization. Hennessey, like his New York counterpart, Police Lt. Joseph Petrosino, wrote to authorities in Palermo, Sicily, sending them names and descriptions of suspected Sicilian criminals residing in New Orleans. He learned, by return mail, "that more than one hundred escaped convicts are in New Orleans." Hennessey went on to state: "I am now prepared to break the Mafia in New Orlenas . . . The Mafia doesn't scare me. I will tear it out by the roots before I'm finished." The burly policeman never got to the witness stand.

Peter Hennessey was a tall, fearless cop who brazenly walked New Orleans' most perilous streets alone. He defied the underworld to molest him. Usually armed with two pistols, Hennessey marched down the middle of the street late at night, solemn, proud, a Wyatt Earp dangerously out of his own time.

Following this habit, Hennessey, on October 15, 1890, walked to his home around midnight. The giant policeman took no notice of the small boy skipping and whistling a few yards in front of him. As he was about to enter his home, a series of shotgun blasts tore into him. He turned and staggered down the steps, drawing his service pistol and firing at moving shadows on the dark street.

Wounded six times, Hennessey toppled to the ground. One of his assailants rushed up to him, knelt down, and carefully fired a shotgun charge into his back. With a roar, Hennessey got to his feet, blasting away with his pistol, lurching down the middle of the street. Several men ran along the opposite side of the street, following him like wolves and discharging blast after blast from shotguns, many of which found the target.

The raging battle was heard by another off-duty policeman, Captain William J. O'Connor, who came on the run. He found his police chief sitting on a curb, dying; his attackers had disappeared.

"Who did this?" O'Connor said, holding Hennessey in his arms.

Hennessey was close to passing out but managed to blurt: "The Dagoes . . . Billy, oh, Billy, they have given it to me and I gave them back the best I could!" Hours later Hennessey was dead.

The killing of Police Chief Hennessey served to be the undoing of the early New Orleans Mafia faction. It was a rule that local authorities were never to be attacked and the Mafiosi, out of fear that Hennessey would reveal what he had learned of them, had broken their own rule.

Nineteen Mafia members, including the boy who had run in front of Hennessey on the night of the shooting, Aspero Marchese, were indicted for murder. Their number was subsequently reduced to nine by the state—J. P. Macheca, Charles "Millionaire Charlie" Matranga, Aspero Marchese, Antonio Bagnetto, Antonio Marchese, Bastiano Incardona, Pietro Monastero, Antonio Scaffidi, and Manuel Polizzi (who confessed to the crime but whose confession was not accepted by the district attorney, who insisted on a mass conviction).

The grand juries that indicted these men studied Hennessey's elaborate records and came forth with a statement that shocked the country and made the ensuing trial the hub of national attention: "The extended range of our research has developed the existence of the secret organization styled 'Mafia.' The evidence comes from several sources fully competent in themselves to attest its truth, while the fact is supported by the long record of bloodcurdling crimes . . .

"As if to guard against exposure, the dagger or the stiletto is selected as the deadly weapon to plunge into the breast or back of the victim and silently do its work . . . The officers of the Mafia and many of its members are known

When several thousand New Orleans citizens stormed the Parish Prison on March 14, 1891, Antonio Marchese attempted to hide with other prisoners but was rooted out by the mob and lynched.

Mafioso Pietro Monastero, lynched.

Mafioso Antonio Banetto, lynched.

Mafioso Antonio Scaffidi was shot in the throat in the visitor's room of New Orleans' Parish Prison by an irate friend of Chief Hennessey's.

... The larger number of the Society is composed of Italians or Sicilians [it was not then known that the Mafia was an exclusive Sicilian society] who have left their native land, in most instances under assumed names to avoid conviction for crimes there committed..."

The astounding aspect of this indictment is that the organization was exposed in 1890, decades before U.S. Senate crime committees began their probes.

To determine the existence of the Mafia and learn its secrets, police and Pinkerton Detective operatives were placed in jail cells next to the Sicilians in custody. One, Frank Dimaio, a Pinkerton operative, was put in with the Mafia prisoners in the Old Parish Prison at Conti and Orleans Streets. He befriended Polizzi, posing as a convicted Sicilian counterfeiter under the alias of Anthony Ruggiero.

Polizzi was the most frightened of the Mafia group, telling Dimaio that the leader, "Millionaire Charlie" Matrango, wanted to kill him because of his nervousness. Dimaio convinced Polizzi that the Mafiosi intended to poison his prison food and the terrified Mafioso began to talk.

"Why me, Tony?" Polizzi asked Dimaio. "Why are they picking on me? I did a lot for them. They know that."

"What did you do for them?"

"Murder, Tony, murder." Later, Polizzi became more explicit, telling Dimaio that "we murdered Hennessey... They think I will betray the Society."

The widespread publicity on the case circulated by the local and national press had whipped public indignation over Hennessey's murder into frenzy. Thomas Duffy, the eighteen-year-old son of a prominent New Orleans businessman and friend of the slain police chief, took matters into his own hands, went to the prison, and asked to see Antonio Scaffidi. When the prisoner arrived, Duffy drew a gun and promptly shot Scaffidi in the neck, wounding him severely.

Arrested, Duffy was given a mild six-month sentence. "I'm willing to hang," Duffy shouted at the warden, "if one of those Dagoes die and I wish there were seventy-five men more like me." There were.

When 1800 more Sicilian immigrants landed on the

Mafioso Bastiano Incardona, lynched and shot.

Manuel Polizzi, Mafia member, admitted to killing Hennessey but his confession was ignored, the prosecution insisted on the conviction of all nine murder suspects being held.

docks of New Orleans days later, the town panicked. Coupled to the arrival of the immigrants (many of whom Mayor Shakespeare stated were known criminals) was the surprising fact that a jury exonerated nine men standing trial for Hennessey's killing. The nine, however, were still held in jail pending technical arrangements for their release.

Dozens of angry citizens formed groups and talked openly of lynching the nine Sicilians. Suddenly, posters appeared all over New Orleans asking "all good citizens to appear at Clay Statue to remedy the failure of Justice in the Hennessey case." Thousands of citizens did appear on March 14, 1891, at which time W. S. Parkerson, a New Orleans attorney and firebrand, mounted a tree stump and yelled: "When courts fail, the people must act!" Parkerson studied the quiet throng and then began to harangue the crowd with a loud and throaty speech.

"What protection or assurances of protection is there left us when the very head of our police department, our chief of police, is assassinated in our very midst by the Mafia Society, and his assassins again turned loose on the community? The time has come for the people of New Orleans to say whether they are going to stand these outrages by organized bands of assassins, for the people to say whether they permit it to continue." The attorney stopped talking and then exploded with: "Will every man here follow me and see the murder of Hennessey vindicated? Men and citizens of New Orleans, follow me! I will be your leader!" The mob roared its approval and set off down the street behind the fast-walking Parkerson.

First, the crowd broke into the city arsenal and withdrew weapons. Next, the mob stormed the Old Parish Prison, tossing aside what few guards were on duty. The cries of "We want the Dagoes!" echoed through the gloom-filled corridors of the prison. Captain of the guards, Lem Davis, ordered all prisoners out into the back courtyard. The Sicilians, housed on the second floor, were to be kept separate. Davis opened their cells and told them to "hide the best you can" inside the prison.

Of course, there was no place to hide. Marchese, Scaffidi, and Macheca ran to the third floor, hoping to hide with prisoners there, but they had been removed. Alone in the cell block, the three men were easily visible to the mob in the street who began shooting at them. Macheca was hit several times and killed.

Outside, a large black man came at one of the locked doors with a massive paving stone; the door was broken to bits on impact. Thirty of the vigilantes ran into the building and raced up the stairs for the prisoners.

Polizzi was found by a man named Ross, hiding in a doghouse the warden kept beneath a stairwell. He was dragged to the corner of Treme and St. Anne streets where he was quickly hanged. Dozens of armed men in the mob shot at him with rifles until he dangled lifeless in the March breeze. Bagnetto was next, hanged next to Polizzi. Eleven men (two of whom were not under the final murder indictment) were shot and hanged.

With the dead bodies of the Mafiosi hanging from trees and littering the ground about the prison, Parkerson once more addressed the crowd: "Mob violence is the most terrible thing on the face of the earth. I called you together for a duty. You have performed that duty. . . . I have performed the most painful duty of my life today. . . . Now go to your homes and if I need you, I will call you. If you have confidence in me and in the gentlemen associated with me, I ask you to disperse and go quietly to your homes. God bless you."

"God bless you, Mr. Parkerson," echoed the massive crowd. The good citizens of New Orleans dispersed and trundled home.

The New Orleans incident ignited international explosions felt in Italy, Sicily, and Washington, D.C. Though the White House chastised the residents of New Orleans for the lynchings, Italy was not offered a formal apology despite the demands of Baron Fava, the Italian Ambassador. Neither Parkerson nor any of his followers was ever arrested for the lynchings.

The purge of the Mafia in New Orleans far from stamped out the Society's growth in the U.S. By 1905 there were huge Mafia families in almost every major American city, with networks of communications connecting each faction. Outside of the usual vendettas practiced between the Mafia and its rival Camorra, there were no internecine battles inside the brotherhood until 1909 when a New Orleans grocer, Pietro Pepitone, shot and killed Mafia boss of the city, Paul di Cristina (nee Marchese) who was attempting to extort funds from him through Black Hand threats.

After serving six years in the Louisiana State Penitentiary for the shooting, Pepitone was released. The Mafia had not forgotten. A paid killer, known only as "Doc" Mumfre (whether or not his background was Italian was never learned) was sent to kill Pepitone. This was done in 1915. The Pepitone family struck back and several small-time Mafiosi were slain. Between 1916 and 1920 Mumfre, on orders from the Mafia faction, then systematically murdered, according to reports, twelve members of the Pepitone family, using an axe to bash in each victim's head. More than two dozen Mafia members met their violent deaths in this tribal vendetta which subsided when Prohibition was established.

Kansas City, not Chicago, became the Mafia's Midwestern hub during the 1920s. Capone ruled Chicago in those days and Capone was a Neapolitan and therefore a non-Mafia criminal who was never admitted into the Society even though some reported that he attempted to gain membership on numerous occasions.

Under Boss Tom Pendergast's protection, Mafia chieftains such as Frank "Chee Chee" DeMayo and Johnny Lazia (murdered in 1934) ostensibly ran the rackets in K.C. during the roaring Twenties. Vincenzo Carrollo headed the family until 1940 when he was sent to prison. Charles Binaggio's gambling and narcotics rackets alone brought him in an estimated $34,000,000 a year.

The real power in K.C. was Joseph "Scarface" DiGiovanni, who, along with his brother Pete "Sugarhouse Pete" DiGiovanni and James Balestrere, headed up the Black Hand rings, dominated bootlegging during Prohibition, and then controlled the narcotics traffic and gambling.

In nearby St. Louis, the Mafia throughout the Prohibition era was led by John and Vito Giannola and Alphonse Palizzola, whose family members were referred to as "The Green Ones" because its leaders immigrated from Sicily's farming communities. The Green Ones infiltrated labor unions and the food industry, levying tribute on every item sold in Italian and Sicilian groceries.

Once established, the Mafia battled openly with such independent groups as Egan's Rats, led by Dinty Colbeck, for control of the lucrative bootleg business in St. Louis. Dozens of bootleggers were slaughtered. The Mafia's favorite methods then consisted of stabbing their victims to death and working over the dead bodies with baseball bats. Many times the victims were dragged by the neck behind cars. Colbeck's crew was finally eliminated when The Green Ones arranged a police trap for the gang at the moment its members were enacting a mail robbery. The entire mob was sent to prison.

A gang called "The Cuckoos," a group of ambitious young St. Louis toughs, then took on The Green Ones in bloody gang warfare that lasted until 1930, at which time the Cuckoos were all but eliminated. St. Louis became a Mafia fiefdom.

The larger cities, New York and Chicago, did not come under the criminal control of the Mafia until after the Second World War. There were too many non-Italian, non-Sicilian gangsters, absorbed by the National Crime Syndicate at its inception in 1933, who opposed its domination. Neapolitans such as Vito Genovese and Charles "Lucky" Luciano also resisted a complete Mafia takeover during the period of their reign.

Not until Luciano was deported, Lepke Buchalter executed, and other non-Mafia gang leaders such as Meyer Lansky, Bugsy Siegel, and Abner "Longy" Zwillman were conveniently killed or shuttled to the sidelines, did the Mafia dominate organized crime in the U.S.

The last war of any consequence within Mafia ranks occurred in the early 1960s when New York gangster-brothers Larry ("The Blond"), Joseph ("Crazy Joe"), and Albert ("Kid Blast") Gallo, all members of the Joseph Profaci family, rose up against their leaders and forced many slayings. All three brothers were defeated while attempting to take over this family, which subsequently came under the leadership of Joe Columbo following the death by cancer of Profaci in 1962.

The date of the Mafia's complete takeover of the national crime syndicate was November 14, 1957, when more than 100 top Mafia members from across the country met, following Vito Genovese's order, at the Apalachin, N. Y. estate of Joseph Barbara. By then the American Mafia had relaxed its nationalistic exclusivity and Genovese, a Neapolitan, was elected *capo de tutti capi*. His image of power was punctured moments after the voting when state police raided the Barbara home on a tip that the gangster conclave was meeting there. The most feared criminals in America went dashing through doors and slipping out of windows, racing madly through the woods, shredding their $500 suits, and scuffling their imported shoes. Dozens were arrested.

Since then Genovese has died in prison and the old leaders of the Mafia families in New York have followed him. Ailing Carlo Gambino is now the Mafia's elder statesman in America, if not its boss of bosses.

The statements of long-time Mafia member Joseph Valachi, who turned informer in 1962 and disclosed the rites and existence of the American Mafia under the nom de guerre of *La Cosa Nostra*, presented few new facts about the Society other than the details of the Maranzano-Masseria war in New York during the early 1930s.

[ALSO SEE The Black Hand, Al Capone, Salvatore Maranzano, *Unione Siciliane*; Vito Genovese, Charles "Lucky" Luciano, The Syndicate, Joseph Valachi, *Bloodletters and Badmen*, Book 3.]

MARANZANO, SALVATORE
Founder of La Cosa Nostra • (1868-1931)

BACKGROUND: BORN IN CASTELLAMMARE DEL GOLFO, SICILY. COLLEGE-TRAINED, STUDIED FOR PRIESTHOOD EARLY IN LIFE. IMMIGRATED TO U.S. FOLLOWING FIRST WORLD WAR. ORIGINAL OCCUPATION, REAL ESTATE BROKER. DESCRIPTION: TALL, DARK, SLENDER. ALIASES: UNKNOWN. RECORD: A BOSS OF THE CASTELLAMMARESE FACTION OF THE MAFIA BEFORE IMMIGRATION; CONTINUED IN THIS ROLE WHEN RESETTLED IN U.S.; OPERATED VARIOUS ILLEGAL ENTERPRISES INCLUDING GAMBLING, ILLEGAL DISTRIBUTION OF LIQUOR DURING PROHIBI-

TION, PORTIONS OF THE ITALIAN LOTTERY IN NYC, BURGLARIZING WAREHOUSES; ORGANIZED RESISTANCE TO JOE THE BOSS MASSERIA IN 1930-31 IN WHAT WAS TO BE LATER KNOWN AS THE CASTELLAMMARESE WAR WHICH BEGAN IN NYC AND SPREAD TO VARIOUS OTHER STATES SUCH AS NEW JERSEY AND ILLINOIS; ORDERED THE DEATHS OF SEVERAL MASSERIA HENCHMEN 1930-31, AND MASSERIA HIMSELF ON 4/15/31; KILLED BY LUCIANO-GENOVESE MURDER SQUAD 9/10/31.

Maranzano held a deep grudge against members of the Sicilian Mafia when he immigrated to the U.S. following the First World War. The society had paid little or no attention to his Mafia faction in remote Castellammare; members from his district, including clan chief Maranzano, were looked upon as country bumpkins, hinterland primitives, incapable of ever assuming responsible roles in the organization's hierarchy.

Once established in New York, Maranzano gathered about him those Sicilian-born American criminals who, like himself, came from Castellammare, seeking vindication and honor for their Mafia chapter. A rank egomaniac, Maranzano was enamored and steeped in the life and times of Julius Caesar, a man who set for him an inspired example of benevolent dictatorship and whose death enacted unparalleled political fratricide.

Maranzano's aim in the American underworld was to bring the Mafia to dominance under a new code of ruthless ethics, strict organization, and the establishment of regimented allegiance to a super boss, a *capo de tutti capi*, a dictator, himself. He carried with him into the New World warped concepts of old-line Napoleonic honor which he childishly but eloquently foisted upon those who thought him sage. He demanded the practice of his high theories of crime, theories totally incongruous with the new breed of American criminals. Clearly, Salvatore Maranzano was behind and ahead of his time.

Though a Mustache Pete himself, a Mafia man filled with the Old World traditions, he advocated the destruction of all Mustache Petes in America so that his New Order of crime could flourish unhampered by plodding customs.

Naturally, the elimination of all Mustache Petes allowed for the existence of only one remaining Mafia patriarch. That man would be Salvatore Maranzano.

Maranzano busied himself during the 1920s with interests in gambling, bootlegging, and burglaries, which he directed from his real estate office in Manhattan. His gang of freebooters roamed the city, invading the territory of jealous gangsters, but he was tolerated as an ineffectual and aging Sicilian mob man merely trying to turn a dollar. Non-Italian hoodlums such as Owney Madden, Dutch Schultz, Waxey Gordon, Legs Diamond were unaware of his presence. Sicilian and Italian gangsters like Joe the Boss Masseria, Luciano, and others merely shrugged at his name—"Yeah, old man Maranzano. . . ."

With the rise of Giuseppe "Joe the Boss" Masseria as crime overlord of New York, Maranzano grew apprehensive. Masseria, on many occasions, had talked of his dislike for Mafiosi from Castellammare. Masseria also coveted the rich spoils certain Castellammarese men such as Brooklyn's Joseph "Joe Bananas" Bonanno and Joseph Profaci reaped from their Italian-based rackets. At the zenith of his criminal stature, Masseria declared war on them. The year was 1930 and the Castellammarese War, as the internecine battle would later be termed by informant Joseph Valachi, would cause dozens of gang deaths throughout the country, sweep Masseria's gun-wagging regime away, and establish a newly-constructed Mafia, much like the one that presently exists in the U.S.

Gathering such Mafia sub-dons as Profaci, Bonanno, Stefano Magaddino from Buffalo, and Joe Aiello in Chicago to his ranks, Maranzano organized and fought back. Death squads on both sides established machinegun nests throughout Manhattan and waited for their prey to arrive. Opposing gangsters patroled the streets daily, searching for each other and, upon confrontation, opening up with shotguns, machineguns, and pistols. The toll was excruciating.

Both sides suffered the loss of top men: Gaetano (Tom) Reina, a Masseria man, killed August 15, 1930; Joseph Pinzolo, a Maranzano man, murdered September 9, 1930; Maranzano ally Joe Aiello, killed in Chicago, October 23,

1930; Steven Ferrigno (alias Sam Ferraro), and Al Mineo, Masseria gunmen, killed November 5, 1930; Masseria lieutenant Joseph Catania (alias Joe Baker), murdered February 3, 1931; Joe the Boss Masseria himself executed by his own men at Lucky Luciano's orders on April 15, 1931.

Only upon Masseria's death would Maranzano make peace with Joe the Boss' lieutenants Charles Lucky Luciano and Vito Genovese. This done, Maranzano pompously called the members of both factions together in late 1931. He rented a large hall on Washington Avenue in the Bronx to which flocked more than five hundred gunmen involved in the war.

Maranzano, conservatively dressed in vested suit with silver watch chain dangling and wing collar jutting, looked more like a professor than an overlord of crime. He sat in a throne chair on the stage with a huge cross mounted on the wall behind him. "He had done this," Valachi stated, "so that if outsiders wondered what the meeting was about, they would think we belonged to some kind of holy society."

Once the phalanxes of gunmen were seated, Maranzano stood up and delivered an attack on the recently murdered Masseria, stating that Joe the Boss was destined to die because he had been "shaking down" Italians everywhere and because he had dared to declare war on the all-powerful Castellammarese, unjustly sentencing them to death.

"Now it will be different," Maranzano roared. "I will be your *capo de tutti capi* [boss of bosses]. New families will be set up and each family will have a boss and an underboss. Under them will be *caporegimes* [lieutenants]. The rest of you will be soldiers. You will each be assigned to a lieutenant. When you learn who he is you will meet all the other men in your crew."

The boss of bosses then outlined the order of command and explicitly pointed out that soldiers of this new crime federation must never go to the boss of a family without first seeking the permission of his immediate superior, his lieutenant. For minor infractions of the new fraternity's rules, each man would be judged by a tribunal and given punishment, such as being cut off from the Society's payroll for long periods of time.

There were cardinal rules in the new organization that could never be broken, unless a member wished to face death. For violating any member's wife, death! For talking about the Society and its secret rites, death! For talking to wives about the Society, death! For failing to obey an order from a superior, death!

Such crafty murderers as Luciano, Genovese, Thomas Lucchese, squirmed in their seats at such *ex cathedra* directives, but nodded approval just the same.

Maranzano concluded with: "Whatever happened in the past is over. There is to be no more ill feeling among us. If you lost someone in this past war of ours, you must forgive and forget. If your own brother was killed, don't try to find out who did it or get even. If you do, you pay with your life!"

Throughout the speech, Maranzano employed a term colloquially used in Castellammare to describe the Mafia—"La Cosa Nostra." Literally translated, it meant, "this thing of ours." The term would be one of the most closely guarded secrets in the Italian underworld for more than thirty years, revealed later by Joseph Valachi. The Cosa Nostra was, however, a term strictly used by New York Mafia members and was not adopted universally throughout the country.

It was really Maranzano's personal term, many concluded, and Salvatore Maranzano was to die in the same fashion he had ordained for others. Luciano and his scheming Iago, Genovese, had no intention of serving a boss of bosses (although they did later adopt Maranzano's five family plan for the New York Mafia as well as his system of authority).

Guarded only by a small troop of men, which included Valachi, Steve Runnelli, and the infamous Girolamo Santucci (alias Bobby Doyle), Maranzano became extremely vulnerable, although he felt confident of his authority after triumphing over Masseria. Luciano paid him lip service and planned his death.

The boss of bosses was not unaware of Luciano and Vito Genovese. "I can't get along with those two guys," he once told Valachi. "We got to get rid of them before we can control anything." His "hit" list also included Al

Capone, Frank Costello, Willie Moretti, Joe Adonis, and Dutch Schultz.

Thomas "Three-Finger Brown" Lucchese learned that Maranzano, not trusting the inner circle of his self-invented Cosa Nostra, had gone outside Mafia ranks to employ Vincent "Mad Dog" Coll to kill Luciano, Genovese, and others. Luciano was in no mood to wait for Coll to come calling.

At 2:50 p.m. on September 10, 1931, four men entered the Manhattan offices of real estate broker Salvatore Maranzano in the Eagle Building at 230 Park Avenue. The four men flashed police badges, asking for the boss. Bobby Doyle, who was sitting in the outer office, shook his head, as if nonplussed. Maranzano opened the door to his office.

"Who can we talk to?" one would-be policeman asked him, flashing the badge.

"You can talk to me," Maranzano answered and waved them into his office. Once inside, the fake policemen pulled pistols, but Red Levine of Meyer Lansky's troop—loaned out especially for the occasion—told the others that a knife would be silent and yanked out a blade. He advanced on Maranzano who surprisingly turned on him, hitting Levine several times. Levine kept plunging the blade into the boss of bosses, six times in all. Still alive, Maranzano cursed the quartet and dove for the three men holding pistols. They fired at the same time and Maranzano fell to the floor dead, his dream of being another Julius Caesar blubbering incoherently from frothy lips.

Levine, who watched, fascinated for a moment by Maranzano's death throes, then ordered the other three men from the room. Various reports identified the other killers as Bugsy Siegel, Albert Anastasia, and Thomas Lucchese.

When police arrived they found Maranzano dead of four bullet wounds and six knife thrusts. There were no witnesses. Bodyguard Bobby Doyle had fled after hearing the first gun fired. Doyle, Valachi, and other Maranzano guards went into hiding. Some did not.

Two hours after Maranzano's bloody execution, one of his lieutenants, James Marino (alias James LaPore) was shot six times and killed as he emerged from a Bronx bar-

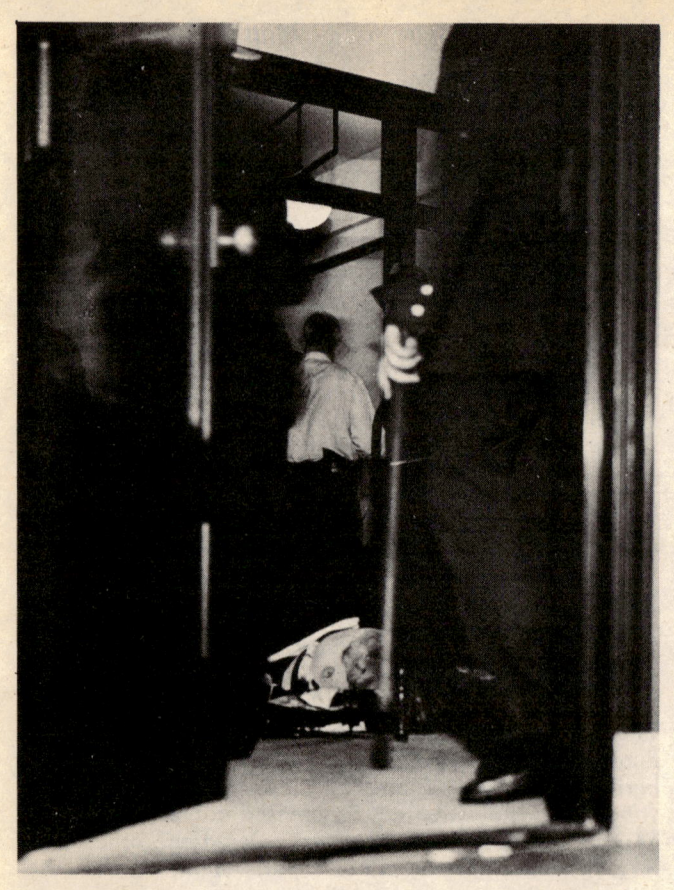

The knife-gashed, bullet-riddled body of Salvatore Maranzano, founder of New York's **Cosa Nostra,** lies sprawled in his private office, 9/10/31. (UPI)

bershop. Three days later, the bodies of two more Maranzano supporters, brutally mangled, washed ashore in Newark Bay. They were identified as Samuel Monaco and Louis Russo. Both men showed signs of horrible torture. Their heads were crushed, their throats slashed, and parts of their bodies were missing, hacked away as if by a cleaver. Valachi, terrified for his own life, heard, in gory details, of the twin slaying. He later reported that "Sam [Monaco] had an iron pipe hammered up his ass."

Luciano had carefully worked out the mass extermination of Salvatore Maranzano's allies throughout the country. The same day Maranzano was killed more than forty Cosa Nostra leaders were slain nationwide. They were killed in their beds, at lunch tables, in washrooms, on the streets, and sitting on their front porches.

It was the beginning of the modern era of organized crime and the end of the Mustache Petes.

[ALSO SEE Vito Genovese, Thomas "Three Finger Brown" Lucchese, Charles "Lucky" Luciano, Joseph Valachi, *Bloodletters and Badmen, Book 3*.]

MINER, WILLIAM ("OLD BILL")
Stagerobber, Trainrobber • (1847-1913)

BACKGROUND: BORN IN JACKSON, KY. MOTHER A SCHOOLTEACHER, FATHER A MINER. MINOR PUBLIC EDUCATION. RAN AWAY IN 1860 TO BECOME A COWBOY. BECAME A MESSENGER FOR THE U.S. ARMY IN 1863. LATER ORGANIZED A ONE-MAN PONY EXPRESS FROM SAN DIEGO TO POINTS EAST. DESCRIPTION: TALL, SLENDER, THICK MUSTACHE. ALIASES WILLIAM MORGAN, GEORGE ANDERSON, SAM ANDERSON, G. W. EDWARDS, CALIFORNIA BILLY, BUDD, OLD BILL. RECORD: ROBBED THE SONORA STAGE IN 1869 ($200); CAPTURED AND SENTENCED TO FIFTEEN YEARS IN SAN QUENTIN; RELEASED IN 1879; ROBBED WITH WILLIAM LEROY A HALF DOZEN TRAINS AND COACHES IN THE COLORADO AREA; VIGILANTES CAPTURED LEROY AND HANGED HIM; TRAVELED TO TURKEY AND SPENT A BRIEF TIME AS A SLAVE TRADER; TRAVELED TO SOUTH AMERICA WHERE HE RAN GUNS TO INSURRECTIONISTS FOR A SHORT TIME; RETURNED TO U.S. AND ROBBED THE SONORA STAGE 11/8/80 ($3,000); ROBBED THE DEL NORTE STAGE IN COLORADO IN LATE NOVEMBER, 1880 ($2,000 IN GOLD DUST); ROBBED WITH STANTON T. JONES THE DEL NORTE STAGE THE FOLLOWING YEAR; ROBBED THE SONORA STAGE 11/7/81; CAPTURED AND SENT TO SAN QUENTIN PRISON FOR TWENTY-FIVE

YEARS; PAROLED 6/17/01; ROBBED A TRAIN ALONE AT CORBETT, ORE., 9/23/03; ROBBED A CANADIAN PACIFIC TRAIN AT MISSION JUNCTION, BRITISH COLUMBIA, IN SEPTEMBER, 1904 ($10,000); ROBBED THE TRANSCONTINENTAL EXPRESS OF THE CANADIAN PACIFIC 5/8/06, NEAR FURRER, B.C.; CAPTURED BY NORTHWEST MOUNTED POLICE; RECEIVED A LIFE SENTENCE; ESCAPED FROM THE NEW WESTMINSTER PENITENTIARY 8/9/07; ROBBED A PORTLAND, ORE., BANK IN JULY, 1909 ($12,000); ROBBED THE SOUTHERN RAILWAY EXPRESS WITH FIVE OTHER BANDITS NEAR WHITE SULPHUR, GA., 2/18/11 ($3,500); SENTENCED TO LIFE IMPRISONMENT; ESCAPED THREE TIMES FROM THE GEORGIA STATE PENITENTIARY AT MILLEDGEVILLE; RECAPTURED EACH TIME; DIED IN HIS CELL IN 1913.

The criminal profession of William "Old Bill" Miner spanned almost a half century and three continents. At the height of his career as a robber he was a wizened geezer who doggedly refused to follow any other path than that of an armed bandit. More than thirty years of his adult life were lived behind bars, but imprisonment failed to reform him. He was still robbing banks and trains when well into his sixties.

After running away from his home in Jackson, Kentucky, Miner rode west in the early 1860s. He reached San Diego in 1863 just as a savage war between the U.S. Army and the Apaches broke out, and he soon became a messenger for General Wright. The hazards Miner faced while riding through hostile Indian territory convinced him that he should be paid handsomely. He agreed to deliver letters from San Diego citizens to points east for hefty charges that ranged up to $25 per letter. Miner accumulated a small fortune, which he promptly spent on liquor and women. He soon realized that to maintain his newly developed standard of living, he had to earn more money. There was big money to be had, he concluded, in robbing stages.

Alone, in 1869, he stopped the Sonora stage, getting $200. Miner had selected a poor mount, however, and the horse dropped dead from overexertion a few miles beyond the site of the robbery. A posse took him without a fight. Sentenced to fifteen years in San Quentin, Miner got out in ten for good behavior.

California was unlucky for Miner, so he rode to Colorado, where he teamed up with Bill Leroy, an experienced bandit. The two robbed several stages and trains, obtaining small amounts of money. Vigilantes closed in on the outlaws' camp one night and a fight took place. Miner shot three possemen who rushed him and fled into the night. Leroy was captured and hanged on the spot.

Packing his bags and loot, Miner took a leave of absence from crime and went to Europe, where he treated himself to a grand tour. He wound up in Turkey in early 1880 and, according to his memoirs, did a brief stint as a slave trader. Later that year he sailed to Rio de Janeiro and employed himself as a gunrunner. He then sailed back to the United States in time to rob the Sonora stage of $3,000 in late November. Days later, in Colorado, he stopped the Del Norte stage, taking about $3,000 from the strongbox.

Again Miner went sightseeing, this time to Chicago, where he met a young bankrobber named Stanton T. Jones. The pair rode back to Colorado and stopped the Del Norte stage, but the take was poor. They went away with only a few hundred dollars and a giant posse on their trail. At one point, the lawmen drew close enough for Jones and Miner to twist in their saddles and shoot three of them from their horses.

Miner returned to California, where his luck ran out again when he once more robbed the Sonora stage and was captured days later by a posse. This time Miner got twenty-five years in San Quentin.

On June 17, 1901, at age fifty-four, Old Bill was released. He tried his hand at various legitimate pursuits for two years and then gave up, returning to outlawry. His first strike was near Corbett, Oregon, on September 23, 1903, where, alone, he stopped a small passenger train and carried off only a few hundred dollars. Miner then decided to test his luck in Canada and rode into British Columbia in 1904. He stopped the Canadian Pacific express at Mission Junction and took $10,000 from the safe, a gigantic haul for those days.

Dressed in the finest clothes, Miner lived in the best hotels and passed himself off as a rich, retired cattleman. His money ran out in 1906, and on May 8, 1906, he again hit the Canadian Pacific, holding up the Transcontinental

Express near Furrer, B. C. It took the Mounties one month to capture him, and he was sentenced on June 1, 1906, to life imprisonment in the New Westminster Penitentiary at Victoria. In less than a year Miner had dug a thirty-foot tunnel from his cell to the other side of the prison wall. He successfully made his escape on August 9, 1907.

Two years later, in July, 1909, Miner robbed a Portland, Oregon, bank of $12,000. He next appeared in White Sulphur, Georgia, on February 18, 1911, and with several other men stole $3,500 from the Southern Railroad Express.

The railroad hired the redoubtable Pinkerton Detective Agency to track down Old Bill, and he was captured in a swamp by several operatives led by agent W. H. Minster. Miner received a life sentence at the Georgia State Penitentiary. This time, there would be no escape—not that Old Bill didn't try. Following his capture after a third break attempt, Miner was led through the swamps back to prison. On the way, he remarked caustically to one of his guards: "You know, I'm really getting too old for this sort of thing."

Old Bill Miner died in his cell in 1913, a recalcitrant bandit to the end.

MOLINEUX, ROLAND B.
Murderer • (1868-1917)

BACKGROUND: BORN AND RAISED IN NEW YORK, N.Y., THE SON OF A BRIGADIER GENERAL WHO HAD A DISTINGUISHED SERVICE RECORD, NOTABLY IN THE CIVIL WAR. COLLEGE-TRAINED. MARRIED BLANCHE CHEESEBOROUGH, 1898. ORIGINAL OCCUPATION, MANAGER OF A COLOR FACTORY; LATER A NEWSMAN AND WRITER. DESCRIPTION: ABOUT 5'10", BROWN EYES, BROWN HAIR, ATHLETIC BUILD. ALIASES: NONE. RECORD: POISONED HENRY C. BARNET IN 1898, N.Y.C.; ATTEMPTED TO POISON HARRY CORNISH, 1898, N.Y.C. (KILLING MRS. KATH-

ARINE ADAMS, CORNISH'S LANDLADY, BY ACCIDENT); CONVICTED AND SENTENCED TO DEATH AT SING SING PRISON AT OSSINING, N.Y., WHERE HE WAS IMPRISONED FOR EIGHTEEN MONTHS AWAITING EXECUTION IN THE ELECTRIC CHAIR; GRANTED A NEW TRIAL IN 1902 AND RELEASED ON A TECHNICALITY; DIED IN KING'S PARK HOSPITAL FOR THE INSANE, 1917.

Molineux was the product of New York society in the Gay Nineties. He flaunted his wealth, prestige, and power. He was an aloof aristocrat used to having his own way. When his way was barred, he chose the ungentlemanly art of murder to dispose of his foes.

The seven-story Victorian building squatting at the corner of Madison Avenue and 45th Street in 1898 represented everything opulent and powerful in New York. It was the exclusive Knickerbocker Athletic Club, which catered solely to members of high society.

One of these was Roland B. Molineux, age thirty, whose father, General Molineux, was a club member and had wangled his son's admission. Roland spent a great deal of time at the club, occasionally traveling to Newark, New Jersey, where he managed a factory that made color dyes, a family business interest.

A handsome, well-built man, Molineux was later described as having a "feline appearance." This, no doubt, stemmed from the fact that his movements were graceful and catlike.

There was something catty about his personality, too. Molineux was constantly plaguing the club's board of directors to get rid of certain members who displeased him. His charges were dismissed as the whims of an eccentric young man yet to discover his purpose in life, or, as the super rich of those days put it, his destiny.

But Roland would not be put off when it came to matters of the heart. A fellow member, Henry C. Barnet, who resided at the club, was courting a beautiful, young debutante, one Blanche Cheeseborough, a girl Molineux secretly planned to marry.

In October, 1898, Barnet died. The club's doctor diag-

Wealthy, aristocratic Roland B. Molineux, a prominent member of New York's high society in the 1890s, chose to poison those he didn't like; he died in an insane asylum. (N.Y. Historical Society)

nosed Barnet's death as being caused by diphtheria, but there was a great deal of rumor and mystery surrounding the passing of Henry Barnet. While delirious, he had mumbled to the doctor something about receiving a strange bottle sent by mail. The doctor ignored the remark. A few weeks later, Roland Molineux married Blanche Cheeseborough.

Weeks later, Molineux had a run-in with the club's athletic director, Harry Cornish. It seems that Cornish had bested Molineux in a dumbbell-lifting contest. Such public humiliations were unbearable to handsome Roland, who rushed to the club's board members, demanding that they put Cornish on the street. "Fire him or I resign," he shouted.

The athletic director stayed and Molineux quit the club. On December 23, 1898, Cornish recieved a bottle of Bromo Seltzer along with a silver holder generally used for toothpicks. Cornish thought it a joke, one of the members undoubtedly pointing out his need for relief at the height of a champagne holiday.

Cornish took the bottle home with him to his boarding house and forgot about it. When his landlady, Mrs. Katharine Adams, awoke on December 28, 1898, with a thumping headache, Cornish remembered the Bromo Seltzer and poured out a glass, giving it to Mrs. Adams.

"It tastes bitter," she said.

"Let me try," Cornish replied and took a sip. "Seems all right."

Mrs. Adams then gulped down the potion. To Cornish's amazement, his landlady suddenly fell from her chair in wild convulsions. He himself became so queasy that he barely managed to stagger outside for help. A doctor arrived, but could do nothing. Mrs. Adams was already dead. Cornish, who was taken to his club, was deathly ill for days but survived.

The club's doctor now remembered Barnet's ravings about receiving a bottle and went to Cornish's boarding house. There, he analyzed the Bromo Seltzer and discovered it was loaded with cyanide of mercury, a deadly poison. He called in detectives who virtually ransacked the Knickerbocker Club, much to the annoyance of its crusty members.

In Cornish's office they found the original wrapper used to mail the poison. Comparing the writing on the wrapper with the writing of club members, they quickly determined that Roland B. Molineux was their man.

A sensational trial ensued. The prosecution spent over $200,000 to convict Molineux. His father spent even more to save him. The young man steadfastly cried out his innocence, but his case was hopeless.

Fourteen experts testified that it was Molineux's handwriting on the package Cornish had received. Moreover, the prosecution proved that Roland had, before the poisonings, rented two mailboxes. One was in the name of H. C. Barnet. The other was in the name of Harry Cornish.

Using Barnet's name, Molineux, it was proved, ordered a shipment of Kutnow's Stomach Powder from a Cincinnati firm (the handwriting on this order was also identified as Molineux's). Roland, the prosecution insisted, had replaced the powder with poison and sent it to Barnet.

The prosecution also proved that Molineux had ordered a shipment of cyanide of mercury, ostensibly for his factory.

Roland the handsome was doomed. Though more than 500 persons, all males, were interrogated about their open-mindedness before the jury was formed, the twelve jurists carefully selected and screened by the defense found Molineux guilty, and he was sentenced to die in the electric chair at Sing Sing.

He sat on death row for eighteen months until he was granted a new trial on a technicality. The court ruled that testimony concerning Barnet in the Cornish-Adams case was inadmissible. While watching one condemned man after another walk to the electric chair, Molineux coolly penned a small book entitled *The Room With the Little Door*. It was published and was heralded as a minor masterpiece.

Shrewdly, Molineux's lawyers dragged their feet, stalling off the second trial, which did not occur until 1902. By then public rage had subsided. Witnesses were missing. When Roland Molineux entered the courtroom, he was the picture of a victimized man, suffering from the oppression of the masses jealous of his wealth and prestige (as would be the case with Harry Thaw), a sensitive writer of great talent whose attractive wife had been visited by unjust misery.

Molineux was relaxed and smiling in court. A jury, reportedly unconcerned with the real facts of the case, responded emotionally and set him free in four minutes, a record deliberation.

Life was good to Roland Molineux after that, kinder than he had been to it; he prospered and his stature as an author grew. Ironically, he became a writer for several newspapers, exclusively covering murder stories. Theatrical impresario David Belasco even produced one of his plays.

After Blanche divorced him, Molineux remarried. For a while his life appeared stable, but following a relapse, Molineux was committed to an insane asylum in 1913, where he died four years later.

A curious footnote to the Molineux case was his biography in *Who's Who*. For the years 1898 to 1902—the time of the poisonings and his imprisonment—the biographical sketch merely stated: "out of employment."

NELSON, EARLE LEONARD
Murderer • (1897-1928)

BACKGROUND: BORN IN PHILADELPHIA, ORPHANED AT AN EARLY AGE, RAISED BY AN AUNT. HIGH-SCHOOL EDUCATION. MARRIED A SCHOOLTEACHER 8/12/19, SEPARATED SHORTLY THEREAFTER. DESCRIPTION: 5'6", BLUE EYES, BLOND HAIR, STOCKY BUILD. ALIASES: ROGER WILSON. RECORD: ARRESTED AND CONVICTED OF RAPE, PHILADELPHIA, 1918, SENT TO THE STATE PRISON FARM FOR TWO YEARS; ESCAPED, 1918, RECAPTURED THE SAME YEAR; ESCAPED AGAIN IN LATE 1918 FROM THE STATE PENITENTIARY; MURDERED AND RAPED MRS. CLARA NEWMAN 2/20/26 IN SAN FRANCISCO; STRANGLED TO DEATH AND RAPED MRS. LAURA BEALE 3/2/26; KILLED AND RAPED MRS. LILLIAN ST. MARY 6/10/26; MURDERED AND RAPED MRS. GEORGE RUSSELL 6/26/26 IN SANTA BARBARA; STRANGLED AND RAPED MRS. MARY NESBIT 8/16/26 IN OAKLAND, CAL.; MURDERED AND RAPED MRS. BETA WITHERS 10/19/26 IN PORTLAND, ORE.; KILLED AND RAPED MRS. MABEL FLUKE 10/20/26 IN PORTLAND; STRANGLED AND RAPED MRS. VIRGINIA GRANT 10/26/26 IN PORTLAND; KILLED AND RAPED MRS. WILLIAM EDMONDS 11/10/26 IN SAN FRANCISCO; STRANGLED AND RAPED MRS. BLANCHE MYERS 11/15/26 IN PORTLAND; MURDERED AND RAPED MRS. JOHN BERARD 12/23/26 IN COUNCIL BLUFFS, IOWA; KILLED AND RAPED MRS. GERMANIA HARPIN AND HER EIGHT-MONTH-OLD CHILD 12/28/26 IN KANSAS CITY, MO.; MURDERED AND RAPED MARY MCCONNELL 4/27/27 IN PHILADELPHIA; MURDERED AND RAPED JENNIE RANDOLPH 5/1/27 IN BUFFALO, N.Y.; MURDERED AND RAPED TWO SISTERS, MINNIE MAY AND MRS. M. C. ATORTHY, 6/1/27 IN DETROIT, MICH.; KILLED AND

RAPED MARY SIETSOME 6/3/27 IN CHICAGO, ILL.; MURDERED AND RAPED LOLA COWAN 6/8/27 IN WINNIPEG, MANITOBA; STRANGLED AND RAPED MRS. EMILY PATTERSON 6/9/27 IN WINNIPEG; ARRESTED IN KILLARNEY, MAN., IN JUNE, 1927; ESCAPED, RECAPTURED HOURS LATER; CONVICTED OF MURDERING MRS. EMILY PATTERSON 11/14/27 IN WINNIPEG; EXECUTED BY HANGING 1/12/28.

America has never seen anything like him before or since. There have been killers who were just as methodical and who carried out their brutal murders with just as much religious fervor—but none had the transcontinental intensity that overflowed from the poisonous wells inside Earle Leonard Nelson.

He was a killer apart, a killer's killer, a mass murderer who worked from coast to coast with a Bible in his hand.

Earle Nelson loved God. He said he did. His words oozed with sanctimonious tones, and his Bible was thumb-worn and ink-stained at his favorite passages.

Nelson carried his Bible everywhere, especially when trying to rent a room from a landlady. It was a disarming device which worked effectively—so effectively that it cost eighteen landladies their lives.

Earle Nelson was a common-looking little boy when his mother died. The orphan was taken in by a kindly aunt, Mrs. Lillian Fabian, whose religious beliefs bordered on fanaticism and who constantly chanted that "Earle will be a minister someday."

Mrs. Fabian encouraged her young charge to read his Bible and say grace at every meal. His whole appearance exuded purity, from his sensitive, slightly quivering mouth to his unblinking blue eyes.

If it hadn't been for a trolley car, Earle Leonard Nelson might have lived up to his aunt's pious expectations.

While playing catch with a playmate one day, Earle raced after a runaway ball and was snared by the cowcatcher of a passing trolley car. The trolley dragged him fifty feet, his head bouncing on the cobblestones, before the car could be braked.

Aunt Lillian and Earle's cousin Rachel stayed at his bedside for five days as little Earle fought death. He recovered slowly, battered and broken as he was. His bones mended, but the doctors continued to worry about the terrible blow to his skull.

Six weeks later, Mrs. Fabian reported that Earle was "all mended and all well. The accident hasn't changed him a bit."

But had Aunt Lillian had the psychic gift to see into Earle's mind, her blood would have run cold. For the little boy's brain had been grotesquely altered, distorted into some unrecognizable blob of horror.

At first, Earle lapsed into sullen moods of brooding silence. He would take his Bible to his room and read it, underscoring passages.

Then he began pulling his cousin's pigtails so viciously that the little girl screamed in pain. At such times, a twisted smile would dart across Earle's mouth.

His aunt scolded him for this, and Earle, playing upon the naive ignorance of his guardian, would drop to his knees and plead for forgiveness, groveling and sniveling. He would then run off to his room and babble over his Bible for hours.

Nothing Mrs. Fabian attempted altered the dark course Earle followed. She began to find him peeping at his cousin Rachel through a keyhole while the blossoming girl was undressing for bed.

Even as a child Earle's hands had been big, almost outsized, and extremely powerful. In celebration of his twenty-first birthday in 1918, Earle Nelson used those massive hands to drag a neighbor girl to her basement, where he tore away her dress and tried to rape her.

Her screams were heard by her father, who raced to the basement. It took two policemen to hold Nelson after he was arrested.

Authorities no longer agreed with Mrs. Fabian that Earle was merely an odd young man whose peculiar manners and attitudes were the result of a tragic accident. He was dangerous, a powerful bully and a threat to the safety of those around him.

The rape charge was upheld, and Nelson was convicted and sent to the state penal farm for two years. Within a week Nelson escaped, only to be recaptured immediately.

Six months later, he broke out again, and police tracked

him to Mrs. Fabian's home. They found him standing in the rain, leering at his cousin Rachel as he watched her undress for bed through a bedroom window.

The penal farm couldn't hold Nelson, so he was transferred to the state penitentiary. But the penitentiary couldn't hold him either. He escaped on December 4, 1918.

After that, Earle Leonard Nelson disappeared and didn't resurface for nine years. Police files later revealed that Nelson married a young schoolteacher on August 12, 1919, using the alias Roger Wilson.

The young couple's marital life was anything but blissful. Nelson constantly raged at his wife over the smallest if imagined slights. He accused her of flirting with every male on the street, from salesmen to streetcar conductors.

Like a preaching prophet of old, he screamed in full public view that his wife was a woman of sinful ways, a whore.

The girl finally had a nervous breakdown. But she found no peace in the hospital. Nelson visited her there and, with vulgar expressions pouring from his mouth, tore the sheets from her bed and threw himself on her.

Doctors and nurses ran to Mrs. Nelson's room after hearing her screams. Nelson raved at the doctor for interrupting his carnal pleasures. Then he accused the doctor of having intercourse with his wife. Indignant, Earle left the hospital. His wife, luckily for her, did not see him again for seven years.

The next six years of the life of Earle Nelson remain a blank, a curtain of obscurity that has never been lifted.

Nelson stepped from this maw on February 20, 1926, appearing on the doorstep of a boarding house in San Francisco.

The landlady, Mrs. Clara Newman, watched the young man in rather drab clothes approach her front door.

"Are you Mrs. Clara Newman?" the young man asked. Mrs. Newman looked him over, noticing that he was neat, clean, and of medium build and had piercing blue eyes.

"Are you the lady who has advertised a room for rent?"

"I have three rooms vacant at the moment," Mrs. Newman said.

Something red-hot entered Earle Nelson's mind and caused a glow in his eyes as he watched the attractive

Mrs. Newman lead him up the stairs to the room. He ravaged her body with his eyes—the neatly turned ankle, the swaying buttocks beneath her dress.

On the third floor, Mrs. Newman suddenly felt the young man's arm around her throat. He yanked the struggling woman to him and grabbed the pearl necklace around her neck, twisting it into her soft flesh until she hung limp and dead from his arm.

As the pain in his head reached a white-hot-pitch, Nelson gave himself up to necrophilia and ravaged the dead woman again and again.

The murdered woman's nephew, Richard Newman, found her and rattled off his story to the police later that evening.

Richard had passed both Nelson and his Aunt Clara on the stairs as the landlady took her prospective boarder to his room. His description was limited because he had only glanced at Nelson: a man standing five-foot-six with dark complexion and blue eyes. That was all.

But the San Francisco officers knew something more about Nelson. He was a maniacal sex pervert with a taste for murder. From the looks of Mrs. Newman's ravished body, he had enjoyed himself and would want more of the same.

Nelson moved South and on March 2, 1926, struck again. Mrs. Laura Beale, strangled and raped, was found dead and naked in one of the rooms of her boarding house. Again, witnesses described a short, dark-complexioned man with strange blue eyes.

On June 10 Mrs. Lillian St. Mary was found ravished and stuffed beneath a bed in her rooming house. Sixteen days later, Nelson's insatiable appetite for sexual fulfillment through death was appeesed with the murder of a Santa Barbara landlady, Mrs. George Russell.

On August 16 Nelson raped and strangled an Oakland landlady, Mrs. Mary Nesbit. Then, for several months, he held back. Police thought that his sexual perversion had subsided.

But it had taken Nelson time to work his way up to Portland, Oregon, where he attacked Mrs. Beta Withers on October 19. The following day Nelson killed Mrs. Mabel Fluke. Both victims were boarding-house landladies and both were strangled and ravished after being murdered.

Police intensified their search, but that didn't stop Nelson from killing and then raping Mrs. Virginia Grant, also a Portland landlady.

Nelson's ninth victim was in San Francisco, Mrs. William Edmonds. He then raced back to Portland and murdered and raped Mrs. Blanche Myers.

Ten victims and still no clues. The state of California was panicking, and the heat was so intense that Nelson decided to leave the West Coast. He ambled across the Plains States, and before the year was out, he murdered and violated two more landladies, Mrs. John Berard of Council Bluffs, Iowa, on December 23, and Mrs. Germania Harpin of Kansas City, Missouri, on December 28.

With this last stop, Nelson added one more gruesome and perverted act to his ghoulish list: he strangled and ravished Mrs. Harpin's eight-month-old daughter.

Nelson's bloody trail can be charted by the bodies he left from coast to coast. He struck in the East on April 27, 1927, in Philadelphia, where he strangled Mary McConnell.

The berserk killer moved to Buffalo, New York, where he killed and raped Jennie Randolph. Then he swung back to Detroit and murdered Minnie May and Mrs. M. C. Atorthy on June 1.

While the entire nation was throwing dragnets out for the blue-eyed killer, Nelson moved to Chicago, where he murdered Mrs. Mary Sietsome on June 3. She was his last victim in the United States, and like all his other victims except the Harpin baby, she was a landlady.

Earle Nelson realized he could not forever elude the armies of police looking for him. He headed for Canada, and on June 8 he rented a third-story room from a Winnipeg landlady, Mrs. August Hill.

Mrs. Hill was impressed with her new and devout lodger. He even appeared at her doorstep carrying a Bible.

That night, sixteen-year-old Lola Cowan disappeared. Lola was widely known and loved in Winnipeg. The lovely girl sold artificial flowers made by her crippled sister to support their family.

On June 9, 1927, police began combing the city for the girl. The following evening, a Winnipeg man returned home to find his children at play.

"Where is your mother, children?" William Patterson asked.

The children broke into sobs when they informed him that she had been gone all day. In a quick check of the neighborhood, Patterson could find out nothing.

A devoutly religious man, Patterson went to his bedroom and knelt at his bed in prayer for his wife's safe return. After finishing, he glanced down and saw his wife's hand protruding from beneath the bed. He peered under and gasped in shock.

Emily Patterson lay naked beneath the bed, dead. She had been strangled and then raped after death.

George Smith, Winnipeg's chief of detectives, told his men: "I think that we must operate on the assumption that the madman who has been killing all those landladies in the States has crossed over into Canada. Mrs. Patterson had been strangled by a man with extremely powerful hands and then, after death, she had been sexually molested. It is the same pattern."

Someone pointed out that Mrs. Patterson was not a landlady, and Smith countered that the killer had changed his *modus operandi*. He not only had killed and ravished the Patterson woman but this time had done something he had not done before—he had stolen things: a complete set of Mr. Patterson's clothes, $70 in currency, Mrs. Patterson's wedding ring, and a Bible.

He had also done another strange thing—he had left behind his old clothes.

"Then we do have some clues," a lieutenant put in.

"The clothes he left behind were probably stolen from a clothesline somewhere," Smith said.

Smith kept his men working around the clock for the next few days, and issued bulletins all over Canada that the sex fiend had struck in Manitoba and was probably trying to escape from Winnipeg.

On a routine check of boarding houses detectives interviewed a Mrs. Hill, who denied taking in any suspicious borders recently.

"You're certain that no new lodgers have come to your house lately?" one asked her.

"None since Mr. Wilson last Wednesday."

Mrs. Hill described Mr. Wilson as "rather on the short side, dark, with blue eyes."

The detectives immediately realized that this matched the killer's description and raced to Wilson's room.

There, a thick and sickening smell greeted them. Mrs. Hill apologized for the odor and opened a window.

"Good God, man" an officer cried out to his partner. "Look here!"

Under the bed, they discovered the body of a naked girl. Her body was mutilated almost to the point of obliteration. It was the flower girl, Lola Cowan.

Mrs. Hill's husband, August, comforted his hysterical wife and then turned to the officers, saying, "To think that that fiend lay sleeping in that room for three nights with that poor dead girl under his bed!"

The dragnet that went out for "Roger Wilson" was the most desperate and intense in Canadian history.

But Earle Leonard Nelson was now an expert at escape. He showed up in Regina, 200 miles west, the next day and rented a room. This time, he went after a fellow boarder, an attractive girl who worked at the telephone company.

Her screams, as he tore at her, brought an alert landlady, and Nelson fled, police on his trail within minutes.

In Winnipeg Smith got the report and told his men, "my hunch is that he's trying to get back to the States. Things are becoming much hotter in Canada than he had anticipated. If he's heading for the border, he'll have to cross prairie country. That should make him easy to spot."

Smith was right, and for the first time police began closing in on the most murderous strangler on the American continent.

Two constables, Grey and Sewell, on the alert for the strangler, were patrolling twelve miles north of the international border, outside the small farming community of Killarney.

There they saw a man walking leisurely down the roadway. He wore a plaid shirt and corduroy pants.

Pulling up alongside of him, the officers asked him who he was.

"My name is Wilson. I'm a stock hand and I work on a ranch near here."

"We're looking for a man who is responsible for the deaths of twenty women," Constable Grey blurted. He watched for some telltale sign from the stranger in the road.

A loud laugh greeted him as Nelson coolly said, "I only do my lady-killing on Saturday nights."

"I think you'd better ride back to Killarney with us," Grey said, "so we can check on your story."

Nelson was nonchalant. "That's fair enough. I guess you fellows have to play it safe when there's a killer on the loose."

Constables Grey and Sewell locked Nelson in the small local jail. They handcuffed him to the bars of his cell and took away his shoes. Then they called Chief Smith in Winnipeg.

Sewell thought they had the wrong man and told Smith so as he and Grey stood in the telephone office. "He sure looks like he might be the killer but he says that his name is Roger Wilson and he works on a ranch near here. Besides that, he is just too calm to be guilty of anything."

Smith exploded. "That must be the strangler!" he shouted wildly at Sewell. "He used the name Roger Wilson here in Winnipeg and once before in San Francisco. It may be a coincidence but I am coming down there to question the man. Is Constable Grey with him now?"

"No, sir. He's here with me in the telephone office."

"What! Don't let that man out of your sight! I want one of you with him at all times! And don't be taken in by his calmness and innocent appearance. Remember, twenty women are now dead because they made the same mistake."

It was only fifteen minutes since the constables had locked up Nelson, but when they rushed back to the jail, he was gone. He had picked the locks from the handcuffs and the jail doors.

A 500-man posse was quickly formed, and all the women

of Killarney were locked safely behind doors. Chief Smith sent detectives to the area by plane, and he led fifty men to the isolated village on the next train.

While the frantic search for Nelson went on, he was sleeping like a baby in William Allen's barn, only one block from the jail.

Nelson rose in the morning and calmly walked to the train station. He lounged in the waiting room until the morning express came into view.

With the air of a man confident of escape, Nelson walked slowly to the train. Just as he was about to board it, dozens of men rushed down the steps of the car, Chief Smith pointing out their target.

With his hands bent behind his back, the powerful little man was led away.

Nelson faced trial in Winnipeg for the murder of Mrs. Patterson. All through the damning testimony, the brutal killer displayed not the slightest bit of emotion. His blue eyes gazed in a stare at some inner vision and a smile played subtly about his lips.

Earle Leonard Nelson (center), who made a habit of strangling landladies in the late 1920s.

His aunt and wife came to visit him in Winnipeg, but he only stared blankly at them, saying nothing.

A verdict of guilty was brought in on November 14, 1927, and he was condemned to death.

Earle Leonard Nelson mounted thirteen steps to the gallows on January 12, 1928. He stood on the gallows, and just before the hangman lowered the black hood over his sensitive face, he broke his strange silence.

His voice was high-pitched, the words tumbling and joining rapidly: "I am innocent. I stand innocent before God and man. I forgive those who have wronged me and ask forgiveness of those I have injured. God have mercy!"

The hood went down, the trap snapped open, and Earle Nelson swung into space.

NELSON, GEORGE ("BABY FACE")
Murderer, Bankrobber • (1908-1934)

BACKGROUND: BORN IN CHICAGO AS LESTER GILLIS. MINOR PUBLIC EDUCATION. MARRIED HELEN WAWZYNAK, 1928. **DESCRIPTION:** 5'4¾", BLUE EYES, LIGHT-BROWN HAIR, STOCKY BUILD. **ALIASES:** GEORGE NELSON, BABY FACE NELSON, ALEX GILLIS, LESTER GILES, "BIG GEORGE," "NELSON," "JIMMIE." **RECORD:** ROBBED A CHICAGO, ILL., JEWELRY STORE 1/15/31; ARRESTED DAYS LATER BY CHICAGO POLICE; TRIED, CONVICTED, AND SENTENCED TO ONE YEAR TO LIFE AT THE STATE PENITENTIARY IN JOLIET (INMATE 5437); ESCAPED 2/17/32; ROBBED WITH TOMMY CARROLL AND EDDIE GREEN SMALL-TOWN BANKS IN IOWA, NEBRASKA, AND WISCONSIN DURING 1933; SHOT AND KILLED ST. PAUL, MINN., RESIDENT, THEODORE KIDDER, MARCH, 1934; ROBBED TWO BANKS EARLY IN 1934 WITH JOHN DILLINGER; SHOT AND KILLED FBI AGENT W. CARTER BAUM NEAR LITTLE BOHEMIA LODGE, RHINELANDER, WIS., 4/23/34; SHOT AND KILLED FBI AGENTS HERMAN HOLLIS AND SAM COWLEY 11/27/34 NEAR FOX RIVER GROVE, ILL., AT WHICH TIME NELSON WAS ALSO KILLED.

Lester Gillis looked innocent from the day he was born in 1908 next to the reeking Chicago stockyards.

He grew up tough in the Chicago street gangs, but his height was always a source of agitation to him. Snubbed, bullied, and beaten as a boy, Lester wanted recognition more than anything in the world. He got it—as the most bloodthirsty, death-seeking bandit of the Public Enemy Era.

His fame came to him under another name—Baby Face Nelson. As one criminal historian put it, he "was something out of a bad dream." Nightmare would be more apt. Where outlaws such as Pretty Boy Floyd and the Barkers would kill to protect themselves when cornered, Nelson went out of his way to murder—he loved it.

Lester strutted a lot, and his angelic, pear-smooth face never betrayed his instant ability to kill. He wanted to be known as "Big George Nelson," but the underworld called him "Baby Face"—though never, never to his face.

Baby Face learned how to make a fast buck the easy way. He graduated from petty thieving to sticking up brothels and bookie joints and then selling the same establishments protection against his own trespassing.

While working his heist and protection rackets in 1928, he met a petite girl named Helen Wawzynak. She was selling hardware in a Chicago Woolworth's store. He said she was his "Million Dollar Baby from the Five and Ten Cent Store."

By 1929 Nelson was working for the racket czar Al Capone. His specialty was labor relations. He could always be counted on to line up labor unions to kick back part of their union dues to gangsters.

Sometimes he got too ambitious and his usually severe beating of a balking labor leader turned into murder. It was all the same to Baby Face.

His strong-arm tactics were finally too much for syndicate operators, and he was dropped from the muster rolls of reliable gunmen in 1931. He went back to his old heist trade, but was apprehended that year for a jewelry store robbery.

Joilet prison couldn't hold Nelson, and he made his escape, running out of Illinois all the way to the West

George "Baby Face" Nelson, berserk bankrobber who killed three FBI agents in 1934. (UPI)

Coast. Once there, Baby Face went to work as a gunman for bootleg boss Joe Parente.

Nelson's right-hand man was John Paul Chase, who chauffered, ran errands, and cleaned up after him. Chase wasn't too bright, but Nelson thought he could count on him. He was loyal.

Nelson left California in 1932 and headed for an underworld gathering place, Long Beach, Indiana, to recruit a bankbusting mob. After Chase, his first member was topnotch machine gunner Tommy Carroll, a light-hearted character who had once been a promising boxer.

Eddie Green, known in the trade as a "jugmarker"—the man who picked and scouted a bank marked for robbery—also joined Nelson. These men were professionals. They had robbed banks all over the Midwest.

With these men, Nelson hit banks in Iowa, Nebraska, and Wisconsin during the fall and winter of 1933.

The take was good, but Nelson was outraged because the publicity mistakenly went to others. All of his jobs were attributed to the Dillinger gang or to Pretty Boy Floyd.

Baby Face felt credit should be given where credit was due. Although he admired the work of the levelheaded Dillinger, he also hated him because of Dillinger's publicity and the impressive rewards offered for his capture.

Dillinger was too big to overshadow, Nelson figured, so he went to John's right-hand man, Homer Van Meter, and asked if Dillinger needed another gun.

"We don't know you, Nelson," Van Meter told him. "And we don't trust you."

The story was different the following February, when Van Meter and John Hamilton were the only Dillinger gangsters still at large. The "Super Gang" that Dillinger had led through several bank robberies had broken up.

Bank-busters Harry Pierpont, Charles Makley, and Russell Clark were all in custody in Ohio. Dillinger himself was languishing in the so-called escape-proof Crown Point Jail in Indiana.

This time, Van Meter and Hamilton went to Nelson. They were now interested in a merger. "Johnny's breaking out of that tin can soon," Van Meter explained. "Do you have any big action for us?"

"Yeah," the bantam rooster replied. "Eddie Green has marked two jugs in Sioux Falls, South Dakota, and Mason City, Iowa. Big dough there." Nelson gave Van Meter and Hamilton the once over, squinted his eyes, and then said, "Can Dillinger take orders?"

"Why you little . . ."

"They're my men and my jobs," Nelson said, stopping Hamilton.

"Johnny will go along with it," Van Meter said diplomatically.

Little did John Dillinger realize what he was in for when he broke out of Crown Point in early March, 1934, and joined Nelson in St. Paul.

When the five men met in Nelson's hotel room, the

runty gangster was obviously star-struck by Dillinger. He covered this up by delivering an insane diatribe on robbing banks.

His theory was basically to roar into a bank, shoot everybody in sight, and then roar out of town, guns blazing.

Van Meter laughed at him, and Nelson went for his machinegun. Only Dillinger's cool presence prevented the two of them from killing each other.

The following day Dillinger was in a car with Nelson as they traveled to Van Meter's room. Nelson, always a poor driver, hit another car in an intersection.

The other driver, Theodore Kidder, jumped from his auto and ran back to Nelson. "Are you blind?" he raged. "You had a stop sign . . ."

Baby Face's gun was already drawn. He sent a .45 slug into Kidder's head right between the eyes, killing him instantly. Then he backed up wildly and roared off.

"Did you have to do that?" Dillinger said.

"Hell, yes!" Baby Face yelled hysterically. "He recognized you."

"Well, a citizen got your number back there," Dillinger said. This threw Nelson into a frenzy of curses.

Baby Face's temperament didn't improve. On March 6, 1934, just three days after his Crown Point break, Dillinger, with Nelson, Hamilton, Van Meter, Green, and Carroll, hit the bank in Sioux Falls, South Dakota.

Though the take was slightly under $50,000, it was a disaster. Dillinger was astounded at the insanity Nelson displayed. No sooner were they in the bank than a teller nudged a security button which touched off a loud, clanging burglar alarm.

Nelson went berserk. While Dillinger, Van Meter, and Green emptied the cages, they could hear the banty outlaw scream over and over again, "I'm gonna kill the bastard who hit that alarm!"

Nelson's attention was distracted by an off-duty policeman who sauntered by a window. Baby Face hurled himself over a railing, jumped on a desk, and blasted four quick shots through a window. The cop fell dead.

"I got one of them! I got one of them!" Nelson yelled in glee.

It was a typical Dillinger getaway, with hostages crowded

onto the running boards of his car and roofing nails strewn behind on the road.

The next bank, in Mason City, Iowa, was another setting for Nelson's lunatic tantrums. Here, after the outlaws had scooped up $52,000, Baby Face wounded the bank's vice president and was only stopped from killing him by Dillinger.

After weeks of running in separate directions, Dillinger collected his gang at the Little Bohemia Resort in northern Wisconsin. On a tip, federal agents raided the place on April 22, 1934. Everybody ran for it but Nelson.

He traded shots with several FBI men and then, ignoring the escape plan, ran the wrong way to Koerner's Resort. Just as he was about to steal Koerner's car, a coupe containing two G-men and a constable roared into the lot.

Nelson leaped from Koerner's car and ran over to the coupe. He held two .45s in his hands. As the agents started to get out, he yelled: "I know you bastards wear bulletproof vests so I'll give it to you high and low!" He emptied his guns into them, killing Special Agent H. Carter Baum.

He then hopped into the agents' car and drove off at high speed, first to hide out on an Indian reservation, then to find his way back to expensive hideouts in Chicago.

After the Biograph shooting in Chicago in which Dillinger was claimed to have been killed, Nelson went to California to cool off.

He was now Public Enemy Number One, but it made him crazy to think that the reward on his head was a lot less than that offered for Dillinger. He'd fix that, he told John Paul Chase. He would go back to the Midwest and really give the yokels something to remember.

Nelson planned to rob a bank a day for a month! But Tommy Carroll was dead, killed in a gunfight in Waterloo, Iowa. Eddie Green was also dead in St. Paul, Minnesota, at the hands of G-men. John Hamilton was dead, too, in an Illinois quarry, his body almost destroyed by acid to avoid identification. In August, 1934, Homer Van Meter was caught in a St. Paul blind alley and riddled with fifty bullets. Nelson was on his own.

With only John Paul Chase and his wife, Baby Face returned to the Midwest in September, 1934. He skidded about, hotter than burning griddlecakes. The underworld wanted nothing to do with him. "Die," they told him.

Two FBI agents—Sam Cowley and Herman Hollis—spotted Nelson's car on November 27, 1934, along a lonely country road near Fox River Grove, Illinois. Then began a wild chase with bullets flying from both cars.

Just outside Barrington, Baby Face braked his car. Helen ran into a nearby field to hide. Nelson jumped out with his trusty machine gun. Chase had a BAR.

The FBI car halted, too, and one of the wildest gun battles in modern crime history ensued.

Hollis crouched behind the FBI car with a shotgun, and Cowley threw himself into a ditch, his machine gun ready. Then everyone opened up. Highway-construction workers nearby belly-flopped to the ground as the air was suddenly thick with bullets.

After several minutes, Nelson got disgusted. He swung his machine gun to his hip, stood up, and told Chase, "I'm going over there and get those bastards!"

When the construction workers looked up, their eyes almost popped as they watched Nelson walking casually toward the two G-men, his Thompson spitting death.

"It was just like Jimmy Cagney," one of the workers breathlessly recalled later. "I never seen nothin' like it. That fellow just came right a-comin' at them two lawmen and they must a hit 'im plenty, but nothin' was gonna stop that fellow."

As Nelson plodded forward, Cowley sprayed him several times with his own machinegun. But he did keep coming, like a man in a dream, walking and firing. He reached the ditch where Cowley was and fired directly down at him, almost cutting him in half.

Then he turned and went after Agent Hollis, who pumped several rounds from his shotgun into Nelson's legs. The little gangster walked on, firing short bursts. "Come on, you yellow-belly sonofabitch!" he screamed, delirious. "Come and get it."

Hollis threw down his empty shotgun and ran for the cover of a telephone pole, drawing his pistol.

He emptied his gun at Baby Face, who seemed to grin as he walked forward. One long burst from his machine gun cut Hollis down like a cracked sapling.

Almost as calmly, Nelson went back to the G-men's car,

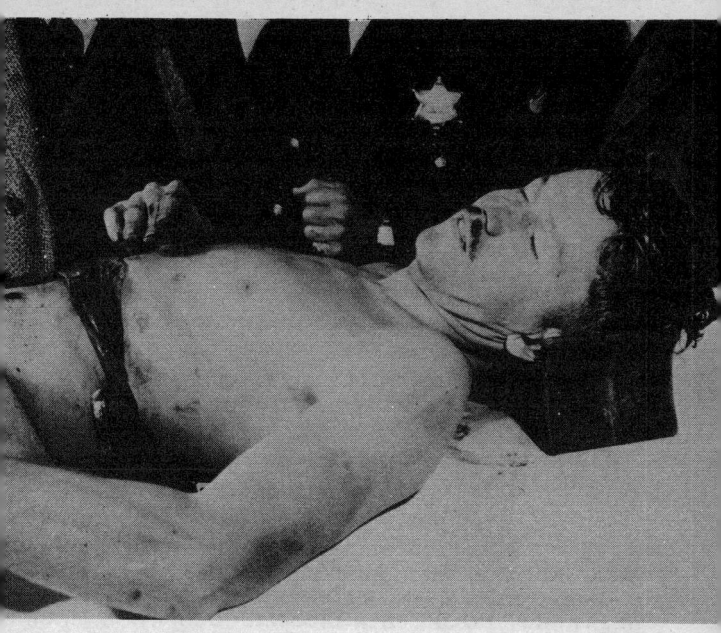

Nelson's naked and bullet-torn body was found on a deserted country road in Illinois, 11/27/34, where his wife and best friend had left him. (UPI)

staggering the last few steps. Chase and Helen joined him, and as they piled in, Nelson said, "You'll have to drive. I'm hit." There were seventeen slugs in him.

Baby Face's shredded body was found the next day in a ditch near Niles, Illinois. Chase had stripped him naked to avoid immediate identification. It didn't matter. John Paul Chase was taken a month later and so was Helen Gillis.

Chase is still in a federal penitentiary today. Helen Gillis, alias Mrs. George "Baby Face" Nelson, did a year in the Madison, Wisconsin, women's prison and then faded into oblivion.

But little Lester Gillis got his wish after all. Baby Face Nelson would be remembered for a long, long time.

[ALSO SEE John Dillinger.]

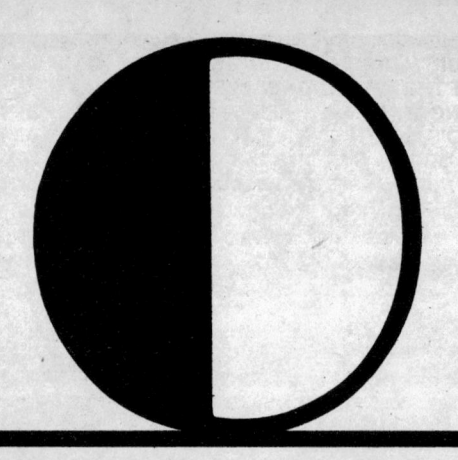

O'BANNION, CHARLES DION ("DEANIE")
Bootlegger • (1892-1924)

BACKGROUND: BORN IN AURORA, ILL. MOVED WITH PARENTS TO CHICAGO, CIRCA 1899. MINOR PUBLIC EDUCATION. MARRIED VIOLA KANIFF, NO CHILDREN. ORIGINAL OCCUPATION, SINGING WAITER. DESCRIPTION: 5'8", BLUE EYES, LIGHT-BROWN HAIR, SLENDER, LEFT LEG SHORTER THAN RIGHT AS A RESULT OF A BOYHOOD ACCIDENT, WALKED WITH LIMP. ALIASES: UNKNOWN. RECORD: JOINED THE LITTLE HELLIONS, A JUVENILE DIVISION OF THE MARKET STREET GANG WHICH OPERATED ON CHICAGO'S NORTH SIDE IN 1902; BECAME A PICKPOCKET AND DRUNK-ROLLER IN EARLY TEENS; BECAME AN ENFORCER FOR WILLIAM RANDOLPH HEARST'S "HERALD-EXAMINER" IN 1909, BEATING UP NEWSSTAND OWNERS WHO REFUSED TO SELL THE PAPER; ARRESTED FOR ASSAULT, 1909, SERVED THREE MONTHS IN HOUSE OF CORRECTION; ARRESTED FOR ASSAULT, 1911, SERVED SIX MONTHS IN HOUSE OF CORRECTION; ARRESTED IN MARCH, 1921, FOR BURGLARY, STRICKEN OFF WITH LEAVE TO REINSTATE; ARRESTED, MAY, 1921, FOR BURGLARY, STRICKEN OFF WITH LEAVE TO REINSTATE; ARRESTED AGAIN IN MAY, 1921, FOR POSSESSING BURGLAR TOOLS, STRICKEN OFF WITH LEAVE TO REINSTATE; ARRESTED, JULY, 1922, FOR ROBBERY, POSTED BOND OF $10,000, CASE NOLLE PROSSED; ORGANIZED A GANG OF THE MOST FEARED MOBSTERS, NEXT TO CAPONE'S, IN CHICAGO, ABSOLUTELY CONTROLLING THE 42ND AND 43RD WARDS; GANG INCLUDED SUCH NOTORIOUS THIEVES, HIJACKERS, ROBBERS, SAFECRACKERS, AND KILLERS AS GEORGE "BUGS" MORAN, EARL "HYMIE" WEISS, VINCENT

"THE SCHEMER" DRUCCI, SAMUEL J. "NAILS" MORTON, LOUIS "TWO-GUN" ALTERIE, MAXIE EISEN, PETE AND FRANK GUSENBERG; AT THE ADVENT OF PROHIBITION BEGAN BREWING BEER, DISTILLING WHISKEY, AND DISTRIBUTING SAME THROUGHOUT CHICAGO'S NORTH SIDE, OPERATING FROM A HEADQUARTERS AT 738 NORTH STATE STREET, A FLOWER SHOP; KILLED 11/10/24 IN HIS FLOWER SHOP BY AL CAPONE'S GANGSTERS—REPORTEDLY ALBERT ANSELMI, JOHN SCALISE, AND NEW YORK MOBSTER FRANKIE YALE (UALE).

He was a disarming fellow, lovable almost. Chicago's newspaper reporters fawned over him, chronicling his zany antics and quoting his wisecracks and butchered *bons mots*. He was delightfully macabre copy, a walking fiction, the storybook gangster of the 1920s—Charles Dion "Deanie" O'Bannion. He was also, according to Chief of Police Morgan Collins, "Chicago's arch criminal who has killed or seen to the killing of at least twenty-five men."

From the beginning, O'Bannion strove heartily to be unique, despite his dirt-common background. Deanie's father was a hard-drinking Irish immigrant who became a plasterer in Aurora, Illinois. Thankfully, his mother never saw her son rise to the top of his profession, dying when O'Bannion was five. Upon moving to Chicago, Deanie's playground was the street, and his youthful games consisted of pick-pocketing and rolling drunks as a member of the Little Hellions Gang, a division of the Market Streeters.

At the same time, O'Bannion sang in the choir of Holy Name Cathedral—he possessed a fine, lilting Irish tenor voice. Each Sunday he served as an altar boy for Father O'Brien, who thought Deanie's religious zealousness might lead to the priesthood. Although a practicing Catholic, O'Bannion kept his religion in its place, reserving a few hours for God on Sunday mornings throughout his brief life and devoting his remaining hours to robbery and murder.

Graduating to the Market Street adult gang, O'Bannion shunned jackrolling for burglary—"a man's profession." His legitimate front was that of an enforcer for William Randolph Hearst's *Herald Examiner*. His job was to convince various newsstand proprietors to carry the Hearst paper instead of McCormick's *Tribune*. Those who resisted his commercial cooing were beaten senseless by Deanie's hamhock fists.

It was during this period of his life that O'Bannion befriended the knight-errant newspaperman Charles MacArthur, who would pole-vault to fame as the coauthor of such plays as *The Front Page* and *Twentieth Century* and a host of film scenarios written with the prolific Ben Hecht. Later, when Deanie became a sort of underworld *cause célèbre*, he would pick up MacArthur at whatever saloon or poolroom the writer happened to be in, and the two of them would race O'Bannion's flivver down the sidewalks of posh Michigan Avenue as the dawn broke. It was all great fun, but not to MacArthur's editor, the indomitable Walter Howey. On one occasion, when O'Bannion stood like a ghostly Charon framed in the steamy light of a saloon door beckoning to his friend MacArthur, Howey shouted at his protégé: "You're not going with that murderous son-of-a-bitch! You're going home and go to bed."

Almost obediently, MacArthur put down his pool cue, yawned, and said to his editor: "Deanie's my sandman. He'll take me home." He then strolled away with O'Bannion for some early morning high jinks.

In Deanie's newspaper-slugging days, he was arrested only twice for assaulting news dealers. He was thrown into jail for short terms, each time being released in the shadow of the powerful Hearst lawyers. One story has it that O'Bannion stole a mail truck thinking it was a *Tribune* lorry and, upon discovering that it contained sacks full of negotiable bonds, went into the crime business in a big way.

During his early twenties Deanie became a singing waiter at the McGovern brothers' café and saloon on North Clark Street, hobbling between the tables on his bad left leg (his left leg was noticeably several inches shorter than his right one as a result of falling from a trolley car as a boy) and singing "Where the River Shannon Flows" while balancing a hefty tray of foaming beer steins. McGoverns' was the worst sort of dive. Every other customer was a crook working on a future score.

It was here that Deanie met and befriended such notorious safecrackers and hijackers as George "Bugs" Moran, Earl "Hymie" Weiss, Vincent "The Schemer" Drucci, and Samuel J. "Nails" Morton.

With this crew of fearless Fagins, O'Bannion put together one of the most devastating gangs in Chicago, centering his activities on the northeast side of the 42nd and 43rd wards. O'Bannion's power in these wards, commonly referred to as the Gold Coast—its eastern fringe was lined with the most exclusive homes and apartment dwellings in the city—was overwhelming by the late 1910s.

His political control of this area was best summed up in an old refrain: "Who'll carry the Forty-Second and Forty-Third?" The answer was always: "O'Bannion in his pistol pockets."

During election time Deanie's boys swarmed through polling places, stuffing ballot boxes, herding floaters and repeaters through the lines, and bribing officials to dump votes for the opposition. If none of these methods achieved O'Bannion's ends, he resorted to employing strong arm squads who bashed in the heads of stubborn election judges and counters.

Seldom did the O'Bannion gang flash any of their heavy equipment, although Deanie alone carried three pistols on his person at all times. He was ambidextrous and could reach to the left armpit of his suit jacket, the left-outside coat pocket, or his right-front pants pocket for a pistol.

When Prohibition came into being, O'Bannion purchased several of the best distilleries and breweries on the North Side. Where Capone and Torrio on the South Side were compelled to either import beer or whiskey into Chicago at high prices or rely on the rotgut produced by the Genna stills to supply their outlets, O'Bannion had the finest booze and beer available. "The real McCoy," he called it.

Throughout the city, society people and owners of the better restaurants bought from O'Bannion. The quality of his bootlegging wares was superior to anyone else's, and it was thought that he was more trustworthy than

Capone, who avidly insisted that his customers also patronize his brothels and floating gambling operations. O'Bannion once signed an agreement to keep his interests north of "The Dividing Line"—Madison Street—but continued to service his special customers south of the line.

At first this encroachment upon Torrio-Capone territory was tolerated. Next, Capone argued that if O'Bannion was to continue running booze into his area, he should, at least, agree to the establishment of Torrio-Capone whorehouses in the Gold Coast. "I ain't no pimp!" O'Bannion snorted to Capone one night in the latter's headquarters, the Four Deuces, at 2222 South State Street. "Besides," he added sincerely, "running prostitutes is against the Holy Mother, the Church!"

Interestingly enough, not one professional brothel was operated in the opulent Northeast section of Chicago during the tenure of the O'Bannion-Weiss-Moran gang. O'Bannion's religious compunctions, however, did not apply to hijacking Capone's trucks, wholesale robberies, gambling casinos, and the killing of anyone who got in his way.

Wide-open bootlegging practiced by O'Bannion did not alter his attitude about liquor. He hated alcohol and beer. He did love flowers, so much so that he purchased a half-interest in the Schofield Flower Shop operated by William Schofield at 738 North State Street, directly across from Holy Name Cathedral, which Deanie continued to visit each morning, stuffing the poor box with fistfuls of dollars culled from his criminal sorties.

"My money goes to those who need it," he once remarked. To prove his point and to ease his sin-struck conscience, O'Bannion filled his large touring car each week with foodstuffs and clothing and drove into the shabby parts of his district to distribute these to the needy. "Deanie's always good for a touch," his devoted bodyguard "Two-Gun" Louis Alterie once said. "The old guys, people who don't have no jobs, the crippled kids, these are the ones Deanie doles his dough to. He's a swell guy, ain't he?"

There was even a story describing how O'Bannion once sent a crippled child to the Mayo Clinic for extensive operations and, learning that the boy was beyond help, provided a trust fund for him for life. O'Bannion once shot a citizen by mistake and paid for the hospital bills.

The shooting became part of Chicago folklore. O'Bannion stopped Edward Dean Sullivan of the *Examiner* one day and asked: "Where can a guy buy a boxful of the best cigars around here?"

"Who's sick?" Sullivan inquired.

Deanie gave Sullivan his saddest face. "This morning I'm going across the Madison Street bridge and I got plenty on my mind. Somebody's been tailing me lately. An automobile crossed the bridge and backfired. I didn't know what it was. I popped at the only guy I saw. I got to send some smokes over to him." O'Bannion had shot Arthur Vadis in the leg when Vadis was on his way to work.

Such indiscriminate shooting on O'Bannion's part was commonplace. A nightclubber who sipped soda, Deanie donned his tuxedo almost every evening, and with his top hat tilted on his head, led his boys into bistros and theaters to enjoy themselves. Moran, Weiss, and Alterie all aped their boss, their tuxedos snug at their hips and bulging from the weight of pistols near their hearts.

One evening, while watching a play at the LaSalle Theater, O'Bannion happened to spot Davy "Yiddles" Miller, a prizefight referee and ex-boxer who had publicly insulted an O'Bannionite, one Yankee Schwartz, weeks before.

O'Bannion excused himself from his party just before the play ended and walked to the lobby. There, as Miller emerged, Deanie calmly withdrew one of his pistols and shot the referee in the stomach. Miller's younger brother Max rushed forward and O'Bannion shot him, too. The second shot, however, did no damage other than paralyzing Max Miller with fright after it bounced harmlessly off his belt buckle.

Then the "Cock-of-the-Walk," as the newspapers called O'Bannion, turned with a grin on his face and strolled from the theater unmolested. He was never arrested, but he did send a nice floral piece to Davy Miller, who was recovering in a nearby hospital.

Next to tending his flowers, O'Bannion's love for safecracking never ceased. He had been a box man most of his adult life and derived great pleasure in splitting cribs, particularly with George "Bugs" Moran (who had been captured several times and convicted of safecracking, taking the fall for O'Bannion, who always managed to escape) and Earl "Hymie" Weiss.

In early 1922 O'Bannion and Weiss were interrupted by police detective John Ryan just at the moment they were about to blow open a Postal Telegraph safe. On the way to the station O'Bannion smilingly explained that "You got it all wrong, Paddy. Me and Hymie were waiting for the manager. You see, Paddy me boy, we heard about what good pay these telegraphers get and wanted to hire on."

"You mean to tell me that you were in that office in the middle of the night to apply for jobs?"

"Ah, that's it, Paddy boy. That's the very thing, you see."

Ryan turned to another detective in the squad car and clucked his tongue. "I've never heard of anything so disgusting in all my days."

The attempted-robbery charge came to nothing, which was usual in O'Bannion's case. Alderman Titus A. Haffa of the 43rd Ward rushed to O'Bannion's side and put up $10,000 bond so that he and Weiss could swagger free out the police-station doors. With an additional $30,000 in well-placed bribes, O'Bannion had indictment No. 28982 on the Chicago Police Department's blotter nol-prossed in court.

Haffa's gesture was not surprising. Politicians throughout Chicago catered to O'Bannion. His power in delivering his borough into Republican hands at each election was so omnipotent that no political favor was too large to grant him. "I deliver my wards as per requirements," O'Bannion once boasted, and the service brought him and his criminal activities unlimited immunity.

A prime example of the way Chicago politicians coddled the Irish gangster was a party given in his honor at the swanky Webster Hotel during the embattled election year of 1924. The guests filing into the dining hall would have caused the eyes of any law-abiding citizen in Chicago to pop.

On one side of a long, long table sat O'Bannion, Weiss, Moran, and Alterie; Cornelius P. Con Shea, murderer and labor racketeer; burglar and gunman Frank Gusenberg;

Maxie Eisen, union thug and manager of O'Bannion's Cragin distillery; gambler Jerry O'Connor (not to be confused with the Chicago gunman of the O'Donnell clan of the same name); and William Scott Stewart, Alterie's lawyer and former assistant state's attorney.

The other side of the table was occupied by County Clerk Robert Schweitzer, Chief of Detectives Michael Hughes, Police Lieutenant Charles Egan, and Colonel Albert A. Sprague, the Democratic nominee for U.S. Senator and Commissioner of Public Works. Lesser party hacks trailed to the end of the exquisitely set table.

Sprague spoke briefly and then sat down to enjoy himself. The best Scotch, wines, and beers began to flow. Everyone commented favorably on the decorous red-white-and-blue bunting adorning the walls and chandeliers.

O'Connor, who was vice president of the Theater and Building Janitors' Union, received a $2,500 stickpin from his federation. O'Bannion was given a $1,500 platinum watch "for services rendered." The end of the festivities was highlighted by Louis Alterie's gun act.

The gangster took note of a waiter passing the hat among the guests for tips, which was the usual custom at the Webster. Alterie jumped up with both pistols in his hands. "Hey you!" he shouted at the startled waiter. "None of that racket stuff goes here!"

Jaws dropped and mouths opened in disbelief. Alterie glanced about him at the distinguished company and asked: "Shall I kill him?"

O'Bannion sat back in his chair in peals of laughter and finally blurted: "Naw, let 'em suffer, Louis lad."

When the "Belshazzar feast," as the clergy dubbed the meeting, was made known, reform mayor Dever exploded and called Hughes before him to explain. The chief of detectives mumbled that he thought the dinner was to be for Jerry O'Connor. He didn't know O'Bannion and his mob would be there, he claimed. "When I recognized a number of notorious characters I had thrown into the detective bureau basement a half dozen times I knew I had been framed, and withdrew almost at once."

Such hand-in-hand fraternization between gangsters and politicians blithely continued in Chicago all the same. O'Bannion flagrantly used the police to cover up one of the most sensational thefts in Chicago history. In 1924 he engineered the robbery of the Sibley warehouse, carting off 1,750 cases of bonded whiskey worth $1 million. The startling aspect of this theft was that a grand jury indicted police lieutenant Michael Grady and four of his sergeants from the detective bureau for providing a protective convoy of police cars which accompanied O'Bannion's truck drivers to their various distribution points. (The charges were subsequently dismissed, and Grady was made a captain.)

Chief Collins was not on O'Bannion's payroll and attempted to foil the bootlegger at every turn, even placing a wiretap on the Irish mobster's flower-shop phone. One evening the tap recorded a call to O'Bannion by one of his truckers who had been stopped on the West Side by two enterprising policemen. "That load of beer we're bringing in, Deanie," he said. "Well, there's two bulls here who want three hundred bucks to release it."

"Three hundred dollars!" O'Bannion screamed. "To them bums? Why, I can have them knocked off for half that much!"

While squads of police sent out by Collins to arrest the rogue cops and, perhaps, save their lives, were searching frantically through West Side streets, the trucker again called O'Bannion, stating: "Hey, Dion, I just been talkin' to Johnny and he says to let the cops have the three hundred. He says he don't want no trouble."

O'Bannion grunted a reluctant approval and hung up. The "Johnny" referred to in the phone conversation was none other than Johnny Torrio. Only months before, O'Bannion had joined forces with Torrio and Capone in a triumvirate that controlled the entire bootlegging operation in Cicero. His association with the "spaghetti-benders," as he called them, agitated his independent nature. He was also partners with Capone and Torrio in a gambling casino called The Ship, and bitterly complained each week when the three owners met to divide the earnings that certain Sicilian gangsters were allowed to lose heavily without redeeming their markers.

O'Bannion was referring, of course, to Angelo Genna of the murderous Genna brothers, a Capone-Torrio ally and a notoriously poor gambler. When O'Bannion learned that Genna had lost $30,000 at The Ship's roulette table,

Bootlegger Dion "Deanie" O'Bannion was considered "Chicago's arch killer" of the 1920s; he attended church regularly.

he called "Bloody Angelo" and told him: "You got one week to pay up, spaghetti-bender!"

Hatred for Italian and Sicilian gangsters ran deep in O'Bannion. At every opportunity, he attempted to ridicule and undermine Capone and Torrio. In May, 1924, Deanie went to the gangster captains of the South Side and offered to sell the lucrative Sieben's brewery to them for $500,000, explaining that he was going to quit the rackets and settle down in his flower shop.

Torrio paid O'Bannion in cash and on May 19, 1924, drove to the brewery to take charge. He was not inside the place for more than twenty minutes before dozens of policemen swarmed through the brewery, arresting Torrio for violating the Prohibition Act.

O'Bannion roared with laughter. He had learned that the police planned to close down his operation and dumped the property on Torrio and Capone for a handsome profit. Between guffaws, O'Bannion told Weiss: "I guess I rubbed that pimp's nose in the mud all right."

Weiss, a cunning gangster with above-average intelligence, pleaded with his boss to "take it easy with them guys."

"Aw, Hymie," O'Bannion snickered. "When you gonna learn, lad? Those people are gutter rats, dumb bastards all of 'em, Torrio, Capone, them Gennas . . . To hell with them Sicilians!"

Capone and the Gennas raged against such insults from O'Bannion, and they told Torrio Deanie would have to be killed. Torrio tried to soothe Scarface and then warned, "It means war, Al." He reminded Capone that Mike Merlo, the founder and president of the all-powerful *Unione Siciliane*—an ethnic federation that controlled Sicilian gangster operations which Capone sought for years to dominate—was a close friend of O'Bannion's. Capone thought better of his intent and waited. When Merlo died in November, 1924, Capone felt his way was clear to kill the Irish gang leader.

On November 10, 1924, James Genna and Carmen Vacco, a city sealer, entered O'Bannion's flower shop and ordered a large wreath for Merlo's funeral. They gave Deanie $750 for the floral arrangement. "We'll send some boys to pick it up later," Genna told him.

Five minutes later the phone rang, and an unknown caller wanted to know if O'Bannion had the flowers ready. "At noon," O'Bannion told them. A few minutes after twelve a blue Jewett touring car pulled up in front of the shop.

Negro porter William Crutchfield, who was at that moment sweeping petals into the back room, glanced up to see three men get out of the car and walk into the shop while another stayed at the wheel.

O'Bannion, dressed in a long white smock and holding a pair of florist's shears in his left hand, lurched forward in his curious rolling limp, his left hand outstretched in greeting.

"Hello, boys," Deanie said. "You from Mike Merlo's?" The three men, walking abreast, approached O'Bannion with smiles. The man in the center was tall, clean-shaven, and wearing an expensive overcoat and fedora; the other two were dark-complexioned, short, and stocky.

"Yes . . . for Merlo's flowers," Crutchfield heard the tall man say before he stepped into the back room. The tall man grabbed O'Bannion's hand in greeting. The two men at his sides moved around Deanie and drew pistols. Then, at close range while the tall man held O'Bannion in a viselike grip, bullets ripped into the Irish gangster—two in the right breast, one through the larynx, another next to that one, another in the right cheek, and a final *coup de grace* shot through the left cheek. So close were the shots fired that powder burns were later found at the opening of each wound.

The three men fled to the car, which drove away slowly once they were inside. O'Bannion crashed, dead on his feet, into a row of geraniums, his three pistols still tucked away unfired in his specially made pockets. The first victim of the handshake-murder method sprawled among his flowers, an incongruous sight for a man known as Chicago's "arch criminal."

Years later O'Bannion's executioners were determined to be Frankie Yale (the man in the center) and John Scalise and Albert Anselmi, the sinister Genna killers loaned to Capone for the occasion. James Genna had placed the order for Merlo's floral piece; it was only logical that when O'Bannion saw the two Genna men enter his shop, he would think they were there to pick up the order.

At least that's what Detective Captain William Shoemaker ("Old Shoes") thought. Although he didn't name Scalise and Anselmi as the murderers, he did state: "O'Bannion, above all things, knew he was marked for death. He knew it might come at any moment. Ordinarily, when talking to strangers, he stood with feet apart, the right hand on the hip, thumb to rear and fingers down in front. The left was usually in his coat pocket. In this position he was ready for instant action with the automatics in the specially tailored pockets.

"But we have him advancing to meet these fellows without hesitation—his right hand extended. He felt safe. He knew them—at least by sight—and did not suspect them."

The Genna brothers, Capone, and Torrio were all arrested on suspicion of homicide, but were soon released after supplying concrete alibis. Frankie Yale, a good Capone friend from New York, was arrested at La Salle Station as he was about to depart for points east only hours after the shooting. He, too, was ultimately released.

At an elaborate funeral ceremony O'Bannion's minions filed past his body, tough gangsters weeping as they went past his bier in Sbarbaro's Funeral Home. He was placed inside a $10,000 bronze casket filled with bronze-and-silver double walls. A heavy plate-glass window allowed visitors to peer down at Deanie's patched-up face. "They did a good job on Deanie," Louis Alterie said. "He looked great."

O'Bannion reposed on white satin cushions with a purple cushion beneath his mounted left hand, his shooting hand. One reporter wrote: "Silver angels stood at the head and feet with their heads bowed in the light of ten candles that burned in solid golden candlesticks they held in their hands. Beneath the casket, on the marble slab that supports its glory, is the inscription: 'Suffer little children to come unto me.'"

Deanie's funeral was the most lavish in gangland history, a gaudy show topped with twenty-six truckloads of flowers, his favorite blossoms, worth $50,000, leading the hearse's way to Mount Carmel cemetery. One small wreath among the deluge was labeled "From Al."

The scene at the cemetery was more bizarre than the everyday confrontations occurring between the North and South side gangster factions. On one side of the grave, lowering the body to its rest, were Earl "Hymie" Weiss, George "Bugs" Moran, and Vincent "The Schemer" Drucci; on the other, Al Capone, Johnny Torrio, and Angelo Genna. The O'Bannionites glared at the Italian gangsters, but made no move toward their guns. That would come within days.

Torrio had been right. By killing O'Bannion, Capone had started a war that would claim the lives of at least five hundred gangsters (which the police would appreciate). Following the ceremony, Torrio, Capone, and Genna raced off in their cars. Within six months Torrio would nearly be killed in an ambush by Weiss, Moran, and Drucci; Angelo Genna would be shot to pieces; and Al Capone would slip behind a barricade of gunsels, where he would remain in terror for four years before ordering the slaughter of the entire North Side gang on St. Valentine's Day in 1929.

"If I had known what I was stepping into in Chicago," Capone was later to lament, "I would never have left the Five Points outfit [in New York]."

Fifteen thousand people attended O'Bannion's funeral. "It was one of the most nauseating things I've ever seen happen in Chicago," remarked reform judge John H. Lyle. Though Cardinal George Mundelein refused to allow O'Bannion to be buried in consecrated ground or any last rites administered to his corpse, Father Malloy of Holy Name Cathedral knelt next to O'Bannion's casket as it was being lowered into the unblessed earth by his gangster friends and enemies and said three Hail Marys and the Lord's Prayer. The priest remembered O'Bannion only as the smiling, blue-eyed choirboy in his church, not as the gangster.

Above it all, Viola O'Bannion, the gangster's pretty widow, wailed, "Why, why, oh tell me why?" Why would anyone want to kill her peace-loving husband, a gentle man who enriched people's lives with his beautiful flowers?

To her, he was a quiet businessman whose North Pine Grove Avenue apartment possessed a $15,000 player piano, a symbol of his love for music. "Dean loved his home and spent most of his evenings in it," Viola O'Bannion told the world. "He loved to sit in his slippers, fooling with the radio, singing a song, listening to the player-piano. He never drank. He was not a man to run around nights with women. I was his only sweetheart. We went out often to dinner or the theater, usually with friends. He never left home without telling me where he was going and kissing me goodbye."

[ALSO SEE Louis "Two-Gun" Alterie, Al Capone, Vincent "The Schemer" Drucci, Genna Brothers, Frank Yale; George "Bugs" Moran, John Torrio, *Bloodletters and Badmen*, Book 3.]

O'DONNELL BROTHERS (CHICAGO, SOUTH SIDE)

"When arguments fail, use a blackjack!" This was the motto of Edward "Spike" O'Donnell, and the advice he gave to his gun-toting brothers—Steve, Walter, and Tommy—when selling their bootleg beer. The brothers, and a small but devoted group of strong-arm men, centered their bootleg operations in southwest Chicago, in a traditional Irish neighborhood known as Kerry Patch.

They were squeezed between the Torrio-Capone area and the back-of-the-yards southwest section claimed by the dreaded Saltis-McErlane gang. While the oldest brother Spike was in Joliet penitentiary doing a long stretch for complicity in the $12,000 robbery of the Stockyards Trust and Savings Bank, peace reigned between Capone and the O'Donnells. Then, in the summer of 1923, Spike was released from Joliet.

The O'Donnell clout was heavy. Spike's release had been petitioned by no less than six state senators, five state representatives, and a judge of the Cook County Criminal Court. Governor Len Small was only too happy to sign the parole papers for his old friend O'Donnell.

O'Donnell's return to Kerry Patch marked a brief but bloody gang war between Capone and the South Side Irish gang under Spike's leadership. O'Donnell bolstered his bootleg crew with such gunmen as George "Spot" Bucher, George Meeghan, and Jerry O'Connor, who had been doing a life term in Joliet until he, too, was paroled. A New York marksman named Henry C. Hasmiller was imported to provide additional gunfire.

At the time of the O'Donnell uprising and encroachment into foreign bootlegging territories in Chicago, the Capone-Torrio organization was closely allied with Polack Joe Saltis and his gun-happy sidekick, Frankie McErlane. After a brief meeting, Scarface convinced Saltis to handle the O'Donnells. "If they get to be too much for you," he said, "we'll come in, too."

The O'Donnells weren't too much for Frankie McErlane. He eagerly waited for an opportunity to put the O'Donnells in their place. His chance came on September 7, 1923.

On that day, Steve, Walter, and Tommy O'Donnell, accompanied by Meeghan, Bucher, and O'Connor, strolled into a saloon operated by ex-pug Jacob Geis at 2154 West

51st Street. Meeghan and Bucher, acting as drummers for O'Donnell beer, had tried to convince Geis to take the Irishmen's brew instead of Capone's. Geis was adamant. He was staying with Capone. Next, Spike sent in his six-man contingent.

Steve O'Donnell approached Geis and his apelike bartender, Nick Gorysko. "We're giving you one more chance," the O'Donnell brother stated. "What say?"

Geis snarled, "Nothin' doin'!"

Six pairs of hands reached across the bar for the two men, and in the presence of a half-dozen witnesses, Geis and Gorysko were beaten senseless and left unconscious on the floor. Geis' skull was fractured, and he barely survived the beating after lying in Deaconess Hospital for two weeks.

The Irish gang moved off to four more bars that night, slugging owners and bartenders as they went. After knocking Frank Kveton through a plate-glass window when he, too, proved reluctant to switch from Capone beer to O'Donnell brew, the clan withdrew to one of their strongholds, a bar operated by Joseph Klepka at 5358 South Lincoln Street.

Spike was waiting for his bravos in Klepka's with sandwiches and beer, O'Donnell beer naturally. No sooner had the gang entered than Cook County Deputy Sheriff Danny McFall followed them into Klepka's and shouted to them: "Stick up your hands or I'll blow you to hell!" As a way of emphasizing his point, McFall, with two pistols in his hands, sent a bullet whining past Spike O'Donnell's derby.

"Scram!" Spike yelled to his minions, and they dove out the back and side doors. Waiting at the side entrance for whomever might attempt that escape route was a short, stocky man holding a sawed-off shotgun. He was Frankie McErlane. Within seconds, Jerry O'Connor ran right into him and McErlane shot him in the heart.

The O'Donnells dwindled fast after that. On September 17, 1923, beer drummers Bucher and Meeghan stopped their touring car for traffic at Garfield Boulevard. A green auto drew alongside and a stocky man holding a shotgun—Frankie McErlane—blew off their heads. Another killer wielding a pistol, Polack Joe Saltis according to one report, fired several more bullets into Meeghan and Bucher.

"I can lick this bird Capone," Edward "Spike" O'Donnell said in 1923, but he and his brothers were run out of the Chicago rackets within two years. (UPI)

Police found the dead men minutes later, cigarettes still burning in their hands.

Mayor William E. Dever was incensed over the killings and issued a statement reading: "Until the murderers of Jerry O'Connor and the murderers of these two men have been apprehended and punished and the illegal traffic for control of which they battle has been suppressed, the dignity of the law and the average man's respect for it is imperiled, and every officer of the law and every enforcing agency should lay aside other duties and join in the common cause. . . . The police will follow this case to a finish as they do all others. This guerrilla war between hijackers, rum runners and illicit beer peddlers can and will be crushed. . . ."

Dever's noble intent was but a grunt in a hurricane. Though Daniel McFall was indicted for O'Connor's death, he was speedily acquitted in January, 1924. McErlane wasn't even picked up for questioning.

Spike's hearties continued to fall. In the next few months, Spike O'Donnell was shot at by the McErlane troop at least ten times. Once, his brother Tommy was wounded as he and Spike were driving to church on Sunday. Spike, who readily gave out colorful interviews to the press, commented: "I've been shot and missed so often I've a notion to hire out as a professional target. Life with me is just one bullet after another."

In December, McErlane caught up with Morris Keane, stopping his beer truck and shotgunning him to death. Another O'Donnell driver, William "Shorty" Egan, was also stopped by McErlane and wounded several times. Frankie also got Philip Corrigan, shooting him on the wing as his beer truck sailed past. Dead at the wheel, Corrigan and the truck crashed into an all-night diner, luckily injuring no one.

McErlane was busy throughout 1924 tracking down the O'Donnells. He found Walter O'Donnell and hotshot gunner Henry Hasmiller in a roadhouse in Evergreen Park. Barging through the crowded tables, he walked up to the two men as they were eating and emptied his shotgun into them.

When Spike heard of the double murder, he roared to a sob sister on one of the newspapers: "I can whip this bird Capone with my bare fists any time he wants to step out in the open and fight like a man!" But the days of bare-knuckle battles were long ended, and Spike's enthusiastic but thinning platoon of bootleggers was soon destroyed.

Spike O'Donnell lingered inside Chicago's gang wars for another year, until McErlane took to using a machinegun, the first ever employed by the underworld, on September 25, 1925, when he sprayed a storefront where O'Donnell was standing. Spike, wounded and shaken, decided to quit the rackets and soon settled for more mundane enterprises.

[ALSO SEE Al Capone.]

O'DONNELL BROTHERS (CHICAGO, WEST SIDE)

The West Side O'Donnells were no less fierce, but perhaps a bit more tactful, than the O'Donnells of the South Side (no relation) in controlling their bootleg barony during the 1920s—a vast area between Madison Street and Grand Avenue that stretched as far west as Cicero. The three brothers—William "Klondike," Bernard, and Myles—were anything but standup gunfighters; rather, they would needlessly and recklessly potshoot at members of the Torrio-Capone forces to make their point.

Their all-Irish gang was small, and they preferred to negotiate their future with Scarface rather than slug it out. When Capone and Torrio took over the suburb of Cicero in the early 1920s to evade pressure from Chicago's new reform mayor Dever, the O'Donnells were placated with promises of sharing the spoils. They would be allowed to retain their own "milk runs"—speakeasies serviced with O'Donnell beer and booze—but all other saloons and casinos would come under Scarface's domination.

Klondike O'Donnell even agreed to provide some muscle for Capone if any of the old-line saloonkeepers refused to take his needle beer. One such was Eddie Tancl, a broken-nosed ex-prizefighter. Myles O'Donnell, Thomas Duffy, and James J. Doherty paid Tancl a call on Klondike O'Donnell's orders and tried to convince him to go along with Capone.

"I buy my beer from the guys I want to buy my beer from," Tancl truculently told them. "That Capone guy makes bad stuff, I don't serve no needle beer in my joint."

"You don't get it, Eddie," Myles O'Donnell reasoned. "If you don't take Al's beer, you don't take no beer at all."

"And you leave Cicero besides," Doherty said.

"Yeah, you leave Cicero in maybe not a healthy state," Myles added.

Tancl gripped the bar and shouted: "Try and put me out! I was in Cicero long before youse guys came!"

Days later, Myles and Doherty were back, entering Tancl's saloon at about 8 a.m. after an all-night drinking bout. Both were half drunk and knocked over several chairs before sitting down and ordering breakfast from waiter Martin Simet.

Chicago's gang wars took its toll of nerves as well as lives; here, the once fearless Myles O'Donnell goes into a screaming faint after hearing the popping of news cameras; he thought they were pistols. (UPI)

Tancl and his burly bartender Leo Klimas stood at the bar, alerted for an O'Donnell outburst. It came a half hour later when Myles O'Donnell tore up the check Simet brought him. "You overcharged us, you bastard!" He hit Simet in the face. Tancl rushed forward. "Wait a minute, Myles—"

O'Donnell and Doherty drew their guns. So did Tancl. Four shots went into Eddie Tancl, but before he crashed to the floor of his saloon, he had sent three bullets into Myles O'Donnell and two into Doherty.

O'Donnell, who sagged against the bar, lurched out of the saloon and, to the surprise of the Sunday-morning churchgoers walking by, staggered down the street, his blood splotching the sidewalk. Tancl, with four chest wounds, raised himself from the floor of his bar with superhuman strength and ran wobbly-legged after O'Donnell. He tackled the gangster halfway down the block. Both men lay gasping when bartender Klimas dashed up.

"Leo," Tancl choked, "kill the rat! He got me!" Klimas jumped on O'Donnell's back and began to club him with the gangster's own gun. At that moment, the wounded Doherty struggled past the two and, almost as an afterthought, fired a bullet into Klimas' head, killing him. O'Donnell and Doherty then half-crawled to their car and drove away. Both survived, but Eddie Tancl and his loyal bartender Klimas were quite dead. Neither O'Donnell nor Doherty was arrested for the murders, although there were several eyewitnesses to the shootings.

By the spring of 1926 the O'Donnells were no longer in the good graces of Capone. They had sided with George "Bugs" Moran in his war with Scarface, and Jim Doherty had helped Moran's pal Vincent "The Schemer" Drucci shoot down a Genna-Capone ally, Samuzzo "Samoots" Amatuna, in a Chicago barbershop on November 13, 1925. In addition to several other killings of Capone gunsels by the O'Donnells, Klondike O'Donnell, tired of taking orders from Capone, began to distribute his own beer and booze to Cicero saloons then under Scarface's control.

There was hatred for Capone's strong-arm tactics and bad booze in Cicero. One saloonkeeper, Harry Madigan, stated to the police: "When I wanted to start a saloon in Cicero more than a year ago, Capone wouldn't let me. I finally obtained strong political pressure and was able to open. Then Capone came to me and said I would have to buy his beer, so I did.

"A few months ago Doherty and Myles O'Donnell came to me and told me they could sell me better beer than Capone beer, which was then needled. They did and it only cost $50 a barrel, where Capone charged me $60. I changed and, upon my recommendation, so did several other Cicero saloonkeepers."

Madigan's political connections might have been explained by the presence of assistant state's attorney William H. McSwiggin, who was sitting in a car parked outside his bar on the night of April 27, 1926. Also inside the car, which had just parked, were Myles O'Donnell, Thomas Duffy, James J. Doherty, and Doherty's chauffeur, Edward

William "Klondike" O'Donnell. (UPI)

Hanley. Ironically, McSwiggin had prosecuted Doherty earlier on a murder charge which was dropped.

As Doherty, Duffy, and McSwiggin stepped from the car, another auto, first traveling at top speed and then slowing to a crawl when it came abreast of Madigan's saloon, began to spit lead. A fat, balding machine gunner, shouting obscenities as he fired, leaned from a window.

McSwiggin, Doherty, and Duffy hit the cement, riddled with bullets. Hanley and Myles O'Donnell ducked and were uninjured. Duffy, though bleeding from several wounds, crawled down the block and propped himself against a tree, mumbling and fidgeting with a piece of paper which listed sixty bars that carried O'Donnell beer. He died halfway through his odd inventory.

Myles O'Donnell and Hanley dragged McSwiggin and Doherty back into their car and drove off at high speed, thinking the two men could be saved. They died of their wounds in the car, and their bodies were thrown into a ditch in the suburb of Berwyn. The car was abandoned in Oak Park.

Capone, who was identified as the machine gunner, had apparently decided to handle the O'Donnell uprising personally, which he was wont to do in matters he deemed important. Witnesses who spotted him during the shooting, however, predictably vanished, though several newspapers claimed "a secret warrant was issued for Al Capone charging him with murder." Scarface was never indicted.

When reached for comment, affable Al smilingly complained that "they made me the goat. McSwiggin was a friend of mine. Doherty and Duffy were my friends. Why, I used to lend Doherty money. Just a few days before the shooting, my brother Ralph, Doherty, and Myles and Klondike O'Donnell were at a party together."

The O'Donnells ceased to exist as an organized gang following the triple killing, and Capone dominated Cicero and points south and west completely. For years, however, the cry of "Who killed McSwiggin?" became part of the police idiom in Chicago. Of course, everybody knew.

[ALSO SEE Al Capone, Vincent "The Schemer" Drucci.]

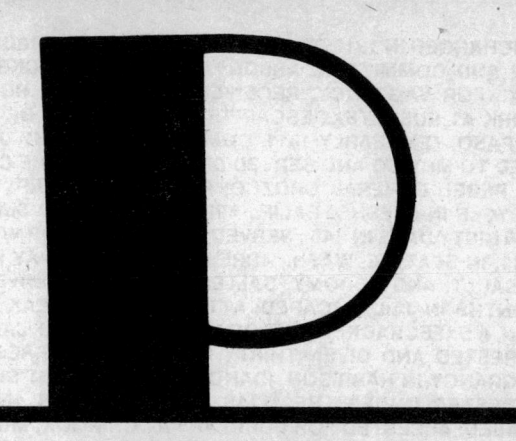

PANZRAM, CARL
Murderer, Burglar, Robber •
(1891-1930)

BACKGROUND: BORN 6/28/91 ON A FARM NEAR WARREN, MINN., TO MATHILDE ELIZABETH (BOLDEN) AND JOHN PANZRAM, PRUSSIAN IMMIGRANTS WHO MOVED TO THE U.S. IN 1888. MINOR PUBLIC EDUCATION. THREE BROTHERS—PAUL, ALBERT, LOUIS; ONE SISTER—LOUISE. ORIGINAL OCCUPATION, FARMER. DESCRIPTION: 6', BROWN EYES, BROWN HAIR (RECEDING), HEAVYSET, MUSTACHE. ALIASES: JEFF DAVIS, JACK ALLEN, JEFFERSON RHOADES, JEFF BALDWIN, JOHN O'LEARY, COPPER JOHN II. RECORD: ARRESTED AT AGE EIGHT FOR BEING DRUNK AND DISORDERLY, DISMISSED; AFTER GOING ON A ROBBING RAMPAGE AT AGE ELEVEN, SENT TO MINNESOTA STATE TRAINING SCHOOL IN RED WING IN 1903; SET FIRE TO A WAREHOUSE IN THE SCHOOL 7/7/05, RESULTING IN $100,000 DAMAGE; RELEASED JANUARY, 1906, TO THE CUSTODY OF HIS MOTHER; AFTER THREATENING A PREACHER WITH A PISTOL IN GRAND FORKS, N.D., RAN AWAY FROM HOME 3/29/06; ARRESTED IN BUTTE, MONT., FOR BURGLARY AND JAILED FOR TWO MONTHS; TRIED, CONVICTED, AND SENT TO MONTANA STATE REFORMATORY AT MILES CITY, MONT.; ESCAPED IN LATE 1906 WITH ANOTHER INMATE, JAMES BENSON; ROBBED AND BURNED, WITH BENSON, SEVERAL CHURCHES IN MONTANA; JOINED THE U.S. ARMY IN 1907; COURT-MARTIALED 4/20/07 FOR ATTEMPTING TO STEAL GOVERNMENT PROPERTY, SENTENCED TO THREE YEARS IN LEAVENWORTH; SERVED THIRTY-SEVEN MONTHS,

DISCHARGED IN 1910; TRAVELED THROUGH COLORADO, STEALING AND COMMITTING ARSON; ARRESTED IN JACKSONVILLE, TEX., FOR VAGRANCY, RECEIVED THIRTY DAYS' ROAD-GANG WORK AT RUSK, TEX., ESCAPED; ROBBED A MAN OF $35 NEAR EL PASO, TEX., EARLY 1911, COMMITTING SODOMY UPON HIM; FLED TO MEXICO AND SERVED BRIEFLY UNDER THE COMMAND OF REBEL GENERAL OROZCO; RETURNED TO U.S., STOLE A BICYCLE IN FRESNO, CALIF., APPREHENDED AND SENTENCED TO THIRTY DAYS IN JAIL; SERVED THIRTY DAYS FOR VAGRANCY, 1911, IN SEATTLE, WASH.; ARRESTED FOR HIGHWAY ROBBERY, ASSAULT, AND SODOMY, DALLES, ORE., 1912, SERVED THREE MONTHS IN JAIL, ESCAPED: ATTEMPTED TO BREAK CAL JORDAN, A SAFECRACKER, OUT OF A MOSCOW, IDAHO, JAIL IN 1912, ARRESTED AND GIVEN THIRTY DAYS IN JAIL; ARRESTED FOR VAGRANCY IN HARRISON, IDAHO, RECEIVED LIGHT SENTENCE; ARRESTED UNDER THE ALIAS JEFF DAVIS FOR ARSON, RELEASED; ARRESTED FOR BURGLARY AT CHINOOK, MONT., SENTENCED TO ONE YEAR IN THE STATE PRISON AT DEER LODGE, MONT., ESCAPED IN EIGHT MONTHS; ARRESTED, 1912, IN THREE FORKS, MONT., FOR BURGLARY, UNDER THE ALIAS OF JEFF RHOADES, SENTENCED TO ONE YEAR IN STATE PRISON AT DEER LODGE; RECEIVED AN ADDITIONAL YEAR FOR PREVIOUS ESCAPE; SERVED TWENTY-THREE MONTHS OF SENTENCE; RELEASED IN 1914, MOVED TO ASTORIA, ORE., ARRESTED THERE FOR BURGLARY, SENTENCED TO SEVEN YEARS IN THE STATE PRISON AT SALEM; LED RIOTS AND BECAME INCORRIGIBLE, PROVOKING SEVERAL INCIDENTS, HAD AN ADDITIONAL SEVEN YEARS ADDED TO HIS SENTENCE; ESCAPED MAY, 1918; ROBBED A HOTEL IN FREDERICK, MD., OF $1,200; JOINED THE MERCHANT MARINE UNDER THE ALIAS JOHN O'LEARY, SAILED TO PANAMA ON "JAMES S. WHITNEY," JUMPED SHIP IN PERU, WORKED BRIEFLY IN COPPER MINES THERE; MOVED TO BOCAS DEL TORO, PANAMA, AND WORKED FOR THE SINCLAIR OIL COMPANY; BURNED DOWN AN OIL RIG IN 1919; RETURNED TO U.S., SHIPPED OUT ON ANOTHER FREIGHTER AND SAILED TO SCOTLAND; TRAVELED THROUGH EUROPE AFTER JUMPING SHIP; RETURNED TO U.S. IN EARLY 1920; ROBBED A JEWELRY STORE IN BRIDGEPORT, CONN., 1920 ($7,000); ROBBED THE NEW HAVEN, CONN., HOME OF WILLIAM HOWARD TAFT IN JULY, 1920 ($40,000 IN JEWELRY AND LIBERTY BONDS); PURCHASED SMALL YACHT "AKISTA," 1920; LURED SAILORS TO YACHT DURING 1920 ON THE PROMISE OF WORK, AND, BY HIS OWN ADMISSION, ROBBED AND MURDERED TEN MEN; ARRESTED FOR BURGLARY IN BRIDGEPORT, CONN., SENTENCED TO SIX MONTHS IN JAIL, RELEASED; ARRESTED IN PHILADELPHIA FOR AGGRAVATED ASSAULT, RELEASED ON BAIL, JUMPED BOND AND SAILED TO EUROPE ON FREIGHTER; JOURNEYED TO AFRICA, WORKING FOR THE SINCLAIR OIL COMPANY, CLAIMED TO HAVE KILLED A NEGRO BOY OF TWELVE IN QUIMBAZIE AFTER PERFORMING

ACTS OF SODOMY UPON HIM; ALSO CLAIMED TO HAVE KILLED SIX NEGRO MEN NEAR LOBITO BAY (CLAIMED TO HAVE KILLED A TOTAL OF TWENTY-ONE PERSONS IN HIS LIFETIME); RETURNED TO U.S., CIRCA 1922, KILLED TWELVE-YEAR-OLD HENRY MCMAHON IN JULY, 1922, AT SALEM, MASS.; ROBBED SEVERAL YACHTS AT THE NEW HAVEN YACHT CLUB (WHERE HE WORKED AS A WATCHMAN) IN APRIL, 1923; STOLE A YACHT IN PROVIDENCE, R.I., MAY, 1923; KILLED A MAN IN KINGSTON, N.Y., BY HIS OWN ADMISSION, IN JUNE, 1923; ARRESTED WEEKS LATER IN NYACK, N.Y., ON CHARGES OF BURGLARY, ROBBERY, AND SODOMY, RELEASED ON BOND, JUMPED BAIL; KILLED, BY HIS OWN ADMISSION, A BOY IN NEW HAVEN, CONN.; ARRESTED WEEKS LATER IN LARCHMONT, N.Y., BEING CAUGHT IN THE ACT OF ROBBING AN EXPRESS OFFICE; SENTENCED TO FIVE YEARS IN SING SING PRISON; TRANSFERRED TO CLINTON PRISON AT DANNEMORA, N.Y., AS A HARD-CASE INMATE; RELEASED IN 1928; WITHIN A MONTH'S TIME, BY HIS OWN ADMISSION, COMMITTED ELEVEN BURGLARIES AND ONE MURDER IN THE BALTIMORE, MD./WASHINGTON, D.C., AREA; ARRESTED FOR HOUSEBREAKING 8/16/28 IN WASHINGTON, D.C.; WROTE OUT CONFESSION IN JAIL AND AS A RESULT OF THIS RECEIVED A TWENTY-FIVE-YEAR SENTENCE AT LEAVENWORTH; MURDERED CIVILIAN FOREMAN OF LEAVENWORTH'S LAUNDRY, ROBERT G. WARNKE, 6/20/29; HANGED AT LEAVENWORTH 9/5/30.

Carl Panzram was the complete misanthrope. Nowhere in the annals of American crime has there been anyone so dedicated to the wholesale destruction of mankind than Panzram. He enjoyed crime. There was no penance in him for the countless hideous deeds he performed. "I have no desire whatever to reform myself," he stated in his self-written confession-autobiography. "My only desire is to reform people who try to reform me. And I believe that the only way to reform people is to kill 'em."

In a rather blasé fashion, an approach obviously designed to evoke terror and dread in the reader, Panzram callously admitted: "In my lifetime I have murdered 21 human beings. I have committed thousands of burglaries, robberies, larcenies, arsons and last but not least I have committed sodomy on more than 1,000 male human beings. For all of these things I am not the least bit sorry. I have no conscience so that does not worry me, I don't believe in man, God nor Devil. I hate the whole damned human race including myself."

There was a subtle pride in Panzram's didactic diatribe, similar in many respects to the maniacal passion for killing expressed by Los Angeles' mass murderer of the late 1950s, Stephen Nash, who, at age thirty-three, had killed a half-dozen skid-row bums, children, and unemployed workers. After killing ten-year-old Larry Rice (with twenty-eight knife wounds), Nash told police: "He was a kid. It was all there in front of him . . . His whole life . . . sex, fun, all of it! Why should he have it when I never did? I took it all away from him . . . Besides, I never killed a kid before. I wanted to see how it felt."

Panzram took great delight in murdering, too, but his self-admitted goal in life was the slaughter of whole cities. He stayed awake nights in his cell plotting the demise of thousands. "I used to spend all my time figuring how I could murder the most people with the least harm and expense to myself, and I finally thought of a way to kill off a whole town. . . ." He devised macabre murder systems, such as poisoning a town's reservoir or blowing up passenger trains like the National Limited.

His counterpart, Stephen Nash, thirty-odd years later would say: "Killings are cheap. They cost about $1.35 or $1.40. . . . It's like being on a quiz show . . . When you get to ten, you go for twenty . . . You always want more. . . . When I was in Quentin [San Quentin prison], I borrowed books from the prison library. I was studying the operation of railroads. I planned to run a whole train off a bridge and watch them monkeys go swimming. I'd lie on the river bank and enjoy myself laughing at them."

Panzram was a Minnesota runaway, Nash a New York foundling. Panzram went to the gallows, describing himself as "the most criminal man in the world." Nash entered San Quentin, sentenced to the gas chamber, describing himself thusly: "I'm the king of killers! I'll go to my death like any king should. I have nothing to die for because I had nothing to live for."

Where Nash's life had been but a series of vagrancy arrests, drifting, and unemployment, a lifetime of looking through windows as the total outsider, Panzram was brutalized early in life by what he called "Bible-back" disciplinarians and a medieval prison system where heinous tortures and spiritual degradation were the backbone of penal reform.

In one prison where he spent four years, the archaic state prison at Salem, Oregon, Panzram was placed in a strait jacket until his blood ceased to circulate; a torture known as "The Humming Bird" was applied to him—the victim was placed in a steel bathtub filled with water, chained hand and foot, and rubbed down with a sponge connected to an electric battery ("The agony is intense . . . Two or three minutes and the victim is ready for the grave or the mad house")—whipped on the bare back and buttocks and then salt applied to the wounds (done to Panzram while he was working on a road gang in Rusk, Texas); beaten on the bare back, buttocks, and legs by a baseball bat while strapped face down on a cot (in the Montana State Training School); strapped across the chest and by the hands to a steel wall and forced to dangle barefooted for hours (in the U.S. Military Prison at Leavenworth); chained naked to a wall and hosed down with a water hose that caused his eyes to blacken, his body to welt, and his genitals to swell to enormous proportions (in the Oregon State Prison).

There is no doubt, when viewing Carl Panzram's subsequent crimes, that such unthinking prison bestiality created an unreasoning monster of wrath who killed and pillaged without mercy, a malevolent demon who serenely slumbered untroubled by Coleridge's "avenging angel—dark misgiving, an ominous sinking at the inmost heart."

Born to lower-class parents, Panzram's stark youth was lived in rural Minnesota. His father deserted the family, and one by one, his brothers slipped away from the farm to let his mother till the soil alone (his brother Albert did work in the fields for a while before becoming a policeman). Given little or no attention at all by his slaving mother, little Carl first grew envious of common emotions such as love and compassion; then he developed an early hatred for any kind of affection.

He was brought into juvenile court in 1899 at the age of eight on a charge of being drunk. Dismissed, he quickly began to steal from neighbors and was finally sent as an incorrigible to the Minnesota State Training School in Red

Wing, Minnesota. The school was rigid and demanding. Panzram was ordered about in military fashion, made to toil in workshops in his bare feet, and wound up endlessly scrubbing dishes. He reacted by urinating and masturbating into beverages he served officers of the school. He was caught trying to insert rat poison into the coffee of a commander named John Moore.

Seeking to punish those he thought were punishing him, Panzram set fire to the school's warehouse which stored winter clothes and blankets on July 7, 1907. "That night," he stated, "the whole place burned down at a cost of over $100,000. Nice, eh?"

Whipped, beaten, and often starved, Panzram's hatred went down to bone marrow, and by the time he was released in January, 1906, he was well on his way to homicide. He later commented: "I have met thousands of graduates of those kinds of institutions and they were either in, going into or just leaving jails, prisons, mad houses, or the rope and the electric chair was yawning for them as for me."

Panzram went home briefly after being discharged, stole a pistol and threatened to kill a preacher with it, and then, on March 29, 1906, hopped a freight train in the yards of East Grand Forks, North Dakota. The rest of his short life was a Gorgonian odyssey into crime.

Stealing and burglarizing his way west (after being gang-raped by four men in a boxcar), Panzram was arrested several times and put into jail, but he always escaped. He and another inmate of the Montana State Reformatory, one James Benson, broke out and robbed and burned several churches throughout the state.

For some inexplicable reason—the future killer attributed it to a fascination for uniforms—Panzram joined the Army in 1907 while drinking beer in a Helena, Montana, bar and listening to an impassioned recruiting sergeant. He was soon punished for insubordination, and on April 20, 1907, he was court-martialed and sentenced to three years in the military prison at old Fort Leavenworth for attempting to steal government property. Panzram served thirty-seven months breaking up rocks under a blistering Kansas sun and was discharged in 1910 ("I was the spirit of meanness personified").

Bumming and robbing across Texas, Panzram reached

Mexico, which in 1911 was torn with several revolutions, and served briefly with the insurrectionists led by Pascual Orozco, a satellite of Venustiano Carranza. He then moved on to California, Washington, and Idaho, served several minor sentences for sodomy, assault, highway robbery, safecracking, burglary, and vagrancy.

Under the name Jeff Davis, Panzram was arrested in Chinook, Montana, for burglary and received a year in the Montana State Prison, where he was tortured and beaten; he escaped in eight months. The following year he was arrested under the alias of Jeff Rhoades and sentenced to one year for a burglary in Three Forks, Montana. Authorities learned of his previous escape and added another year to his sentence in the Montana State Prison. Upon his release in 1914, Panzram went to Astoria, Oregon, and was there arrested for burglary. He was sentenced to seven years in the state prison at Salem.

Leading a constant revolt against the horrible prison conditions in Salem earned Panzram another seven years. Serving his time under the alias of Jeff Baldwin, Panzram attempted several escapes. In retaliation he was placed in a cage and fed bread and water which he more than once threw into the face of his guard. He was then beaten and sprayed with a fire hose. In May, 1918, Panzram sawed his way to freedom with crudely made instruments and traveled east.

He next appeared in Frederick, Maryland, using the name John O'Leary. He held up a hotel, taking about $1,200, and then went to New York, where he joined the Marine Firemen's, Oilers', and Water Tenders' Union. He signed on board the *James S. Whitney*, a tanker en route to South America. Jumping ship in Peru, Panzram worked briefly in the copper mines. He traveled to Chile and then to Panama, where he got a job as a foreman for the Sinclair Oil Company.

In Bocas Del Toro, Panzram, out of pique, spite, or whim, burned down an oil rig. The firm offered a $500 reward to anyone who could identify the arsonist, but Panzram went unnoticed as he shipped out in another freighter headed for the United States. His travels then widened. He sailed to Europe and, after robbing his fellow seamen, returned to the United States.

Early in 1920 Panzram robbed a jewelry store in Bridgeport, Connecticut, getting $7,000. That summer he went to New Haven and burglarized the home of William Howard Taft, taking $40,000 worth of jewels and Liberty Bonds. Using the loot from this robbery, Panzram purchased a yacht under the name John O'Leary.

He then lured several sailors (ten in all, he later admitted) to his boat and robbed and killed them. After they had worked hard refitting his ship, the sailors were invited to spend the night on board the docked yacht. ". . . we would wine and dine and when they were drunk enough they would go to bed. When they were asleep I would get my .45 Colt Army Automatic . . . and blow their brains out." He would then take their bodies to the middle of the harbor in his rowboat and drop the weighted corpses into the water.

When Bridgeport police began to grow suspicious of Panzram, he sailed his boat to New Jersey, where it was destroyed in a gale. Days later, like a homing pigeon, Panzram was back in Bridgeport, where he was arrested for burglary and sentenced to spend six months in the local jail, which he did without incident. He next hopped a freight to Philadelphia where he was tossed in jail for inciting a riot in a union dispute. He posted bond and then jumped bail, sailing to Europe on a freighter. From there he went to Africa.

By his own account Panzram worked briefly for the Sinclair Oil Company in Portuguese West Africa, where he murdered a twelve-year-old Negro boy (". . . first I committed sodomy on him and then I killed him . . . His brains were coming out of his ears when I left him and he will never be any deader . . .")

In Lobito Bay, Panzram thought it would be exciting to hunt crocodiles and hired six Negro porters to pole him through the backwaters. (". . . I shot all six of these niggers and dumped 'em in . . . The crocks done the rest . . . It was very much easier for me to kill those six niggers than it was for me to kill only one of the young boys I killed later and some of them were only eleven or twelve years old.")

Murder became an avidly pursued pastime for Panzram. He worked his way back to the United States, and in Salem, Massachusetts, in July, 1922, he attacked twelve-year-old

Henry McMahon, killing him with a rock. (". . . I tried a little sodomy on him first . . . I left him laying there with his brains coming out of his ears . . .")

Obtaining a night watchman's job at the New Haven Yacht Club, Panzram looted several ships and then stole a yacht in Providence, Rhode Island, and sailed it to New York. In June, 1923 a man attempted to rob Panzram while on board his boat. He shot the robber twice and dumped the body into the bay at Kingston, New York.

He returned to New Haven after jumping bail for an arrest in Nyack, New York, where he was charged with burglary, sodomy, and robbery. Once again in New Haven, Panzram claimed to have killed another boy. A few weeks later, he decided to rob an express office, but was caught in the act and sentenced to five years in Sing Sing. He proved to be such a thorough malcontent that he was quickly transferred to Clinton Prison at Dannemora in remote upstate New York, a jail especially reserved for hardened criminals.

Carl Panzram was released in 1928 and went on a crime spree in the Baltimore/Washington D.C. area, committing, by his own count, eleven burglaries and one murder. Washington police arrested him for housebreaking on August 16, 1928, and he was thrown into the local jail.

It was there that Panzram wrote out his gruesome memoirs and handed them to a friendly jailer, Henry Lesser. At his subsequent trial, the mass murderer taunted and threatened the jury with: ". . . If I live I'll execute some more of you!" After Judge Walter I. McCoy sentenced him to twenty-five years in Leavenworth, Panzram smiled and shouted to the justice: "Visit me!"

Panzram told Leavenworth's deputy warden Fred Zerbst upon arrival: "I'll kill the first man who bothers me." He was put to work in the laundry.

The prison's laundry at that time was run by a civilian named Robert G. Warnke, a squat, taciturn man who efficaciously went about his business. He never shouted at the prisoners working under his direction, but did scribble out daily infractions on a penalty sheet which was turned into authorities and brought minor punishments to inmates. It may have been for this reason, or because the laundry foreman merely got in Panzram's way, as he had warned, that the killer of twenty men and boys added Warnke to his list. On June 20, 1929, Panzram bashed in Robert Warnke's head with an iron bar, killing him instantly.

He then walked calmly across a prison yard with blood-smeared hands still gripping the iron bar. He stared through the bars of a door leading to the isolation cells. "I just killed Warnke," Panzram told guard Dale Ballard. "Let me in."

Ballard could not take his eyes from the bloody iron bar. "I'll never let you in with that in your hand," he finally managed.

Panzram looked at the bar, as if for the first time, and then said, "Oh. This must be my lucky day." He threw the bar aside and was admitted to the cell block, where he was promptly locked in a cell.

Following a quick trial, Panzram was sentenced to die on the gallows. When the Society for the Abolishment of Capital Punishment attempted to obtain a commutation for Panzram, the convicted murderer wrote to them telling them that he wanted to hang and that in no way should they attempt to save him. He insisted that he was sane and said: "I do not believe that being hanged by the neck until dead is a barbaric or inhuman punishment. I look forward to that as real pleasure and a big relief to me . . . when my last hour comes I will dance out of my dungeon and on to the scaffold with a smile on my face and happiness in my heart . . . the only thanks you or your kind will ever get from me for your effort on my behalf is that I wish you all had one neck and that I had my hands on it . . . I believe the only way to reform people is to kill 'em . . . My motto is: 'Rob 'em all, rape 'em all and kill 'em all!' " He signed his letter COPPER JOHN II, in memory of a copper statue that once stood in front of Auburn Prison in New York.

To ensure his execution, Panzram wrote to President Herbert Hoover, demanding that his "constitutional rights" be observed and that he be hanged on schedule. "I absolutely refuse to accept either a pardon or a commutation should either one or the other be offered me," Panzram wrote Hoover.

Neither was forthcoming. Panzram was true to his word. He fairly bullied his way to death, shoving guards to hurry up as they led him to the gallows in Leavenworth on September 5, 1930. "Let's get going. What are we stalling around for?" he asked Warden T. B. White.

The hangman ran the rope through his hands, eyeing Panzram, and then asked, "Anything you want to say?"

"Yes," the arch-killer replied. "Hurry it up, you Hoosier bastard! I could hang a dozen men while you're fooling around!" He then pulled the hangman up the scaffold steps, spat twice, and was quickly hanged, dying at 6:20 a.m. in the prison yard.

PERRY, OLIVER CURTIS
Trainrobber • (1864-1930)

BACKGROUND: BORN IN NEW YORK. NO PUBLIC EDUCATION. RAN AWAY TO THE WEST, CIRCA 1881, SETTLING BRIEFLY IN WYOMING. ORIGINAL OCCUPATION, COWBOY. DESCRIPTION: TALL, SLENDER, SOMETIMES WORE MUSTACHE. ALIASES: JAMES CURTIS PERRY, CURT PERRY, OLIVER MOORE. RECORD: ALONE, STOPPED THE NEW YORK CENTRAL NO. 31 ON 9/29/91, STEALING SEVERAL THOUSAND DOLLARS' WORTH OF JEWELS AND CASH FROM THE EXPRESS CAR NEAR ALBANY, N.Y.; ROBBED THE NEW YORK CENTRAL TRAIN NEAR SYRACUSE, N.Y., 2/21/92 FOR SMALL AMOUNT OF CASH; ROBBED NEW YORK CENTRAL TRAIN NEAR LYONS, N.Y., FOR SMALL AMOUNT OF CASH; CAPTURED BY A POSSE HOURS LATER NEAR LYONS; SENTENCED TO FORTY-NINE YEARS IN AUBURN PRISON, N.Y.; TRANSFERRED IN 1893 TO THE STATE HOSPITAL FOR THE CRIMINALLY INSANE AT MATTEAWAN, N.Y.; ESCAPED 4/10/95 AND RECAPTURED DAYS LATER IN WEEHAWKEN, N.J.; SENT TO CLINTON PRISON AT DANNEMORA; AFTER SEVERAL ESCAPE ATTEMPTS, PLACED IN SOLITARY CONFINEMENT FOR TWENTY-FIVE YEARS; DIED IN HIS CELL 9/10/30.

I was only a lad without schooling so I had to take bold strokes with big chances." Thus spoke Oliver Curtis Perry, who claimed to be related to Oliver

Hazard Perry of the Battle of Lake Erie fame, and who was also considered "the nerviest outlaw in New York."

Early in his youth, Perry fled the tenement life he was born to in New York and bummed his way west. When he reached the broad, green plains of Wyoming, he became a cowboy, his lifelong dream. The incessant rounds of chores and gulping dust kicked up by cattle soon bored Perry. He quit and then committed several small robberies in the area before traveling back east.

The thought of robbing trains had often occurred to Perry. The success of Wyoming's Wild Bunch convinced him to enter the same profession. Perry wandered through Texas, up to Nebraska, and into Minnesota, robbing, he later claimed, several coaches and trains (this was never verified). When he reached New York State in late 1891, he was determined to rob a train single-handedly.

He bought a ticket on the New York Central's fast flyer, No. 31.

On September 29, 1891, Perry cut a hole in the wall of the baggage car while the train was en route to Albany, New York, squeezed through and held up the express guards, taking about $2,000 in jewelry and cash. Just outside of Albany, Perry, hanging on by one hand, sawed the train's air hose between two cars, bringing it to a halt. He quickly ran to a nearby woods and escaped.

Small amounts were turned over to the lone bandit when he robbed two more New York Central trains the following year—one on February 21, 1892, near Syracuse, another on September 20, 1892, near Lyons. Perry's last train robbery, reckless though it may have been, possessed all the grit and gumption of latter-day Western film heroes.

Perry had learned that the New York Express Company's car would be carrying more than $100,000 in gold and jewelry in its safe. He purchased a ticket to Lyons on the day of that shipment and, during an eye-scratching hailstorm, climbed to the top of the express car while the train was hurtling through mountain gorges. He drilled a hole in the top of the car and then screwed a hook into the hole. Through the hook, the bandit threaded a rope. He then slowly let himself down the rope to the side of the express car and, with a spring of his legs, pushed himself outward away from the train and then, returning with full force to its side, crashed through one of the express car windows.

Guard Daniel T. McInerney blinked in amazement, said, "My God," and then tenaciously threw himself upon the outlaw. The two fought wildly through the length of the car for several minutes until Perry managed to withdraw his pistol, which he bashed against McInerney's head, knocking him senseless. During the fight, however, the valiant guard had pulled the signal rope, and this brought conductor Emil Leass on the run. He found Perry fumbling with the combination of the safe.

Perry, who had robbed the guard and the petty-cash box, looked up, startled, at the conductor, and then dashed to the door of the express car, flung it open, and dove out near Jordan, New York. By the time the train reached Lyons, authorities had been warned of the robbery, and a posse was waiting to board a train to take them back down the line to Jordan. Just as the lawmen were about to embark, the sedulous conductor, Leass, saw Perry calmly waiting for a train outside the station.

With Leass' shriek, the lawmen poured out of the train and began to chase the bandit across the yards. Perry, dashing frantically over the rails, reached a freight engine that already had a full head of steam, its cab deserted. He jumped on board and yanked the throttle. The locomotive ground out of the yards.

The amazed possemen boarded another train and gave pursuit. The chase was risky, especially for Perry, since his locomotive was running on the opposite track and an oncoming train would mean certain collision. When the pursuing locomotive loaded with lawmen came abreast of Perry's engine, the bandit and possemen began trading shots. Perry drove his locomotive with one hand and fired a pistol with the other. Though a dozen rifles were trained on him, the lawmen proved poor shots, their bullets missing Perry repeatedly.

The outlaw threw his locomotive into reverse in an effort to shake off his pursuers, but the experienced engineer in the other engine stayed with him. Back and forth, forward and reverse, the engines huffed and hissed. Stale-

The most inventive trainrobber in the business, Oliver Curtis Perry. (Pinkerton, Inc.)

mated, Perry finally gave up and brought his engine to a halt after spying a large stand of timber. He raced for cover. The lawmen were right behind him.

Perry stole a buggy from a nearby farmhouse and drove it wildly down a country road. The lawmen commandeered carriages and chased him, shots from their rifles echoing strangely through the valley at dusk.

After changing horses several times, Perry quit the twenty-five mile buggy chase and waded into a swamp. The lawmen went in after him. Sheriff J. Collins knew a showdown was at hand, and when he spotted Perry attempting to hide behind a log, he shouted: "Do you want to fight it out, Perry?"

The hard-breathing possemen staunchly clutched their rifles, preparing for a fight to the death. For a full minute nothing stirred in the shadowy swamp, and then Perry's high, almost girlish voice broke the lull: "No. I'm out of bullets . . . I guess it's all up with me."

Once in custody, the lone train robber was rushed to trial and quickly convicted. Perry recieved forty-nine years in Auburn Prison. The newspapers played up the bandit's clawing fearlessness. Pinkerton's superintendent George

Bangs was quoted as saying Perry's ingenious method of breaking into the New York Central's express car was "the most daring train robbery attempt in criminal history. I would call Perry the nerviest outlaw I ever heard of. There are few western badmen who possessed his courage."

The press fawned over Perry, and his reputation became such that several women proposed marriage to him in long, maudlin letters. One young lady, swept into the mawkish emotion whipped up by the newspapers' inflating of Perry's career, was moved to send him a saw secreted inside a Bible. The prisoner had been removed from Auburn Prison after creating several disturbances and sent to the State Hospital for the Criminally Insane at Matteawan, New York. Here, poorly paid guards were less inclined to check gifts sent to inmates, and the lovesick lady's saw went undetected. Before making his escape on April 10, 1895, the bandit penned a bit of doggerel and placed it on his bunk:

> I don't intend to serve this out,
>   Or even let despair,
> Deprive me of my liberty
>   Or give me one gray hair.

Within an hour, Perry sawed his way through the bars of his cell, stole a set of keys from a sleeping guard, and released a number of other prisoners. He then forced a window and spotted a drainpipe running down the side of the building. Once again, Perry relied on his athletic prowess. He stood on the windowsill, jumped sideways to grapple the pipe, and then rode it downward for eighty feet to the ground and freedom.

Penniless and hunted by hundreds of lawmen, Perry tramped his way to New York City and then moved to Weehawken, New Jersey. He was arrested by a town constable while roasting over a small fire a rabbit he had killed with a rock.

Authorities took no further chances with Perry. He was sent to the maximum-security prison at Dannemora. The train robber never gave up hope of escaping, but after several futile attempts he was permanently isolated in a narrow solitary-confinement cell where he stayed for twenty-five years.

Driven half-mad by the solitude, Perry built an odd contraption consisting of a block of wood and two nails which he evenly spaced so that when he dropped the gruesome machine with weights onto his face, both his eyes were pierced, causing permanent blindness.

Weeks later, he dictated a letter to a friend which read: "I was born in the light of day, against my will, of course. I now assert my right to shut out the light."

Perry, totally blind and without speaking a word for six years to his guards, died quietly in his Clinton Prison cell on September 10, 1930.

PONZI, CHARLES
Swindler • (1878-1949)

BACKGROUND: BORN IN ITALY, IMMIGRATED TO THE U.S., CIRCA 1893. MINOR PUBLIC EDUCATION. MARRIED ROSE PONZI. ORIGINAL OCCUPATION, TRANSLATING CLERK FOR AN IMPORT-EXPORT FIRM. **DESCRIPTION:** 5'2", BLACK EYES, BLACK HAIR, SLENDER. **ALIASES:** NONE. **RECORD:** ARRESTED FOR FORGERY IN MONTREAL, QUE., 1905, RECEIVED MINOR SENTENCE; ARRESTED FOR SMUGGLING ALIENS IN ATLANTA, GA., 1908, RECIEVED MINOR SENTENCE; PERPETRATED A GIANT FINANCIAL INVESTMENT SWINDLE BETWEEN 12/20/19 AND 8/13/20 IN BOSTON; ARRESTED BY FEDERAL AGENTS AND CONVICTED OF USING THE MAILS TO DEFRAUD; SENTENCED TO FOUR YEARS IN PLYMOUTH PRISON; ARRESTED UPON RELEASE FROM FEDERAL PRISON BY MASSACHUSETTS AUTHORITIES AND CONVICTED OF FRAUD; SENTENCED TO A SEVEN-TO-NINE YEAR TERM; POSTED BOND PENDING APPEAL AND FLED TO FLORIDA WHERE HE WAS ARRESTED IN 1925 ATTEMPTING TO DEFRAUD REAL-ESTATE INVESTORS; RECEIVED A YEAR IN JAIL; REARRESTED BY THE STATE OF MASSACHUSETTS UPON RELEASE AND SENT TO PRISON TO SERVE OUT PREVIOUS SENTENCE OF NINE YEARS; RELEASED IN 1934 AND DEPORTED TO ITALY; DIED IN RIO DE JANEIRO IN 1949.

Charles Ponzi was never anything more than a common swindler. His checkered career, however, failed to be lost to the oblivion of petty thievery and awkward frauds because he perpetrated with nerveless emotions and a permanent grin the simplest yet most gigantic financial hoax of the twentieth century. P. T. Barnum's axiom that there was a sucker "born every minute" was not lost on Ponzi.

To put across his fantastic scheme, Ponzi banked on the avariciousness of investors, the gullibility of the press, and the naiveté of Americans who believed all things possible in the free-enterprise system. It was terribly simple: he borrowed from Peter and paid Paul. And it worked . . . until Peter got wise.

After emigrating from Italy to the United States in the early 1890s, Ponzi became a waiter but was soon fired for being garrulous with customers. A Chaplinesque figure, Ponzi longed to dress like the elegantly tailored diners he had served. Jobless, he saw the promised riches of the New World fade. With two dollars in his pocket, he boarded a train bound for Canada. He was there only a short while before he was picked up for forging a check and sentenced to jail for a short term.

Undaunted, Ponzi rode the rails to Atlanta, where he convinced leaders of the Italian community that he could arrange to have members of their families still in Italy transported to America without the bother of immigration regulations. He apparently did manage to slip a few immigrants into the country, because he was shortly arrested and jailed briefly on a charge of smuggling aliens.

In 1914 Ponzi traveled to Boston, disgusted with his faulty get-rich-quick schemes. He met and married the daughter of a wholesale grocer and soon took over the business. The firm, under Ponzi's wacky procedures, floundered almost immediately. "The market just fell out," he explained to his despondent wife, Rose.

A year later, Ponzi became a $16-a-week translator for an import-export firm, J. P. Poole. His knowledge of Italian landed him the job. For two years the little schemer sat at his desk and worked out elaborate plans to bilk people out of millions, but he gave them up as impractical moments after they had hatched in his plotting brain. Then, in June, 1919, the "Ponzi Plan" materialized.

Little Charlie noticed a packet of International Postal Union reply coupons in the office. Upon inquiring, he learned that the coupons were purchased abroad and then sent to the United States or other countries not suffering economic depression and redeemed for a considerably higher rate than when purchased. In Italy or Germany, for instance, where depressed rates for these coupons were in effect, one could purchase a coupon for a penny. These could be redeemed for five cents in the United States, for more than that in other countries.

Ponzi's brain exploded. Here it was, the scheme of a lifetime. He quit his job and went home to work out the details. He first borrowed money and sent this to relatives in Europe, instructing them to buy postal coupons and return them to him. This was done, but when Ponzi attempted to redeem the coupons here, he met with horrendous red tape and his scheme was foiled.

Still, he would not give up the idea. Ponzi went to several Boston friends and told them as he waved his postal coupons on high that he could double their money in ninety days. His elaborate plan made little sense to his first investors, who had never even heard of postal-reply coupons, but they gambled small amounts with him. In ninety days Ponzi had paid back $750 interest on the first due date from initial investments totaling $1,250.

"Incredible . . . I can't believe it," one friend told him.

Ponzi smiled knowingly. "Re-invest and tell your friends."

In days, hundreds rushed to Ponzi with fistfuls of dollars with which to purchase postal-reply coupons. In weeks, thousands were flocking into the offices of Ponzi's new Financial Exchange Company on School Street in the heart of Boston's financial district. The affable wizard couldn't hire people fast enough to count the money, so he stuffed it into desk drawers, suitcases, filing cabinets, wastebaskets.

Forty thousand frenzied investors, mostly little people, dumped their life savings into Ponzi's coffers. The amazing thing was that from December 20, 1919, until he was exposed the following year, Ponzi paid off, first at 50 per cent interest every ninety days and then at 50 per cent interest every forty-five days. His harried clerks—mostly members of his wife's family who barely spoke English let alone knew how to handle delicate investment data— scooped up an estimated $200,000 a day from investors during the firm's peak period.

A financial writer on one of Boston's newspapers dared to suggest that Little Charlie's financial dealings were questionable and that no financier, even the "Great Ponzi," as Charlie liked to be called, could legitimately provide such earnings in so short a time.

Ponzi read the article and sued the writer and the paper for $500,000 damages. His brazenness stunned and quieted the press, nullifying any probes into his business matters for some time. Meanwhile, the Great Ponzi realized his dream of riches and luxury. He bought a twenty-room mansion in Lexington for $100,000; he bought a $12,000, chauffeur-driven Locomobile; he bought the Poole firm where he had spent two years at a job he hated (and upon taking over, fired his old employer); he bought two hundred suits, one hundred pairs of shoes, four dozen Malacca canes with solid-gold handles, two dozen diamond stickpins, one hundred five-dollar ties—Charlie Ponzi bought everything in sight and still he couldn't spend money fast enough to clear it out of every nook and cranny in his spacious offices.

He continued to pay his incredible interest rates on old investments with the money from new investments. By the summer of 1920 Ponzi, who spent most of his time posing for pictures while smoking through a diamond-studded cigarette holder and hustling bags of money to his car, thought it wise to invest elsewhere. He walked into the esteemed Hanover Trust Company with two suitcases full of large bills, totaling $3 million, and bought a controlling interest.

When the *Boston Post* asked for an interview with the financial genius, Ponzi grew leery and hired a public-relations man, William McMasters, to deal with the press. McMasters became suspicious of his employer from the first moment he walked into Ponzi's offices.

"The man was a financial idiot," the PR man later stated. "He could hardly add. There was money stuffed into every conceivable place in his offices. He sat around with his feet on the desk, talking complete gibberish about postal coupons."

McMasters went to the state authorities, who were already interested in the blossoming financial Ponzi empire that had spread with electrifying rapidity through New England, New York, and New Jersey, where branch offices of the Financial Exchange Company were doing brisk business. At the PR man's urging, state investigators called in Ponzi and his books.

He arrived at the State House in Boston in late July, 1920, carrying a stack of moth-eaten ledgers. Hundreds of his fanatically loyal investors were at the entrance to greet and encourage him. He posed on the steps waving confidently.

"You're the greatest Italian of them all!" one man yelled.

"Oh, no," Ponzi modestly offered. "Columbus and Marconi. Columbus discovered America. Marconi discovered the wireless."

"Sure, but you discovered money!" came the reply.

State auditors labored over Ponzi's labyrinthine books and distractedly reported that they could make nothing out of them. Enormous sums had been entered in the ledgers without dates and the names of investors. Investors' names had been entered without the amounts of their investments.

When some of Ponzi's workers were interviewed, they responded to the simplest questions with stares of wonder. They had no idea how Mr. Ponzi worked his business. They merely paid people who showed up with notes at collection time and took money from those who wanted to give it to Mr. Ponzi.

At this point the *Boston Globe*, whose reporters had been quietly investigating Ponzi's background for months, exposed the financial wizard, citing his former arrests and convictions for smuggling and forgery. The balloon burst, and the Ponzi exchange was inundated with thousands of investors demanding the return of their money on August 13, 1920. Ponzi ordered his clerks to "pay everybody off." Inside of eight months, the diminutive tycoon had taken in $20,000,000. After paying off $15,000,000, his clerks ran out of money.

Thousands of investors trailed from his offices into the

Charles Ponzi at the zenith of his multi-million dollar swindle in 1920. (UPI)

street and around several corners, all on the verge of rioting. Desperately, Charlie Ponzi ran about his office, muttering and peeping into boxes, drawers, and cabinets. "There's more here," he was heard to say, "there's gotta be more here." He knew there wasn't; only two days previously, according to one report, he had packed close to $2,000,000 in a suitcase and driven to Saratoga Springs in a last-ditch effort to win enough at the gambling tables to shore up his company. He had lost it all.

Federal agents arrested Ponzi in his mansion days later on charges of using the mails to defraud. He had sent some of his investors letters reminding them to reinvest in his swindle. He got four years in Plymouth prison. On his release in 1925, Ponzi was arrested by Massachusetts authorities for his swindle and convicted in a speedy trial. He was sentenced to nine years in jail, but posted bond pending appeal and then skipped to Florida, where he attempted to defraud investors in the feverish land boom there. He was again arrested and jailed for a year. Upon his release, the State of Massachusetts claimed him, and he served out his original nine-year term, being paroled in 1934. With his parole went an automatic deportation order to Italy.

Reporters who interviewed him before he sailed saw a different Charles Ponzi. His mouth drooped, his hands twitched, he was dressed in an old suit and unpolished shoes with the heels worn down. His wife Rose had left him, and he was returning to the land of his childhood with empty pockets.

"I bear no grudges," he told reporters. "I hope the world forgives me."

If the world didn't, dictator Benito Mussolini certainly did. He gave Ponzi a high-ranking job in the financial section of his government, but soon learned that little Charlie was unreliable as well as inept. Before charges were brought, Ponzi skipped to South America with a large unstated sum from Mussolini's treasury.

His name all but disappeared until 1949, when his death in a Rio de Janeiro charity ward was reported. There was still a matter of $3,000,000 Ponzi never accounted for, money he took from investors but failed to return. These "Ponzi millions" vanished as completely as did little Charlie's dream of wealth and his amorphous money machine.

PURPLE GANG

Detroit was plagued by this vicious gang of murderous thugs during the Prohibition years. Hundreds of killings in Detroit's bootleg wars were attributed to the Purples, who were led by Abe Bernstein. Other notorious members of the gang included Ed Fletcher,

Purple Gang members Abe Axler and Ed Fletcher were taken for a one-way ride in 1933 when the national syndicate took over Detroit. (UPI)

George F. Lewis, and the brothers Harry and Phil Keywell, the latter two suspected of being loaned out to Al Capone as spotters for the hit men who shot down seven of George "Bugs" Moran's gangsters in the St. Valentine's Day Massacre.

The Purples concentrated on bootlegging hijacking, jewelry thefts, and widespread extortion. The proximity of Detroit to Canada placed the Purple Gang in a strategic position to supply Chicago gangs with Canadian liquor. Capone became the chief importer of Purple Gang whiskey, which was shipped to him under the label "Log Cabin."

Though the gang exported booze and killers to other towns, Bernstein and his lieutenants found it necessary to bring safecracking specialists like Morris "Red" Rudensky to Detroit for important jewelry thefts. Rudensky was paid a straight fee for the jobs he pulled, all marked in advance by the Purples. His fees ran from $5,000 to $15,000. The gang also marked and cased several out-of-town "jugs" and "cribs" (safes) to be broken into by Ru-

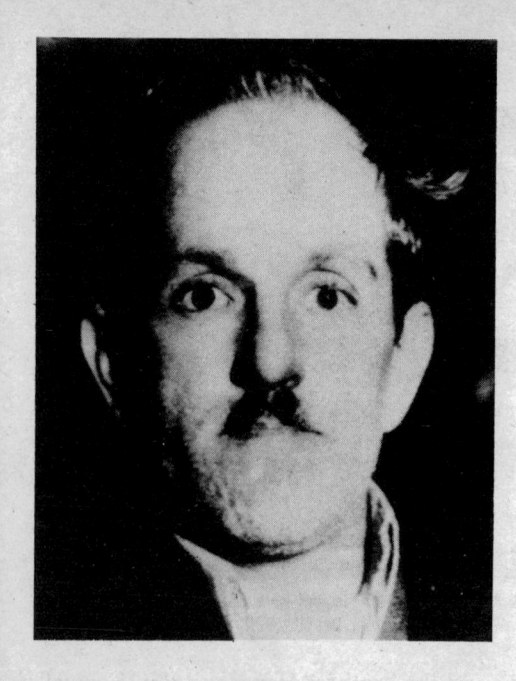

Detroit mobster George F. Lewis, a Purple Gang member, was held for questioning by police in the 1929 St. Valentine's Day Massacre. (UPI)

densky and his safecracking partners, Smitty Krueger and "Dago" Vanelli, such as the $1,500,000 jewelry theft in St. Louis in the 1920s.

Later, Bernstein and other Purple Gang members became partners in several Miami gambling casinos with Meyer Lansky and Joe Adonis. When the national crime syndicate was formed by Luciano, Lansky, Lepke, and others in 1934, the Purple Gang was systematically incorporated into the new crime cartel.

[ALSO SEE St. Valentine's Day Massacre.]

ROTHSTEIN, ARNOLD
Gambler • (1882-1928)

BACKGROUND: BORN AND RAISED IN NEW YORK, N.Y., THE SON OF A SHOPKEEPER. MINOR PUBLIC EDUCATION. MARRIED, NO CHILDREN. **DESCRIPTION:** 5'10", BROWN EYES, BROWN HAIR, HEAVYSET. **ALIASES:** MR. BIG, THE BRAIN, MR. A., A. R., THE MAN TO SEE, THE MAN UPTOWN, THE BIG BANKROLL. **RECORD:** ARRESTED UNDER SUSPICION OF FENCING THE NOTORIOUS MAIL-BOND-ROBBERY BONDS STOLEN FROM WALL STREET BANKS IN 1918, DISMISSED; ARRESTED IN NEW YORK, JANUARY, 1919, FOR HOLDING AN ILLEGAL CRAP GAME AND WOUNDING TWO CITY DETECTIVES MAKING THE ARREST, DISMISSED; APPEARED BEFORE A CHICAGO GRAND JURY IN 1920 ON SUSPICION OF FIXING BASEBALL'S 1919 WORLD SERIES, DISMISSED WITHOUT INDICTMENT; FINANCED ILLEGAL SPEAKEASIES THROUGHOUT MANHATTAN AND GANGS LED BY JACK "LEGS" DIAMOND, JACOB "LITTLE AUGIE" ORGEN, AND LARRY FAY WHICH INVADED THE UNIONS THROUGHOUT THE 1920S; SHOT IN A POKER GAME AT THE PARK CENTRAL HOTEL IN NEW YORK 11/4/28, DYING AT POLYCLINIC HOSPITAL WITHOUT NAMING HIS KILLERS.

Arnold Rothstein was Mr. Big for so long that gamblers, murderers, and common prostitutes alike had only to whisper his initials, "A. R.," up and down the Broadway strip for anyone to get the meaning.

And the meaning was always clear. Rothstein, who had been a millionaire gambler in Manhattan for twenty years, could fix anything. A. R. could fix a bet, a night in bed with a Broadway star—or someone's violent death.

Rothstein's criminal gift, and the reason why he remained Mr. Big on Broadway for so long, was that no one could ever prove anything incriminating against him. His hands were always clean, his henchmen took the falls for him. And nobody ever disagreed or talked back to Mr. Big.

But Rothstein began small, as the son of a respected Jewish immigrant merchant. The father was called Rothstein the Just for his high-principled life and business transactions, but Arnie was completely different.

Rothstein began to gamble impulsively as a child. He had a quick mind that could handle numbers like a modern-day computer. All day long he figured odds.

His friend Nicky Arnstein (Jules W. Arndt Stein, who later became Fanny Brice's lover) tossed random numbers to him. Rothstein added, multiplied, or subtracted the lengthy numbers instantly and belched out the correct answer.

"It isn't good for you, A. R.," Nicky said. "It isn't normal and you'll hurt your brain."

"Just exercise," Rothstein replied.

As a teenager, Rothstein gambled his way into a fortune. His nerves and ruthless composure betrayed no emotion whether he was shooting craps in a Manhattan alleyway or drawing three cards at poker. He always won.

He was a close friend of gambler Herman Rosenthal, who was killed by Charles Becker in 1912.

By the time he was twenty, Rothstein was half-owner of a high-toned New York gambling den which sported thick carpets, glass chandeliers, and champagne at every table. Upstairs, Rothstein had a string of sultry, expensive whores for customers wanting more diversion.

His take at such a tender age was more than $10,000 a week. For most, this kind of super-livelihood would have been more than enough. But A. R. was greedy. Money was power in New York, and power was what Rothstein most lusted after.

He began to steal from his partner by skimming off huge gobs of money from the nightly take. His partner discovered the thefts and told Rothstein to beat it or take a bullet in the head. Rothstein went elsewhere.

Probably the greatest scandal in American sports—the fixing of the 1919 World Series by bribing eight Chicago White Sox players (afterward called "The Black Sox")—was attributed to Rothstein.

The fixing of the 1919 World Series was a bumbling, awkward affair handled by ex-featherweight boxing champion Abe Attell and almost certainly masterminded by his good friend and employer, Arnold Rothstein. Eight players of the winning Chicago White Sox—Eddie Cicotte, "Shoeless" Joe Jackson, Charles "Swede" Risberg, George "Buck" Weaver, Claude Williams, Oscar "Happy" Felsch, Chick Gandil, and Freddie McMullin—were bribed by Attell (for approximately $70,000) to throw the first and second games of the series.

The cry that went up for Rothstein's head after the fix was discovered was mighty, but the nerveless gambler, acting under the advice of his shrewd lawyer, William Fallon, traveled to Chicago in 1920, where he faced a grand jury investigating the baseball scandal.

Rothstein leaped to the attack, challenging the city's pride. "Gentlemen," he roared at the jurors, "what kind of courtesy is this? What kind of a city is this? I came here voluntarily, and what happens? A gang of thugs bar my path with cameras [newsmen], as though I was a notorious person—a criminal even! I'm entitled to an apology. I demand one! Such a thing couldn't happen in New York. I'm surprised at you."

This audacity proved to be the right ploy, and Rothstein was not indicted.

Though no one ever proved that A. R. did the bribing, Mr. Big never denied it; he liked having that kind of fame. Fixing a World Series was big-time crime, and that's where Rothstein wanted his name and image.

Friends meant nothing to Rothstein. For instance, his closest associate for years was Nicky Arnstein. But when police captured a gang of killers and heistmen who were robbing Wall Street messengers carrying securities between brokerage houses, Rothstein threw Nicky to the wolves.

The thieves only knew their boss, they said, as "Mr. A." They told police that Mr. A. directed all the robberies and killings from a comfortable office uptown. They had never met him.

But they had glimpsed him—or so they thought.

Before the thefts, when the thieves demanded Arnstein's stooges to tell them who Mr. A. was, Rothstein sent another stooge to take them to an all-night restaurant. The flunky told the thieves that Mr. A. sat in the big window table there every evening.

The man in the window was hapless Nicky Arnstein.

Arnstein was identified as Mr. A. after the thieves were caught. He was sent to a federal penitentiary in 1922. That was the way Mr. Big dealt with his "friends."

As the twenties roared, so did Rothstein. He bet heavily on just about anything, fixing the odds and, when possible, the outcome. He never seemed to lose.

Rothstein's interests grew. He bought race-horses, nightclubs, gambling casinos, and red-plush whorehouses.

To protect this ever-increasing empire, he hired one of the most fanatical killers in America—Jack "Legs" Diamond, who saved his life on numerous occasions.

For instance, when Dutch Schultz tried to take over some of Rothstein's gambling interests, Legs—at A. R.'s orders—killed six of the Dutchman's boys within three days.

Dutch Schultz got the message and backed off. Rothstein became such a power in the New York underworld that his orders were obeyed even by rival gangs. For example, when the Owney Madden and Waxey Gordon gangs began blasting each other in an all-out war, it was Rothstein who arranged a truce.

He settled the argument—with Legs Diamond standing behind him—in twenty minutes. It was his singular pride that he could wield such power. His plan was simple; he described how the boys could carve up the rackets and all make money.

Reportedly, A. R. got $500,000 to mediate the first gangland summit conference in America.

No one got in Rothstein's way now. He lived high, with an estimated fortune of $50 million salted away in banks.

Every night his chauffeur-driven limousine pulled to the curb at Broadway and 49th Street. Rothstein got out and walked down to 42nd and back. On his walk, Rothstein laid down his bets with sharpers waiting on the street. He carried $200,000 on him all the time in crisp $1,000 bills. He collected and paid off as he walked. Mostly, he collected.

Sometimes, to keep his name in kingly status, Rothstein would pass on a tip. Within minutes, thousands of tongues were wagging: "Get in on this. A. R.'s got the fix in."

Rothstein, after making the rounds of several nightclubs, wound up at Lindy's and continued to take bets there until dawn.

Then he drove either home to his beautiful wife or to one of the two-dozen plush apartments he kept and the showgirl mistresses waiting there for him.

The money rolled in so fast that Rothstein couldn't find enough ways to gamble or invest it. So he loaned it for more power. He loaned vast sums to judges, police captains, commissioners, stage stars, and politicians. His interest rates were high, and Legs Diamond did the collecting.

But some of A. R.'s loan-shark clients—judges especially—were not pushed to repay. Instead, he took his interest in other ways, such as having indictments quashed against his hired killers, gambling-den managers, and call girls.

He literally owned Broadway and almost all of Manhattan. And he dressed like it. All of his suits cost $400 or more. His shoes were $50 a pair.

At forty-six, Arnold Rothstein had not only arrived, he was uncrowned king of the underworld and almost everything on top of it.

Then, for reasons no one has ever explained, Rothstein went to pieces in 1928. His face took on a sickly pallor, his dress became unkempt, his hands shook. His confidence seemed to fade.

Worse, Rothstein started to lose and lose big.

His bets still went down, but now he was coming up a loser. He dropped tens, then hundreds of thousands of dollars on the horses and at poker tables.

The financial crash came in September, 1928. Between the 8th and 10th of that month, Rothstein tried to recoup his losses in what was, perhaps, the biggest poker game of the decade.

Sitting in the expensive apartment of George "Hump"

Gambler Arnold Rothstein was known as Mr. Big in New York until his luck ran out in 1928. (UPI)

McManus at the Park Central, Rothstein lost hand after hand to two newcomers from California—sharp, fast gamblers "Nigger Nate" Raymond and "Titanic" Thompson.

For two days, these men battled back and forth, with A. R. losing consistently. He lost his nerve and his sophistication. He screamed that they were cheating. They laughed. Laughed! At Mr. Big!

After forty-eight hours, the play came down to Rothstein and Nigger Nate. A. R. foolishly bet $50,000 on a high-card draw. Nigger Nate agreed.

Rothstein drew a queen and smiled.

Nigger Nate drew an ace.

Rothstein jumped from his chair, exploding in a hail of curses. McManus tallied A. R.'s losses. They came to $320,000.

Snarling, Rothstein headed for the door. "I'll pay off

in a day or two," he yelled over his shoulder. "I don't carry that sort of dough under my fingernails!"

He was lying, of course. Rothstein had that and more in his inside coat pocket. Nigger Nate nodded coolly.

In twenty-four hours, A. R. told waiters from his reserved table at Lindy's that the game was fixed. "I don't pay off on fixed poker," Rothstein said.

His words were like a shock wave down Broadway. Arnold Rothstein was welshing on a bet!

Weeks went by, and Rothstein was contacted by unknown parties who wanted the account closed.

"I won't pay off!" several heard him yell over the phone. "The game was rigged!"

On November 4, 1928, Rothstein laid down more than half a million dollars that Herbert Hoover would beat Al Smith in the Presidential election. He took bets that night in Lindy's.

A. R. was called to the phone.

Soon he was putting on his coat. "I'm going up to the Park Central," he told intimates, "to see Hump McManus."

Less than a half hour later, a bellboy in the Park Central found Mr. Big holding his stomach in the service entrance. Blood was gushing from a bullet wound.

Detectives later followed the trail of blood to the suite rented by Hump McManus. Rothstein was rushed by police ambulance to the Polyclinic Hospital, where police asked him to name his killer. But A. R. kept the underworld code to the last. Smiling, he raised his finger to his lips. Then his head slumped forward and he was dead.

Nigger Nate Raymond was arrested but released. He had a beautiful alibi—a blonde who told the judge brassily that Nigger Nate was her bed partner at the time A. R. was being killed.

Hump McManus had no blonde, and he went to trial. But there was no substantial evidence against him either and he, too, was released.

The story that A. R. had drawn a royal flush in his last poker hand was untrue. There were five sets of cards on the table in McManus' room. One hand was a disaster—not even an ace high. It had A. R.'s blood on it.

SCHULTZ, DUTCH
(ARTHUR FLEGENHEIMER)
Bootlegger • (1902-1935)

BACKGROUND: BORN IN BRONX, N.Y., 8/6/02 TO EMMA (NEU) AND HERMAN FLEGENHEIMER, OWNER OF A SALOON AND STABLE. ATTENDED P.S. 12 IN THE BRONX THROUGH 4TH GRADE. WIFE, FRANCES, NO CHILDREN. ORIGINAL OCCUPATION, PRINTER. DESCRIPTION: 5'9", BLUE EYES, LIGHT BROWN HAIR, STOCKY BUILD. ALIASES: THE DUTCHMAN, DUTCH SCHULTZ. RECORD: BECAME A MEMBER OF THE BERGEN AVENUE GANG AT AGE 14 (FOLLOWING HIS FATHER'S DESERTION OF THE FAMILY); COMMITTED SEVERAL PETTY HOLDUPS AND BURGLARIES; ARRESTED IN 1919 FOR BURGLARY AND CONVICTED, SENTENCED TO FIFTEEN MONTHS IN JAIL WHICH HE SERVED; UPON RELEASE PURCHASED A BRONX SALOON AND ADOPTED THE NAME DUTCH SCHULTZ FROM AN INFAMOUS MEMBER OF THE DEFUNCT FROG HOLLOW GANG WHICH HAD OPERATED IN THE BRONX BEFORE THE TURN OF THE CENTURY; ENLISTED SUCH TOUGHS AS JOEY RAO AND FORMED A GANG THAT CONTROLLED BOOTLEGGING IN THE BRONX AND PARTS OF MANHATTAN FROM THE MIDDLE 1920S TO HIS DEATH; ALSO TOOK OVER CONTROL OF THE POLICY GAME IN HARLEM; WENT INTO SLOT MACHINES THROUGHOUT NEW YORK WITH DANDY PHIL KASTEL, JOEY RAO AND FRANK COSTELLO; PROMINENT IN RESTAURANT RACKETS IN MANHATTAN FROM LATE 1920S TO EARLY 1930S; ORDERED GANGSTER RIVAL JACK "LEGS" DIAMOND SHOT TO DEATH IN 1931; ORDERED GANGSTER VINCENT

"MAD DOG" COLL KILLED THE FOLLOWING YEAR; TRIED FOR INCOME-TAX EVASION (REPUTEDLY MADE $481,000 FROM 1929 TO 1931 FROM THE SALE OF HIS BOOTLEGGED NEEDLE BEER ALONE) IN 1933; ACQUITTED; ORDERED HIS FIRST LIEUTENANT, BO WEINBERG, KILLED (MURDERED BY BENJAMIN "BUGSY" SIEGEL) IN 1933; DEMANDED THAT SPECIAL PROSECUTOR THOMAS E. DEWEY OF N.Y.C. BE KILLED BUT THE BOARD MEMBERS OF THE NEWLY-CREATED NATIONAL CRIME SYNDICATE, NOTABLY LOUIS LEPKE BUCHALTER AND CHARLES LUCKY LUCIANO VETOED THE ACTION; WHEN SCHULTZ INSISTED UPON KILLING DEWEY, THE BOARD CONDEMNED HIM TO DEATH; SHOT AND KILLED WITH THREE BODYGUARDS IN THE PALACE CHOPHOUSE IN NEWARK, N.J., 10/23/35 BY CHARLES "THE BUG" WORKMAN AND MENDY WEISS.

New York's mobsters in the 1920s were slick. In Capone's wild and woolly Chicago 1,000 rival gangsters died in the streets over a ten-year period. But in Little Old New York, "the boys" knew better. You only killed for business, not pleasure or loyalty or anger. Kid stuff. Kill for money!

At first such suave mobsters as Owney Madden, Waxey Gordon (Irving Wexler), Vannie Higgins, and Little Augie Orgen ran things. No pistol-smoking shootouts on busy corners. Keep it smooth, work with Tammany Hall and the politicians. Is everybody happy?

There was one who wasn't. He was a wild Third Avenue punk named Arthur Flegenheimer. The Roaring Twenties and all its bootleg riches were passing him by.

A product of Bronx's Bergen Avenue Street Gang, Flegenheimer stole his nickname from a once-feared thug named Dutch Schultz. Schultz's early years were misspent in gang battles but he did manage to go through four years of grade school at P.S. 12 in the Bronx. Oddly enough, his principal then was Dr. J. F. Condon who was to become famous years later as the mysterious "Jafsie," the go-between who handed the Lindbergh ransom money over to kidnapper-murderer Bruno Richard Hauptmann.

The Dutchman turned bad shortly after his father deserted the family in 1916. His mother, a pious, warm-hearted woman who worked hard to keep Schultz in clothes and food, took in washing. Dutch took up a bag of burglar tools.

He began by opening a few speakeasies, supplying them with hooch run down from Canada in his own trucks. He also manufactured his own needle beer, the worst in town.

He lined up his own gunsels, over one hundred of them, and he muscled in on the bigger boys. Jack "Legs" Diamond worked for him briefly, then branched out on his own.

At fist Dutch didn't care. It was when Legs and his troop started hijacking Schultz beer that the Dutchman blew his top. New York's first full-scale gang war broke out.

Legs, who got his nickname by turning on the speed after swiping packages from horse-drawn delivery wagons, was also known as the Clay Pigeon. Diamond carried so many bullets in him that he jingled when he walked.

For years, the Dutchman and Legs battled it out while Luciano, Genovese, and Costello bided their time.

Then, on December 19, 1931, luck ran out for Legs. Celebrating with his girl, Kiki Roberts, after being released on a kidnapping charge, Diamond saw his number come up. An ace Schultz gunner, Bo Weinberg, slipped the latch on the door of his dingy room, quietly crept up on the sleeping Legs and pumped seventeen steel-jacketed shells into him.

Dutch Schultz's epitaph for Legs was succinct: "Just another punk caught with his hands in my pockets. That's why Bo took him." The Dutchman's philosophy in a nutshell.

As his debonair mouthpiece, Dixie Davis (also rubbed out later), once said about Dutch, "You can insult Arthur's girl, spit in his face, push him around—and he'll laugh. But don't steal a dollar from his accounts. If you do, you're dead."

Another young man with ideas, Vincent Coll, didn't believe Dixie. He and his brother Pete went to work as part of Dutch's army of hired guns. But in three months Coll went single.

"The Mick," as Dutch called Coll, wasn't content with his own operation; he wanted Dutch's $20 million-a-year booze and policy racket empires, too.

The Dutchman's war with Vincent Coll was brief but bloody. In one attempt to kill Schultz lieutenant Joey Rao,

Coll sprayed a crowded Manhattan street with machinegun bullets, killing a small child and wounding a half dozen more.

This kind of insanity earned for Coll his nickname "Mad Dog" and the Dutchman's fear. Once, in June, 1931, while being accompanied by his bodyguard Dannie Iamascia, Schultz spotted two figures lurking in the shadows near his headquarters on upper Fifth Avenue.

"The Mick!" he hissed to Iamascia and both drew their guns, popping away at two city detectives, Steve DiRosa and Julius Salke, who had been keeping the Dutchman under surveillance. The policemen returned the fire and Iamascia fell to the pavement, critically wounded.

Schultz, after glancing at his fallen henchman, threw his pistol down an alleyway and ran. DiRosa charged after him (although one well-aimed bullet could have rid the city of Schultz) and tackled him. Dutch quickly yanked $18,600 from his pockets and offered it to DiRosa as a bribe to let him go.

"Here, take it all," he said.

DiRosa became incensed. "You miserable bum!" he yelled. "I'll shove that dough down your throat!" When Sergeant Salke ran up, he found DiRosa trying to do exactly that.

It was darkly clever, the way they got Coll. The movies have used it a thousand times since. While Dutch's friend, Owney Madden, stalled the Mad Dog on the phone (Coll was blackmailing Owney at the time) Schultz had the call traced. Several minutes later three men pulled up to a drugstore on West Twenty-Third Street. Coll stood in the phone booth threatening Madden. Bo Weinberg hauled out a machinegun from beneath his long overcoat and opened up.

The glass booth exploded, and Coll tumbled out dead.

The Dutchman's troubles were just beginning. He was charged with income-tax fraud and went to trial. After getting a change of venue to a small town court in upstate New York, Dutch became a nice guy. He hired a public relations firm to spread his money around to needy charities. He became a model family man.

One admirer seeing him in his drab, cheap clothes said he should improve his attire. "Such display is vulgar,"

Schultz said. "Personally, I think only queers wear silk shirts . . . I never bought one in my life. A guy's a sucker to spend fifteen or twenty dollars on a shirt. Hell, a guy can get a good one for two bucks!"

His thrifty chatter hoodwinked the hayseeds. They said he wasn't guilty.

While Schultz was on trial, Luciano, Genovese, and the others of the newly-established crime syndicate seized his rackets. Bo Weinberg complained to Lucky Luciano, "But what if Schultz comes back?"

"That loudmouth is never coming back," Luciano promised. But the Dutchman did come back. With murder in his eyes. He knew that he was outnumbered but he wasn't out. So Dutch went across the river to Newark, N.J. to lick his wounds and rebuild his forces. Bo Weinberg was the first order of business—he had his disloyal minion stabbed to death.

In 1935, Special Prosecutor Thomas E. Dewey was appointed to bust up the N. Y. rackets. Mayor Fiorello LaGuardia wanted the Dutchman's blood.

Dewey went to work attacking and raiding Schultz's policy rackets with a vengeance. The Dutchman went crazy. He called a meeting of the syndicate's board members. "Dewey's my nemesis," he told the crime lords. "He's gotta go."

Johnny Torrio, who'd left the palmy-though-bloody Chicago days behind, tried reasoning with Schultz. "You just can't go around bumping off big shots like him, Dutch."

"It'll bring down the heat on all of us," Luciano said.

"It's bad for business," Joe Adonis said.

Schultz went berserk. He shouted, he waved his arms. "You guys stole my rackets and now you're feeding me to the law. Dewey's gotta go. I'm hitting him myself . . . and in forty-eight hours!" He stomped out.

Every eye in the room turned to the deadly-looking Albert Anastasia, the new head of Murder, Incorporated, the syndicate's enforcer arm. "Okay," he said coldly. "Schultz goes tonight."

Dutch was in the Palace Chophouse in Newark with some of his men that night, plotting how he'd kill Dewey. Outside a car pulled up. Charlie "The Bug" Workman,

Mendy Weiss, and a man named Piggy got out and, like little boys, pressed their faces to the window of the restaurant. "He's in there!" Piggy said.

"You guys wait here," the Bug said, "I'll hit the Dutchman alone." Piggy sat behind the wheel of the car. Mendy stood watch on the sidewalk.

Workman sauntered through the half-empty bar area, heading toward the rear where the Dutchman held court. "I'd better check the john," he told himself. He kicked the door open, gun drawn, and saw a heavy-set man washing his hands. He looked familiar but the Bug didn't ask his name. He fired rapidly and the man crashed to the floor.

Then, like a Western marshal, Workman waded into the back area of the Chophouse, two .38's blazing. Schultz's startled gunsels returned fire but missed. In ten seconds Abe "Misfit" Landau, Lulu Rosencranz, and Otto "Abbadabba" Berman were all dead.

"But where's Schultz?" the Bug wondered. "The guy in the john!" He went back to the washroom and rifled the Dutchman's pockets, taking several thousand dollars. Workman still resides in the New Jersey State Prison for this mass slaying.

The Dutchman was hit all right, but he wasn't dead. Rushed to the Newark City Hospital, Schultz lay dying and raving. His last words, as he slipped in and out of a coma, his body leaking blood like a sieve (five hundred cubic centimeters of blood were administered to him in fruitless, massive transfusions), was a grim ode to the short, brutal life of a gangster.

The Dutchman's last words (taken down by police stenographer, F. J. Lang): "George, don't make no full moves. What have you done with him? Oh, mama, mama, mama. Oh, stop it, stop it; oh, oh, oh. Sure, sure, mama.

"Now listen, Phil, [possibly referring to his ex-partner policy king Dandy Phil Kastel], fun is fun. Ah, please, papa. What happened to the sixteen? Oh, oh, he done it. Please.

"John, [a reference to Johnny Torrio?] please, oh, did you buy the hotel? You promised a million, sure. Get out. I wished I knew.

"Please make it quick, fast and furious. Please. Fast and furious. Please help me get out. I am getting my wind back, thank God. Please, please, oh, please. You will have to please tell him, you got no case.

"You get ahead with the dot-dash system. Didn't I speak that time last night? Whose number is that in your pocket book, Phil—13780.

"Who was it? Oh—please, please. Reserve decision. Police, police. Henry and Frankie.

"Oh, oh, dog biscuits and when he is happy, he doesn't get snappy . . . please, please to do this. Then Henry, Henry, Frankie you didn't meet him, you didn't even meet me. The glove will fit what I say. Oh, Kayiyi, Kayiyi. Sure, who cares when you are through? How do you know this?

"How do you know this? Well, then—oh, Cocao know—thinks he is a grandpa again. He is jumping around. No Hobo and Poboe. I think it means the same thing."

Police Sergeant L. Conlon attempted to quiz Schultz about the shooting at the Chophouse. "Who shot you?" he asked Dutch.

"The boss himself."

"He did?"

"Yes, I don't know."

"What did he shoot you for?"

"I showed him boss. Do you hear me meet him? An appointment. Appeal stuck. All right, mother."

"Was it the boss who shot you?"

"Who shot me? No one."

"We will help you."

"Will you get me up? Okay, I won't be such a big creep. Oh, mama, I can't go through with it. Please. Oh—and then he clips me; come on. Cut that out. We don't owe a nickel. Hold it. Instead, hold it against him. I am a pretty good pretzler. Winnifred. Department of Justice. I even got it from the department. Sir, please stop it. Say listen the—last night."

"Don't holler," Conlon told the delirious gangster.

"I don't want to holler."

"What did they shoot you for?"

"I don't know, sir, honestly I don't. I don't even know who was with me, honestly. I went to the toilet. I was in the toilet and when I reach the—the boy came at me."

"The big fellow gave it to you?"

"Yes, he gave it to me."

"Do you know who this big fellow was?"

"No." Schultz rolled back into raving: "If we wanted to break the ring . . . No, please—get a month. They did it. Come on,——[name garbled], cut me off and says you are not to be the beneficiary of this will. Is that right? I will be checked and double checked and please pull for me. Will you pull? How many good ones and how many bad ones? Please, I had nothing with him; he was a cowboy in one of the seven days a week fight. No business. No hangouts. No friends. Nothing. Just what you pick up and what you need.

"I don't know who shot me. Don't put anyone near this check. You might have. Please do it for me. Let me get up, heh? In the olden days, they waited and they waited. Please give me shot. It is from the factory. Sure, that is a bad—well. Oh, good, ahead. That happens for trying. I don't want harmony. I want harmony. Oh, mama, mama! Who give it to him? Who give it to him? Let me in the district—fire—factory that he was nowhere near. It smoldered.

"No, no. There are only ten of us. There are ten million fighting somewhere of you, so get your onions up and we will throw up the truce flag. Oh, please let me up. Please shift me. Police are here. Communistic—strike—baloney—honestly this is a habit I get. Sometimes I give it and sometimes I don't. Oh, I am still in. That settles it. Are you sure? Please let me get in and eat. Let him harness himself to you and then bother you.

"Please don't ask me to go there. I don't want to. I still don't want him in the path. It is no use to stage a riot. The sidewalk was in trouble and the bears were in trouble and I broke it up. Please put me in that room. Please keep him in control. My gilt-edged stuff and those dirty rats have tuned in. Please, mother, don't tear, don't rip; that is something that shouldn't be spoken about. Please get me up, my friends. Please look out, the shooting is a bit wild and that kind of shooting saved a man's life.

"No payrolls. No walls. No coupons. That would be entirely out. Pardon me, I forgot. I am plaintiff and not defendant. Look out. Look out for him. Please. He owes

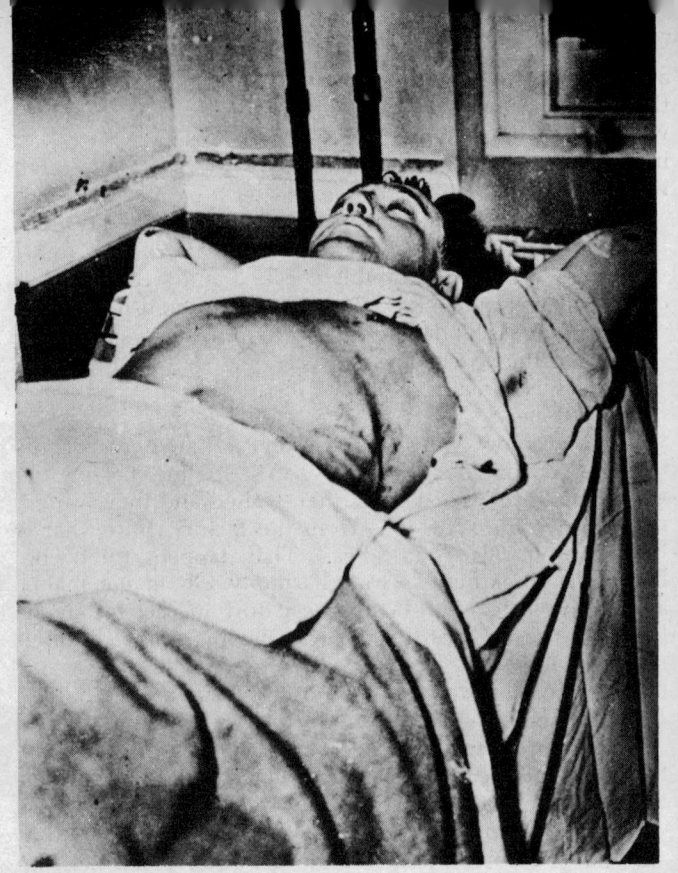

New York gangster Dutch Schultz mortally wounded, 10/23/35, babbled and raved before dying. (UPI)

me money; he owes everyone money. Why can't he just pull out and give me control?

"Please, mother, you pick me up now. Please, you know me.

"No, don't scare me. My friends and I think I do a better job. Police are looking for you all over. Be instrumental in letting us know. They are Englishmen [a possible reference to British-born Owney Madden] and they are a type and I don't know who is best, they or us. Oh, sir, get the doll a roofing. You can play jacks and girls do that with a soft ball and do tricks with it. It takes all events into consideration. No. No. And it is no. A boy has never wept nor dashed a thousand kim. Did you hear me?"

"Who shot you," Conlon again asked the Dutchman.

"I don't know."

"The doctor wants you to lie quiet."

"That is what I want to do."

"How many shots were fired?"

"I don't know."

"How many?"

"Two thousand. Come on, get some money in that treasury. We need it. Come on, please get it. I can't tell you to. That is not what you have in the book. Oh, please, warden. What am I going to do for money? Please put me up on my feet at once. You are a hard-boiled man. Did you hear me? I would hear it, the Circuit Court would hear it, and the Supreme Court might hear it. If that ain't the payoff. Please crack down on the Chinaman's [Chink Sherman, a Schultz rival] friends and Hitler's commander. I am sore and I am going up and I am going to give you honey if I can. Mother is the best bet and don't let Satan draw you too fast."

Conlon persisted in his questioning. "What did the big fellow shoot you for?"

"Him? John? Over a million, five million dollars."

"You want to get well, don't you?"

"Yes."

"Then lie quiet."

"Yes. I will lie quiet."

"John shot you," Conlon said, "and we will take care of John."

"That is what caused the trouble. Look out. Please get me up. If you do this, you can go on and jump right here in the lake. I know who they are. They are French people [perhaps a reference to Owney Madden's chief enforcer, Big Frenchy DeMange]. All right. Look out, look out. Phhhh . . . my memory is gone. A work relief. Police. Who gets it? I don't know and I don't want to know, but look out. It can be traced. He changed for the worse. Please look out; my fortunes have changed and come back and went back since that. It was desperate. I am wobbly. You ain't got nothing on him but we got it on his helper."

Conlon leaned forward. "Contol yourself."

"But I am dying."

"No, you are not."

"Come on, mama. All right, dear, you have to get it."

At this point, Schultz's wife entered the room and sat next to the babbling gangster. "This is Frances," she said.

"Then pull me out. I am half crazy. They won't let me get up. They dyed my shoes. Give me something. I am so sick. Give me some water, the only thing that I want. Open this up and break it so I can touch you. Dannie [obviously Dannie Iamascia], please get me in the car."

Mrs. Schultz left the room and Conlon resumed his questioning.

"Who shot you?"

"I don't know. I didn't even get a look. I don't know who could have done it. Anybody. Kindly take my shoes off."

"They are off."

"No, there's a handcuff on them. The Baron says these things. I know what I am doing here with my collection of papers. It isn't worth a nickel to two guys like you or me, but to a collector it is worth a fortune. It is priceless. I am going to turn it over to . . . Turn your back to me, please. Henry, I am so sick now. The police are getting many complaints. Look out. I want that G-note. Look out for Jimmy Valentine for he is an old pal of mine. Come on, come on, Jim. Okay, okay, I am all through. Can't do another thing.

"Look out, mama, look out for her. You can't beat him. Police, mama, Helen, mother, please take me out. I will settle the indictment. Shut up, you got a big mouth! Please help me up, Henry. Max, come over here. French-Canadian bean soup. I want to pay. Let them leave me alone."

Then, for two hours, the Dutchman said nothing. He died at 8:40 p.m.

[ALSO SEE Vincent "Mad Dog" Coll, John T. "Legs" Diamond; Louis "Lepke" Buchalter, Meyer Lansky, Charles "Lucky" Luciano, Oweny Madden, Benjamin "Bugsy" Siegel, The Syndicate, *Bloodletters and Badmen, Book 3.*]

ST. VALENTINE'S DAY MASSACRE

The battle for control of Chicago's North Side between Al Capone and George "Bugs" Moran reached its peak in 1929. Several of Capone's top lieutenants had been killed by Moran's gunners while Scarface retreated to his home in Palm Island, Florida. Capone decided that drastic measures were called for and ordered Moran's entire gang annihilated. His scheme was diabolically clever.

Through a contact in Detroit, reportedly Abe Bernstein, leader of the Purple Gang, Capone arranged for someone to call Bugs Moran on the phone, telling him that a special shipment of hijacked bonded whiskey was going to be delivered to Moran's North Side headquarters, a garage at 2122 North Clark Street. Adam Heyer, a Moran flunkie, owned the garage, a front with the sign "S.M.C. Cartage Company" plastered on its street window.

Moran received a call at the garage on the morning of February 13, 1929, probably from Abe Bernstein. The caller told Moran that he had a wonderful load of booze available, recently hijacked "right off the river."

"How much?" Moran asked.

"Fifty-seven dollars a case."

"Okay, deliver it to the garage."

"When?"

"By ten-thirty tomorrow morning. All the boys will be here. We're short and they'll want a cut."

Bernstein, who had previously been Capone's chief supplier of Canadian liquor, probably had begun to send Moran shipments of quality booze months before, working his way into the leery gangleader's confidence. The caller was both known and trusted by Moran.

The following morning, February 14, 1929—St. Valentine's Day—Moran's gang, such as it was after years of being ravaged by the bootleg wars, assembled at the garage. Thief and bootlegger Adam Heyer attended. Also waiting were Moran's top gunners, the deadly brothers Frank and Pete Gusenberg. John May, a safe-blower, speakeasy owner

Al Weinshank, bankrobber James Clark, and Dr. Reinhardt H. Schwimmer, an optometrist fascinated by gangsters, lounged about on the premises. A German shepherd named Highball, belonging to May, scampered about the trucks and cars parked in the garage. The men impatiently waited for Moran to arrive with Willie Marks and Ted Newbury.

Moran was late. He, Newbury, and Marks had stopped to attend to some business and just as he rounded a corner he saw a black Cadillac, similar to that used by police detectives, roll up to the curb and stop before the garage. Five men, three dressed as policemen, two in plainclothes, went inside. Bugs waved Newbury and Marks into a nearby coffee shop. They waited until the expected pinch was over. Moran talked of sending Newbury down to precinct headquarters with bond money. The Gusenbergs always went armed and were sure to be arrested for carrying concealed weapons, he said.

Neighbors in adjoining buildings then heard what they later described to police as "pneumatic drills." The police emerged minutes later with two men apparently under arrest. The "squad car" drove off leisurely. Then May's dog began to howl.

The landlady in the next building, Mrs. Jeanette Landesman, was disturbed at the dog's whining and sent one of her roomers, C. L. McAllister, to the garage to investigate. He came outside two minutes later, his mouth gaping, his face ashen. McAllister ran up the stairs to tell Mrs. Landesman: "The place is full of dead men!"

The police were called and, upon entering the garage, stepped back in shock at the sight of the carnage. It was obvious to police that seven men had been lined up against the north brick wall of the building and machine-gunned while their backs had been turned. One reporter later described the victims as models of "upkeep and dress—shave, hair trim, manicure; the silk shirt, the flashy tie; here and there a diamond stickpin and ring; in Dr. Schwimmer's case a carnation boutonniere; fedoras with brims slanted down over the right eyes; spats; tailored suits and overcoats; each with the customary roll—Heyer, $1,135; Weinshank, $1,250; May $1,200. . . ."

Capone's killers had not bothered to rummage through their victims' pockets. Their assignment was mass murder

Seven men (five shown) were lined up against the wall in the North Clark Street garage by Capone's machinegunners on 2/14/29 and slaughtered. It was the end of the Moran gang. (UPI)

plain and simple. They performed their duty so adroitly, using the police raid ruse, that they were never completely identified. The only person named without reservation as one of the machinegunners was Fred "Killer" Burke, an out-of-town gunsel who was never brought to trial for the St. Valentine's Day slaughter. Others thought to be part of the extermination party were John Scalise, Albert Anselmi, and "Machine Gun" Jack McGurn, all top Capone hit men.

One man survived the slaughter for a few hours. Frank Gusenberg had worked his way from the blood-splattered wall where his brother Pete had died kneeling, slumped

Fred R. "Killer" Burke (with cigar and manacles) was the only man positively linked with the St. Valentine's Day shooting; he was never tried for this crime. (UPI)

against a chair, where James Clark had fallen on his face with half his head blown off, where Heyer, Schwimmer, Weinshank, and May sprawled lifeless on their backs, their brains spilling onto the greasy garage floor.

Sergeant Tom Loftus found Gusenberg crawling toward the garage door and called an ambulance. An hour later police sergeant Clarence Sweeney, at a bedside in Alexian Brothers Hospital, his head bent close to the mortally wounded gangster, asked Gusenberg; "Who shot you, Frank?"

Gusenberg could only whimper a reply: "No one—nobody shot me."

The gangster was tough but he was dying and he knew it. He had been with O'Bannion since the beginning and upon that gangleader's assassination, had gone on working for Earl "Hymie" Weiss and then Bugs Moran. He had been part of the car cavalcade that drove past Capone's Cicero headquarters and sprayed the place with machine-gun bullets in broad daylight. He had, with his brother Pete, cornered "Machine-Gun" Jack McGurn in a McCormick Hotel phone booth and shot him to pieces only to see McGurn recover and swear revenge; he had helped to shoot down Capone's *Unione Siciliane* appointee as president, Pasqualino Lolordo.

"You don't have long to live, Frank," Sweeney told him. "They got Pete and all the others. Tell us who did it. We'll get them for you."

Gusenberg's eyes flashed open for a moment. "Nobody shot me."

Sweeney could see Gusenberg slipping into death. "Want a preacher, Frank?" he asked.

The gangster moved his lips and the word "No" was barely heard in a last sigh.

Gusenberg died at 1:30 p.m., bringing the Clark Street toll to seven.

Moran exploded when he heard of the almost total destruction of his gang. When police asked him who the caller was who set up the gang, "he raved like a madman." Where Frank Gusenberg staunchly upheld the underworld's code of silence, even on his deathbed, Moran did not. Pressured by newsmen for a comment, he finally blurted: "Only Capone kills like that!"

The St. Valentine's Day Massacre marked the end of any significant gangland opposition to Capone in Chicago. It also heralded a wave of reform in reaction to the slaughter that would sweep Scarface from power forever.

[ALSO SEE Al Capone; "Machine-Gun" Jack McGurn, George "Bugs" Moran, *Bloodletters and Badmen, Book 3.*]

STARR, HENRY
Bankrobber • (1881-1921)

Allegedly a nephew of Belle Starr, Henry began a life of crime while a teenager living in the Oklahoma Strip; he rustled cows and horses. The part Cherokee Indian organized a small band of hard-riding desperadoes in the late 1890s and began to rob one-horse banks in Oklahoma, Texas, and Arkansas, forty-eight of them by the end of his career according to one literary accountant.

In 1903, Starr shot and killed one of Judge Isaac Parker's deputies, Floyd Wilson. He was convicted and sentenced to death by the rope but was saved through appeals. Judge Parker tried him again for the same crime and sentenced him to death again. President Theodore Roosevelt stepped in and pardoned Starr.

A month later, Starr, Kid Wilson, and three others held up the Bentonville, Arkansas bank, getting more than $11,000 from the vault. Posse members trapped Starr and Wilson in Colorado Springs, Col. in July, 1903 as they were eating steaks in the Cafe Royal. The lawmen asked the outlaws where they had hidden their loot. Starr stared at them in silence.

When asked his real name Kid Wilson replied: "My kinfolks have never done a thing to place me where I am, so I prefer to say nothing of them." He, too, refused to turn over the stolen money.

Starr's young wife, however, was found sleeping in a nearby hotel. Possemen plucked close to $2,000 in gold from beneath her pillow. She had been safeguarding it for him. Starr was sentenced to five years in the State Penitentiary. He was far from reformed when he was released in 1908. Starr continued to rob banks regularly. In 1914, Henry was thunderstruck with an idea. The automobile, he had seen, could certainly outdistance any posse on horseback. He purchased one and used it in his next bank raid, becoming the first American criminal to employ

Bankrobber Henry Starr was the first bandit to use the auto in a robbery. (Oklahoma Historical Society)

a car in a robbery. The new gimmick worked successfully for six years until lawmen also equipped themselves with autos. After he robbed the bank in Harrison, Arkansas in 1921, Henry Starr's car broke down on a dusty road. A sherriff's posse, riding a string of cars, caught up to him and he was killed in a wild gun battle.

THAW, HARRY KENDALL
Murderer • (1872-1947)

Probably the most famous of murder cases involving America's super rich was Harry K. Thaw's murder of the architectural genius, Stanford White.

Thaw was a product of an ambitious Pittsburgh family who engineered a vast fortune—close to $40 million—in a short time by cornering the coke market and forcing their way into New York high society.

Though well-educated, Thaw was weird. Harry's wild behavior caused his tycoon father to cut his considerable allowance to $2,000 a year. His doting mother, however, supplemented this paltry income with an additional $80,000 annually. Thaw whined that such pin money was hardly enough for a man of his stature and manner of living. His manner of living was anything but normal.

He was at times insane with rage and strange sexual compulsions. He kept an apartment in a New York brothel to which he enticed young girls under the promise of a show business career.

Once there, as the house madam Susan Merrill later testified, he ravished the girls and beat them senseless.

Thaw's victim, world famous architect Stanford White.

"I could hear the screams coming from his apartment," she later testified, "and once I could stand it no longer. I rushed into his rooms. He had tied the girl to the bed, naked, and was whipping her. She was covered with welts. Thaw's eyes protruded and he looked mad."

At times, a jury later concluded, Harry K. Thaw indeed was mad.

Still, Thaw probably would never have been known to the American public if it had not been for a sultry lovely, Evelyn Nesbit, who came from Pittsburgh to New York at age sixteen. Evelyn became one of the Floradora Chorus, and the mistress of millionaire Stanford White.

The corpulent White, a red-haired, 250-pound girl-chaser, was the most distinguished architect of his day. More than fifty of New York's most elegant buildings were monuments to his talents, including the resplendent Wash-

371

ington Square Arch. White was a spectacular rake who kept several mistresses at once. In one of his many love nests—in the tower of Madison Square Garden—was a red velvet swing hanging from the ceiling. In this, he would swing his women wildly to peer lasciviously up their billowing skirts as a prelude to more primitive passions, according to Miss Nesbit.

White fell madly in love with chorus girl Nesbit almost at first sight and gave her large amounts of money and expensive jewels. He gave Evelyn's mother considerable money, too.

From poverty to fame and wealth was not enough for Miss Nesbit. At nineteen, she left White to marry multi-millionaire Harry Thaw.

Evelyn Nesbit, one-time Floradora Girl, became "The Girl in the Red Velvet Swing" and the reason Thaw gave for killing White.

For almost three years, Thaw persecuted Evelyn about her relationship with White. He forced the girl to never use White's name but to refer to him as "The Beast," or "The Bastard."

At these times, Thaw became insane. Once, while crossing the ocean on a European vacation, Thaw chained his young wife to the bed in their stateroom and took his belt to her for hours until she confessed every horrible atrocity of the flesh she could imagine Stanford White had ever done to her.

She told her insanely jealous husband that White had lied to her with promises of marriage to get her to come to his New York love nest and, once there, stripped her and raped her and made her pose and swing naked on the red velvet swing.

Later, at Harry's murder trial, Evelyn Nesbit Thaw stated that White had invited her and a girl friend to his love nest one evening. She and another girl had gone to his Madison Square Garden penthouse and, after mounting two flights of stairs, they had entered a strange room: ". . . and in this room was a red velvet swing and Mr. White would put us in this swing and we would swing up to the ceiling. He would put the other girl in the swing, and then it would be my turn . . . He would push us until we would swing to the ceiling. There was a big Japanese umbrella on the ceiling, so when he pushed us our feet would crash through."

A few nights later, Evelyn recounted, White invited her to a big party. The architect had given her mother a large amount of cash to return to Pittsburgh for a visit with relatives. When Evelyn arrived at White's place, she discovered no one present except the architect. He proceeded to get her drunk with champagne, she claimed, until she blacked out.

"When I woke up all my clothes were pulled off me. I was in bed. I sat up in bed and I started to scream. Mr. White got up and put on one of his kimonos which was on a chair. I moved up and pulled some covers over me, and there were mirrors all around the bed; mirrors on the sides of the wall and on the ceiling. Then I looked down and saw blotches of blood on the sheets. Then I screamed and screamed and screamed, and he came over and asked me to please keep quiet, and that I must not make so much noise. He said, 'It's all over, it's all over.'

"Then I screamed, 'Oh, no!' and then he brought a kimono over to me and he went out of the room. Then as I got out of the bed, I began to scream more than ever. Then he came back into the room and tried to quiet me. I don't remember how I got my clothes on or how I went home. But he took me home and left me and I sat up all night."

This is essentially the story Harry Thaw whipped out of his wife while the couple sailed the Atlantic to Europe and the same story she would repeat at her husband's trial.

Such was the intensity of his madness that Thaw, who had whipped the accusations against White out of his wife, believed every word and vowed revenge.

Revenge came on the warm summer evening of June 25, 1906. That night Harry and Evelyn, accompanied by two effeminate males, attended the opening of a light Victorian musical farce, *Mam'zelle Champagne* at the dining theater on the roof of Madison Square Garden.

It was the gathering place for high society, most of whom were attending this play.

In the audience was architect Stanford White. He sat alone at one of the tables. Evelyn placed a gloved hand on her husband's sleeve. Harry, dressed in a heavy overcoat even though it was a balmy summer night, turned his boyish face to her. "The Bastard is here," she told him. As he glared at White, Thaw's whole being seemed to change.

During one of the production numbers, Thaw calmly got up from his table, walked over to White and fired three shots. The architect took two bullets in the brain and died immediately, his heavy frame crashing to the floor.

Thaw changed his grip on the pistol, holding it by the muzzle to signify that he meant no harm to anyone else. He was arrested, hurried off to the Center Street Station, charged with murder, and locked in the Tombs.

While awaiting trial, Thaw had all his meals catered from the finest New York restaurant, Delmonico's. He had whiskey smuggled to him and he continued to play the stock market, visiting with his broker in the jail at all hours.

After his arraignment for murder, Harry's mother pub-

Millionaire murderer Harry K. Thaw in his N.Y. Tombs cell, dining on catered meals from Delmonico's after slaying Stanford White in 1912.

licly announced that she would spend all of her $40,000,000 fortune to save her boy from dying in the electric chair. Mrs. Thaw imported the famous trial lawyer Delphin Delmas from California to defend her son. Delmas was called "The Little Napoleon of the West Coast Bar."

The equally famous William Travers Jerome, New York's district attorney, opposed him. When Jerome learned that the Thaw millions would be spent down to the last penny to save Harry, he thundered: "With all his millions, Thaw is a fiend! No matter how rich a man is, he cannot get away with murder—not in New York County!"

It seemed like an open-and-shut case but from the first moment of his lengthy seven-month trial, Thaw claimed that he was innocent, that a form of insanity took him over and made him kill White.

"I never wanted to shoot that man," Thaw pleadingly

told a jury. "I never wanted to kill him . . . Providence took charge of the situation."

This claim of being controlled from the great beyond was supported, strangely enough, by a doctor of medicine and member of the American Association for the Advancement of Science, Dr. Carl Wickland of Chicago.

Dr. Wickland's wife, it seems, was endowed with powerful visions of mediumship. Three weeks after Thaw's arrest and months before his trial, on July 5, 1906, Mrs. Wickland insisted, a spiritual voice admitted through her that he had killed White!

At this seance, the spirit stated, "I killed Stanford White. He deserved death. He had trifled too long with our daughters."

According to Mrs. Wickland, the voice that spoke through the medium identified himself as a man named Johnson. The manners and articulation of his speech indicated he was from a low social scale, the same as Evelyn Nesbit.

Johnson denounced the rich such as White as society rakes and ne'er-do-wells. "They steal our children from us and put fine clothes on them, and the parents do not know what becomes of them."

Another spirit broke into Mrs. Wickland's busy trance, speaking rapidly. He identified himself as the long-dead father of Harry K. Thaw!

Thaw's spiritual father fought for his son's innocence. "He is sensitive to spirit influence and has been all his life. He was always erratic and so excitable that we were afraid to correct him for fear he would become insane. But I see our mistake now."

The voice claiming to be Thaw's father went on to add that though he never understood his son's actions when he was alive, he now knew that Harry "had been a tool in the hands of earth-bound spirits, evil spirits that ordered death.

"He was obsessed by revengeful spirits when he killed Stanford White," the voice went on.

Incredibly, the Wicklands reported that the spirit-father implored Wickland to write to Thaw's attorney informing him of these spiritual truths.

Counsel Delmas and other attorneys representing Thaw apparently ignored the Chicago mediums but did advance the theory to the court that Harry, at the moment of killing White, suffered a severe attack of what they termed "dementia Americana," a singularly American neurosis among males in the U.S. who believed that every man's wife was sacred.

Apparently, the jury listening to evidence in the White killing came to the conclusion that something had taken temporary control over Thaw's reasoning at the time of the murder.

They returned the verdict, "Not guilty, on the ground of his insanity at the time of the commission of the act."

But Thaw was not free. He was imprisoned for life in the New York State Asylum for the Criminally Insane at Matteawan, N. Y. He spent years in this institution while his mother spent tens of thousands of dollars attempting to get him judged sane. Harry grew tired of waiting for psychiatrists to make up their minds and escaped from the Matteawan asylum in 1913. He was captured in Canada and returned.

Evelyn Nesbit went on to become a vaudeville attraction. A son was born to her which she stubbornly insisted was Harry K. Thaw's offspring (she filed for huge support money). When newsmen politely pointed out that Mr. Thaw had been inside a mental institution for the past seven years, Evelyn blithely told them that Harry had bribed a guard at Matteawan to allow her to spend a heavenly and quite fruitful night with her.

When Thaw was finally pronounced sane by a New York court in 1915, he barreled out of Matteawan, cursing Evelyn Nesbit and denying he had anything to do with fathering her child. He divorced her and went on a buying spree.

In 1916 Thaw was again arrested, this time for horse-whipping a teenager named Frederick B. Gump. He attempted to buy the Gump family off and made a huge settlement reported to be a half million dollars. He was nevertheless returned to Matteawan and kept under close security until his second release in 1922. Fifty, Harry Thaw then embarked on another career of fast living, which would not end until his death in 1947.

He roamed the world, a pathetic playboy, sporting attractive young girls on his arm, billing himself to reporters as a producer of plays and motion pictures.

Of course, it was all imagination—or something else, especially when Harry would get that wild stare in his eyes, his mouth would sag, and strange words would tumble incoherently from him.

THOMPSON, GERALD
Murderer, Rapist • (1910-1935)

BACKGROUND: BORN AND RAISED IN PEORIA, ILL. HIGH SCHOOL EDUCATION. OCCUPATION, FACTORY WORKER. DESCRIPTION: 5'8", BROWN EYES, BROWN HAIR, SLENDER. ALIASES: NONE. RECORD: RAPED SIXTEEN WOMEN IN THE PEORIA, ILL., AREA BETWEEN NOVEMBER AND JUNE, 1935, HIS LAST VICTIM BEING MILDRED HALLMARK, WHOM HE ALSO MURDERED 6/16/35; APPREHENDED 6/22/35 BY POLICE AND CONFESSED TO THE MURDER AND RAPES; CONVICTED OF MURDER AND SENTENCED TO DEATH, EXECUTED AT THE ILLINOIS STATE PENITENTIARY IN JOLIET, ILL., IN THE ELECTRIC CHAIR, 10/15/35.

He was an ineffectual-looking young man with a weak chin. Fingerwaves of hair poked from the top of his high forehead. Quiet, soft-spoken, he lived with his grandmother and labored diligently as a toolmaker for the Caterpillar Tractor company in Peoria, Ill. His name was Gerald Thompson.

Another toolmaker at the same factory, John Hallmark, had just lost his daughter, an attractive young woman who had been a hostess in a popular Peoria restaurant. Mildred Hallmark had not died of natural causes. She had been brutally raped, beaten, and murdered a few days before.

Her naked body had been found in a shallow ravine in Peoria's Springdale Cemetery on June 17, 1935.

Someone came to Gerald Thompson while he was at work in the plant and asked for a donation for flowers and mass cards for the murdered girl. He gave willingly.

Meanwhile an army of police and reporters were trying to sift the grisly facts surrounding the discovery of the corpse. The pretty auburn-haired girl had had her neck broken. Police, inspecting the body, noticed that human skin was curled in shreds under the dead girl's fingernails.

Another curious item: Mildred Hallmark's fountain pen had a badly bent point. It wasn't much to go on, but the town of Peoria—where rape and murder was not the norm of, say, Chicago—demanded instant apprehension of Mildred's killer. The police stepped up the manhunt, frantically scooping up suspects.

Gerald Thompson watched as startled young men all over Peoria were arrested as murder suspects. He watched and waited and said nothing.

As a result of the widespread publicity and waves of gossip buzzing through the community, dozens of young women and girls came forward with bizarre tales of being raped by a lone, charming young man who used his auto as a bedroom.

The stories the young women told about this lone wolf dated back several years and were mostly the same. The young man carried a pair of razor-sharp scissors in his glove compartment. After charming his female victims into his car, he prevented their escape through a cleverly devised wiring system hooked from his battery to the car's door handle. If a young woman attempted to flee, she was jolted back into the arms of the unwanted lover, trapped.

Then the young man would go to work with his scissors, carefully cutting away with precision the bra straps and panties of each woman. After satisfying himself against their unwilling flesh, he would switch on the lights of the car and the beams would poke eerily into the dark reaches of lonely roadways he always chose.

He would then force each woman to the front of the car and in the glare of car lights, while a self-timing camera clicked lewdly away, compelled each victim to pose naked with him in wildly-invented sexual positions.

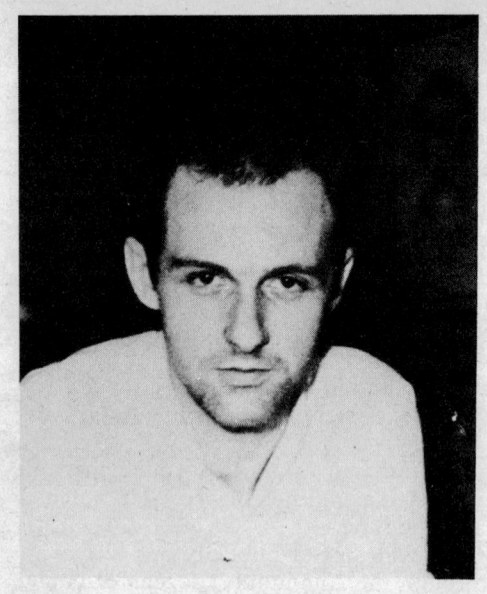

Mass rapist and murderer Gerald Thompson in 1935. (UPI)

The rape victims told Peoria's enraged police officials that these pictures would subsequently be used by the young pervert to blackmail them into silence.

Gerald Thompson, meanwhile, reported to work at the Caterpillar factory promptly, performed his duties conscientiously, and went home each evening to dine with his elderly grandmother.

The police frantically pulled in more suspects.

The man hunt went on and Gerald Thompson waited and waited. Six days after the murder, on June 22, 1935, the police, on a tip, came for him. They grilled Thompson for hours and he finally broke down.

Thompson explained that he had picked Mildred up as she was waiting for a streetcar after having left her date, John McGinnis. Thompson explained that he had joked and charmed her into his car with the promise of a lift home. Once in the car, he drove immediately to his favorite deserted spot, the cemetery, and took out his trusty scissors.

Mildred had not been submissive and frightened like the other young women. As Thompson cut her clothes away, Mildred did the unexpected—she fought back, clawing desperately at his face with her fingernails, gashing and slashing him. Thompson told police he laughed at her. As they struggled, the not-so-helpless girl slashed Thompson's neck with her long fingernails and he felt his hot blood run out.

Seething with anger, Thompson smashed the girl blindly and her head whipped back with a snap and she collapsed unconscious. He then went at the limp body again with his scissors.

Mildred awoke screaming and struggling as Thompson groped at her body. Again she clawed at his face and more of the rapist's blood ran down his face. In desperation she reached into her purse and using her fountain pen, jammed the needle-sharp point again and again into Thompson.

He went wild, he admitted, and began to hammer the young girl's face with flailing fists until she sagged silent against the now blood-splattered car seat. She was dead.

Thompson said he threw the girl's naked and battered body into the ravine next to the cemetery and drove away to his home where he went to bed. Police asked Thompson how he felt after killing Mildred Hallmark. His only remark was: "I slept like a baby."

But there were more shocks to come. Gerald Thompson's trial was a regular circus with angry mobs threatening to lynch him. The self-admitted rapist and murderer had to be spirited away to another town until Peoria citizens quieted.

The prosecution had more evidence to convict Thompson than was really necessary. On top of his signed confession, police investigators produced Thompson's bloodstained trousers, a bloodstained car cushion from his auto and a diary that would have made Bluebeard blanch.

Thompson had recorded in his diary the names and addresses of sixteen pickup and rape victims. Along with the list of names were many obscene photos showing Thompson and his victims naked under the glare of his car's headlights.

It was enough to convict him ten times over. One more startling detail was added by a former friend of Thompson's. The ex-friend stated from the witness stand: "Thompson boasted that he would use this sinister pattern of action to rape fifty-two girls within the year. By the middle of November last year he told me he had already exceeded his quota—one for every week of that year."

Gerald Thompson's twisted calendar ended abruptly on October 15, 1935, when he was strapped into the electric chair at Joliet State Penitentiary and three massive electrical charges were sent through his body.

THURMOND, THOMAS HAROLD
Kidnapper, Murderer • (1909-1933)

BACKGROUND: BORN AND RAISED IN SAN JOSE, CALIF. ONE BROTHER, A MINISTER. GRADUATE OF SAN JOSE HIGH SCHOOL, BRIEFLY ATTENDED SAN JOSE STATE COLLEGE. ORIGINAL OCCUPATION, FILLING STATION ATTENDANT. DESCRIPTION: 5'10", BROWN EYES, BROWN HAIR, SLENDER. ALIASES: NONE. RECORD: KIDNAPPED WITH JOHN MAURICE HOLMES, A HIGH SCHOOL CLASSMATE, 22-YEAR-OLD BROOKE HART, SON OF A WEALTHY HOTEL AND DEPARTMENT STORE OWNER ON 11/9/33, KILLING HIM BY THROWING HIM BOUND INTO SAN FRANCISCO BAY THAT SAME NIGHT; ARRESTED BY POLICE 11/15/33 IN SAN JOSE, INFORMED AUTHORITIES OF HOLMES' COMPLICITY IN THE MURDER, BOTH MEN IMPRISONED IN THE SANTA CLARA COUNTY JAIL IN SAN JOSE. ON 11/26/33 HART'S BODY WAS FOUND; THAT NIGHT A MOB, ESTIMATED TO BE 15,000 OR MORE, LYNCHED BOTH PRISONERS.

Thurmond came from a middle-class family in San Jose where he had lived all his life. He had never committed a crime and the only explanation he ever gave for kidnapping and killing 22-year-old Brooke Hart, scion of a department store fortune, was that he was "driven half crazy" by the thought of not being able to marry his high school sweetheart for lack of funds. He later changed this story, insisting that he was in love with another woman several years his senior who rejected him because he was poor. "I don't even know that man," the woman said when confronted.

Whatever the reason, Thurmond and a boy who had gone to school with him, John Maurice Holmes, abducted blonde-haired Brooke Hart as he drove away from his father's store (where he had recently been made a vice president following his graduation from Santa Clara College). The two forced Hart's Studebaker to the side of the road.

Then, using Hart's car, the three men drove to the San Mateo-Hayward Bridge arching across the southern part of San Francisco Bay. They stopped on the bridge late on the night of November 9, 1933 and Hart was forced to get out. He was then hit by a brick and knocked unconscious. Thurmond and Holmes then bound him tightly with wire and tied chunks of cement to his body to weight it down. They threw him into the Bay. Regaining consciousness, Hart began to scream that he couldn't swim. Thurmond fired several shots at him and his body quickly disappeared.

An hour later Thurmond was on the phone to Alex Hart demanding $40,000 for the release of his son. "Keep the police out of this," Thurmond said, "if you want to see him alive."

Hart, however, instantly called the police after talking to the kidnapper. Authorities at first did not believe the tale. Hart was probably kidding around with some college chums, they said.

The kidding theory exploded when Hart failed to return to his home in several days and two more ransom notes followed, one reading: "We have Brooke and are treating him right." The second note instructed Alex Hart to put an "L" in the window of his department store if he was willing to pay the $40,000 ransom. Hart did as directed. Next, Hart was told to drive a car south on the Los Angeles highway bringing the money in small bills. This Alex Hart did not do.

He received a call the next day. "What gives, Mr. Hart?" Thurmond said. "You didn't show up last night. You got one more chance."

Kidnapper and murderer Thomas Harold Thurmond in custody (center); to his right is FBI agent R. E. Vetterli, who had guarded gangster Frank Nash in 1933 and survived the Kansas City Massacre. (Wide World Photos)

"I don't drive," Hart said.

There was a pause. "We'll call you back," Thurmond said and hung up. This time the police were ready. When Thurmond rang up the Hart residence again on November 15, 1933, his call was traced while Alex Hart stalled him on the phone. Officers located Thurmond in a San Jose garage, still arguing on the phone with Hart about a pickup spot for the ransom money. They entered and arrested him.

Thurmond quickly confessed, signing a statement which put most of the guilt for the kidnapping and murder on his partner Holmes. When Holmes was arrested, he, too, confessed but blamed Thurmond for planning and executing the crime. The two were locked up in separate cells in the Santa Clara County Jail in downtown San Jose.

Nine days later Brooke Hart's body washed ashore and was found by duck hunters. Upon hearing the news, the citizens of San Jose, especially the college community where Hart was well-liked, went berserk with rage. By early evening a giant crowd of at least 15,000 collected in a park across from the jail.

Women with babies, small boys, elderly men with canes joined the students in shouting thunderous calls like "We want a touchdown!" and "Get that ball!" Staring down from his second floor office, Sheriff William Emig got jittery. Days before he had stated: "We are not at all alarmed at the threat of possible violence." Now it was at hand and he turned out his men to guard all windows and doors on the first floor of the jail. He then got on the phone and asked California Governor James "Sunny Jim" Rolfe for troops.

Rolfe said no, it wasn't necessary. Emig glanced out the window to see dozens of youths pick up planks and pipes from a nearby construction area. The mob was now howling for the blood of Thurmond and Holmes. "You hear that?" Emig said, holding the phone's mouthpiece toward the window. Rolfe heard nothing. No troops, he repeated. Then he hung up.

At about 9:30 p.m., the crowd surged forward with its pipes and planks, battling the state and local police officers on duty for close to two hours. The police did everything but fire on the jostling vigilantes. They sprayed them with high-powered hoses and drove them back. The mob came on again. They bombarded the mob with tear gas shells. Again, the crowd pushed forward, demanding Holmes and Thurmond be turned over to them. Alex Hart appeared and begged the self-appointed avengers to go home, but he was brushed aside and within two hours, a young boy of about sixteen appeared and shouted as he waved an iron bar: "I want fifty men with guts enough to follow me!" At least that number raced after him in a charge against the front door of the jail; it was promptly battered down.

They poured into the jail, sweeping past the handful of guards. When members of the lynch mob flung wide Holmes's cell door, the young man snarled like a trapped cougar. Several went in after him and he put up a terrific fight. His clothes were stripped from him in the raging battle and he was beaten so badly that his face was turned to raw pulp. He was led half unconscious out of his cell with an eyeball dangling from its socket.

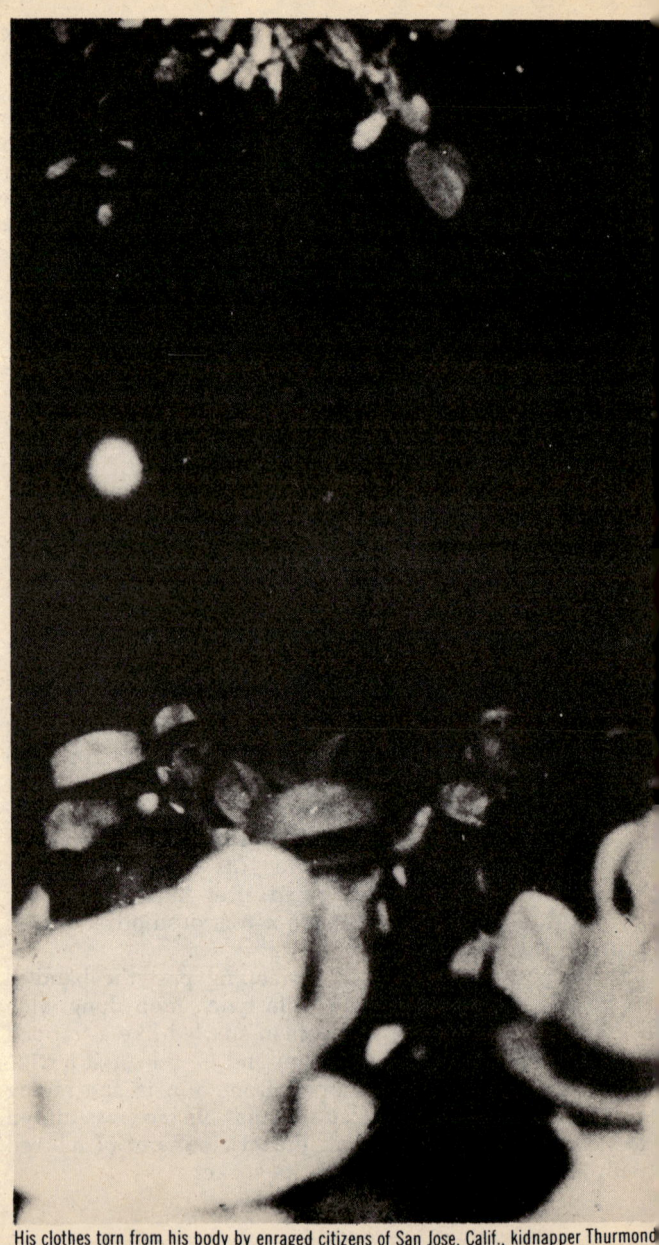

His clothes torn from his body by enraged citizens of San Jose, Calif., kidnapper Thurmond was lynched, 11/26/33. (Wide World Photos)

Someone called down from a second-floor window to the hooting mob below: "We've got Holmes and he's coming down to you! Now we'll get Thurmond!"

Thurmond was no where to be found. His cell was empty and the vigilantes foraged through the cell block looking for him. One of them entered his open cell and stood silently listening. Then he heard the heavy breathing and looked up. There, hanging high from the water pipes above the cell's toilet, was Thurmond. He was dragged down. The lynch mob punched him senseless as they descended the jail stairs and then into the park.

The two largest trees in the park facing each other were used to string up the two prisoners. First Thurmond was lynched as he pleaded with his captives. As his lifeless corpse swayed in the breeze, Holmes was led over to him and made to look at the dead body. "How do you like your pal now?" someone asked him.

"For God's sake, give me a chance?" Holmes said.

A roar of laughter greeted his plea.

He was led to the other tree and promptly hanged. Spotlights were trained on both bodies. The two dead kidnappers, half naked and almost unidentifiable from beatings swung solemnly in the midnight air as the stark and eerie lights played upon them.

A small army of state police arrived on motorcycles and bullied its way through the hostile crowd. Boos and jeers greeted them when they cut the bodies down and placed them on stretchers.

"Throw them into the Bay, too!" someone shouted.

"Why waste time? They're headed for hell anyway," another said.

As the bodies passed through the throng, men, women and small boys spat on them and punched them with vicious swipes. No one was ever indicted for the killings.

Though newspapers throughout California condemned the mob violence, Governor Rolfe stated that the lynch mob provided "the best lesson ever given the country. I would pardon those fellows if they were charged. I would like to parole all kidnappers in San Quentin and Folsom to the fine patriotic citizens of San Jose."

For years after the lynchings, members of the mob held

onto grisly souvenirs taken that November night in 1933, pieces of clothing from the prisoners, bits of bark of the trees from which they were hanged. It was a night to remember.

TOURBILLON, ROBERT ARTHUR
Swindler, Robber • (1885- ?)

BACKGROUND: BORN IN ATLANTA, GA., 1885. MINOR PUBLIC EDUCATION. ORIGINAL OCCUPATION, CIRCUS PERFORMER. DESCRIPTION: 5'9", BROWN EYES, BROWN HAIR, SLENDER. ALIASES: DAPPER DON COLLINS, HARRY HUSSEY, CROMWALL, RATSY. RECORD: ARRESTED FOR THEFT IN NYC, 1908, RELEASED; ROBBED THE HOTEL ROY. 6/15/11 ($160), RECEIVED A MINOR SENTENCE; BECAME A MEMBER OF A TELEPHONE COIN BOX RING; ARRESTED 1916 AND SENTENCED TO TWO YEARS IN THE FEDERAL PRISON OF ATLANTA AFTER BEING CONVICTED OF INTERSTATE WHITE SLAVE BLACKMAILING; ROBBED A WEALTHY MERCHANT IN UPSTATE NEW YORK, 1918; ARRESTED AND FREED; ARRESTED, TRIED AND CONVICTED OF ROBBING AN AMERICAN EXPRESS GUARD, FREDERICK C. ROBB, OF $5,000 CASH AND SOME JEWELRY; RELEASED ON $5,000 BOND PENDING APPEAL; JUMPED BOND; SUSPECTED OF SHOOTING JOHN H. REID IN NYC OVER A WOMAN ON 5/15/21; BECAME AN IMPORTANT RUMRUNNER ALONG THE EAST COAST IN THE EARLY 1920S; FLED TO PARIS, FRANCE TO AVOID ARREST AFTER BEING INDICTED FOR ROBBING FREDERICK C. ROBB: ARRESTED IN PARIS IN 1924 AND RETURNED UNDER GUARD TO THE U.S.; ARRESTED FOR SWINDLING AN APPLE FARMER, THOMAS WEBER, IN EGG HARBOR, N.J.; AND SENTENCED TO THREE YEARS IN THE NEW JERSEY STATE PRISON AT TRENTON ON 4/26/29; RELEASED ON PAROLE, AUGUST, 1930; DISAPPEARED.

Tourbillon's first known job was that of riding a bicycle down a chute, through a hoop, and past a cage loaded with well-fed lions; his act was known as "The Circle of Death." Life with a Southern circus, however, bored Bobby Tourbillon. Seeking higher adventure, he made his way to New York, arriving at Curly Bennett's celebrated pool hall in 1908 where, at the age of 23, he promptly and happily fell in with thieves.

Within a month Tourbillon was arrested for burglary, but the charge was dismissed. Tourbillon's reputation as a clothes horse and highly-polished con man grew among the shifty denizens who inhabited off-Broadway haunts. They dubbed him "Rat," an unsavory moniker derived from the initials of his three names, an appellative he understandably refused to cherish.

Late on the night of June 15, 1911, accompanied by two gunmen, Tourbillon entered the Hotel Roy in mid-town Manhattan and robbed the clerk of $160. The three were caught hours later and convicted. Receiving a light sentence, Tourbillon heard his reputation dramatized by Judge Edward Swann, who told reporters that "He is as smooth a rascal as ever came before me . . . He is a real Raffles. I consider this man a very dangerous character, for he is a smooth talker and such a fine dresser."

Four years later, Tourbillon was back on the crime circuit, this time allied with a ring who robbed telephone coin boxes. Detectives apprehended the gang but Tourbillon was turned over to federal authorities holding a warrant for his arrest on a charge of interstate white-slave blackmail. He was convicted of this charge and given two years in the Atlanta federal penitentiary.

Once back on the streets, Tourbillon decided to bilk an upstate New York landowner named Julius Scholtz. Bobby had learned that Scholtz kept a trunk full of savings which was purported to be in the neighborhood of $20,000. He obtained a fake badge and journeyed to the Scholtz farm with an accomplice. The penny-pinching farmer met them without alarm when the two con men informed him that they were "from the Department of Internal Revenue." Tourbillon quickly flashed his badge.

"Mr. Scholtz, we are compelled to search your farm," Bobby told him.

"I gat nuddings," Scholtz insisted.

Bobby told the farmer that they were looking for illegal caches of liquor. Scholtz replied that all he had on hand was apple cider and offered the two men some. After having downed several tart-tasting cups, Tourbillon searched the premises, discovered the farmer's much-vaunted trunk, and was horrified to learn that it contained nothing more than old German newspapers. He apologized to the farmer for the inconvenience, took his hand and said: "Goodbye, Julius."

After the pair left, the farmer grew suspicious. He concluded that the men were imposters by the fact that they knew his first name. Scholtz went to the local police, repeating to officers: "How he know I gat name Julius?"

Tourbillon was arrested for impersonating a federal officer, but this time he took the precaution of enlisting the services of the greatest criminal lawyer in the land, William Fallon. The agile Fallon speedily won an acquittal, but Tourbillon, being sought by police for robbing an American Express guard of $5,000 in 1920, was convicted of this charge. Fallon arranged bail pending an appeal; Tourbillon jumped bail and went into hiding. Police intensified their search for Tourbillion after one John H. Reid was shot on May 15, 1921, since it appeared that Bobby had performed the marksmanship. He and Reid had been vying for the same woman, a curvacious cutie, Mrs. Hazel D. Warner.

In the summer of 1921, Tourbillon went into rum-running on a large scale. He purchased a luxury yacht, the *Nomad*, noted for its speed (some say its price was paid by gambler and Tourbillon friend, Arnold Rothstein), and began smuggling Canadian liquor into New York harbor.

No one could match Tourbillon for sheer brazenness. He once sailed up to a New York dock and informed the suspicious night watchman that the *Nomad* was putting in for repairs, that the ship would be lifted onto the Marine railway in the morning.

"You can't dock here," the watchman ordered.

"Do you want to be responsible for us sinking here?" Tourbillon said.

"No, you can dock," the watchman said.

A truck then appeared and the watchman returned. "Now what's going on?" he said anxiously.

"We're taking off the furniture, stupid," Tourbillon griped, injecting annoyance into his words.

"Oh, sure," the watchman mumbled and sauntered away.

Two hours later, Bobby Tourbillon and his rum-runners loaded more than 1,800 bottles of whiskey into the truck and then quietly sailed out to sea.

Accumulating a small fortune, Bobby decided to visit Europe, his move undoubtedly prompted by the fact that he was about to face a charge of grand larceny. By 1924, Tourbillon was residing in Paris, living under the alias of Harry Hussey and bilking gullible, wealthy, expatriate women.

Mrs. Helen Petterson, the estranged wife of an American industrialist, fell madly in love with the sneak thief. She plied him with money and even gave him some of her own jewelry. Nothing Tourbillon did daunted her affection for him. One festive New Year's Eve party culminated when Bobby pushed Mrs. Petterson, according to authorities, off her third-floor balcony at the Hotel Majestic. She broke her leg in the fall, yet when Tourbillon was thrown into debtor's prison for failing to pay his hotel bill, the indomitable Mrs. Petterson hobbled each day to the jail to visit her Bobby, telling reporters: "We are going to be married."

Coincidence and luck worked against the adventurous thief in early 1924, while he was serving out the last days of his sentence in Sante Prison. Two American police officers, Lieutenants McCoy and Kane of the NYPD, arrived to extradite an American burglar named Mourey to the U.S. The warden's courtesy extended to showing the officers his well-disciplined inmates.

McCoy was startled to see Tourbillon in the line-up. "I'll be damned if that isn't Ratsy Tourbillon," he told Kane.

"Hello, Rats," McCoy called and wiggled his index finger

in Tourbillon's direction, indicating he wanted him to walk forward.

Bobby arched his eyebrows. "Are you addressing me?" he said airily.

"Yes, Rats, you." McCoy smiled. "You remember us, don't you?"

"Never had the pleasure," the suave Bobby replied.

Minutes later, the two officers were arranging Tourbillon's extradition to the U.S.

Tourbillon returned home in a first-class cabin aboard the luxury liner, *Paris*, accompanied by a detective named Daley whom Bobby referred to as his "secretary." The good-natured cop played out the role rather than embarrass his prisoner.

The wacky and ironic Roaring Twenties were never more in evidence than at the moment the *Paris* docked. A cluster of reporters, hearing that Tourbillon was on board, rushed to the smoking lounge where they found the criminal coolly puffing a cigar.

One newsman showed him a clipping and photo of Mrs. Petterson. "You going to marry this dame?"

"Ask my secretary." Bobby turned to his "secretary" and quipped: "I suppose every milk bottle and door mat stolen since I went away will be attributed to me."

The wily crook was taken to Tombs Prison. While Tourbillon was being booked, an officer asked the accompanying detective what charge was being leveled against the prisoner.

"Moprey!" the insouciant Bobby responded. (Moprey, a joke among criminals, consists of exhibiting the naked body before a blind woman.)

Tourbillon's odd fame faded in the late 1920s when he was sentenced on April 26, 1929 to three years in the New Jersey State Prison for swindling a New Jersey farmer, Thomas Weber, out of $30,000. He served sixteen months.

Upon his release, reporters once again interviewed the dapper con man.

"This was an excellent prison," he told them. "I recommend it as a wonderful vacation spot." When asked what his plans were, Tourbillon became pensive and then replied: "I'm going back to Paris." No one knows whether he ever did. Bobby Tourbillon, or Dapper Don Collins, completely disappeared at this time, leaving behind many news-hungry reporters and a lovesick Mrs. Petterson.

UNDERHILL, WILBUR
Bankrobber • (1901-1934)

Underhill was an impulsive bankrobber who belonged to the genre that produced Charles Arthur "Pretty Boy" Floyd of the Oklahoma Cookson Hills. He was known as the "Tri-State Terror" and robbed dozens of banks in Oklahoma, Kansas, and Arkansas with such other notorious bad men of the 1930s as Ford Bradshaw, Bob Brady, Ed Newt Clanton, Aussie Elliott, Troy Love, Jim Benge, Jim Clark, and Tom Carlisle.

After robbing a number of small town banks in the late 1920s, Underhill was sent to the Kansas State Penitentiary at Lansing. In September, 1933, Underhill, Bob Brady, and Jim Clark escaped and went into hiding in the Cookson Hills. Underhill joined the Ford Bradshaw gang, and Brady and Clark decided to strike out on their own. On October 7, 1933 Clark was apprehended in Tucumari, N. M. Brady lasted until the following year, being surrounded by a posse on January 9, 1934 in Paoloa, Kan. He chose to make a fight of it and was torn to ribbons by a dozen shotgun blasts.

During the fall of 1933, Underhill, Bradshaw, and others

Bankrobber Wilbur Underhill was known as the "Tri-State Terror." (UPI)

went on a bankrobbing spree which included the banks in Stuttgart, Arkansas; Coalgate, Okla.; Helena, Kan.; and Okmulgee, Okla. On November 2, 1933, they took more than $13,000 from the Okmulgee bank vault.

Underhill decided to marry his childhood sweetheart and with his loot moved to Shawnee, Okla. His honeymoon was interrupted by federal agents under the command of R. H. Colvin, who surrounded his cottage on New Year's Day 1934 and ordered him to surrender. Underhill answered them with two pistols spitting bullets. He darted from window to window for nearly a half hour, battling the agents who poured more than one thousand shells into the cottage. Leaking from a dozen wounds and wearing only his long underwear, Wilbur dashed from the house firing a shotgun and broke through the police cordon.

He staggered down a street, dove through the plate glass window of a furniture store, and there passed out. Taken to a hospital, he lingered for five days, dying in McAlester, Okla. on January 6, 1934. Told he was about to die, Underhill cryptically said with a sigh: "Tell the boys I'm coming home."

UNIONE SICILIANE

In the late 1880s, the Sicilian immigrants in New York organized a fraternal organization, the *Unione Siciliane*, to look after their special interests. Members paid small dues and received life insurance and attended social affairs sponsored by the *Unione*. Through the years the *Unione* became a political power and could exercise enough voting strength to win over several wards during elections.

Before the First World War, Ignazio Saietta ("Lupo the Wolf"), a vicious blackhanding terrorist, took over the *Unione* through murder and beatings. He turned the once peace-loving fraternity into a national crime cartel secretly operating among Sicilians in dozens of cities and active in white slavery, extortion, kidnapping, robbery, labor and union rackets, and murder, with umbilical ties to the Mafia.

Under Saietta's direction *Unione* thugs murdered close to seventy people in a six year period, according to the U.S. Secret Service, using the organization's offices in Harlem as a murder den where Saietta installed meathooks from which he would dangle his victims. The basement afforded another avenue of disposing bodies; Lupo the Wolf burned alive at least six Black Hand victims in the furnace there.

When Saietta was sent to prison in 1918, Brooklyn gangster Frankie Yale, a one-time partner of Johnny Torrio's in extortion, took over the *Unione* and broadened its criminal activities. Yale was to hold this all-powerful position for ten years until he was murdered by Al Capone's gunmen in New York.

Capone, a Neapolitan, was much disliked by many Sicilians. He therefore attempted to dominate the *Unione* in order to shore up his own criminal interests.

In the early 1920s, Mike Merlo was president of the *Unione* branch in Chicago. He was an on-and-off Capone ally and when he died in 1924, Angelo "Bloody Angelo"

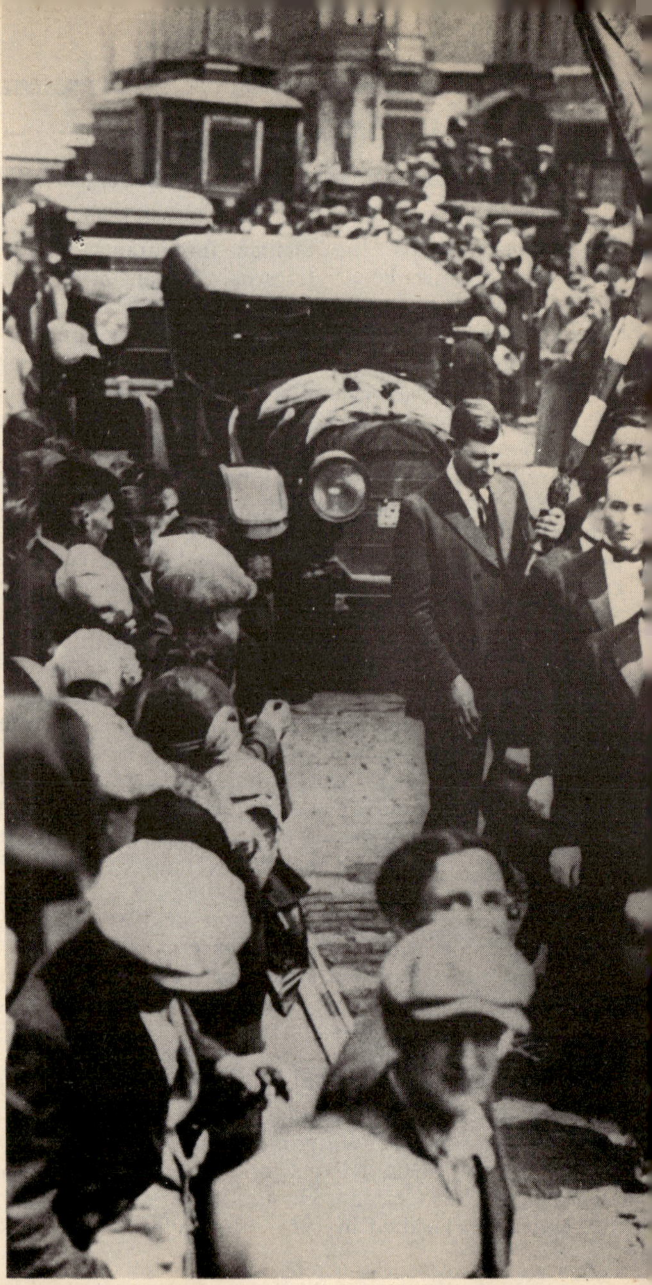

The 1925 gangster funeral of **Unione Siciliane** president Angelo "Bloody Angelo" Genna in Chicago. (UPI)

Genna of the six terrible Genna brothers, appointed himself president of the *Unione*. Genna was quickly killed in early 1925 by the North Side mob run by Earl "Hymie" Weiss, Bugs Moran, and Vincent Drucci. He was replaced by another self-appointed president, Samuzzo "Samoots" Amatuna. Vincent Drucci killed Samoots in a barber shop months later. Upon Amatuna's death, Capone moved in and appointed Anthony Lombardo to the exalted post. Tony was a modest fellow who immediately penned his own brief autobiography and sent it out as a press release to all Chicago newspapers. It read:

"Chicago owes much of its progress and its hope of future greatness to the intelligence and industry of its 200,000 Italians, whose rise in prestige and importance is one of the modern miracles of a great city.

"No people have achieved so much from such small beginnings, or given so much for what they received in the land of promise to which many of them came penniless. Each life story is a romance, an epic of human accomplishment.

"Antonio Lombardo is one of the most outstanding of these modern conquerors . . . Mr. Lombardo came to America twenty-one years ago. He was one of hundreds who cheered joyously, when, from the deck of the steamer, they saw the Statue of Liberty, and the skyline of New York, their first sight of the fabled land, America. With his fellow countrymen he suffered the hardships and indignities to which the United States subjects its prospective citizens at Ellis Island without complaint, for in his heart was a great hope and a great ambition.

"After he landed, he paid his railroad fare to Chicago, and came here with just $12 as his initial capital . . . Mr. Lombardo, however, accepted the hardships as part of the game, and with confidence in his own ability and assurance of unlimited opportunities, began his career . . . He became an importer and exporter . . . His political influence is due largely to his interest in civic affairs and his championship of measures for maintaining and improving standards of living, as well as his activity in the support of charities and benevolent institutions. Like most successful men, he has received much, but has given more to the community in which he lives. It is to such men that Chicago owes her greatness."

One of Lombardo's "interests in civic affairs" was apparently acting as a go-between for Blackhanders and their victims. A sewer contractor, A. Frank Ranieri, was informed by Blackhanders that they had kidnapped his ten-year-old son, William, and were holding him for $50,000 ransom. Desperate, Ranieri attempted to raise the money, gleaning only $10,000 from every available source. He spread the word that he was unable to raise more and begged advice.

An unidentified caller phoned Ranieri on September 6, 1928 and said only two words before hanging up: "See Lombardo."

Ranieri raced to the *Unione* headquarters and, after he had explained his mission, was told by a secretary to return the following day. "The Chief will have some word for you by then," the girl told him.

The distraught father waited the next day in Lombardo's office but Tony Lombardo was absent. Ranieri never did see Lombardo until the day after, when he spotted a newspaper picture of his lifeless body lying on the sidewalk at State and Madison. He did, however, pay off the Blackhanders and retrieve his son.

Lombardo had taken an evening stroll September 7, 1928 on Dearborn Street with two bodyguards, Joseph Lolordo and Joseph Ferraro. As they turned onto the "World's Busiest Corner," State and Madison, with thousands of people streaming by, two men came up behind the trio and opened fire. Two dum-dum bullets crashed into Lombardo's brain, killing him instantly. Ferraro, wounded in the spine, was helpless next to him. He drew his .45 automatic but was so weak from the loss of blood that he feebly dropped the weapon. He, too, died that day. Lolordo, unharmed, drew his gun and chased the killers, but Patrolman John Marcusson, thinking him to be one of the murderers, arrested him.

Pasqualino Lolordo assumed the presidency of the *Unione* next; he, too, met Lombardo's fate. Joseph Aiello and his brothers much coveted the *Unione* leadership and the three Aiellos went calling on Lolordo on January 8, 1929.

Thinking the Aiellos his close friends, Lolordo invited

them into his home at 1921 W. North Avenue. Lolordo' wife, Aleina, brought the four men sandwiches, relishes, pastries, wine, and a box of cigars.

Lolordo closed the door to his den and his wife could hear the foursome enjoying themselves for close to an hour. There was much laughter and toasting. Joseph Aiello lifted his glass and shouted, "Here's to Pasqualino!"

Beaming, the *Unione* president lifted his glass of wine to his lips and at that precise moment three guns barked in unison. The Aiellos emptied their revolvers into the shocked Lolordo, eleven bullets hitting him in the face, neck, and shoulders. He fell dead.

Mrs. Lolordo ran down the hall and threw open the door to the den. The Aiellos rudely shoved her aside. Joe Aiello tossed a .38 revolver into the room and the brothers departed, casually stepping into the street and talking unexcitedly among themselves. Later, Mrs. Lolordo told police she had never met them before.

Joseph Aiello took over the *Unione* the following day. He lasted until October 23, 1930 when Capone machine-gunners found him leaving a friend's home on Kolmar Avenue and stitched his body with a hundred shells.

The position of President of the *Unione* became so lethal that occupants became increasingly hard to find. The *Unione*, which had changed its name to the Italo-American National Union in 1924, began to ebb as a power in the early 1930s and became totally impotent when the great, dark Depression settled over the land.

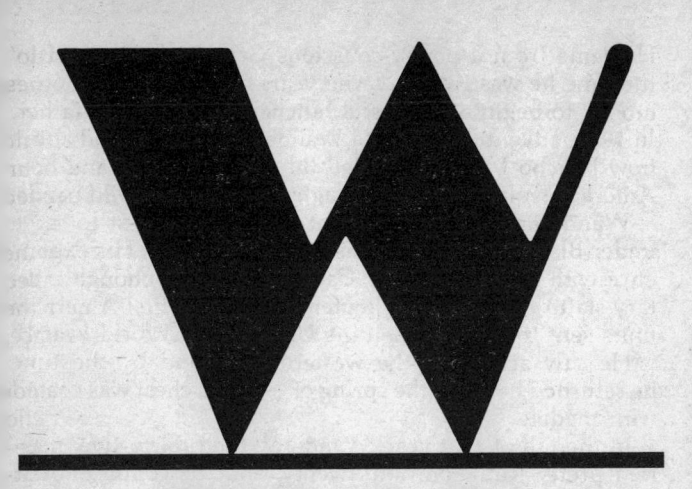

WANDERER, CARL OTTO
Murderer • (1887-1921)

BACKGROUND: BORN AND RAISED IN CHICAGO. GRADE SCHOOL EDUCATION. ORIGINAL OCCUPATION, BUTCHER. SERVED IN THE FIRST ILLINOIS CAVALRY DURING PERSHING'S CAMPAIGN AGAINST PANCHO VILLA IN 1916; SERVED AS A LIEUTENANT OF INFANTRY IN WORLD WAR I ON THE WESTERN FRONT, EARNING SEVERAL IMPORTANT CITATIONS FOR HEROIC DUTY. DESCRIPTION: 5'10", BROWN EYES, BROWN HAIR (BALDING), SLIGHT BUILD. ALIASES: NONE. RECORD: SHOT AND KILLED HIS WIFE AND AN UNKNOWN DRIFTER 6/21/20 IN A BIZARRE PLOT DESIGNED TO THROW GUILT ON ANOTHER MAN; APPREHENDED THROUGH THE EFFORTS OF NEWSMEN AND CONVICTED OF MURDER; EXECUTED BY HANGING ON THE GALLOWS IN CHICAGO, 3/19/21.

Probably no other murder case in the country was solved in a more colorful manner than the one that dealt with the Ragged Stranger. Thanks to the ingenuity, suspicious natures, and natural cunning of two of America's finest reporters, Ben Hecht and Charles MacArthur, one of Chicago's most ruthless murderers was brought to justice.

Carl Otto Wanderer looked like anything but a murderer.

He came from a penny-conscious German family and by the time he was twenty-seven years old had saved enough money to begin a successful butcher shop with his father. In 1916, adventure called to Wanderer when he read about how Pancho Villa had raided the United States, and how American volunteers were sought to pursue his wild bands.

Wanderer enlisted and went to the Southwest to serve under Black Jack Pershing as a cavalry soldier. His experience with the First Illinois Cavalry gave him enough military stature to become a lieutenant with the first American units sent to France when the U.S. entered World War II.

He saw action on the western front and by the time he returned home in the spring of 1919 his chest was coated with medals.

In the fall of that year, Wanderer, then thirty-two, married pretty Ruth Johnson, twenty, and the couple moved into an apartment shared by Ruth's parents. Before Christmas, Ruth told her husband that he would be a father the following summer.

Wanderer did not rejoice. Instead he fell into somber, sullen moods, rarely speaking. This went on for several months until the night of June 21, 1920.

That night Wanderer and Ruth were returning from a movie. They didn't notice the man who followed them into the dark vestibule of their apartment building.

"My wife was feeling for the hall switch," Wanderer later reported to police, "when I heard a voice say, 'Don't turn on the light.' I reached for my gun."

The war hero said that he heard the man shout out a string of obscenities and then the stranger fired once at them. This was followed by several more shots from the stranger's gun. Carl whipped out his Colt .45 service automatic which he habitually carried with him, emptying the clip in the direction of the intruder.

Fourteen bullets roared in heavy explosions in the space of a few seconds. Ruth's mother rushed down to the small vestibule to find Ruth on the floor with two bullets in her. Wanderer was berserk with rage, smashing his gun and fists against a man dressed in rags who was also on the floor, shot full of holes.

Ruth Wanderer lived just long enough to utter the pathetic words: "My baby. . . . my baby is dead."

The stranger in the hallway was rushed to Raveswood Hospital where he died without speaking. In his pockets, police found only $3.80.

It was an unspeakable crime, especially in 1920. Here was a great war hero who had fought to protect America from its enemies left destitute by the murder of his lovely wife and unborn child, even though he valiantly fought and slew the killer.

It was a heartless, devastating crime and the public reacted in shock and outrage. Wanderer was praised for his bravery. Poor, poor Carl Wanderer.

The story was big for the Chicago press. Every newspaper in town gave it great gulps of space. Even the two weapons used in the shooting, both big .45-caliber automatics, were photographed side by side.

Ben Hecht was sitting at his desk in the vast city room of the *Daily News*, looking over the story. He kept turning back to the picture of the two automatics. Something was not right with the photo.

Then he remembered that the Ragged Stranger had but $3.80 in his pockets when killed by Wanderer. It occurred to Hecht that a man down on his luck would hock a hefty automatic for $15 or more rather than risk being shot up by a war hero known to carry a gun.

It didn't make sense. Hecht reasoned that Wanderer's automatic was merely his army-issued sidearm which he kept with him out of habit. But it was more than curious that the Ragged Stranger had an identical weapon in his hand at the time of the murder.

Charles MacArthur, who worked for the rival *Examiner*, also thought the story of the two automatics suspicious. He called the Colt Arms Manufacturing Company and gave the firm the serial number of the stranger's gun. He was told that the weapon was first sold in 1913 to a sporting goods store in Chicago.

MacArthur checked with the store and found that the gun had been bought by one Peter Hoffman, a telephone repairman who lived on Crawford Avenue.

The next day, MacArthur went to see Hoffman and discovered that Hoffman had sold the gun to a mailman several years before. The mailman was Fred Wanderer, Carl's cousin.

MacArthur confronted Fred Wanderer who told him that the weapon was his and that he had loaned it to his cousin the day Ruth Johnson Wanderer was murdered. When he realized the implication of such information the cousin collapsed in a dead faint.

There was still a chance that Wanderer was not involved. The guns might have gotten mixed up. Hecht, who had interviewed the war hero several times after the shooting, went to see Carl Wanderer. He walked up the back porchway. The Johnsons' back porch door was open and Hecht stood there as he listened to Carl Wanderer hum and happily whistle through the screen door.

When Hecht showed himself he could see Wanderer, shirtless, ironing a pair of pants.

"Hi," Hecht said amiably. "Mind if I come in?"

"Oh, Mr. Hecht," Wanderer said in a pleasant voice. "Sure come in. What is it?"

"Just a few more routine questions for a follow-up story. I hope you don't mind."

Wanderer smiled. "No, not at all."

It was unreal. Only a few days ago, Hecht thought, this man's young wife and unborn child had been shot to death by a cold-blooded killer and here he was happy as a lark.

"Mind if I use your bathroom, Carl?"

Wanderer pointed to a small door off the hall. "Help yourself, Mr. Hecht."

Hecht went into the washroom and as he pondered the curiosities of the weapons and Wanderer's attitude he noticed something strange sticking from a bathrobe that belonged to the war hero. He reached forward and withdrew a woman's silk stocking from the pocket. Then another. Then he discovered lipstick, rouge, mascara, all the essential makepup items that women habitually carry around.

Then he found some incriminating letters Wanderer had written . . . to a man. Love letters of deep devotion. Standing there in that cramped little bathroom, holding these strange items all taken from Wanderer's bathrobe pocket, Hecht realized that the war hero was a wild-eyed homosexual.

That would account for a lot of things, Hecht reasoned. He walked out to Wanderer and talked to him briefly and then he raced to police headquarters. MacArthur arrived at about the same time. MacArthur told Lieutenant Mike Loftus of the discrepancies in the gun traced to the Ragged Stranger. Hecht felt Wanderer was a confirmed homosexual and that he had arranged for his wife's death.

The police brought Wanderer in for questioning.

Wanderer told the police that, sure, Fred's weapon was the one he used. The other one used by the Ragged Stranger, who was yet to be identified, was mistakenly identified as his.

That was a possibility. The other .45 automatic had been part of a massive shipment sent to several training camps during the war.

"It's all a mistake, don't you see?" Wanderer said innocently.

While police interrogated Wanderer, Hecht had learned that Ruth Wanderer had withdrawn $1,500 from her own account—money she had saved before marrying Carl—at the Second Security Bank the morning before she was killed.

Hecht ran back to the Johnson apartment and ransacked Wanderer's bedroom. He found the money taped to the back of Wanderer's bureau behind a shirt drawer.

He took his find to the police.

Confronted with this, Wanderer still protested his innocence. Then Hecht threw down the female items he had found in Wanderer's room and the letters to his homosexual lover whose name was James.

"James is coming to see you," Hecht bluffed. "I just talked with him." Hecht had no idea who and where James was.

Wanderer's hands shook, the blood drained from his face. "No, not here. Don't let him come here . . . Oh, My God!"

Then Carl Otto Wanderer confessed. He told the police that he had always been homosexual and that he had married Ruth for her money, that he hated her, he hated all women. The idea of having a child by a woman, he said, was repugnant to him. It disgusted him and sickened him. He was in love with James.

He arranged for her death very simply. He said he hung

around several skid row bars until he met a drifter named Al Watson, a Canadian ex-soldier down on his luck. Wanderer had a way for him to make money.

His wife had begun to doubt his war record and his image as a hero, Wanderer said he told Watson. It was his feminine manner that upset her. He couldn't help it; he had always been that way. But he needed to pull a stunt to revive the romantic image of himself as a hero in her eyes.

Wanderer told Watson that he would pay him to stage a holdup. He would hand Watson a gun when the couple went into the dark hallway and when Ruth turned on the light, he would floor him with a punch. Watson would then run away and he, Carl Wanderer, would once again be the hero of his wife's dreams.

Watson thought it was a harmless way to make a few bucks; he agreed. It was to mean his death. That night when Wanderer came into the hallway with Ruth, he did not hand any gun to Watson. Instead he cocked both weapons and fired at both his wife and Watson. After they had fallen he fired several more bullets into them to make sure they were dead.

Then he went into his avenging husband act for the benefit of Mrs. Johnson, who he knew would race to the scene.

After two sensational trials, one for the murder of Ruth Johnson Wanderer and the other for Al Watson, Carl Wanderer was sentenced to death on the gallows.

Hecht and his friend, fellow newsman Charles MacArthur, stood on the gallows on March 19, 1921 when Wanderer approached the dangling rope.

Hecht and MacArthur became quite chummy with Wanderer during his last days on death row, playing poker with him into the early dawn (they won). They convinced the killer to read attacks on their editors which they had meticulously written just before he was to be hanged on the gallows.

The newsmen, however, forgot that those executed on the gallows were tied hand and foot and the pathetic Wanderer could only glance down helplessly to the typewritten speeches strapped to his side. He did the next

War hero and wife killer Carl Otto Wanderer was trapped into confessing by two nimble-witted reporters—he sang loudly for the press when standing on the gallows. (UPI)

best thing. Throwing back his head he burst into an old ditty entitled, "Dear Old Pal O' Mine."

The hangman came forward after the first chorus. Wanderer warded him off with a shake of his head and went into the second. By this time, pranksters Hecht and MacArthur were unnerved to see tears streaming down the murderer's cheeks, his eyes rolling crazily in his head like a man whose mind has snapped once and for all.

Carl was still singing when the hangman placed the black shroud on his head and lowered the rope to his neck. The pathetic voice sang on behind the mask. "Glub . . . glub . . . glub" were his last words.

The trap sprung open and Wanderer shot down till the rope snapped him up into space and instant death.

The world-hardened MacArthur turned to his friend and co-author Ben Hecht and said, "You know, Ben, that son-of-a-bitch should have been a song plugger."

WEIL, JOSEPH ("YELLOW KID")
Swindler • (1877-   )

"I never cheated an honest man, only rascals," said the greatest confidence man of them all after his retirement. "They may have been respectable but they were never any good. They wanted something for nothing. I gave them nothing for something."

With that philosophy ever in mind, Joseph "Yellow Kid" Weil embarked at an early age to take the wealthy suckers of this country through the most ingenious schemes ever concocted. Born and raised in Chicago, the Kid became famous early when members of the press adopted him, delighting in Weil's highminded confidence games.

The Kid often operated with confederates such as Fred Buckminster, but generally preferred to pull his swindles alone. His greatest asset was his presence. Weil's sartorial splendor was unequalled in his trade. He was always immaculately dressed and was partial to silk cravats spliced with pearl stickpins, winged collars, expensive vested suits, and spats. His sobriquet stemmed from his youthful habit of reading the Ocault cartoon strip character, "Yellow Kid" in the 1890s.

From about 1900 to 1934, when the Kid claimed to have gone straight, Weil was involved with so many bunco plots that he often had to perform some frenzied juggling to keep up with them. His quick wit, razor sharp tongue, and stolid appearance pulled him through colossal bluffs.

One of his more ambitious schemes involved the buying of a bank, or rather the renting of one. Upon hearing that the Merchants National Bank in Muncie, Ind., was moving to a new location, he went to Muncie and set in motion an elaborate swindle. Before the teller cages and other banking accouterments were removed, the Kid rented the vacated bank building. He then had children go to other banks and snatch piles of deposit and withdrawal slips which were placed in the slots of his bank. Streetcar conductors were hired to act as bank guards. His tellers were, of course, some of the most notorious confidence men in the Midwest.

Into this bear trap, the Kid led his lamb. Days before renting the old Muncie Bank Building, Weil had primed an out-of-town millionaire with the prospect of investing $50,000 in a fake land deal. After his bank was established, the Yellow Kid approached his sucker and stated "Why, the president of the Muncie Bank vouches for it."

The sucker was led into the bank by the austere-looking Weil. The building was jammed with customers who hauled sacks of money across the floor and thrust wads of greenbacks upon the tellers as deposits. To Weil's victim the phony bank appeared to be booming with business. Of course, the customers were prostitutes, racetrack touts, and gamblers Weil had employed purposely for his swindle.

After waiting an hour, Weil and his pigeon were shown into the bank president's office. The president, a Weil associate who acted with great dignity and sophisticated bearing, sanctioned the $50,000 investment while spouting financial gibberish. By the evening of that day, Yellow Kid was far from Muncie with $50,000 in his pocket.

Another scheme enacted in Youngstown, Ohio, also involved a bank, a real one. Here Weil approached the president of the bank pretending to be a millionaire passing through town. He talked of depositing a great deal of money in the bank but intimated that there was a pressing matter to be cleared up first. "Please be kind enough to use my office for any business transactions," the bank president obligingly said.

Weil used the offices for an hour—just enough time for him to pass himself off as the bank president and take another sucker in a quick swindle.

The Kid was publicity-minded, convinced that most people were gullible and believed almost anything that appeared in print. He stumbled across a financial magazine of great repute which carried the story of an investor who had purchased an abandoned gold mine and subsequently made millions from it. Weil took the magazine to a friend who was a printer. His friend ingeniously reprinted the page in the magazine that dealt with the mining millionaire

The greatest con man of them all—Joseph "Yellow Kid" Weil, shown here in 1924 in the palmy days of his fabulous swindles. (UPI)

and substituted Weil's picture for the investor, and then carefully rebound the magazine.

Armed with this tool, Weil traveled throughout the Midwest. His first stop in each town was the library. There he would take out an authentic copy of the magazine, substituting it with his doctored copy. He would then buttonhole his victims with a stock pitch, pretending to be the mining millionaire. "You can find it in the library," he would point out to the sucker. When the prospective victim checked, he found the article with Yellow Kid's picture and invariably foisted his money upon Weil within hours. Before leaving town, the Kid was careful to replace the doctored copy of the magazine with the original.

The Kid plotted and schemed his way into some of the most fantastic swindles imaginable. One story had it that he took a Detroit car manufacturer for several thousand dollars by selling him pills that could turn water into gasoline.

Not all of the Kid's swindles were successful. He served

a number of prison terms in local and federal jails. The Yellow Kid looked upon these periodical jolts of incarceration as temporary setbacks. Fame became his ultimate undoing. Addicted to a pince nez and a full, luxurious, and carefully combed and trimmed beard, he soon realized that his appearance had become a trademark and caused him to be identified by his victims. After serving a long term in the Illinois State Prison at Joliet, Weil attempted to bilk youthful Detroit millionaire George Malcolmson, of $30,000 in a fake copper mine proposition. Malcolmson recognized Weil and brought charges on February 11, 1924.

Outwardly, such police rousts did not ruffle Weil, but he became increasingly aware that the great glut of stories concerning his activities stripped away his most important tool, anonymity.

In Peoria, Ill. on February 3, 1934, the Kid's hotel room was invaded by an army of local police just as he was preparing another swindle. Weil had been in town only a few days with two partners, both named Smith. The trio had been negotiating the rental of a whole floor of the largest business building in Peoria. Weil had asked real estate brokers to locate "a palatial residence" for him in town. The Kid and his partners then received dozens of telegrams at their hotel which reported the meteoric rise of something called "Soviet Gold Mine Stock."

That's as far as Weil's intended swindle got. Police recognized the dapper crook and stormed into his room, finding in one suitcase bundles of paper cut to bank bill size and carefully wrapped and marked: "$20,000." Whatever the Kid's scheme was, it never materialized.

He was hauled into jail but police authorities were nonplussed. There was no real evidence upon which to convict the Kid of a crime. Police Chief Walter Williams realized his raid had been premature.

"Give me proof that I've broken the law," the Kid insisted.

"I don't have any," Williams said, "but you're up to something." Williams was compelled to free Weil and his associates.

It was a close shave and for Weil spelled the end of his career. He had been defeated by his own notoriety. The Yellow Kid decided to go straight.

The Kid disappeared after that and did not emerge until the late 1940s. A policeman passed him on a Gold Coast street in Chicago while he was walking his dog. Weil recognized the officer and waved at him. The policeman recognized the Kid and arrested him. Taken to court on "suspicion," Weil grew indignant and then, with an impassioned speech made before the judge, the Kid insisted that he had gone straight years ago and the pinch was a miscarriage of justice.

"Just what are you doing now, Mr. Weil?" the judge asked the chipper 72-year-old confidence man.

"I'm writing my memoirs," Weil announced proudly.

He was telling the truth. The Yellow Kid's autobiography, written with W. T. Brannon, appeared in 1948. Apparently the old master had not lost his touch. One report stated that "a legal battle is expected between Brannon and a moving picture company over film rights to the book, as the Kid has been up to his old tricks and sold the rights to both Brannon and the film company."

Still alive at this writing, The Yellow Kid at ninety-five walks the streets of Chicago, dapper and as meticulously dressed as ever, no doubt dreaming of the more than $8,000,000 he won and lost in his fabulous confidence games.

WHITE HAND GANG

The White Handers were river terrorists who extorted money from dockworkers and boat captains alike on the East River, centering activities along the Brooklyn shore from 1900–1925. They were led by Wild Bill Lovett and Dinny Meehan. In 1920, White Hand lieutenant Meehan was stabbed to death by an un-

Two leaders of the Brooklyn White Hand Gang of the early 1920s—W. L. "Wild Bill" Lovett and Richard "Peg Leg" Lonergan.

derling who aspired to his rank. Wild Bill was shot to death in 1923, ambushed one evening as he made his way to his Brooklyn home.

Richard "Peg Leg" Lonergan, a scabrous murderer with twenty killings to his credit, then took over the White Hand mob. On the night of December 26, 1925, Lonergan entered the Adonis Social Club, a South Brooklyn saloon patronized by Italian gangsters. With him was Cornelius "Needles" Ferry, Jimmy Hart, Patrick "Happy" Maloney, and Aaron Harms.

By coincidence, Al Capone, who had become ganglord of Chicago, had returned to his old stomping grounds in Brooklyn for a brief nostalgic visit (and also to cement relationships with *Unione Siciliane* president Frankie Yale) and happened to also be in the club. With him were Italian mobsters Fiore "Fury" Agoglia, Jack "Stick-'em-Up" Stabile, George Carozza, Ralph Demato, Frank Piazza, and Tony Desso.

Lonergan was apparently spoiling for a fight, even though

he and his band were considerably outnumbered. He slammed the bar for service and made loud, insulting remarks about "dagoes" and "ginzos." When he spotted two Irish girls entering the club on the arms of Italian youths, he chased them out, shouting after them: "Come back with white men!"

At 2 a.m., as if on cue, the lights of the Adonis Club suddenly went out. The place then lit up with blazing, snapping gunfire. When the lights went back on again, Lonergan, Harms, and Ferry were lying in the middle of the floor, all of them shot in the head. The rest of the Irish gangsters had fled in the dark.

A gruesome jester had, while the lights were out, pinned some sheet music to Peg Leg's suitcoat. The title of the song was "She's My Baby."

The White Handers faded after that and disappeared altogether in 1928.

WHYOS GANG

Following the Civil War, the Whyos came into existence in New York and they soon proved to be the most vicious and terrifying street gang ever seen in the city. The origin of the name of the gang remains a mystery but one writer advanced the idea that it resulted from a "peculiar call sometimes employed by gangsters."

Evolving from the Chichesters and the old Five Points Gang, the Whyos dominated the Fourth Ward of the Lower East Side and headquartered at Mulberry Bend. Unlike any other gang in New York, the Whyos considered the whole of Manhattan their province and some of their five hundred members were, at one time or other, constantly raiding the territories of Greenwich Village or West Side

Some deadly members of the dreaded New York Whyos Gang (left to right) Big Josh Hines, Piker Ryan, Red Rocks Farrell, Slops Connolly.

gangs. Their central drinking spa was aptly named The Morgue and was the scene of at least one hundred violent murders.

Gang fights between the members were not unusual. Often, Whyos factions drew guns on each other and blasted away for hours in The Morgue. Among the broad ranks of the Whyos were to be found the arch criminals of the day: Big Josh Hines, Hoggy Walsh, Bull Hurley, Fig McGerald, Baboon Connolly, Googy Corcoran, Red Rocks Farrell, Slops Connolly, Piker Ryan, Dorsey Doyle, and Mike Loyd: Irish to a man and not only professional killers, but also master burglars, pickpockets, and bandits.

Big Josh Hines delighted in holding up stuss games (a variation of faro), marching from one gambling den to another like a man following a milk route each night. He openly wore a brace of pistols and was utterly amazed by a police detective who stopped him one night and said "The boys are getting mad with your stickups."

"What?" Hines bellowed. "Them guys must be nuts. Don't I always leave 'em somethin'? All I want is me fair share!"

At the peak of the Whyos' reputation and power in the 1880s and 1890s, it became mandatory for an apprentice Whyo to kill a man before gaining full membership. This decree was handed down by gang captain Mike McGloin in 1883 when he was quoted as saying: "A guy ain't tough until he has knocked his man out!"

Living up to his own code, McGloin attempted to rob a West Twenty-fifth Street saloonkeeper named Louis Hanier, killing Hanier in the process before he was captured by police. McGloin died on the gallows in the Tombs prison on March 8, 1883.

Whyos killers hired out at all hours of the day to administer beatings and murder. One of the gangleaders, Piker Ryan, was arrested in 1884. In his pocket was found a printed list of services the Whyos offered and the cost of each. It read:

"Punching	$ 2
Both eyes blackened	4
Nose and jaw broke	10
Jacked out (knocked out with a blackjack)	15
Ear chawed off	15
Leg or arm broke	19
Shot in leg	25
Stab	25
Doing the big job [murder]	100 and up."

Danny Lyons and Danny Driscoll headed the Whyos by 1887. The latter hanged on January 23, 1888. Driscoll had gotten into an argument with gangster John McCarthy over a prostitute named Beezy Garrity. They both drew guns in the girl's presence and banged away at each other. Though they missed each other, one of Driscoll's bullets struck Beezy and killed her. Lyons followed Driscoll to the gallows six months later on August 21, 1888 after shooting a fellow gangster, Joseph Quinn, in a noonday gun battle in the middle of Paradise Square at the Five Points on July 5, 1887. The duel was fought over a prostitute named Pretty Kitty McGown.

Two of Lyons' prostitutes, Lizzie the Dove and Gentle Maggie, were so upset by the gangleader's subsequent execution in the Tombs that they donned mourning black and refused customers for a whole week. Months later the two women fell to arguing in a bar over whose sadness at the loss of Lyons was greater.

"I'll settle it," Gentle Maggie said; she drew a knife and plunged it into Lizzie the Dove's throat.

As she was dying, Lizzie gurgled: "I'll meet you in hell soon and scratch your eyes out there!"

One of the Whyos gangsters turned inventor. Dandy John Dolan created a host of deadly implements for the gang members with which they could gouge out eyes and stomp the faces of gang rivals. Dolan used his eye gouger, made of copper and worn on the thumb, on many occasions. He once robbed, in the summer of 1875, a store owned by wealthy manufacturer James H. Noe. When Noe caught him in the act, Dolan crushed his skull with an iron bar and gouged out Noe's eyes for good measure. Dolan carried the eyeballs around in his vest pocket for a week, showing them to his pals.

Police Detective Joseph M. Dorcy tracked Dolan down and found Noe's jewelry in Dolan's pockets. Dolan was convicted of the murder and was hanged April 21, 1876.

For forty years the Whyos ruled the criminal underworld in New York but faded at the turn of the century with the coming of newer gangs led by Monk Eastman and Paul Kelly.

YALE, FRANKIE
Gangster • (1885-1927)

Brooklyn-born Frankie Yale (christened Frank Uale) began his criminal career as a member of the Five Points gang in the late 1890s and several gangland killings were attributed to him before he was twenty. He joined Johnny Torrio in a Brooklyn blackhand ring in 1908, extorting money from fellow Italian residents under threats of kidnapping, bombings, and murder.

Yale took over the *Unione Siciliane*, the powerful Sicilian fraternal organization turned crime cartel, in 1918, following the imprisonment of its former president, Ignazio Saietta, a bloodthirsty killer. Yale assumed the presidency and began taking murder contracts to supplement his income. When asked by police what he did for a living, Yale wryly stated: "I'm an undertaker."

He owned the Harvard Inn with Torrio before Johnny went West to work for Big Jim Colosimo. Yale continued to run this dive throughout his criminal career. At least two dozen men were murdered on the premises of this Brooklyn bar from 1918 to 1928.

In addition to bootlegging and rumrunning during the 1920s, Yale forced tobacconists to buy cheap brands of

Murderer, extortionist, blackhander, and national president of the **Unione Siciliane**, Frankie Yale.

cigars he manufactured, his company serving as a front for illegal activities. Yale's countenance—that of a smirking, pudgy-faced man with slick-downed hair, wearing a high starched collar and a narrow black tie—was stamped on each cigar box. His product was universally condemned; in the Brooklyn argot of the 1920s, "A Frankie Yale," meant anything cheap and rotten.

Yale functioned as Al Capone's chief supplier of bonded whiskey during Prohibition. He also did little favors for Capone, who had palled about with him as a fellow Five Pointer before the First World War. The favors consisted of murdering Capone's Chicago-based enemies. It was generally accepted that Yale was the man who held Dion O'Bannion's hand in a vise-like grip while Capone's gunmen, Albert Anselmi and John Scalise, shot the Irish mobster to death in his flower shop on November 10, 1924.

Chicago police picked up Yale and his bodyguard Sam Pollaccia at the LaSalle Street train station just after O'Bannion was killed, three minutes before Yale's New York-bound train was scheduled to depart.

To police questions, Yale replied: "I came here for Mike Merlo's funeral. Sure I know Capone. No, I don't know Torrio. I stayed over for a swell dinner that my friend Diamond Joe Esposito gave for me."

A machinegun death for Frankie Yale in Brooklyn.

Police took two revolvers from Yale and Pollaccia. When Chief Morgan A. Collins confronted Yale with the weapons, he nonchalantly replied: "I have a permit from a Supreme Court justice of New York to carry it. I collect lots of money in New York."

He was let go, but Chief Collins felt with "moral certainty" that Yale had helped to kill O'Bannion.

When Yale refused to endorse Capone-sponsored candidates for the branch office presidency of the *Unione Siciliane* in Chicago, their relationship deteriorated. Capone began to suspect Yale was selling him liquor shipments and then having the trucks hijacked before they ever left New York State.

Yale told Johnny Torrio, who had returned from his brief

exile in Italy in 1927, that Capone was complaining about his liquor shipments. "The bastard is beefing that I'm giving him a short count," Yale said.

Capone did suspect Yale of the short shrift and sent one of his hoodlums, James F. DeAmato, to Brooklyn to spy on Yale. DeAmato relayed information to Capone that his suspicions were correct, but he did not live long enough to report personally to Scarface. Yale had DeAmato killed.

Capone then sent Yale an unsigned wire stating: "Some day you'll get an answer to DeAmato."

On July 1, 1927, the answer came. In the early afternoon of that day Yale was called to the phone in a Brooklyn speakeasy and then rushed out to his car. The jaunty Yale—attired in a soft gray fedora, pinstripe suit, and spats—wheeled his roadster down Forty-fourth Street and was suddenly overtaken by a large touring car bristling with gunmen. They opened up on Yale who was half blown through the seat of his car by the blizzard of shotgun, rifle, pistol, and machinegun bullets.

Yale's car crashed wildly off the street and ploughed into a house, tearing half the facade away. The killers threw their weapons out on the street blocks away. A machinegun, the first to be used in New York in a gangland killing, was traced to Chicago gun shop owner, Peter von Frantzius, who was well-known as Capone's gun supplier. Obviously, Scarface wanted the New Yorkers to know who had taken care of Yale.

The funeral of Frankie Yale was the most impressive ever seen for Manhattan mobsters. Following Dion O'Bannion's lavish funeral of 1924, Yale had commented: "Boys, if they ever get me, give me a sendoff that good." The boys saw to it. Yale's silver and copper-lined casket cost $12,000 and twenty-eight trucks of flowers followed him to the cemetery.

On the last truck, a giant wreath bore the ominous inscription: "We'll See Them, Kid."

[ALSO SEE Al Capone, Dion O'Bannion, *Unione Siciliane*; John Torrio, *Bloodletters and Badmen*, Book 3.]

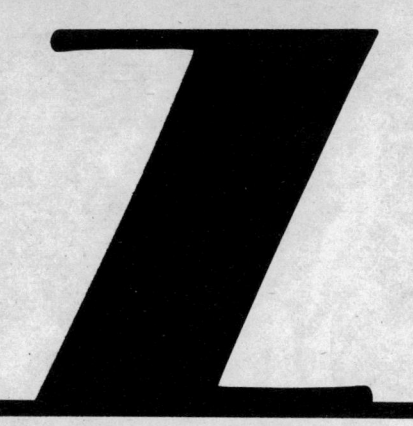

ZANGARA, JOSEPH
Assassin • (1902-1933)

An unemployed New Jersey mill hand, Zangara hoboed his way to Miami, Florida in early 1933 where he attempted to find work. Unable to locate employment, as was the plight of most people in America at that time, Zangara began to rave wildly about "capitalists" and babbled Marxist double-talk to strangers on the street.

In the second week of February, 1933, newspapers in Miami announced that President-elect Franklin D. Roosevelt would arrive there accompanied by Chicago Mayor Anton J. Cermak. Zangara decided to kill Roosevelt.

The diminutive Zangara was plagued with stomach cramps on the morning of February 15, 1933, the day of Roosevelt's arrival in Miami. He swallowed several bottles of "medicine" and then loaded his revolver.

As President Roosevelt, with Cermak at his side, rode in the back seat of an open car through the Miami streets, enormous crowds gathered to cheer him. The reception became so enthusiastic that the mobs spilled into the street and pushed forward against the President's car until it was

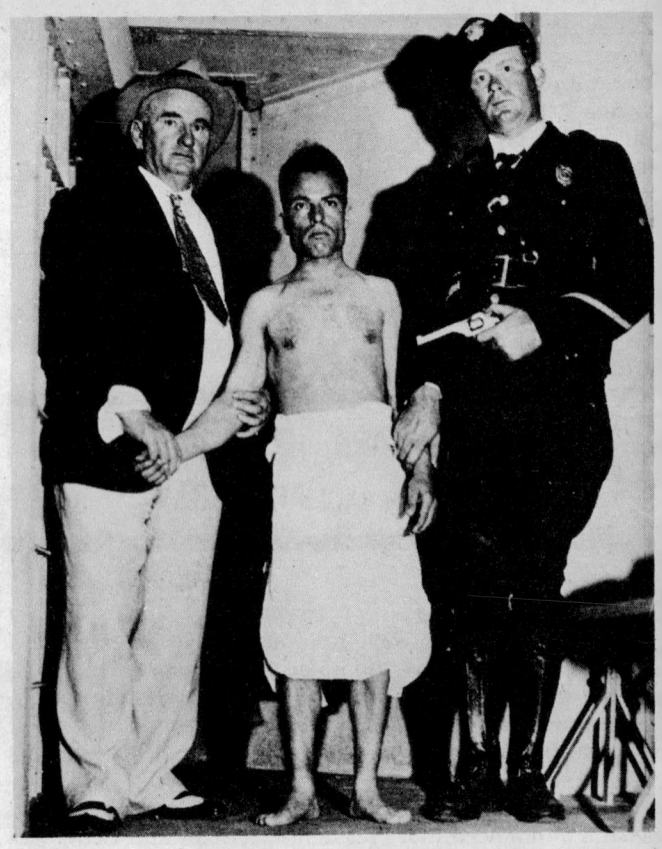

Would-be presidential assassin Joseph Zangara shown only hours after he attempted to kill FDR; he missed, but fatally wounded Chicago Mayor Anton Cermak. (UPI)

reduced to a crawl. At that moment, little Joe Zangara came barreling through the mass, knocking people down and shoving others aside. His mouth dropped and his black eyes smoldered.

One observer shoved aside by Zangara later stated: "It was like he was going to explode. I was going to hit him but something made me stop. He was like a nut."

When he was about eight feet from the President's car,

Zangara raised his pistol and shouted: "There are too many people starving to death!" He fired wildly in the direction of the car. As he was squeezing off his rounds, a woman swung her handbag at him, knocking the pistol upward. Bullets hit 23-year-old Margaret Kruis, who was vacationing in Florida, and 22-year-old Russell Caldwell. Both received head wounds. Two bullets hit Mayor Cermak, wounding him fatally.

Roosevelt's only reaction to the shooting was a withering glance flashed in Zangara's direction. An FDR aide, Raymond Moley, later wrote: "There was not so much as the twitching of a muscle, the mopping of a brow, or even the hint of false gaiety."

Cermak died hours later and Zangara was convicted of murder in a whirlwind trial and sentenced to death. Hours before his execution, Zangara was interviewed by newsmen in his Raiford, Fla. cell.

"Was anyone in on this with you?" a reporter asked.

"No, I have no friends. It was my own idea."

"Do you realize you killed Mayor Cermak? How do you feel about that?"

"I feel nothing about that. Nothing."

"One of your bullets hit a woman, you know."

"She shouldn't have got in the way of the bullet."

"What made you do this? Why do you hate Mr. Roosevelt?"

Zangara stared and then said, "If I got out I would kill him at once."

He was strapped into the electric chair on March 21, 1933. His last words were: "Good-bye. Adios to the world."

ZELIG, JACK ("BIG JACK")
Murderer, Gangleader • (1882-1912)

Born William Alberts, Zelig took over a faction of the Monk Eastman Gang in New York when Monk was sent to prison. Big Jack's two lieutenants were Jack Sirocco (who had introduced Johnny Torrio into the Five Points gang) and Chick Tricker.

A minimum of seventy-five tough gangsters worked for this trio from 1910 until 1912, when Zelig was killed. Most of them had backgrounds similar to Zelig's, who began as a pickpocket at age fourteen and then went on to mugging, rolling drunks, and murdering for profit. Early in his career, Zelig, who always retained a youthful appearance, developed a gimmick used exclusively in courtrooms. He hired a consumptive-looking girl to act as his wife.

Arraigned before a judge, Zelig would hang his head in a remorseful manner, a signal to the girl who would then rush forward and tearfully cry out: "Oh, Judge, for God's sake, don't send my boy-husband, the father of my baby, to jail!" Big Jack was almost always released by a kind-hearted judge who instructed him to return home and take care of his family.

In Zelig's employ were the most unsavory murderers of the era—Gyp the Blood (Harry Horowitz), Lefty Louis (Louis Rosenberg), Dago Frank (Frank Cirofici), and Whitey Lewis (Jacob Siedenschner), all of whom helped to kill gambler Herman "Beansy" Rosenthal on orders from Zelig and the crooked cop, Charles Becker.

When Zelig robbed a brothel of $80 in 1911, he discovered the loyalty of his lieutenants Sirocco and Tricker was sadly wanting. He called them from a police station after the madam had had him arrested and told his men to pay her off. They ignored Zelig's plea, hoping to see him sent to prison so they could take over the gang.

Big Jack, however, called upon his political contacts, who were quite influential; he was freed. He vowed to kill Sirocco and Tricker. They, in turn, sent a gunman named Julie Morrell to kill Zelig. Big Jack was informed of Morrell's intent by Ike the Plug and went hunting his would-be executioner.

On the night of December 2, 1911, several Zelig-paid stooges got Morrell drunk in the Stuyvesant Casino on Second Avenue. Morrell staggered across the dance hall with a gun held limply in his hand and shouted: "Where's

New York gangster Big Jack Zelig; he was gunned down on a Manhattan trolley car in 1912. (UPI)

Zelig? . . . I'll fill that big Yid so full of holes he'll sink! . . . Where's that big Yid, Zelig? . . . I gotta cook that big Yid! . . ."

The casino's lights suddenly went out, and as dancers scattered for the exits they heard two words boom across the dance hall toward Morrell—"Right here!" A single shot followed and Morrell was dead with a bullet in his heart.

Gang warfare then broke out between Zelig's band and that of Tricker and Sirocco. It lasted until the following year when Zelig was shot and killed on a Thirteenth Street trolley car, October 5, 1912, by Red Phil Davidson.

ZWERBACH, MAX ("KID TWIST")
Gangster • (1882-1908)

Zwerbach, best known to the criminal underworld in New York in the early 1900s as Kid Twist, was one of Monk Eastman's top killers. He was responsible for the murder of at least ten men, one of whom was gang rival Richie Fitzpatrick, who was lured to his death by Zwerbach on the promise of settling a gang war.

In tandem with his friend Cyclone Louie (Vach Lewis), Kid Twist then killed five more of Fitzpatrick's men within a week. A sadist by nature, Zwerbach enjoyed punishing others. One of his favorite victims was nineteen-year-old Louie the Lump (Louis Pioggi). Kid Twist and Cyclone Louie ran into Louie the Lump in a second-story bar in Coney Island on May 14, 1908. Zwerbach taunted Louie the Lump with caustic remarks about his girl, a tart named Carroll Terry, stating that he, Kid Twist, had made love to her and that she disliked Louie the Lump's awkward advances.

"She says youse was an active little cuss, Louis," Kid Twist said with a grin. "Always jumpin' around. Let's see how active youse is, kid. Take a jump out the window!" Zwerbach and Cyclone Louie pulled out guns and motioned Louie to jump from the broken second-story window. He did and survived with only a broken ankle.

Louie the Lump called Paul Kelly of the Five Points Gang and screamed: "I got to cook him!"

"Sure you got to cook him," Kelly smoothly assured. "I'll send some boys." Kelly dispatched twenty goons from the Five Points Gang to Coney Island and two hours later, as Zwerbach and Cyclone Louie swaggered from the bar, fifty bullets cut them down. Carroll Terry, the girl in question, suddenly arrived at the scene of the shooting, and Louie the Lump sent a bullet in her direction for good measure, wounding her in the shoulder.

Louie the Lump was apprehended and tried for the double murder. He pleaded guilty to manslaughter and received eleven months in jail.

BLOODLETTERS AND BADMEN
by Jay Robert Nash

A definitive collection—in three volumes—of the most notorious men and women in American history from the eighteenth century to the present. Lavishly illustrated bibliographical listing in Book 3.

__BOOK 1: CAPTAIN LIGHTFOOT TO JESSE JAMES   (l30-150, $3.95)

__BOOK 2: BUTCH CASSIDY TO AL CAPONE   (l30-151, $3.95)

__BOOK 3: LUCKY LUCIANO TO CHARLES MANSON   (l30-152, $3.95)

WARNER BOOKS
P.O. Box 690
New York, N.Y. 10019

Please send me the books I have checked. I enclose a check or money order (not cash), plus 50¢ per order and 50¢ per copy to cover postage and handling.* (Allow 4 weeks for delivery.)

_____ Please send me your free mail order catalog. (If ordering only the catalog, include a large self-addressed, stamped envelope.)

Name _____
Address _____
City _____
State _____ Zip _____

*N.Y. State and California residents add applicable sales tax.   40